Book Synopsis

Soul Stealers address people and practices that claim to have a form of godliness, but do not have God's identity, spirit, or power. Soul stealers thus lead people into sin, bondage, and to HELL, because what they are offering as God or his way, it really "strange fire." This book examines the Soul Stealers of the New Age Movement, their customs, and what God deems as acceptable regarding spiritual practices, eternal life, and worship. Learn how many of the New Age Movements are ancient practices rooted in idolatry, how to be delivered personally, generationally, and regionally, and to witness to those who engage in these practices. Learn what is acceptable to God, and how to align your life and lineage to biblical standards and customs that are pleasing to him.

UNMASKING THE POWER OF THE SCOUTS
Volume II: Soul Stealers

Kingdomshifterscec@gmail.com
(Ministry Website) Kingdomshifters.com
(University & Wellness Website) KSWU.NET
(Book Website) Kingdomshiftingbooks.com

Connect with Taquetta via
Facebook, YouTube or Clubhouse

Copyright 2021 – Kingdom Shifters Christian Empowerment Center. All rights reserved.

Images are either copyright free, public domain images or used with permission of the graphic artist.

This book is protected by the copyright laws of the United States of America. This book may not be reprinted for commercial gain or profit. The use of occasional page copying for personal or group study is permitted and encouraged. Permission will be granted with written request.

Taquetta's Story (abridged edition)

Taquetta was adopted by her aunt at two weeks old. She was raised with four brothers in East St. Louis and has been a fighter since she was a little girl. God has transformed that fighting personality into a spiritual warrior in his kingdom! She has a testimony of having her fists turned into hands of prayer, complete with a gift of healing and faith for miracles, signs, and wonders to manifest. God transformed Taquetta from one who frequented nightclubs and battled alcoholism to one with a strategy to empower others in destiny. Her name means "child of love," and she carries that mantle of unconditionally loving and restoring the unlovable.

Taquetta is gifted at empowering and assisting people with launching ministries, businesses, and books. She provides mentoring, counseling, coach, and destiny development through Kingdom Wellness Counseling and Mentoring Center. She has written her very own Kingdom Wellness Counseling Theory and will be launching a certified program to train mental health leaders, deliverers, and healings, in how to SHIFT people into sustainable wellness.

Taquetta flows through the wells of deliverance, revival reform, warfare, and worship. She carries the mantle, not only of her spiritual mother, Dr. Kathy Williams, but also of her overseer and apostolic mother, Dr. Jackie Green. Her mantle includes an apostolic mandate of judging and establishing God's kingdom in people, ministries, communities, and regions. Taquetta has over 22 years of deliverance and warfare experience. She is skilled at dismantling principalities and strongholds in people, generations, and regions, and is keen in seeking God for strategic insight on how to overthrow the powers and systems of darkness.

Taquetta travels in foreign missions and throughout the United States. She has mentored and established dance, altar workers, deliverance, and prophetic ministries. Taquetta ministers in the areas of fine arts, all manners of prayer, fivefold ministry, deliverance, healing, miracles, atmospheric worship, apostolic reform, and empowers and train people in their destiny and life vision. She walks the walk and rejoices at the expansion of God's kingdom!

Taquetta's Credentials

- Founder of Kingdom Shifters Ministries (KSM), Indiana
- Founder of Kingdom Wellness Counseling and Mentoring Center
- Author of over 50 books and 2 prayer decree CD's
- Doctorate in Ministry from Rapha Deliverance University
- Master's Degree in Community Counseling with an emphasis on Marriage, Children and Family Counseling
- Bachelor's Degree in Psychology
- Associates Degree in Business Administration
- Certified Life Coach, Certified Professional Coach, Certified Executive Leadership Coach through Breakthrough Coaching and Leadership Academy
- Therapon Belief Therapist Certification from the Therapon Institute (faith-based counseling)
- Board of Directors for New Day Community Ministries, Inc.
- Graduate of Eagles Dance Institute under Dr. Pamela Hardy; licensed in liturgical dance.
- Apostolic Ordination by Bishop Jackie Green, Founder of JGM-National Prayer Life Institute (Phoenix, AZ)
- Previous ministry service as prophet, visionary for Shekinah Expressions Dance Troupe, teacher, member of presbytery, overseer for altar workers' ministry

DISCLAIMER: Dr. Taquetta Baker has used best efforts in collecting information and publishing this volume. The presentation of the contents is intended for guidance and understanding. Throughout the book, a wide diversity of religious practices is included, not with intent of slander, but of demonstrating principles and practices that fall outside of the scope of Christianity. In certain portions of the book, information is shared about public figures, once again, with no intent of slander but illustration. Only information commonly available through various media sources is used with no suggestion of having private or personal connections to those individuals. Dr. Baker does not assume, and hereby disclaims any liability for any misuse or misconstruing intent, whether such errors or omissions result from negligence, accident, or other causes. The contents of this book are written for an audience of mature Christian believers. Dr. Baker discourages anyone new to Christianity to not undertake these materials without the guidance of a pastor or other seasoned believer. This book is not intended for anyone under the age of 18 without direct parental or adult participation via conversation and oversight.

Soul Stealers Prayer Charge

**DO NOT SKIP THE PRAYER CHARGE!
IT IS VITAL TO COVERING YOU AS YOU STUDY THIS MANUAL!**

In the name of Jesus, we thank you Father for the Soul Stealers manual and for the revelation you have downloaded to dismantle principalities, powers, rulers of darkness, and spiritual wickedness in high places. We thank you that we wrestle not against flesh and blood; that the blood of Jesus, the works of the cross, and the resurrection power of Jesus Christ dying and rising for our sins, has given us authority over all demons and darkness. In the name of Jesus, we assert our right as kingdom heirs to walk in the fullness of salvation and sonship. We call forth angels to encamp round about us - to fight against those who would fight against us. We hedge ourselves under the eternal banner of *Psalms 91* and declare protection, fortification, fortress, and refuge inside the secret place of you Lord. We declare that as we dwell inside the secret place of the Highest God, we remain protected, refuged, fortified, stable, and fixed, under the shadow of the Almighty whose power no foe can withstand. We decree all powers of witchcraft, idolatry, paganism, ungodly and manmade - all manner of evil and wickedness - is nullified as they partake and utilize the revelation in this manual.

We decree that every attack against this manual, the writers, editors, and readers, is eternally canceled and nullified in Jesus name. We eternally snuff out the strongholds, curses, and powers of witchery, bewitchment, telepathy, clairvoyance, divination, sorcery, magic, incantation, Jezebel, python, Baal, Mammon, satanism, ancestral interferences, familiar spirits, the spirit of stupor and slumber, confusion, strife, quarreling, zapping spirits, mind binding and mind blinding, blurring of pages, spirits that operate in the dark, all pestilences and afflictions, and misunderstanding spirits, in the name of Jesus. We release and decree the spirit of truth, Holy Spirit discernment, clarity, keenness in the spirit, divine kingdom hearing and understanding, true godly awakening, and a desire to be free and set apart in consecration, sanctification, covenant relationship, and sold-out destiny alignment in Jesus name.

We thank you for Lord the eternal deliverance, personal, generational, and regional breakthrough that will take place in our lives through this manual. You are so awesome to care for our souls and our purpose in such a gracious manner. We give you all the glory as we testify of freedom and live and minister in the fullness of truth that will embody us from the wealth of knowledge in the manual. We thank you that it is so, in Jesus matchless name.

Table of Contents

Book Synopsis i
Taquetta's Story (abridged edition) ii
Taquetta's Credentials iii
Soul Stealers Prayer Charge iv
Table of Contents v
Foreword by Dr. Jackie Green vii
Foreword by Dr. Oscar Guobadia ix
Foreword by Prophet Stephen Halliburton xi
DEMON DEALING / SOUL STEALING 1
ANOINTED OPERATIONS OF A SCOUT 4
POWER AND AUTHORITY OF A SCOUT 7
TRUTH ABOUT CONVICTION 9
HONORING THE BOUNDARIES OF GOD 13
WITCHCRAFT AND THE NEW AGE MOVEMENT 27
ANCIENT NEW AGE CUSTOMS 35
CURIOUS ARTS 70
THE ETHNICITY OF JESUS 129
DEMON DEALING ORGANIZATIONS 133
WITCHES AND WARLOCKS 161
COSMIC MEDITATION AND CELESTIAL ACTIVITY 164
CHURCH WITCHES AND WARLOCKS 168
BABYLONIAN CHRISTIANITY 177
COMMUNING WITH DECEASED RELATIVES 182
CHARISMATIC WITCHCRAFT 195
CHRISTIAN GIMMICKS 199
WITCHCRAFT VERSUS PROPHETIC ACTS 204
POLITICAL DEMON DEALING 209
THE POWER OF ALGORITHMS 215
MEDIA DEMON DEALING 219
ENTERTAINMENT DEMON DEALING 225

INTERFAITH PERSECTIVE	233
SHIFTING TO FREEDOM	235
SOUL STEALER DELIVERANCE PRAYER	246
SOUL STEALER TEST	248
SOUL STEALER ANSWER KEY	259
SOUL STEALER DEFINITION INDEX	270
SOUL STEALER DEFINITION INDEX CONT.	271
REFERENCES	272

A comprehensive list of the information available in this manual can be found in the index section at the end of this book. This will allow you to go to a specific page based on the topic you are looking for.

Foreword by Dr. Jackie Green

*"Since the 2020 Presidential Election in America, those with eyes to see and ears to hear in the Spirit, saw charismatic witchcraft on prime-time TV and every form of social media. We saw a pure example of loyalty to a leader, under charismatic witchcraft powers. Loyalty to a man outweighed character, truth, and integrity. This was a "national test" to prepare for the coming of the Anti-Christ, and the Church largely failed the test, America failed the test, and even failure among high profile leaders, senators, capitol police and power thirsty political parties. That is why this book is so important. It will help the Church remove spiritual blinders and reveal the many types and strategies of **Soul Stealers** at work among us." Bishop Dr. Jackie L. Green*

As one of Apostle Taquetta Baker's spiritual mothers, I am again honored to say a word regarding this **_Volume II of the Power of the Scouts- Soul Stealers_**. It is straight *"meat of the Word"* and not for babes. This book will challenge your level of truth and understanding of the meaning of the Lord's Prayer that Jesus taught us," *Deliver Us from Evil."* This book can accomplish that prayer in your life, if you are able to chew it, swallow it and digest hard truths about the condition of our nation and especially the condition of the Church, and the Body of Christ as a whole.

One of the greatest concerns I have after reading the entire book is **"Can today's pastors and church leaders eat all of it?"** Or is the Church in the hands of *demon dealers* and s*oul stealers*, persons that operate like God sent them, but they transform themselves as the devil's ministers, and Satan is their father, and the Church are sheep to the slaughter. _A demon dealer will hate this book_, because it will reveal the truth about who is their father, God, or Satan.

Dr. Baker states: *"Witchcraft will be released at an enormous rate in the coming days. There will be divination and dimensions of witchcraft unveiled that the earth has not seen yet. There is an increase of people becoming witches and warlocks and this is becoming a norm. There will continue to be an increase of people declaring they are Christian witches and warlocks; and this will be received as the lines of biblical standard become blurred, devalued, and outlawed. It is time out for being scared of witchcraft, witches, warlocks and scared to confront and other throw it."*

Dr. Baker's ability and dedication to months and months of research and gathering information is sounding an alarm that the Church is desperately in need of tough truth, that has birthed this book "**_Soul Stealers._**" It is a reliable and user-friendly New Age and Occult encyclopedia. This author's work must be appreciated and valued, along with the realization of immense spiritual warfare that has attacked her while preparing this book for publication. Dr. Baker is a gift to the Body of Christ to *"keep people from perishing for a lack of knowledge"* that can save their lives from *soul snatchers and death.*

In a section titled *"Church Witches and Warlocks,"* Dr. Baker shares that: *"Some saints are now rogue witches and warlocks because they were not taught how to steward their gifts and powers of the prophetic, seed in the church or in life. They go to the dark side where they can at least walk in their calling even if it is not for the true and living God."* As I read the *48*

Characteristics of a Church Witch, it sounds a lot like the people in our churches today from the pulpit to the door.

THIS BOOK WILL BRING THE CHURCH - THE BODY OF CHRIST OUT OF DENIAL. IT WILL DESTROY IGNORANCE AND SPIRITUAL BLINDNESS AND CHALLENGE THE PRESENCE OF BLIND GUIDES IN AMERICAN PULPITS.

Dr. Baker cautions believers to not get entangled and be so gullible of what you hear and see but *"resist the popular word of well-known leaders over God's truth. We must be willing to be the only one in the room that sees truth and separates ourselves from the New Age witchcraft, gimmicks, and idolatry that is being presented to us by platform prophets, apostles, teachers, pastors, evangelists, ministers of this day. We must be willing to stand in truth, go higher in truth, and do whatever is necessary to stand inside the truth of God."*

Today, we are in trouble without God's Holy Spirit of Truth. This book gives the Church and those seeking for truth in this hour a "fact check." Check with the Holy Spirit, for He is the only One that is the Holy Lie Detector for the Believer in Christ. The news, media, and social media avenues is like A SPIRITUAL SUICIDE GUMBO. It is enticing and satisfies the taste buds with spicy flavors, but you do not really know what is in it. We had better start seeking the Holy Spirit about the GUMBO and the KOOLAID we are eating and drinking!

The biggest Soul Stealing demon Dr. Baker addresses is the *Media Demon Dealing and Entertainment Demon Dealing*, namely Hollywood. Dr. Baker so eloquently says, *"With the rise of social media, truth has been replaced!"*

In closing, the terms **Demon Dealing** and **Soul Stealing** might sound scary and non-religious. But the Holy Spirit of Truth is trying to get our attention and He is using Dr. Taquetta Baker as an end-time voice calling the Church back to righteousness, truth, and the Kingdom of God. There is something in this book for every believer, even youth and babes in Christ.

Set the table, get your plates and your knife, spoon, and fork, and get ready to eat a full course meal of God's truth that will surely begin the process of delivering us from all evil. **God's Truth is Marching on!**

Bishop Dr. Jackie L. Green, Overseer
JGM-Enternational Prayer Life Institute
Redlands, California

Foreword by Dr. Oscar Guobadia

The Apostle Paul spent a considerable amount of time addressing the church at Ephesus, giving them a six chaptered epistle on both the wealth and the walk of the Church. As he ends this epistle, he reminds them of the real danger out there: *"Finally, my brethren, be strong in the Lord and in the power of His might. Put on the whole armour of God, that you may be able to stand against the wiles of the devil. For we do not wrestle against flesh and blood, but against principalities, against powers, against the rulers of the darkness of this age, against spiritual hosts of wickedness in the heavenly places" - Ephesians 6:10-12 (NKJV).*

Even in his day, there were systems that Apostle Paul had to contend with as we see both the Pauline and Petrine epistles. Both Paul and Peter had spent a large chunk of their letters to warn the Church against the false teachers and teachings spreading across churches. At a point, Paul wrote to the Corinthian Church warning them to be careful of the so-called apostles: *"But what I do, I will also continue to do, that I may cut off the opportunity from those who desire an opportunity to be regarded just as we are in the things of which they boast. For such are false apostles, deceitful workers, transforming themselves into apostles of Christ. And no wonder! For Satan himself transforms himself into an angel of light. Therefore, it is no great thing if his ministers also transform themselves into ministers of righteousness, whose end will be according to their works" - 2 Cor 11:12-15.*

Paul mentions false Apostles and deceitful workers who transform themselves into apostles of Christ. If they transformed themselves as apostles of Christ, then they are apostles of Satan because their master also transforms himself. There are three beings that transform themselves into: False Apostles and ministers, the devil, and the demons. It is with this scripture I believe this wonderful book – *Soul Stealers* - does justice of discerning the spirits behind these acts.

We experience a life where the dark world is unknown and untaught. People live their lives not considering the consequences of their actions whatsoever. Sadly, even within some of the Christian denominations, the issue of demonology and satanology seems to be alien in those gatherings. There awaits a major disaster when the Church pay no mind to demons, systems, their practices, and impact in the earth. I am grateful that the Lord would allow seasoned voices with an in-depth knowledge of the dark world, to shed light, and bring illumination, so the Church can understand how to engage in spiritual warfare.

Dr. Taquetta Baker has impeccably given language and deep research in this area. Her understanding of the underworld is mind blowing. I thank God for this revelation because I know this resource will be of great blessing to the Church, especially the prophetic apostolic churches, with a mandate for deliverance. I can testify firsthand that she is a naturally gifted teacher and apostle of the Lord who has done the church a great blessing by taking the time to unveil mysteries from both in the scriptures and history of certain demonic practices.

Dr Taquetta's work is a masterpiece as she talks about the dark world, not just in the world we live in, but in the Church. She exposes demonic activities guised as the new prophetic and apostolic movements, practices that has no bearing with scriptures and heretic teachings parading the podium. This work should be on every shelf and cabinet of every serious Christian, especially those called to intercession. She has extensively brought language to the realm of the unseen and I am incredibly grateful to forward this work.

My Prayer is that this book blesses you as it has blessed me.

Dr Oscar Guobadia
Apostolic Leader, The Brook Place, UK.
Author, The Great Misconceptions
Director, Brook School of Prophets, Prophetic mentoring Program.

Foreword by Prophet Steven Halliburton

Throughout my years of ministry, I have come to realize that many believers, cities, regions, and territories are bound and oppressed by demonic powers and demonic systems. I have come to realize that one of the main reasons for such widespread bondage is rooted in the fact that many are ignorant to Satan's devices. In *2Corinthians 2:11*, the Apostle Paul makes a critical statement to the Corinthian believers, *"lest Satan should take advantage of us; for we are not ignorant of his devices."* In this one statement, Paul provides us with an important revelation: Ignorance prevents us from being able to stand against the wiles of the devil. Ignorance prevents us from being able to defeat our adversary, Satan, and his demonic forces.

In this powerful manuscript, *Volume II Unmasking the Power of the Scouts: Soul Stealers*, Apostle Taquetta Baker begins to reveal the multifaceted rank, file, order, and systems of operations of Satan's kingdom, while also empowering the believer with tools and strategies to overcome Satan's tactics. As I began to read her writings, I was reminded of my time of military service in the United States Army. While reading this book, I began to see a direct parallelism between the natural structure of a military fighting force and the structure of a spiritual fighting force. In America, the U.S. Army also employs the use of scouts during combat operations. Each unit of scouts are generally given an area of operations and a scope of jurisdictional authority and functionality. This same principle applies in a spiritual context as well.

In her book, Apostle Baker reveals the identity of scouts as well as their methods of operations and the believers' defense against such forces. I believe that this book is an excellent tool that all believers should add to their libraries. In fact, I highly recommend this book to all believers, and especially those who are called to the ministry of deliverance and spiritual warfare.

As you read this book and journey through its contents, I believe that you will be blessed and empowered to walk in your authority as a believer, while simultaneously being equipped to continue the work of advancing the Kingdom of God here on earth.

~ Prophet Steven Halliburton
Senior Pastor of The Brook Place Clarksville, Clarksville, TN

Chapter 1

DEMON DEALING/SOUL STEALING
Angels of Lights

How witchcraft and idolatry infiltrate our lives:

A demon dealer is someone who presents witchcraft, idolatry, sin, and worldliness as harmless and beneficial to our happiness and overall well-being. They appear to be normal productive citizens of society or of a ministry but are strategically positioned to influence people with witchcraft and demonization. They present themselves and what they are dealing with beauty, glam, and with pertinent necessity so you will be attracted with lust and desire to have it. The attraction evolves into a mesmerizing obsession.

Demon dealers operate subtly as if they have a concern for your wellbeing and as if what they are dealing you will bring healing, prosperity, and other benefits of wellness, success, and progress.

These demon dealers could be your boss, child's teacher, your child's friends, parents, family members (your grandma, auntie, mother), a neighbor, a cashier, doctor, a counselor, the waiter, a Sunday school teacher, minister, your social media sensation, or the food pantry volunteer. *You get my drift????*

***2Corinthians 11:13-14** For such are false apostles, deceitful workers, transforming themselves into the apostles of Christ. And no marvel; for Satan himself is transformed into an angel of light. Therefore, it is no great thing if his ministers also be transformed as the ministers of righteousness; whose end shall be according to their works.*

These demon dealers transform into apostles of Christ. *Apostle* means *"commissioner with miraculous powers, delegate; specially, an ambassador, messenger, a sent one."*

They take on an office of high rank in the spirit realm and believe it their duty to operate like God's "sent one" even though the devil sent them. They transform themselves in appearance, figure, and operation, even though their motive is deceitful and ungodly.

Then they – the devil's ministers - transform into ministers of righteousness.

The definition of the word *minister* is *diakonos*:
1. one who run on errands, an attendant, a waiter (at table or in other menial duties); specially, a Christian teacher and pastor (technically, a deacon or deaconess),
2. deacon, minister, servant,
3. one who executes the commands of another, esp. of a master, a servant, attendant, minister the servant of a king.

Are you hearing this? SHIFT RIGHT NOW!

This minister operates like a Christian teacher, pastor, deacon, minister, servant, but runs errands for the devil, and is, in fact, an attendant of the devil. The devil is the king that they serve.

<u>*Righteousness*</u> is <u>*dikaiosynē* in Greek and means:</u>
1. state of him who is as he ought to be, righteousness,
2. the condition acceptable to God,
3. the doctrine concerning the way in which man may attain a state approved of God, integrity, virtue, purity of life, rightness, correctness of thinking feeling, and acting in a narrower sense, justice or the virtue which gives each his due.

Imagine the following scenario with me. There is a demon dealer, one used by Satan, appearing like a minister of God. They know how to counterfeit integrity, virtue, purity of life, rightness, correctness of thinking, feeling, and justice. The dividing line between a demon dealer and an authentic man or woman of God is exposed in the outcome. The result of their actions is for personal gain, profit, purpose, and motive. The agenda is to glorify and expand the kingdom of darkness rather than the kingdom of God.

Let's be honest. We see this frequently and have come to accept it. We even use the scripture about wheat and tares growing up together (Matthew 13:25-40) to justify why no action is taken. We even discern its true motives, but because it has the perceived fruit of righteousness and appears as a gospel minister - one who is carrying the salvation welfare of God, we cast off our discernment and accept this as God.

- ✓ This is how witchcraft ends up being compared to and likened to Christianity.
- ✓ This is how witches and warlocks are embraced as laborers of the Lord.
- ✓ This is how demons become leaders and ministries, while contending they are godly even though much of their actions demonstrate that they are servants of themselves and the devil.
- ✓ This is how we become desensitized to magic, sorcery, witchcraft, paganism, satanism, yoga, idolatry, and new age practices and think it does not impact us or our children.
- ✓ This is how we are SHIFTING far away from God, his government, covenant with him, and his standards for our lives, families, regions, nations, and spheres of influence.

Desensitizing the people of God has become Satan's most effective tactic.

We have exposed ourselves to the demonic angels of light who operate as demon dealers, we blur the lines of sin, which causes sin to become the norm and standard among us.

While profit and gain are secondary effects, the main purpose of demon dealers is to steal souls. Many people who are demon dealers may not realize who they have become. They may profess they are doing good and have failed to grasp their demonic ideologies and allegiance. They may have started out on the right path but made choices that left them subject to the enemy becoming their ruling influence. ***But the devil knows.***

John 10:10 *says, The thief cometh not, but for to steal, and to kill, and to destroy: I am come that they might have life, and that they might have it more abundantly.*

<u>Thief</u> is *kleptēs* in the Greek and means:
1. a stealer (literally or figuratively): — thief,
2. an embezzler, pilferer,
3. the name is transferred to false teachers, who do not care to instruct men, but abuse their confidence for their own gain.

There are many examples throughout the scripture of leaders who started with right motive but let personal agenda pull them into darkness. The devil is a legalist, and he knows not only when you have stepped into his territory, but he knows his rights. Look at the priests in the Book of Ezekiel 8:1-18 who became saturated with their personal agenda until they were convinced, they could hide it from God. *"The Lord does not see us . . .."*

Ezekiel 8:12 *Then He said to me, "Son of man, have you seen what the elders of the house of Israel do in the dark, every man in the room of his idols? For they say, 'The Lord does not see us, the Lord has forsaken the land.'"*

The devil knows that his workings are not for our good. He understands his goal is to steal our souls so that we will not live abundantly with Christ in this life or in eternity. We must know that what we may conceive as good, may be jeopardizing souls. I decree this book will raise up ***SCOUTS*** who can discern demon dealers quickly and stand for justice in asserting and overthrowing their powers and authorities in the earth.

Chapter 2

ANOINTED OPERATIONS OF A SCOUT

This Chapter is from Dr. Taquetta Baker's Book,
"Unmasking the Power of The Scout Manual I."

When you are called as an intercessory watchman for a person, ministry, business, organization, or region, you are serving in the position of a scout.

A scout operates in the offensive positions of a watchman, seer, prophet, dreamer, intercessor, soldier, stealth bomber, and sniper. Scouts are employed to inspect, observe, or survey the enemy to gain and gather information for military purposes. Scouts observe and report on the following:

- Character, nature, and personality,
- Abilities and capabilities,
- Likes and dislikes,
- Habits and patterns,
- Strengths and weaknesses,
- Movements, locations, and operations,
- Strategies and techniques,
- Environments and habitats to which they maneuver and dwell,
- Identity, purpose, and mission,
- Personal, geographical, and generational power and operation,
- History, culture, language, and communication strategies.

Your intel is beneficial to being offensive against the enemy, while annihilating any present or future attack or counterattack.

A scout is the eyes and ears for the army of the Lord. It is not something you do; it is your identity. When intel is needed on the enemy, you can maneuver around the enemy's camp or on the battleground and collect intel.

Scouts are not meant to be seen and are not trying to be seen. If you have a need to be seen, then you are not a scout. A need to be seen will get you and your team attacked.

If a scout can be seen it is because God is allowing it and has called the scout to continuously confront the powers of darkness with their very existence. A scout with this mandate will have constant opposition with the powers of darkness for the purposes of being God's judgment, justice, authority, exposer, and annihilator of darkness everywhere that they go.

Scouts are fearless and able to detect the salvation of the Lord in a situation. No matter what they observe, they maintain the eyes, ears, goodness, and victories of God. If you are a scaredy cat and are swayed by your emotions, circumstances, and the powers of your enemy, then you are not a scout. Scouts always know God is greater than anything and that they are greater through him.

Scouts encourage others to see God's hand in a situation or to see a situation like God sees it. Scouts are self-sacrificing to the cause, good of the vision, and the people.

Scouts operate under a stealth bomber and a sniper anointing.

Stealth Bomber - A stealth bomber is one who maneuvers into the enemy's camp undetected to save people, recover things that have been stolen, combat the enemy, destroy spiritual covens and high places, etc.

Psalm 18:28-29 For thou wilt light my candle: the Lord my God will enlighten my darkness. For by thee I have run through a troop; and by my God have I leaped over a wall.

Sniper – enters the spirit realm undetected while blending, hiding, and moving about strategically to gain entail and attack the enemy.

Joshua 23:10 One man of you shall chase a thousand: for the Lord your God, he it is that fighteth for you, as he hath promised you.

Chase (*radap*) in this scripture means, *"to pursue, hunt, attend closely to, persecute, put to flight."* A scout possesses capabilities to discern their target, gain intel, and take their enemy out quickly. In the Old Testament, scouting was used as a warfare tactic. Moses and Joshua sent men to scout out the land.

Deuteronomy 1:22 Then all of you approached me and said, 'Let us send men before us, that they may search out the land for us, and bring back to us word of the way by which we should go up and the cities which we shall enter.'

Numbers 13:1-2 And the Lord spoke to Moses, saying, "Send men to spy out the land of Canaan, which I am giving to the children of Israel; from each tribe of their fathers you shall send a man, every one a leader among them."

Joshua 7:2 New International Bible Joshua sent some of his men from Jericho to spy out the town of Ai, east of Bethel, near Beth-aven.

In the New Testament, scouting was used as a tactic to seize Jesus Christ for the purposes of crucifying him and to spy on the disciples.

Luke 20:20-22 So they watched Him, and sent spies who pretended to be righteous, in order that they might catch Him in some statement, so that they could deliver Him to the rule and the authority of the governor. They questioned Him, saying, "Teacher, we know that You speak and teach correctly, and You are not partial to any, but teach the way of God in truth." Is it lawful for us to pay taxes to Caesar, or not?"

Galatians 2:3-5 The Message Bible *Significantly, Titus, non-Jewish though he was, was not required to be circumcised. While we were in conference, we were infiltrated by spies pretending to be Christians, who slipped in to find out just how free true Christians are. Their ulterior motive was to reduce us to their brand of servitude. We didn't give them the time of day. We were determined to preserve the truth of the Message for you.*

Chapter 3

POWER AND AUTHORITY OF A SCOUT

The devil roams about as a scout spying out people and the land seeking whom he can devour and sends demons to spy on us.

1Peter 5:8 Be sober, be vigilant; because your adversary the devil, as a roaring lion, walketh about, seeking whom he may devour:

Scouts are called to understand, know, and contend against wiles of devil and his high-ranking demonic forces and powers.

Ephesians 6:12 For we wrestle not against flesh and blood, but against principalities, against powers, against the rulers of the darkness of this world, against spiritual wickedness in high places.

Scouts do this by understanding and operating in levels of warfare and rankings:

Levels of Warfare

Ground Level Warfare involves casting demons out of individuals, places, and things.

Occult Level Warfare involves witchcraft, idolatry, or strategic organizations that are really powers of darkness, or spiritual wickedness in high places within a community or region. Examples, Freemasonry, Sororities, Fraternities, New Age Practices, Buddhism, Tibetan, Yoga, etc.

Strategic Level Warfare is where principalities and territorial spirits are assigned by Satan to directly bind, influence, and govern the activities of communities, regions, states, and nations. They also coordinate demonic activities in political, governmental, economic, financial, educational, business, and entertainment arenas.

Demon Rankings

Demons are demonic forces, evil spirits or devils that possess, depress, oppress, torment, influence, or establish a stronghold with a person, place, or thing. The way these demonic spirits attack is as follows:

- **Oppress** -to burden, restrain, weigh heavy upon, to put down; press down, subdue, or suppress an atmosphere or the soul, heart, or body of a person.
- **Depress** – to make sad or gloomy; lower in spirits; deject, dispirit, to lower in force, vigor, activity, etc.; weaken, make dull, a person or atmosphere.

> - **Negatively influence** – cause confusion, discombobulation, double mindedness, unexplainable weariness, tiredness or sluggardness, irritation, frustration, ungodly thoughts, thought racing within a person or atmosphere.
> - **Possess** – to occupy, dominate, or control a person or atmosphere.

Strongholds are demonically possessed, demonically depressed, demonically gripping clutches, barriers, fortresses, walls, or entanglements that harass, influence, hinder and/or prevent a person from being free to walk in the full salvation of the Lord (*2Corinthians 10:3-5, Ephesians 4:22-23, Matthew 16:19, Mark 3:27*).

Principalities are satanic princes and territorial spirits ruling over a nation, city, region, and community for the purposes of establishing Satan's demonic plan in people's lives and spheres.

Powers are high ranking supernatural demons or demonic influences that cause evil and sin in the world.

Rulers of Darkness are demonic forces that govern deception and manipulative hardships and catastrophes that are generally produced by witchcraft, manipulation of the weather and worldly systems; they operate in cultures and countries such that idolatry and sin reign in the earth.

Spiritual Wickedness in High Places are evil plots and deceptions, and demonic attacks directed in and against the church and God's people for the purposes of hindering, contaminating and demolishing God's will in the earth.

Witchcraft Practices

Witchcraft is the practice of magic, especially black magic; it is the utilization of spells and the invocation of demons to bind people, families, ministries, businesses, organizations, land, atmospheres, climates, regions, and nations. Some people engage in witchcraft for entertainment, curiosity, or due to ignorance. Those that dedicate their lives to it use it to acquire personal success and advancement, power, fame, rank in spiritual realms, spheres, and to obtain high-ranking positions and platforms in the natural.

As a scout, it is important to study witchcraft and gain intel on their operations. One of your mandates as a scout is to deal with spiritual wickedness in high places and to pull down high places. Witchcraft has become more prevalent and blatant and confrontation of witches, warlocks, and witchcraft is essential for cleansing the land and airways of regions, and dispelling spells sent about the ministers, ministries, organizations, and businesses of God. Witches are known to come to services posing as saints, while releasing spells against the people and purposes of God. They are known to cast spells on ministers and against events. As a scout, you may even encounter witches in your dream realm, during Holy Spirit translations, or during intercessory and spiritual warfare. Scouts are not afraid of witches and witchcraft. Know your authority and gain intel on how witchcraft operates so you can quickly discern and dispel its workings.

Chapter 4
TRUTH ABOUT CONVICTION

Do not rejoice because you have no conviction about a matter thus assuming it is a pass to engage in something that very well might offend God. A lack of conviction could mean:

- You are still immature in the Lord.
- God is tired of talking to you about the matter.
- God is not your Lord.
- You do not have the Holy Spirit.
- You are not guided by the Holy Spirit.
- Flesh, soul, and emotions guide you.
- You are still in a soul-tie to the world and its transgressions.
- God's biblical word is not operable in you.
- You lack the fear of the Lord.
- You have become dull to God's voice or the unction of the Holy Spirit.
- You have a demonic possession or oppression.

Conviction is a spiritual awareness of wanting to live in right standing with the Lord.

Conviction is not a feeling or emotion. It is not guilt, shame, or condemnation, as these are works of our emotions and not the spirit of the Lord.
Conviction is not a quickening because that is flesh that may or may not be responding to our spirit. Depending on the day, flesh can be loud and grievous in its response or have no response.

Psalm 32:1-5 *Blessed is he whose transgression is forgiven; whose sin is covered. Blessed is the man unto whom the Lord imputeth not iniquity, and in whose spirit there is no guile. When I kept silence, my bones waxed old through my roaring all the day long. For day and night thy hand was heavy upon me: my moisture is turned into the drought of summer. Selah. I acknowledged my sin unto thee, and mine iniquity have I not hid. I said, I will confess my transgressions unto the Lord; and thou forgavest the iniquity of my sin. Selah.*

<u>Guile</u> in Hebrew is *remîyâ* and means:
1. remissness, treachery,
2. deceit (-ful, -fully), false, guile, idle, slack, slothful,
3. deceitful, laxness, slackness, slackening, deceit, treachery.

When you have a spirit without guile, you are not trying to see what you can get away with. You are striving to live in the truth, righteousness, and honor of the Lord.

David said it is good when God does not have to impute one to iniquity and that we are blessed when we confess our sins. Impute means that God called us out on our sin. This is what we deem to be conviction. Though the Holy Spirit does this at times, it is usually because we are not self-aware of God's word and sin. Or it is because we have asked for conviction. It is not because we are only sinning if the Holy Spirit convicts us.

David did not glory in sin or the fact that he did not have conviction. He was a man after God's own heart so he was harder on himself than God or anyone else could ever be when he sinned. He had a fear of the Lord's wrath because of his sin.

Psalm 38:1-10 *O Lord, rebuke me not in thy wrath: neither chasten me in thy hot displeasure. For thine arrows stick fast in me, and thy hand presseth me sore. There is no soundness in my flesh because of thine anger; neither is there any rest in my bones because of my sin. For mine iniquities are gone over mine head: as an heavy burden they are too heavy for me. My wounds stink and are corrupt because of my foolishness. I am troubled; I am bowed down greatly; I go mourning all the day long. For my loins are filled with a loathsome disease: and there is no soundness in my flesh. I am feeble and sore broken: I have roared by reason of the disquietness of my heart. Lord, all my desire is before thee; and my groaning is not hid from thee. My heart panteth, my strength faileth me: as for the light of mine eyes, it also is gone from me.*

David desires truth in his inward parts and knew that having inward truth helped him to know the wisdom and standards of the Lord.

Psalm 51:1-6 *Have mercy upon me, O God, according to thy lovingkindness: according unto the multitude of thy tender mercies blot out my transgressions. Wash me throughly from mine iniquity, and cleanse me from my sin. For I acknowledge my transgressions: and my sin is ever before me. Against thee, thee only, have I sinned, and done this evil in thy sight: that thou mightest be justified when thou speakest, and be clear when thou judgest. Behold, I was shapen in iniquity; and in sin did my mother conceive me. Behold, thou desirest truth in the inward parts: and in the hidden part thou shalt make me to know wisdom.*

Psalm 51:7-14 *Purge me with hyssop, and I shall be clean: wash me, and I shall be whiter than snow. Make me to hear joy and gladness; that the bones which thou hast broken may rejoice. Hide thy face from my sins, and blot out all mine iniquities. Create in me a clean heart, O God; and renew a right spirit within me. Cast me not away from thy presence; and take not thy holy spirit from me. Restore unto me the joy of thy salvation; and uphold me with thy free spirit. Then will I teach transgressors thy ways; and sinners shall be converted unto thee. Deliver me from bloodguiltiness, O God, thou God of my salvation: and my tongue shall sing aloud of thy righteousness.*

David so earnestly pursued God's heart that he even repented for his war acts. Blood guiltiness was bloodshed in war. Though he was fighting for God and operating in his calling as a warrior, he understood that some of the casualties were innocent and that all bloodshed was not just or needful and that even though God commissioned war, he also viewed bloodshed as unclean.

To have a clean heart created within you, you must first acknowledge that your heart needs to be clean and then ask God to do the work. You must seek deliverance and healing even when you have not committed blatant or conscious sin or think you are pure before God. David sought a broken spirit and a contrite heart. He understood that is a sacrifice unto the Lord.

Psalm 51:17 *The sacrifices of God are a broken spirit: a broken and a contrite heart, O God, thou wilt not despise.*

<u>Broken is *šâbar* in Hebrew and means:</u>
1. to burst (literally or figuratively),
2. break (down, off, in pieces, up), broken((-hearted)), bring to the birth, crush, destroy, hurt, quench, quite, tear,
3. break in pieces,
    a) (Qal)break, break in or down, rend violently, wreck, crush, quench, to break, rupture,
    b) (Niphal)to be broken, be maimed, be crippled, be wrecked, to be broken, be crushed,
    c) (Piel) to shatter.

<u>Contrite is *dâkâ* in Hebrew and means:</u>
1. to collapse (phys. or mentally),
2. break (sore), contrite, crouch,
3. to crush, be crushed, be contrite,
4. be broken,
    a) (Qal) to be crushed, collapse,
    b) (Niphal) to be crushed, be contrite, be broken,
    c) (Piel)to crush down to crush to pieces.

Jesus came to bring a reproving which means he came to release conviction.

John 16:8 *And when he is come, he will reprove the world of sin, and of righteousness, and of judgment.*

<u>Reprove is *elegchō* in Greek and means:</u>
1. to confute, admonish, convict, convince, tell a fault, rebuke, reprove,
2. to convict, refute, confute generally with a suggestion of shame of the person convicted by conviction, to bring to the light, to expose,
3. to find fault with, correct by word, to reprehend severely, chide, admonish, reprove, to call to account, show one his fault, demand an explanation, by deed to chasten, to punish.

In ***John 16:9-14***, Jesus reveals his reasons bringing conviction:

Verse 9 Of sin, because they believe not on me; (He came to bring enlightenment to unbelievers)

Verse 10 Of righteousness, because I go to my Father, and ye see me no more; (To release righteousness on earth)

Verse 11 Of judgment, because the prince of this world is judged. (To judge Satan and his demons)

When Jesus came, he could not reveal all the reasons he came to convict us but said the Holy Spirit would come and guide us into all truth.

Verse 12 *I have yet many things to say unto you, but ye cannot bear them now. Howbeit when he, the Spirit of truth, is come, he will guide you into all truth: for he shall not speak of himself; but whatsoever he shall hear, that shall he speak: and he will shew you things to come. He shall glorify me: for he shall receive of mine, and shall shew it unto you.*

The Holy Spirit convicts through him being able to guide your life.

1John 2:20 *But ye have an unction from the Holy One, and ye know all things.*

New Living Bible *But you have an anointing from the Holy One, and all of you know the truth.*

The Amplified Bible *But you have been anointed by [you hold a sacred appointment from, you have been given an unction from] the Holy One, and you all know [the Truth] or you know all things.*

This unction is not a fleshing quickening. It is a spiritual oil, a spiritual endowment, where you just know truth or brought into truth.

The Holy Spirit brings enlightenment and conviction as you allow him to be the governor and leader of your life. If you feel no remorse about a matter that is suspect, rooted in sin, sinful, demonic, demonically rooted, the first thing to do is to search whether the Holy Spirit is guiding you. Seek the truth and guidance of the Holy Spirit.

Also, know that if God is placing information in your path then that is part of how he operates. sometimes his guidance comes from an urgency to read and pay attention to something that is put before you. When you immediately reject it with no thought to examine it with him, it was not that you were not unctioned - or quickened - you did not respond to the unctioning of the spirit. You ignored or disregarded it. It became something you did not want to hear or already made up in your mind was not an area of your life you were willing to give up or examine yourself about.

To boast in a lack of conviction for something that is clearly unrighteousness - not the character or nature of God is unwise. It does not mean you have his permission or grace. Only he can tell you what it really means. Therefore, seek him for truth before you think you have God's permission to engage in it.

Grace was not granted so we could be given a free sin card or pass to sin. Grace was granted to empower us to overcome sin (***Study Romans 3:20-31 NIV***).

Chapter 5

HONORING THE BOUNDARIES OF GOD

Many revelations in this book are going to challenge the reader. This is because once reading the revelation, the reader will be pricked by Holy Spirit to be accountable regarding what they learn and to aid others in being delivered and set free. Many of these concepts as it relates to demon dealing is centered around transgressions, sins, ancestral and ethnic customs and traditions, and pleasurable and self-motivating activities, that many people did not regard as ungodly, have been doing a long time, and may not want to rid themselves. I get it. I am not teaching something that I did not first have to live and have my own life purged (over and over).

There have been so many things in my life that I did not know was demon dealing until God revealed it to me. Some of those things were easy to relinquish, and others I released with dread and fear of the Lord more so than wanting to let them go. My desire to please God was more important to me than holding on to something that would jeopardize my life and relationship with him. I admit that the cost and responsibility to change requires conscious effort and intentionality. It required the ridding of customs, people, relationships, material possessions, social settings, and activities, that I was not ready in my own strength to relinquish. Sometimes I had to cry out for a heart that loved what God loved and hate what God hates. And even now, I constantly ask for quick conviction and keen discernment so I can immediately know when I am succumbing into demon dealing as this help me SHIFT immediately to choosing God and what is beneficial to me and others, over what is ungodly no matter how good, innocent, or customary it appears. Let us explore the reasons SHIFTING out of demon dealing can be a challenge:

Sin brings pleasure to our lives. We like to feel good; we will risk a little pleasure, even at the expense of displeasing God, dying, and going to hell.

Proverbs 19:21 *There are many devices in a man's heart; nevertheless the counsel of the LORD, that shall stand.*

Pleasures are rooted in ancestral, family, religious, societal, ethical, and cultural customs, and traditions. We love the pleasures of our traditions and the unity that is symbolizes. Yet unity among a particular group that disregards the principles of God, causes division between that group and God.

Mark 7:8 New International Bible *You have let go of the commands of God and are holding on to human traditions.*

New Living Bible *For you ignore God's law and substitute your own tradition.*

Romans 12.2 *And be not conformed to this world: but be ye transformed by the renewing of your mind, that ye may prove what is that good, and acceptable, and perfect, will of God.*

The Amplified Bible *Do not be conformed to this world (this age), [fashioned after and adapted to its external, superficial customs], but be transformed (changed) by the [entire] renewal of your mind [by its new ideals and its new attitude], so that you may prove [for yourselves] what is the good and acceptable and perfect will of God, even the thing which is good and acceptable and perfect [in His sight for you].*

Pleasures are not considered big sins in man's eyes, but all sin is the transgression against God. Blasphemy against the Holy Ghost is an unforgivable sin. There are also sins that God hates, but sin is sin to God. All sin is despised in God's eyes.

Matthew 12:31-32 *Therefore I say to you, any sin and blasphemy shall be forgiven people, but blasphemy against the Spirit shall not be forgiven. "Whoever speaks a word against the Son of Man, it shall be forgiven him; but whoever speaks against the Holy Spirit, it shall not be forgiven him, either in this age or in the age to come.*

Proverbs 6:16-19 New International Bible *There are six things the Lord hates, seven that are detestable to him: haughty eyes, a lying tongue, hands that shed innocent blood, a heart that devises wicked schemes, feet that are quick to rush into evil, a false witness who pours out lies and a person who stirs up conflict in the community.*

Romans 3:10 *As it is written, There is none righteous, no, not one.*

Romans 3:23 *For all have sinned, and come short of the glory of God.*

James 2:10-11 *For whosoever shall keep the whole law, and yet offend in one [point], he is guilty of all. For he that said, Do not commit adultery, said also, Do not kill. Now if thou commit no adultery, yet if thou kill, thou art become a transgressor of the law.*

Many ungodly pleasures are not specifically listed in the Bible yet spoken clearly in context to them being out of alignment with God. Through this, we know God's commandments, but only want to implement them or obey them when they benefit us. When they do not benefit us, we look for loopholes to insert our will above God's laws. This does not change the law. It changes our relationship and stature in God.

Psalm 102:27 *But You are the same, And Your years will have no end.*

Malachi 3:6 *For I am the LORD, I change not; therefore ye sons of Jacob are not consumed.*

James 1:17 *Every good and perfect gift is from above, coming down from the Father of the heavenly lights, with whom there is no change or shifting shadow.*

Psalm 119:1-5 The Amplified Bible *BLESSED (HAPPY, fortunate, to be envied) are the undefiled (the upright, truly sincere, and blameless) in the way [of the revealed will of God], who walk (order their conduct and conversation) in the law of the Lord (the whole of God's revealed will). Blessed (happy, fortunate, to be envied) are they who keep His testimonies, and who seek, inquire for and of Him and crave Him with the whole heart. Yes, they do no* *unrighteousness [no willful wandering from His precepts]; they walk in His ways. You have commanded us to keep Your precepts, that we should observe them diligently. Oh, that my ways were directed and established to observe Your statutes [hearing, receiving, loving, and obeying them]!*

Psalm 119:168 *I obey your precepts and your statutes, for all my ways are known to you.*

Proverbs 5:21 New Living Bible *For your ways are in full view of the LORD, and he examines all your paths.*

Jeremiah 42:6 *Whether it is pleasant or unpleasant, we will listen to the voice of the LORD our God to whom we are sending you, so that it may go well with us when we listen to the voice of the LORD our God.*

1John 5:2 *By this we know that we love the children of God, when we love God and observe His commandments.*

2Timothy 3:16-17 *All scripture is given by inspiration of God, and is profitable for doctrine, for reproof, for correction, for instruction in righteousness: That the man of God may be perfect, thoroughly furnished unto all good works.*

Our desires seem harmless on the surface, but are sometimes rooted in idolatry, paganism, and witchcraft. We think because we do not feel conviction, complete the idolatrous ritual, or put a 'Christian twist" on the activity, it does not have the same effect. It is all profane to God.

Leviticus 10:1-3 *AND NADAB and Abihu, the sons of Aaron, each took his censer and put fire in it, and put incense on it, and offered strange and unholy fire before the Lord, as He had not commanded them. And there came forth fire from before the Lord and killed them, and they died before the Lord. Then Moses said to Aaron, This is what the Lord meant when He said, I [and My will, not their own] will be acknowledged as hallowed by those who come near Me, and before all the people I will be honored. And Aaron said nothing.*

Numbers 3:4 *Nadab and Abihu, however, died in the presence of the LORD when they offered unauthorized fire before the LORD in the Wilderness of Sinai. And since they had no sons, only Eleazar and Ithamar served as priests during the lifetime of their father Aaron.*

Sin SHIFTS us into a knowledge that God originally did not want us to experience. Satan tricked Adam and Eve into wanting to know more than God allowed. They trusted Satan's direction and ate from the tree that God had forbidden. This opened them to the knowledge of good and evil. They essentially opened a third eye and began to see in ways that God had closed them off too. God put boundaries in place for a reason. Just because something is in the earth and is available or present around us, does not make it lawful or godly. Adam and Eve lived in eternal life and glory. They were clothed in the glory of purity but now knew they were naked. Their awareness of nakedness brought shame and condemnation, such that they sowed leaves to hide their actions. Though now aware of good and evil, they had exposed themselves to hardship and death. When God forbids a thing, it opens doors to challenges that he never intended us to experience. Witchcraft exposes us to things that are available and even knowledgeable, but not godly.

Genesis 2:15-17 *And the LORD God took the man, and put him into the garden of Eden to dress it and to keep it. And the LORD God commanded the man, saying, Of every tree of the garden thou mayest freely eat: But of the tree of the knowledge of good and evil, thou shalt not eat of it: for in the day that thou eatest thereof thou shalt surely die.*

Genesis 3:1-7 *Now the serpent was more subtil than any beast of the field which the LORD God had made. And he said unto the woman, Yea, hath God said, Ye shall not eat of every tree of the garden? And the woman said unto the serpent, We may eat of the fruit of the trees of the garden: But of the fruit of the tree which is in the midst of the garden, God hath said, Ye shall not eat of it, neither shall ye touch it, lest ye die. And the serpent said unto the woman, Ye shall not surely die: For God doth know that in the day ye eat thereof, then your eyes shall be opened, and ye shall be as gods, knowing good and evil. And when the woman saw that the tree was good for food, and that it was pleasant to the eyes, and a tree to be desired to make one wise, she took of the fruit thereof, and did eat, and gave also unto her husband with her; and he did eat. And the eyes of them both were opened, and they knew that they were naked; and they sewed fig leaves together, and made themselves aprons.*

Sin is profitable and we do not want to lose the finances, fame, and success that accompanies sin.

Proverbs 10:2-3 The Amplified Bible *Treasures of wickedness profit nothing, but righteousness (moral and spiritual rectitude in every area and relation) delivers from death.*

Isaiah 57:10-12 The Amplified Bible *You were wearied with the length of your way [in trying to find rest and satisfaction in alliances apart from the true God], yet you did not say, There is no result or profit. You found quickened strength; therefore you were not faint or heartsick [or penitent].*

Of whom have you been so afraid and in dread that you lied and were treacherous and did not [seriously] remember Me, did not even give Me a thought? Have I not been silent, even for a long time, and so you do not fear Me? I will expose your [pretended] righteousness and your doings, but they will not help you.

Matthew 16:26 The Amplified Bible *For what will it profit a man if he gains the whole world and forfeits his life [his blessed life in the kingdom of God]? Or what would a man give as an exchange for his [blessed]life [in the kingdom of God]?*

Luke 9:25 The Amplified Bible *For what does it profit a man, if he gains the whole world and ruins or forfeits (loses) himself?*

We condemn, persecute, and crucify, those that speak truth to SHIFT us out of these abominations, while praising and supporting those who keep us bound.

Galatians 5:1 *Stand fast therefore in the liberty wherewith Christ hath made us free, and be not entangled again with the yoke of bondage.*

Verses 9-12 *A little leaven leaveneth the whole lump. I have confidence in you through the Lord, that ye will be none otherwise minded: but he that troubleth you shall bear his judgment, whosoever he be. And I, brethren, if I yet preach circumcision, why do I yet suffer persecution? then is the offence of the cross ceased. I would they were even cut off which trouble you.*

<u>Leaveneth</u> in Greek is *zymē* and means:
1. ferment (as if boiling up, agitation, unrest, to seethe with excitement, commotion, tumult),
2. leaven - metaph. of inveterate mental and moral corruption, viewed in its tendency to infect others,
3. leaven is applied to that which, though small in quantity, yet by its influence thoroughly pervades a thing; either in a good sense as in the parable ***Mat. 13:33***; or in a bad sense, of a pernicious influence, "a little leaven leaveneth the whole lump."

Proverbs 17:15 *He that justifieth the wicked, and he that condemneth the just, even they both are abomination to the LORD.*

New Living Bible *Acquitting the guilty and condemning the innocent— both are detestable to the LORD.*

Isaiah 30:10 *They say to the seers, "No more visions," and to the prophets, "Do not prophesy to us the truth. Speak to us pleasant words; prophesy illusions.*

Malachi 2:17 English Standard Bible *You have wearied the LORD with your words; yet you ask, "How have we wearied Him?" By saying, "All who do evil are good in the sight of the LORD, and in them He delights," or "Where is the God of justice?"*

> People rise in rebellion to protect what they should be rejecting.

The church and its leaders have practiced, exalted, and mixed paganism, sin, and witchcraft into our lives and allowed it in the church. **I said what I said!** SHIFT RIGHT NOW! When God comes to deliver such profane acts, the people are so rooted in compromise and justification, they do not want to divorce the profane.

Jeremiah 23:1-4 *Woe be unto the pastors that destroy and scatter the sheep of my pasture! saith the Lord. Therefore thus saith the Lord God of Israel against the pastors that feed my people; Ye have scattered my flock, and driven them away, and have not visited them: behold, I will visit upon you the evil of your doings, saith the Lord. And I will gather the remnant of my flock out of all countries whither I have driven them, and will bring them again to their folds; and they shall be fruitful and increase. And I will set up shepherds over them which shall feed them: and they shall fear no more, nor be dismayed, neither shall they be lacking, saith the Lord.*

Jeremiah 50:6 *My people are lost sheep; their shepherds have led them astray, causing them to roam the mountains. They have wandered from mountain to hill; they have forgotten their resting place.*

Ezekiel 13:3 *This is what the Lord GOD says: Woe to the foolish prophets who follow their own spirit, yet have seen nothing.*

Ezekiel 34:2 *"Son of man, prophesy against the shepherds of Israel. Prophesy and tell them that this is what the Lord GOD says: 'Woe to the shepherds of Israel, who only feed themselves! Should not the shepherds feed their flock?*

Proverbs 28:13 *He that covereth his sins shall not prosper: but whoso confesseth and forsaketh them shall have mercy.*

Matthew 7:15-23 *Beware of false prophets, which come to you in sheep's clothing, but inwardly they are ravening wolves. Ye shall know them by their fruits. Do men gather grapes of thorns, or figs of thistles? Even so every good tree bringeth forth good fruit; but a corrupt tree bringeth forth evil fruit. A good tree cannot bring forth evil fruit, neither can a corrupt tree bring forth good fruit. Every tree that bringeth not forth good fruit is hewn down, and cast into the fire. Wherefore by their fruits ye shall know them. Not every one that saith unto me, Lord, Lord, shall enter into the kingdom of heaven; but he that doeth the will of my Father which is in heaven. Many will say to me in that day, Lord, Lord, have we not prophesied in thy name? and in thy name have cast out devils? and in thy name done many wonderful works? And then will I profess unto them, I never knew you: depart from me, ye that work iniquity.*

We have made things that seems good or that feels good be godly when God does not base his principles on what feels good or appears good to man.

Isaiah 5:20 *Woe unto them that call evil good, and good evil; that put darkness for light, and light for darkness; that put bitter for sweet, and sweet for bitter.*

Job 17:12 *They change the night into day: the light is short because of darkness.*

Luke 11:35 New Living Bible *Make sure that the light you think you have is not actually darkness.*

Amos 5:7 English Standard Bible *You who turn justice into wormwood and cast righteousness to the ground.*

Habakkuk 1:4 English Standard Bible *Therefore the law is paralyzed, and justice never goes forth. For the wicked hem in the righteous; therefore, justice is perverted.*

Our standards are based on holiness until we want to do something unholy. God's standards are ALWAYS based on what is holy, has his nature, and what brings him glory.

Leviticus 11:44-45 *For I am the LORD your God. You shall therefore consecrate yourselves, and you shall be holy; for I am holy. Neither shall you defile yourselves with any creeping thing that creeps on the earth. For I am the LORD that bringeth you up out of the land of Egypt, to be your God: ye shall therefore be holy, for I am holy.*

Isaiah 35:8 *And an highway shall be there, and a way, and it shall be called The way of holiness; the unclean shall not pass over it; but it shall be for those: the wayfaring men, though fools, shall not err therein.*

1Peter 1:15-16 *But as he which hath called you is holy, so be ye holy in all manner of conversation; Because it is written, Be ye holy; for I am holy.*

Grace does not give us a free pass to sin. Jesus did not die for us to be unholy and engage in sin. Holiness will always be a standard of God. Sin will never be of God. God will never honor sin as godly or view it as his will. He will always be a holy God seeking a righteous holy sacrifice.

Proverbs 21:3 *To do justice and judgment is more acceptable to the Lord than sacrifice.*

Romans 6:13 *Do not present the parts of your body to sin as instruments of wickedness, but present yourselves to God as those who have been brought from death to life; and present the parts of your body to Him as instruments of righteousness.*

Romans 14:16-18 *Let not then your good be evil spoken of: For the kingdom of God is not meat and drink; but righteousness, and peace, and joy in the Holy Ghost. For he that in these things serveth Christ is acceptable to God, and approved of men.*

Philippians 4:8 *Finally, brethren, whatsoever things are true, whatsoever things are honest, whatsoever things are just, whatsoever things are pure, whatsoever things are lovely, whatsoever things are of good report; if there be any virtue, and if there be any praise, think on these things.*

Romans 12:1 *I beseech you therefore, brethren, by the mercies of God, that you present your bodies a living sacrifice, holy, acceptable to God, which is your reasonable service.*

Titus 1:10-16 *For there are many unruly and vain talkers and deceivers, specially they of the circumcision: Whose mouths must be stopped, who subvert whole houses, teaching things which they ought not, for filthy lucre's sake. One of themselves, even a prophet of their own, said, The Cretians are alway liars, evil beasts, slow bellies. This witness is true. Wherefore rebuke them sharply, that they may be sound in the faith; Not giving heed to Jewish fables, and commandments of men, that turn from the truth. Unto the pure all things are pure: but unto them that are defiled and unbelieving is nothing pure; but even their mind and conscience is defiled. They profess that they know God; but in works they deny him, being abominable, and disobedient, and unto every good work reprobate.*

Jesus broke the powers of the law that SHIFTED us from under death and provided us mercy and grace from paying the debts of the law. We, however, are still accountable for implementing the full redemption of salvation whereby we live in covenant with God on earth and eternally after we SHIFT to heaven; such that we do not perish unto death in hell for sinning.

Matthew 9:10-13 The Amplified Bible *And as Jesus reclined at table in the house, behold, many tax collectors and [especially wicked] sinners came and sat (reclined) with Him and His disciples. And when the Pharisees saw this, they said to His disciples, Why does your Master eat with tax collectors and those [preeminently] sinful? But when Jesus heard it, He replied, Those who are strong and well (healthy) have no need of a physician, but those who are weak and sick. Go and learn what this means: I desire mercy [that is, readiness to help those in trouble] and not sacrifice and sacrificial victims. For I came not to call and invite [to repentance] the righteous (those who are upright and in right standing with God), but sinners (the erring ones and all those not free from sin).*

Titus 12:14 New Living Bible *Who gave himself for us to redeem us from all wickedness and to purify for himself a people that are his very own, eager to do what is good.*

What God defines as an acceptable sacrifice determines its worth and sufficiency.

We have made our personal intent a consideration for whether something is a sin or not when God is about the acceptable sacrifice.

Proverbs 16:12 *All the ways of a man are clean in his own sight, But the LORD weighs the motives.*

Jeremiah 17:10 *I, the LORD, search the heart, I test the mind, Even to give to each man according to his ways, According to the results of his deeds.*

1Kings 8:3 *then hear in heaven Your dwelling place, and forgive and act and render to each according to all his ways, whose heart You know, for You alone know the hearts of all the sons of men.*

Jeremiah 12:3 *But You know me, O LORD; You see me; And You examine my heart's attitude toward You Drag them off like sheep for the slaughter And set them apart for a day of carnage!*

1Chronicles 28:9 *As for you, my son Solomon, know the God of your father, and serve Him with a whole heart and a willing mind; for the LORD searches all hearts, and understands every intent of the thoughts If you seek Him, He will let you find Him; but if you forsake Him, He will reject you forever.*

Psalm 139:1 *O LORD, You have searched me and known me.*

Psalm 44:21 *Would not God find this out? For He knows the secrets of the heart.*

1Samuel 16:7 *But the LORD said to Samuel, "Do not look at his appearance or at the height of his stature, because I have rejected him; for God sees not as man sees, for man looks at the outward appearance, but the LORD looks at the heart."*

God views the motives and intents of man's heart, but it is through his standards not ours. This is where we misinterpret his will and purpose for our lives. We think he is basing his searching on what we believe is right or wrong, good or bad, positive or negative, happy or sad, good or evil. But it is not through our perceptions or standards, it is through his.

Proverbs 19:21 *Many are the plans in a person's heart, but it is the LORD's purpose that prevail.*

Proverbs 4:19-23 The Amplified Bible *The way of the wicked is like deep darkness; they do not know over what they stumble. My son, attend to my words; consent and submit to my sayings. Let them not depart from your sight; keep them in the center of your heart. For they are life to those who find them, healing and health to all their flesh. Keep and guard your heart with all vigilance and above all that you guard, for out of it flow the springs of life.*

Verse 23 in the King James Bible *says Keep thy heart with all diligence; for out of it are the issues of life.*

Issues entail whatever challenges, questions, concerns, perceptions, proceedings, wounds, pains, circumstances, experiences we have in occurring in our lives.

<u>Issues</u> is *totsaah* in Hebrew and means:
1. (only in plural collective) exit, i.e. (geographical) boundary, or (figuratively) deliverance,
2. (actively) source: — border, borders, going(s), outgoings,
3. a going out, extremity, end, source, escape, extremity (of border).

Issues, in and of themselves, are about boundaries, borders, and have the potential to produce life or death. The word is telling us to guard our hearts because what we allow in, determines what flows out of us. The word is also urging us not to trust our heart, but to know the word and do it, so that our heart can be in right standing with God and produce the correct flow.

Jeremiah 17:9-10 *Even declares, "The heart is deceitful (polluted, crooked, fraudulent) above all things, and desperately wicked (sick, incurable, woeful): who can know it? I the Lord search the heart, I try the reins, even to give every man according to his ways, and according to the fruit of his doings."*

This is the reason David cries these words to God in ***Psalm 59:10*** to *"Create in me a clean heart, O God; and renew a right spirit within me."*

In ***Ezekiel 36:26*** Gods declares, *"I will give you a new heart and put a new spirit within you; I will take the heart of stone out of your flesh and give you a heart of flesh."*

The heart must be created and made new and even then, it requires the word of God to trust what flows from it. Boundaries provide a guard over our hearts, so we remain protected from unnecessary pain, hardships, issues, trial, tribulation, and tragedy. When we lack a guard, the issues within us SHIFT us into pathways that God did not intend for us to take.

A *boundary* is defined as:
- a line which marks the limits of an area; a dividing line,
- something that indicates bounds or limits,
- a limiting or bounding line,
- a mark of limits and drawing a line that makes a distinction to what is proper, expected, or reliable.

Boundaries defines our:
- Borders,
- Limits,
- Tolerance levels,
- Expectations,
- Identity - who we are, who we are not, how we value ourselves, what we believe about ourselves, what we are worth, whether we expect to be treated by what we are worth and whether we expect to receive what we are worth.

When we lack boundaries, we are:
- Undefined,
- Unidentified,
- Undetermined and lending to confusion,
- Compromising,
- Inconsistent,
- Indifferent, in opposition - at odds with ourselves,
- Without distinction or clarity regarding ourselves, of others, and of what is appropriate,
- Devaluing or devalued in our worth,
- Wavering and/or without expectation,
- Subject to anything - will fall or give way to anything.

Proverbs 23:19 *Listen, my son, and be wise, and guide your heart on the right course.*

When we or others are drifting off-course, there is an overstepping of God's boundaries. We risk succumbing to demon dealers and even becoming demon dealers. Boundaries are not new. They have always been in place. God established boundaries when he created heaven and earth. God established boundaries from the beginning.

In ***Genesis 1***, God, created the heavens and the earth with defining borders by dividing light from darkness, thus making day and night. God created the firmament from the waters, and calling the firmament heaven, while making evening and morning. God gathered the waters under the heaven together, divided it from dry land and created the seas. God created needful things and animals to dress and live in the earth.

In *Genesis 2*, God created man in His image - Adam and Eve - placed them in the garden and gave them specific boundaries on what to eat and not to eat, and how to sustain in the territory that he gave them rulership over.

Genesis 2:15-19 And the Lord God took the man and put him into the garden of Eden to dress it and to keep it. And the Lord God commanded the man, saying, Of every tree of the garden thou mayest freely eat: But of the tree of the knowledge of good and evil, thou shalt not eat of it: for in the day that thou eatest thereof thou shalt surely die. And the Lord God said, It is not good that the man should be alone; I will make him an help meet for him. And out of the ground the Lord God formed every beast of the field, and every fowl of the air; and brought them unto Adam to see what he would call them: and whatsoever Adam called every living creature, that was the name thereof.

The devil is the first demon dealer. It was the crossing of boundaries through the dealings of the devil that cause the fall of man. He SHIFTED Eve into a demon dealer as she ate of the devil's knowledge, then fed her husband his lies regarding the tree of good and evil.

Genesis 3:5-7 For God doth know that in the day ye eat thereof, then your eyes shall be opened, and ye shall be as gods, knowing good and evil. And when the woman saw that the tree was good for food, and that it was pleasant to the eyes, and a tree to be desired to make one wise, she took of the fruit thereof, and did eat, and gave also unto her husband with her; and he did eat. And the eyes of them both were opened, and they knew that they were naked; and they sewed fig leaves together, and made themselves aprons.

Jesus came to reestablish godly boundaries by restoring us through salvation. He SHIFTED us out of demon dealing into being a blueprint for journeying in a lifestyle of covenant boundaries and principles with God.

John 3:16 For God so loved the world, that he gave his only begotten Son, that whosoever believeth in him should not perish, but have everlasting life.

John 10:10 The thief cometh not, but for to steal, and to kill, and to destroy: I am come that they might have life, and that they might have it more abundantly.

2Corinthians 5:17-21 Therefore if any man be in Christ, he is a new creature: old things are passed away; behold, all things are become new. And all things are of God, who hath reconciled us to himself by Jesus Christ, and hath given to us the ministry of reconciliation; To wit, that God was in Christ, reconciling the world unto himself, not imputing their trespasses unto them; and hath committed unto us the word of reconciliation. Now then we are ambassadors for Christ, as though God did beseech you by us: we pray you in Christ's stead, be ye reconciled to God. For he hath made him to be sin for us, who knew no sin; that we might be made the righteousness of God in him.

Boundaries are connected to our sonship and heritage in Christ Jesus.

Psalm 16:6 The lines are fallen unto me in pleasant places; yea, I have a goodly heritage.

New International Bible *The boundary lines have fallen for me in pleasant places; surely, I have a delightful inheritance.*

We see from this scripture that there is a pleasant and substantial inheritance that derives from not crossing God's boundaries. This is because boundaries keep us away from engaging in behaviors that displease God and that are idolatrous in nature.

When we reject or cross boundaries, we can succumb to inordinacy.

Dictionary.com defines *inordinate* as:
1. not within proper or reasonable limits; immoderate; excessive,
2. unrestrained in conduct, feelings, etc.,
3. disorderly; uncontrolled,
4. not regulated; irregular,
5. to have inordinate affection, to lust.

Colossians 3:5-6 *Mortify therefore your members which are upon the earth; fornication, uncleanness, inordinate affection, evil concupiscence (craving, lust), and covetousness, which is idolatry: For which things' sake the wrath of God cometh on the children of disobedience.*

The Amplified Bible *So kill (deaden, deprive of power) the evil desire lurking in your members [those animal impulses and all that is earthly in you that is employed in sin]: sexual vice, impurity, sensual appetites, unholy desires, and all greed and covetousness, for that is idolatry (the deifying of self and other created things instead of God).*

In the Colossians' passage *inordinate affections* is Greek word *pathos* and means to:

- to suffer, suffering,
- to suffer with an unhealthy passion in concupiscence (one's sexual desires, lust; to be ardent, usually sensuous, or longing constant in one's desires),
- to succumb to whatever befalls a person, whether happy or sad, good or bad (this means that no matter how it makes you feel, you are driven by it, driven to have more, you cannot be fulfilled and continuously lust for more so even if it is good you keep demanding or pursuing more because you are inordinate – you lack boundaries or balance in your passions and desires for it),
- display an unhealthy driven passion or affection for something or someone,
- a feeling in which the mind suffers,
- an affliction in which the mind, emotions, and passions suffer,
- a depraved passion,
- a vile passion.

When we do not have boundaries, we become distorted in our perception. We have no clear vision of what is right or wrong. We can become inordinate in doing whatever feels good or doing whatever to make us feel good. The challenge with that is when we become inordinate, we become like a bottomless pit that has no ending, so we have a difficult time being fulfilled in whatever it is we are seeking. We also have a difficult time deciphering what is good and what is evil, what is of God and what is of the devil.

No matter how much time, attention, blessings, resources, love, companionship, friendship, affection, sex, honor, appreciation, someone or something gives us, we just want more.

- We seek more,
- We lust and thirst for more,
- We are driven to have more,
- We demand to have more,
- We become obsessed and/or compulsive and driven with wanting more.

We then justify why it is needful and even godly. This is how the lack of boundaries open the door to sin and the demonic. Our emotions and thoughts are now being driven by our passions, which causes us to cross even more boundaries and engage in behaviors in effort to fulfill the inordinate longing that is inside of us.

Inordinacy can lead to obsessive and compulsive thoughts and behaviors that can make us appear or act double-minded or mentally unstable. Doublemindedness is when we say one thing but do another or have a desire to do the right thing but do the wrong thing. (*James 1:8 A double minded man is unstable in all his ways*). Mentally unstable refers to speaking and/or behaving with irrational, impulsive, irresponsible, obsessive, compulsive, impure, unrighteous, unhealthy, aggressively, passive aggressively, dramatic or in a way that incites drama. It includes mood swings that are up and down, extreme, unclear, or differentiated in emotions, thoughts, or behaviors (bipolar, schizophrenic, multiple personalities). Inordinacy can also lead to idolatry as now we are striving to be our own god – becoming our own gods - by striving to fulfill our desires at the expense of God's will and plan for our lives. We become covenant breakers as we are focused on making sin fit into our relationship with God, rather than ejecting it from our lives and covenant with God.

Exodus 20:3-5 Thou shalt have no other gods before me. (When you are god in people's lives or they are god in yours, you and/or them are putting yourselves above God). Thou shalt not make unto thee any graven image, or any likeness of any thing that is in heaven above, or that is in the earth beneath, or that is in the water under the earth. Thou shalt not bow down thyself to them, nor serve them: for I the Lord thy God am a jealous God, visiting the iniquity of the fathers upon the children unto the third and fourth generation of them that hate me.

When you become your own god, become someone else's god, or they become your god, you or they have created yourselves as an image of him - you or they are contending you are like him - comparable to him - equal to him - and can be him in one another's lives.

When you have become god, have become someone else's god, or they have become your god, you or they have bowed downed to yourself or to one another where you are now worshipping and serving yourself or one another rather God - your acts towards yourself or one another serve as worship to who you are to yourself or to each other rather than to god. Such sins can provoke the jealousy and judgment of God where he allows curses to prevail in future generations.

If you are always studying the Bible from a posture of proving that it is okay to keep a certain pleasure, activity, or behavior in your life, then you most likely have opened a door to self, intellect, or demonic influence. You will surely find it and many times will engage in using the scriptures in error to justify your desires and behaviors. The Bible was never intended to be used this way. The Bible is not about us trying to fit our will into the scriptures but using the scriptures to align our lives.

2Timothy 3:10-17 But thou hast fully known my doctrine, manner of life, purpose, faith, longsuffering, charity, patience, Persecutions, afflictions, which came unto me at Antioch, at Iconium, at Lystra; what persecutions I endured: but out of them all the Lord delivered me. Yea, and all that will live godly in Christ Jesus shall suffer persecution. But evil men and seducers shall wax worse and worse, deceiving, and being deceived. But continue thou in the things which thou hast learned and hast been assured of, knowing of whom thou hast learned them; And that from a child thou hast known the holy scriptures, which are able to make thee wise unto salvation through faith which is in Christ Jesus.

All scripture is given by inspiration of God and is profitable for doctrine, for reproof, for correction, for instruction in righteousness: That the man of God may be perfect, thoroughly furnished unto all good works.

2Timothy 4:1-5 I charge thee therefore before God, and the Lord Jesus Christ, who shall judge the quick and the dead at his appearing and his kingdom; Preach the word; be instant in season, out of season; reprove, rebuke, exhort with all longsuffering and doctrine. For the time will come when they will not endure sound doctrine; but after their own lusts shall they heap to themselves teachers, having itching ears; And they shall turn away their ears from the truth, and shall be turned unto fables. But watch thou in all things, endure afflictions, do the work of an evangelist, make full proof of thy ministry.

Apostasy means "a falling away;" to abandon previously professed beliefs.

Heresy means division by way of false teaching. It is that which is not orthodox or is not grounded in biblical truth. This book will enable you to identify God's standards effectively where even the subtle ways of the devil can be discerned and cast out of your life and spheres of influence.

DECREEING YOU SAY NO TO DEMON DEALING SOUL STEALING!

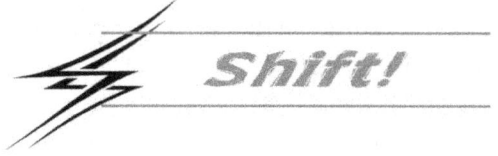

Chapter 6

WITCHCRAFT AND THE NEW AGE MOVEMENT

God put witchcraft to death from the beginning of time. His exact words were,

Exodus 22:18, *"Thou shalt not suffer a witch to live."*

God believed the best way to rid the earth of witchcraft was to kill the witch. He has a no compromise stance regarding witchcraft. This has never changed to this day. His judgment remains the same. **Suffer Not Says the Lord.** The word suffer means to tolerate.

Though we are not physically going to go out and kill anyone, we do have authority in the spirit realm to not tolerate witches and witchcraft, and to release God's judgment on those who engage in witchcraft or operate as witches. When witches are casting spells and evoking evil prayers against God and his people, they are seeking to make sure we experience pain, hardship, and destruction. Many of them are not repentant or remorseful for how their actions impact anyone. They are seeking to fulfill whatever purpose they are aspiring at that time. A plan that is at the expense of others, especially God's kingdom. They are workers of the devil and no toleration for anything or anyone outside themselves. God, therefore, has no toleration for them.

Isaiah 57:1-12 New International Bible *The righteous perish, and no one ponders it in his heart; devout men are taken away, and no one understands that the righteous are taken away to be spared from evil. Those who walk uprightly enter into peace; they find rest as they lie in death.*

But you--come here, you sons of a sorceress, you offspring of adulterers and prostitutes! Whom are you mocking? At whom do you sneer and stick out your tongue? Are you not a brood of rebels, the offspring of liars? You burn with lust among the oaks and under every spreading tree. you sacrifice your children in the ravines and under the overhanging crags. The idols among the smooth stones of the ravines are your portion; indeed, they are your lot. Yes, to them you have poured out drink offerings and offered grain offerings. In view of all this, should I relent?

You have made your bed on a high and lofty hill; there you went up to offer your sacrifices. Behind your doors and your doorposts you have put your pagan symbols. Forsaking me, you uncovered your bed, you climbed into it and opened it wide; you made a pact with those whose beds you love, and you looked on their naked bodies.

You went to Molek with olive oil and increased your perfumes. You sent your ambassadors far away; you descended to the very realm of the dead! You wearied yourself by such going about, but you would not say, 'It is hopeless.' You found renewal of your strength, and so you did not faint.

You were wearied by all your ways, but you would not say, 'It is hopeless.' You found renewal of your strength, and so you did not faint. Whom have you so dreaded and feared that you have been false to me, and have neither remembered me nor pondered this in your hearts? Is it not because I have long been silent that you do not fear me? I will expose your righteousness and your works, and they will not benefit you.

Micah 5:12 New International Bible *I will destroy your witchcraft, and you will no longer cast spells.*

God is unwavering in his disdain for witches and witchcraft and demolishing their practices. When commanding us to suffer a witch not to live, he is wanting us to make sure their workings and plans do not survive, do not prosper, do not advance in the earth. God does not want what they do and who they are to have any affect in life, and no chance of sustaining from generation to generation. We fulfill God's purpose by:

- Breaking free from fears surrounding witches, witchcraft, and the supernatural.
- Getting delivered from personal and generational curses and practices of witchcraft.
- Acknowledging and falling out of agreement with witches and witchcraft practices.
- Discerning and dismantling witches and their practices; ridding them from your life, family, ministries, businesses, regions, nations.
- Consistently confronting and proactively praying to cancel and utterly destroy the assignments, workings, and high places of witches and witchcraft.
- Praying for witches and those who operate in witchcraft practices to have divine encounters with God and start living for him **Proverbs 28:10** *Whoso causeth the righteous to go astray in an evil way, he shall fall himself into his own pit; but the upright shall have good things in possession.*
- Embracing the supernatural, allowing the Holy Spirit to educate, train, and guide you in governing and operating in these realms.
- Learning your governmental rule in the kingdom of God and how the kingdom of God operates to dismantle principalities and powers. Learning effective warfare strategies, ranks and rules within the demonic kingdom to dismantle their systems and operations. Embracing, positioning, training, and releasing those gifted and called to these spheres.
- Flowing in the gifts of the spirit and making them available in your communities and regions so that people will come to the ministry of God for wisdom, guidance, counsel, prophetic knowledge, revelation, strategy, rather than seeking witches and warlocks for these insights.
- Creating businesses and organizations that draw people out of worldly systems and witchcraft high places into the kingdom systems of God.

Biblically, Nimrod is the fathering idol god that released paganism, witchcraft, occult, and the new age movement into the earth. Nimrod was the great-grandson of Noah through the line of Cush. Nimrod is described as the first of the "mighty men," to appear on the earth after the great flood. Mighty men were giants who were larger than the average man. Nimrod was known as a mighty hunter before the Lord. His name means "rebellion" or "the valiant." He declared himself a god. He also built a kingdom that rejected God, was anti-God and that rebelled against God. Much of these practices we see in the earth today derived from Nimrod and his kingdom. His kingdom was full of idol worship, paganism, witchcraft practices, and occultism.

Genesis 10:8-10 *And Cush begat Nimrod: he began to be a mighty one in the earth. He was a mighty hunter before the LORD: wherefore it is said, Even as Nimrod the mighty hunter before the LORD. And the beginning of his kingdom was Babel, and Erech, and Accad, and Calneh, in the land of Shinar.*

In ***Genesis 11:4***, we find Nimrod and his kingdom striving to build a city and a tower to reach heaven. God had to confound their language and scattered them abroad upon the earth, so they would not understand one another, and would not be able to complete this task. The language barrier brought such baffling until the city was called Babel which means mixing and confusion which is the basis for all idolatry and witchcraft. A person may think what they are doing is intelligent, knowledgeable, needful, and advancing, but God declares it as mixture and confusion. As God seek to SHIFT revival reform into the earth, Nimrod is an ancient stronghold he will be using his chosen remnant to uproot in the earth.

NEW AGE MOVEMENT

The New Age Movement encompasses ancient practices, witchcraft practices, occult practices in a modern context. These practices include sorcery, pursue astrology for divine guidance, magic, witchcraft, communication with the dead, worship of Satan, sacrifices to idols and demons and much more. The people usually are very intellectual, explorers, informational pursuers, spiritual, yet lack submission to authority. Many of them are high strung renegades who have a divine calling but have been drawn away from God's original plan and intent of leadership for their lives. They may also deem themselves Christians who desire to hold on to their cultural or ethic roots and customs, or whose pursuit of greater knowledge, healing, and power, has caused them to believe and delve into in different paths to eternal life. Many as well deem witchcraft a practice, not a religion, and therefore believe a person can practice it no matter what their religious beliefs are.

Witchcraft practitioners and New Agers will claim their practices have been here since the beginning of time before Christianity. They will use this as a justification for their usage. This does not make their workings godly, good, or appropriate. Please note that they may have been here before Christianity, but they have not been here before God.

Isaiah 41:4 *Who has performed this and carried it out, calling forth the generations from the beginning? I, the LORD--the first and the last--I am He."*

Isaiah 44:6 *Thus says the LORD, the King and Redeemer of Israel, the LORD of Hosts: "I am the first and I am the last, and there is no God but Me.*

Revelation 22:13 *I am Alpha and Omega, the beginning, and the end, the first and the last.*

Many New Age participants have ascended their desires, beliefs, ideologies, customs, and practices, above God. They have no authority but themselves, and some of them believe all humans are gods. They use the following scripture to justify their perspective.

Psalm 82:6 *I have said, Ye are gods; and all of you are children of the most High.*

John 10:34 *Jesus answered them, Is it not written in your law, I said, Ye are gods?*

They have risen spiritually to be gods or to be seen as gods. They overgeneralize these scriptures, while declaring themselves as gods and being equal to or being the living God. ***Isaiah 40:12-31*** lets us know that God is God alone and has no equal. The scriptures indeed reveal our identity, likeness and sonship as children and heirs of God. But it does not make us equal to God, nor does it give us the authority to operate as gods to a dimension where we create our own deities, worship patterns, and pathways to eternal life. God's word is the standard authority regarding these principles and do not change no matter how evolving we become as his children.

Isaiah 46:5-11 *To whom will ye liken me, and make me equal, and compare me, that we may be like? They lavish gold out of the bag, and weigh silver in the balance, and hire a goldsmith; and he maketh it a god: they fall down, yea, they worship. They bear him upon the shoulder, they carry him, and set him in his place, and he standeth; from his place shall he not remove: yea, one shall cry unto him, yet can he not answer, nor save him out of his trouble.*

Remember this, and shew yourselves men: bring it again to mind, O ye transgressors. Remember the former things of old: for I am God, and there is none else; I am God, and there is none like me, Declaring the end from the beginning, and from ancient times the things that are not yet done, saying, My counsel shall stand, and I will do all my pleasure: Calling a ravenous bird from the east, the man that executeth my counsel from a far country: yea, I have spoken it, I will also bring it to pass; I have purposed it, I will also do it.

Because of the error thought process of being equal to god, the concept of sin is nullified in the new age movement. Many deem themselves pure or engage in activities that they deem draw them into a god state of purity.

Many new age individuals deem the earth, sky, universe, a person, or carved image as god. They may serve gods from Roman, Greek, Egyptian mythology. These believers may be mixed with paganism and idolatrous religions such as Buddhism, Hinduism, and Taoism, or Native American spiritualism. Some of these participants will serve and mix multiple methodologies and religions, while claiming to be devoted Christian believers. They will contend that they are remaining true to their ethnic heritage, while rejecting the part of the Bible that they believe suppresses ethnic identity, beliefs, and customs. They may also reject salvation, Jesus Christ as Lord and savior, and Jesus as the only way to eternal life. Some will want to be used in their local assemblies or in positions within the communities where they provide guidance to people despite engaging in mixture and will seek to convert other believers into their idolatrous practices. They use trances and meditations to connect with their higher beings and as a way of ascending higher into their higher selves. Some of them may use stones, potions, shapes (circles, triangles, squares), numbers, candles, incense, plants, animal sacrifices, human sacrifices, blood sacrifices, point of contact objects collected from other people, crystals, essential oils, herbs, drugs, body positions (Yoga asanas), breathing practices, mantras, etc., connect or sacrifice to the divine force and/or to release and balance their divine energy within themselves and the atmosphere.

Allaboutspirituality.org states the following concerning the New Age Movement:

New Age Thought System
New Age is a compilation of metaphysical, Eastern-influenced thought systems. These thought systems unite theology, nature, and philosophy. This movement comprises countless "theologies" that often center on religious tolerance and moral diversity. The main phrases (or "isms") that reveal the focal point of New Age thought are "feel-goodism" (do whatever feels good, as long as you are not hurting someone else), "moral relativism" (situational ethics), and "pluralism" (universal tolerance). The phrase "New Age" refers to the "Aquarian Age" which, according to New Age supporters, is now beginning. This Age is expected to bring in peace and enlightenment, as well as reunite humans with "god."

New Age: The Doctrine of Evolutionary Godhood
Generally, New Age thought supports the theory of organic evolution, but extends the concept to the evolution of the spirit. This is the concept of "Evolutionary Godhood," where the next step in evolution won't be physical, but spiritual. The principles of evolution are constantly moving mankind toward god-consciousness, where man and reality connect in unified enlightenment. The "fittest" already understand this reality, while the "unfit" (such as Christians and other proponents of dogmatic worldviews) act as a hindrance to evolutionary forces. Many New Age practices are designed to accelerate the evolutionary push into the spiritual realms. These practices include: (i) astral projection, which is training your soul to leave your body and travel around; (ii) channeling spirits, so they may speak through you or guide you; (iii) crystal usage, which purifies the energy systems of your body and mind; and (iv) visualization techniques, which include everything from basic mental imagery to role playing of animals or divine creatures. In a nutshell, Evolutionary Godhood means that mankind will soon see itself as god. This is often referred to as the "Christ principle" or "Christ consciousness." New Age teaches that we are basically good and inherently divine, and ultimately, we can create our own reality.

New Age: The Doctrine of Global Unity
The second major doctrine of the New Age movement is "Global Unity." This concept typically consists of three parts:

Man Unified with Man. *One New Age principle is that we will all realize our proper divine relationship with one another and achieve pure harmony through the acceptance of this divine knowledge. With relational harmony comes economic unity. With economic unity, we can achieve political unity (a single world government) and spiritual unity (a one world religion).*

Man Unified with Nature. *Another New Age principle is that god is everything, and everything is god. Therefore, nature is also part of god. We must be in harmony with nature. We must* *nurture it and be nurtured by it. Mankind is no different than any other animal. We must live in harmony with them, understand them, and learn from them. Many in the New Age movement refer to the union of earth and nature as "Gaia." Gaia is revered, respected, and even worshipped as a god by some. American Indian rituals are also popular in the New Age movement because they focus on the elements of nature and man's relationship to them.*

Man Unified with God. *Since man is divine by nature, all people can realize their "divinity" and contribute to the unified purpose of man, earth and nature. The ultimate goal in life is to fully realize our own divine goodness. The New Age god is impersonal and omnipresent. He (it) has not revealed himself (itself) to mankind, and therefore, mankind is not accountable to any notions of moral law or absolute truth. There is no objective morality in the New Age philosophy. We should have tolerance for all systems of truth, meaning and purpose. We should create a world of pure relativism, where morality and religion are strictly relative to each person's individual notion of reality itself.*

New Age participants are probably some of the boldest demon dealers we have in the earth today. The internet and social media have enabled them to be more efficient with unifying and asserting their right to free speech and openly practicing their beliefs, while contesting and even demanding imprisonment of those who believe contrary to them. They have gained control in high-ranking positions in society where they are now controlling the process of laws, media, trends, culture, and climates, of society. ***Galatians 1:6-12*** warns of new age practices.

The Amplified Bible *I am surprised and astonished that you are so quickly turning renegade and deserting Him Who invited and called you by the grace (unmerited favor) of Christ (the Messiah) [and that you are transferring your allegiance] to a different [even an opposition] gospel. Not that there is [or could be] any other [genuine Gospel], but there are [obviously] some who are troubling and disturbing and bewildering you [with a different kind of teaching which they offer as a gospel] and want to pervert and distort the Gospel of Christ (the Messiah) [into something which it absolutely is not].*

But even if we or an angel from heaven should preach to you a gospel contrary to and different from that which we preached to you, let him be accursed (anathema, devoted to destruction, doomed to eternal punishment)! As we said before, so I now say again: If anyone is preaching to you a gospel different from or contrary to that which you received [from us], let him be accursed (anathema, devoted to destruction, doomed to eternal punishment)!

Now am I trying to win the favor of men, or of God? Do I seek to please men? If I were still seeking popularity with men, I should not be a bond servant of Christ (the Messiah). For I want you to know, brethren, that the Gospel which was proclaimed and made known by me is not man's gospel [a human invention, according to or patterned after any human standard]. For indeed I did not receive it from man, nor was I taught it, but [it came to me] through a [direct] revelation [given] by Jesus Christ (the Messiah).

Many people in the New Age Movements usually have flesh issues or demonic strongholds of:

- **Rebellion** – Presenting and armed resistance to God's true governance and biblical rule. *Isaiah 1:2 New Living Bible Hear, O heavens! Listen, O earth! For the Lord has spoken: "I reared children and brought them up, but they have rebelled against me."*

- **Rejection & Stubbornness** – Strong-willed in ideologies, behaviors, and pursuit to make their perspective be law that others abide by. Rejecting of anyone and anything that presents godly truth.

  1Samuel 15:23-24 For rebellion is as the sin of witchcraft, and stubbornness is as iniquity and idolatry. Because thou hast rejected the word of the Lord, he hath also rejected thee from being king.

- **Deceiver Like the Devil** – Mislead or delude by false appearance, interpretation, or statement. *John 8:44 Ye are of your father the devil, and the lusts of your father ye will do. He was a murderer from the beginning, and abode not in the truth, because there is no truth in him. When he speaketh a lie, he speaketh of his own: for he is a liar, and the father of it.*

- **Anti-Submission to Authority** – Rejecting of godly truth, laws, principles, and standards. *Romans 2:1-3 New Living Bible Everyone must submit himself to the governing authorities, for there is no authority except that which is from God. The authorities that exist have been appointed by God. Consequently, the one who resists authority is opposing what God has set in place, and those who do so will bring judgment on themselves. For rulers are not a terror to good conduct, but bad. Do you want to be unafraid of the one in authority? Then do what is right, and you will have his approval.*

- **Anti-Christ** - Rejecting Jesus Christ as Lord and savior; contending there are more ways to eternal life besides Jesus; rejecting his principles; mixing and distorting godly principles and standards with worldly and ungodly belief and systems. *John 14:6 Jesus said to him, "I am the way, and the truth, and the life; no one comes to the Father but through Me. Romans 6:4 Therefore we have been buried with Him through baptism into death, so that as Christ was raised from the dead through the glory of the Father, so we too might walk in newness of life.*

- **Lukewarm** – Indifferent, mixed, or wretchedly fluctuation between a torpor and a fervor of love. *Revelation 3:15-17 I know your [record of] works and what you are doing; you are neither cold nor hot. Would that you were cold or hot! So, because you are lukewarm and neither cold nor hot, I will spew you out of My mouth!*

- **Detest Believers** – Many have a hatred or strong dislike for believers. *Matthew 24:10 At that time many will fall away and will betray one another and hate one another.*

1Corinthians 9:12 But when ye sin so against the brethren, and wound their weak conscience, ye sin against Christ.

- **Lawlessness** – Unbridled and unrestrained to the people, ways, authorities, and principles, of God. *Nehemiah 9:26 New Living Bible But they were disobedient and rebelled against you; they put your law behind their backs. They killed your prophets, who had admonished them in order to turn them back to you; they committed awful blasphemies.*

- **Reject Godly Counsel** – Dispel, ridicule - verbally and physically kill those who are God's truth bearers. *Psalm 107:11 New Living Bible For they had rebelled against the words of God and despised the counsel of the Most High.*

- **Idolatry** - Serving of self and their own ideologies – *Romans 2:8 But for those who are self-seeking and who reject the truth and follow evil, there will be wrath and anger.*

- **Witchcraft & Divination** – Preach and practice strange fire; operate in a form of godliness, rooted in creation rather than the creator. *Deuteronomy 18:9-12 English Version Bible When you come into the land that the Lord your God is giving you, you shall not learn to follow the abominable practices of those nations. There shall not be found among you anyone who burns his son or his daughter as an offering, anyone who practices divination or tells fortunes or interprets omens, or aa sorcerer or a charmer or a medium or a necromancer or cone who inquires of the dead, for whoever does these things is an abomination to the Lord. And because of these abominations the Lord your God is driving them out before you.*

~ MY GOD ~

Chapter 7

ANCIENT NEW AGE CUSTOMS

Most of the New Age practices are ancient customs resurfacing with a modernized twist, thus becoming even more engrained in the present and future generations. This lets us know that there really is nothing new under the sun and that what we do not overthrow in our generational line, land, and society is still with us, and will eventually rear its head.

Numbers 14:18 The LORD [is] longsuffering, and of great mercy, forgiving iniquity and transgression, and by no means clearing [the guilty], visiting the iniquity of the fathers upon the children unto the third and fourth [generation].

Exodus 20:5 Thou shalt not bow down thyself to them, nor serve them: for I the LORD thy God [am] a jealous God, visiting the iniquity of the fathers upon the children unto the third and fourth [generation] of them that hate me;

Ezekiel 18:20 The soul that sinneth, it shall die. The son shall not bear the iniquity of the father, neither shall the father bear the iniquity of the son: the righteousness of the righteous shall be upon him, and the wickedness of the wicked shall be upon him.

Many people in the New Age Movement believe the following:

MYSTICISM

A mystic is a person who claims to attain, or believes in the possibility of attaining, insight into mysteries transcending ordinary human knowledge, as by direct communication with the divine or immediate intuition in a state of spiritual ecstasy. Mystics do not deem themselves religious. They claim to focus on spirituality where they choose which methodologies, principles, and gods, they are going to follow, thus sort of creating their own religious doctrine that aligns with their needs, desires, and beliefs. As these beliefs are implemented, mystics use mediation and other curious arts to enter a state of mind consciousness, where they experience supernatural encounters, engage spiritual forces, and unify in oneness with their god/s, so they can be further awakened, purified, illuminated, and SHIFTED into ecstasy and rapture, regarding how they are to impact the world through their belief system. As they learn to live a unitive life, they believe they become clear in their purpose where change lives and change the world. Though this sounds exciting, its witchcraft that is accomplished through many of the customs you will learn about in this chapter. One revelation we need to make clear is that Jesus tore the veil between us and God, so we can boldly approach his thrown of grace in prayer, encounter his glorious presence and transformation power, and receive clear insight about our destiny and purpose. We do not need to use gimmicks, tricks, gadgets, or witchcraft.

Hebrews 4:16 *Let us therefore come boldly unto the throne of grace, that we may obtain mercy, and find grace to help in time of need.*

Hebrews 10:19-22 New Living Bible *And so, dear brothers and sisters, we can boldly enter heaven's Most Holy Place because of the blood of Jesus. By his death, Jesus opened a new and life-giving way through the curtain into the Most Holy Place. And since we have a great High Priest who rules over God's house, let us go right into the presence of God with sincere hearts fully trusting him. For our guilty consciences have been sprinkled with Christ's blood to make us clean, and our bodies have been washed with pure water.*

Ephesians 3:12 *New Living Bible Because of Christ and our faith in him, we can now come boldly and confidently into God's presence.*

CONSCIOUSNESS

The idea of ***raising one's consciousness*** is a core belief of the New Age Movement. The perception that you are "conscious" if you defy systems, authority figures, and live by your own increased sense of self-awareness of your philosophical needs, behaviors, attitudes that distinctly identify who you are as a god. Many of these conscious philosophies are centered around the universe, the earth, **vibes or vibrations, energies, and waves.** They may also make references to the earth, sun, moon, and stars, and engage in some practices of observers of moods and times or enchantment. Often when we are discerning, detecting, or sensing someone's vibes, energies, or waves, what is really being perceived is a person's disposition.

DISPOSITION

Dictionary.com defines *disposition* as:
1. the predominant or prevailing tendency of one's spirits; natural mental and emotional outlook or mood; characteristic attitude,
2. state of mind regarding something; inclination,
3. physical inclination or tendency of a person, place, or thing.

Basically, you are perceiving how a person, place, thing, or matter is. You are perceiving its nature, its character, its identity, and how they or it feels, thinks, sees, hears, smells, sounds, which is all about senses – humans using our senses to perceive a matter. This is not spiritual - this is innate. God put it in us to perceive - to know a thing. Adam and Eve ate from the tree of knowledge of good and evil and opened our senses to perceive between these two entities.

Genesis 3:5-7 *For God doth know that in the day ye eat thereof, then your eyes shall be opened, and ye shall be as gods, knowing good and evil. And when the woman saw that the tree was good for food, and that it was pleasant to the eyes, and a tree to be desired to make one wise, she took of the fruit thereof, and did eat, and gave also unto her husband with her; and he did eat. And the eyes of them both were opened, and they knew that they were naked; and they sewed fig leaves together, and made themselves aprons.*

Verse 22 *And the Lord God said, Behold, the man is become as one of us, to know good and evil: and now, lest he put forth his hand, and take also of the tree of life, and eat, and live for ever.*

The Amplified Bible *And the Lord God said, Behold, the man has become like one of Us [the Father, Son, and Holy Spirit], to know [how to distinguish between] good and evil and blessing and calamity; and now, lest he put forth his hand and take also from the tree of life and eat, and live forever.*

If it were up to God, we would never know evil - we would never know sin - we would never know idolatry or witchcraft. We would only know that which was good.

WAVES

There are two different types of waves that the new age believes in: transverse and longitudinal. A transverse wave is when the wave is vibrating perpendicular (vertical; straight up and down; upright) to the direction the wave is traveling. A longitudinal wave, also called a compression wave, is a wave in which the vibration is in the same direction or in the extended length as that in which the wave is traveling. These waves live on the frequencies and airwaves around us. What is in the waves are the words, thoughts, ideologies, trends, emotions, feelings, that have been released by those who have been in that atmosphere or environment, or that have released such dispositions into the atmosphere and environment by sending curses, decrees, prayers, thoughts, emotions, etc. Since these words, emotions, etc., are living on the frequencies and airways, we run into the waves of them and can feel and encounter them when we enter those areas or when we use witchcraft, astral projection, telepathy, or the third eye to peer into those atmospheres and environments.

VIBES OR VIBRATIONS

Dictionary.com defines *vibes* as:
1. supernatural emanation, bearing good or ill, that is sensed by or revealed to those attuned to the occult,
2. often vibrations. a general emotional feeling one has from another person or a place, situation, etc.

Vibes or vibrations are about how our senses and discernment identify the emotional well-being and characteristic of a person, place, thing, situation, matter, experience, atmosphere, environment, climate, region, etc. If a person has a good spirit and is healthy in their character and emotions, we will discern the wellness and positivity of their disposition. If a person has a bad spirit and unhealthy in their character and emotions, we will discern the affliction, ill will, negativity of their disposition. If they have God's Holy Spirit we will discern, sense, feel, and experience, the goodness of the Holy Spirit in them. If they have demonic spirits, we will discern, sense, feel, and experience the negativity and evil of the demonic spirits in them. The same with atmospheres, environments, climates, and regions. The universe is not revealing this to you. The senses God has placed in you when he created you is allowing you to detect the "vibes." Some people will refer to their ability to "sense a matter" intuition. Intuition is our senses judging or perceiving the truth about a matter. God made us in his image. Even without experience, we possess the ability to have a knowing about everything including him and his existence. This knowing usually is revealing to us a caution, conviction, or truth that when submitted to God, can guide us into further truth and covenant relationship with him. However, when submitted to oneself or the devil, can guide us away from God and covenant relationship with him.

Ephesians 1:18 *The eyes of your understanding being enlightened; that you may know what is the hope of His calling, what are the riches of the glory of His inheritance in the saints.*

2Corinthians 4:6 New International Bible *For God, who said, "Let light shine out of darkness," made his light shine in our hearts to give us the light of the knowledge of God's glory displayed in the face of Christ.*

Romans 1:18-21 *For the wrath of God is revealed from heaven against all ungodliness and unrighteousness of men, who hold the truth in unrighteousness; Because that which may be known of God is manifest in them; for God hath shewed it unto them. For the invisible things of him from the creation of the world are clearly seen, being understood by the things that are made, even his eternal power and Godhead; so that they are without excuse: Because that, when they knew God, they glorified him not as God, neither were thankful; but became vain in their imaginations, and their foolish heart was darkened.*

Psalm 149:13 *I will praise You, for I am fearfully and wonderfully made; Marvelous are Your works, And that my soul knows very well.*

ENERGIES
Dictionary.com defines *energies* as:
1. a feeling of tension caused or seeming to be caused by an excess of such power,
2. an exertion of such power,
3. the habit of vigorous activity; vigor as a characteristic,
4. the ability to act, lead others, effect, etc., forcefully,
5. forcefulness of expression.

Energy is the power that moves along the nerves of our body that is release through our character, emotions, and responses to life experiences. Depending on what we are experiencing, our emotional responses can often be felt and seen by others. Also, if we have a strong bold character people can detect that through the force of power emanating through us. If we have a weak cowering character, people can detect that through the weak, minimal power, and low energy, illuminating through is. I have a strong disposition because I am greatly confident. People are usually drawn to me the minute I walk into a room. I am not doing anything to draw attention. My disposition is releasing the power and authority of my identity. Some people love my disposition, some hate it, and some do not know what to do with it. Because I am saved, my disposition is rooted in God so those in my midst may recognized that my disposition is rooted in the Holy Spirit – the presence of God, while new agers may decide I have good or bad energy based on what they believe about my Lord and Savior - Jesus Christ.

Also, because our emotions tend to change depending on the day, situation, experience, my disposition can be good or bad. This is not some spooky energy; it is just the truth of the posture of my emotions at that time. The witches, warlocks, new age movements, the old ancestors' superstitions that are rooted in witchcraft, have folks making vibes and energies be all deep and about the universe gods. This is all manmade - demonized - witchy poo idolatry. It has been passed down through the generations by way of superstitions, wise tails, folklore, Greek mythology, and divination practices. We really need to rid our family lines of this rather than continuing to engage in these practices and superstitions, as even if your momma, daddy, grandma, granddaddy, great aunt engaged in them, its witchcraft. It is demonic and idolatrous and not of God.

When we lend to living a life through vibes and vibrations, and energies, we open the door to familiar spirits operating in and through our personalities, senses, and emotions, and we deal familiar spirit demons to other people with our vibe – energy genre.

Leviticus 19:31 *Regard not them that have familiar spirits, neither seek after wizards, to be defiled by them: I [am] the LORD your God.* A familiar spirit is a demonic entity that can become familiar to a person, place, or thing, and then take on the likeness of it so that it can oppress or possess for impure, deceptive, defiling, or demonic purposes. In this case, it has the person using their senses and perceptions to discern through the soul realm or the third eye which is connected to the second heaven where demonic principalities and powers operate.

Deuteronomy 18:9-12 *When thou art come into the land which the LORD thy God giveth thee, thou shalt not learn to do after the abominations of those nations. There shall not be found among you [any one] that maketh his son or his daughter to pass through the fire, [or] that useth divination, [or] an observer of times, or an enchanter, or a witch, Or a charmer, or a consulter with familiar spirits, or a wizard, or a necromancer. For all that do these things [are] an abomination unto the LORD: and because of these abominations the LORD thy God doth drive them out from before thee.*

Isaiah 47:8-13 *Therefore hear now this, [thou that art] given to pleasures, that dwellest carelessly, that sayest in thine heart, I [am], and none else beside me; I shall not sit [as] a widow, neither shall I know the loss of children: But these two [things] shall come to thee in a moment in one day, the loss of children, and widowhood: they shall come upon thee in their perfection for the multitude of thy sorceries, [and] for the great abundance of thine enchantments. For thou hast trusted in thy wickedness: thou hast said, None seeth me. Thy wisdom and thy knowledge, it hath perverted thee; and thou hast said in thine heart, I [am], and none else beside me. Therefore shall evil come upon thee; thou shalt not know from whence it riseth: and mischief shall fall upon thee; thou shalt not be able to put it off: and desolation shall come upon thee suddenly, [which] thou shalt not know. Stand now with thine enchantments, and with the multitude of thy sorceries, wherein thou hast laboured from thy youth; if so be thou shalt be able to profit, if so be thou mayest prevail. Thou art wearied in the multitude of thy counsels. Let now the astrologers, the stargazers, the monthly prognosticators,* *stand up, and save thee from [these things] that shall come upon thee. Behold, they shall be as stubble; the fire shall burn them; they shall not deliver themselves from the power of the flame: [there shall] not [be] a coal to warm at, [nor] fire to sit before it.*

Isaiah 8:19 *And when they shall say unto you, Seek unto them that have familiar spirits, and unto wizards that peep, and that mutter: should not a people seek unto their God? for the living to the dead?*

1Chronicles 10:14-15 *So Saul died for his transgression which he committed against the LORD, [even] against the word of the LORD, which he kept not, and also for asking [counsel] of [one that had] a familiar spirit, to enquire [of it]; And enquired not of the LORD: therefore he slew him, and turned the kingdom unto David the son of Jesse.*

2Chronicles 33:6 *And he caused his children to pass through the fire in the valley of the son of Hinnom: also he observed times, and used enchantments, and used witchcraft, and dealt with a familiar spirit, and with wizards: he wrought much evil in the sight of the LORD, to provoke him to anger.*

Galatians 5:19-21 *Now the works of the flesh are manifest, which are [these]; Adultery, fornication, uncleanness, lasciviousness, Idolatry, witchcraft, hatred, variance, emulations, wrath, strife, seditions, heresies, envyings, murders, drunkenness, revellings, and such like: of the which I tell you before, as I have also told [you] in time past, that they which do such things shall not inherit the kingdom of God.*

Revelation 21:8 *But the fearful, and unbelieving, and the abominable, and murderers, and whoremongers, and sorcerers, and idolaters, and all liars, shall have their part in the lake which burneth with fire and brimstone: which is the second death.*

Revelation 22:15 The Amplified Bible *[But] without are the dogs and those who practice sorceries (magic arts) and impurity [the lewd, adulterers] and the murderers and idolaters and everyone who loves and deals in falsehood (untruth, error, deception, cheating).*

STAY WOKE
"Stay Woke" is a term originated around 2010, by a group of African Americans in the United States who are pursuing liberation from racial, social, and spiritual injustices, and believe ascending to a higher way of consciousness is the pathway to freedom. Though not always the case, many of these people have experienced spiritual, social, and racial, maltreatment. They have done their homework in the areas of political, social, racial, worldly, and religious oppression. They can quote historical injustices, past and present laws, statistical disparities, religious and biblical discrepancies, regarding the unjust treatment of their people. They may present as radical, lawless, and angry, due to their identity being broken by the pain of their experiences and the generational patterns they identify with. Their willingness to study and equip themselves so they can "STAY WOKE," makes them a dangerous demon dealing force to be reckoned with. When confronted about their new age practices, their passion rages with rebellion and rejection against any ideology that comes for their conscious enlightenment.

Christians have been so focused on the rebellion and rage that they have not taken the time to discern the root causes that could be key factors in bringing healing and restoration to this group of people. If there is power struggling rather than listening compassionately with a heart to restore, the body of Christ will continue to lose this company of people to New Age consciousness.

Proverbs 11:30 *The fruit of the righteous is a tree of life; and he that winneth souls is wise.*

The "STAY WOKE" community, especially Africans and African Americans, have some valid revelation for rebelling against Christianity and not wanting to be fed a gospel and a Bible that was used to suppress their identity, enslaved them for generations, bewitch them into years of profitless living that they are still battling their way out of, and commercialized a "white Jesus" – "a white savior," that does not align with the biblical traits described in the Bible. Such practices are witchcraft within itself. It required constant brainwashing, trickery, manipulation, spell working of words and abusive sadistic rituals of a physical, emotional, and sexual nature, to pull off such godless injustices. The body of Christ will have to acknowledge and correct these wrongs, admit truth, preach truth, and live truth if they want to reach this community of people.

"STAY WOKE" is a mantra for the third eye we will discuss later in this chapter. It is alluring to making sure a person's consciousness is staying woke and alert - always on guard. The "STAY WOKE" community will use scripture to counterattack Christians addressing their New Age witchcraft ideologies. Though some of them contend they are Christians, they deem mainstream Christians as the enemy that has been sent to devour their truth and the purity of their ethnic and individual identity; and right to be little gods for their god. They base this insight on ***Psalm 82:6*** *I have said, Ye are gods; and all of you are children of the most High.* I will state that though we are little gods, as we embody God identity and are the essence and sonship of God, we are not equal to God, neither are we the divine supreme God. God reigns all by himself and everything under the earth is subject to him (***Psalm 113***).

New age practitioners can silence the most efficient bible scholars and pride themselves on embarrassing Christians by using their own biblical principles against them. They misconstrue and misuse the scriptures to justify their consciousness and the oppressions they have endured. Their twisted theories are mixed with biblical and historical truths which makes it difficult for Christians to dismantle their philosophies without becoming appalled by the way they present God and his word, thus behaving like the religious hypocrites this group deem them to be.

PRIVILEGE & ENTITLEMENT
Privilege is a special right, favor, advantage, advancement, immunity granted or available, only to certain persons or groups. For white and upper middle to rich classes of people, privilege entails inherent advantages based on their race, characterized by racial inequality and injustice, and financial classism.

Though the privileged inherently feels entitled to their advantages, entitlement operates in minority groups, particularly, Africans and African Americans, in a vastly different way.

Entitlement is the belief that one is deserving of or entitled to certain privileges or restitutions because of their identity, experiences, and injustices. It is the impression that something is deserved or owed and is usually rooted in generational pride that is really insecurity, unhealed trauma, generational and childhood wounds, abuse, ill treatment, and injustices at the expense of a person's identity, ethnicity, or circumstance. Though some of the mindsets of entitlement can be justified because of slavery, racism, and the continual experience of inequality and injustice, when entitlement is driven by victimization, retaliation, and a demand for repayment, it breeds new age ideologies that cause further division and murder of unity among ALL races rather than healing and oneness.

Privilege is an ancient custom that fuels entitlement in the new age movements and practitioners. Privilege is so ingrained in society and its' expectations about what is proper, until the privileged do not realize they are privileged. Many of them are biased, unconscious, and in denial, about the fact that they are treated differently and favorably than other races and classes of people. Even when the injustices of privilege are revealed, justifications and heartless comments and actions are made to protect the continual operation of privilege. The failure to apologize and acknowledge privilege as an issue that needs to be extinguished from our society, causes new agers to defend, liberate, and pursue justice by any means they deem necessary.

The fact that the majority of the body of Christ has not apologized for slavery and racial injustices within the church and in society, addressed privilege and racism as an issue, and many leaders have been exposed for how they have capitalized on the gifts and callings of minority groups, particularly Africans and African Americans; yet have been reluctant to stand for change regarding the increases of racial injustices and police brutality, has increased wounds and the mindset of entitlement. Essentially there has been a provoking of rebellion that draws the entitled into new age ideologies and customs. Lending them to lawless, sinful, and idolatrous practices, rather than dismantling privilege oppression, and seeking ways to uproot, heal, stand, and combat injustices in our society. Until this is addressed within the body of Christ, we will continue to lose minority groups, especially Africans and African Americans, to new age practices and ideologies.

WITCHCRAFT
Witchcraft is the practice of illusion, deception, impression, spell casting, witchery, for personal gain, power, influence, success, advancement, of oneself, or over a person, place, or thing.

Diagram 7.0 Witchcraft Practices

\multicolumn{4}{c}{Witchcraft practices include, but not limited to:}			
Sorcery	Magic	Witching	Wizardry
Black Magic	White Magic	Candle Magic	Spells
Hexes	Vexes	Hoodoo	Voodoo
Wicca	Mojo	Chants	Demonic Crossroads
Horoscopes	Tarot Readings	Psychic Readings	Chain Letters
Familiar Spirits	Spirit Guides	High Priest/Priestess	Demonic Omens
Necromancy	Yoga	Tibetan	Fortune Telling
Hypnotism	Acupuncture	Psychic Powers	Superstition
Reincarnation	Ouija Boards	Fengshai	Good Luck Charms
Sororities/Fraternities	Psychic Readings	Witchery	Pagan Holidays
Chakras	Kundalini	Astrology	Tarot Cards
Numerology	Dream Catchers	Palm Readings	Fortune Cookies
Ley lines	Incantations	Psychological Warfare	Demonic Crossroads/Spirits of The Crossroads

Source: Baker, 2021

Diagram 7.1 False Religions

\multicolumn{4}{c}{False religions include, but not limited to:}			
Free Masonry	Eastern Stars	Universalism	Black Muslim
Mormonism	Islam	Hinduism	Wizardry
Wicca	Bahai Faith	KKK	White Supremacy
Black Supremacy	Scientology	Jehovah Witnesses	Jesus Only
Satanism	SRA-Satanic Ritual Abuse	Five Percenters	Roman Catholicism
Christian Science	Shamanism	Santeria	New Age Practices
Deism	Yoruba Religion	Buddhism	Sangomas
Omnism	Polytheism	Raelism	Sikhism
Transhumanism Church	Moonies - Unification Movement	Greek Eastern Orthodox And Russian Orthodox	Chrislam
Illuminati	Church of Christ	Episcopal Church	Humanism
Seventh Day Adventist	Kabbalah	Lutheran	Modernism

Source: Baker, 2021

Diagram 7.2 Cults

Recommended further study on the following cults:		
The People's Temple – Jim Jones (1955-1978)	The Branch Dravidians (1955-1993)	Sullivanians (1957-1991)
Children of God – Family International (1968-Present)	Heaven's Gates (1972-1997)	Rajneesh Movement (1980s)
Buddhafield (1960-Present)	The Manson Family	Nation of Yahweh (1979-Present)

Source: Baker, 2021

ALTARS

We will discuss altars all throughout this book this will be a brief overview on altars. There are two types of altars in the Bible - divine altars inspired by God, and satanic altars created by humans who are influenced by Satan or their own manmade ideologies. Altars are a raised platform set aside and dedicated for the purposes of engaging in communion, worship, offerings, sacrifices, and completing ritual practices to a deity. Biblically, God provided insight on the purpose of an altar or his people would be inspired to build an altar for a specific purpose to honor him or commune with him. Biblically, it is illegal to build an altar to honor or commune with an idol God or for manmade purposes.

Witchcraft practitioners build their own altars or purchase entire altars and altar packages on different online websites. These ungodly altars may change and have different items on them depending on what rituals, sacrifices, dedications, covenants, demonic prayers, chants, meditations, and spells, being done on the altar. Depending on the purpose of the altar, how items are strategically placed can be key to engaging the elements of the earth, energies and frequencies, and deities.

In the old testament, God has his people to physically destroy demonic altars.

Deuteronomy 12:2-3 *You shall utterly destroy all the places where the nations whom you shall dispossess serve their gods, on the high mountains and on the hills and under every green tree. You shall tear down their altars and smash their sacred pillars and burn their Asherim with fire, and you shall cut down the engraved images of their gods and obliterate their name from that place.*

Hosea 8:11 *Since Ephraim has multiplied altars for sin, They have become altars of sinning for him.*

Hosea 10:1 *Israel is a luxuriant vine; He produces fruit for himself. The more his fruit, The more altars he made; The richer his land, The better he made the sacred pillars.*

2Kings 21:3 *For he rebuilt the high places which Hezekiah his father had destroyed; and he erected altars for Baal and made an Asherah, as Ahab king of Israel had done, and worshiped all the host of heaven and served them.*

Isaiah 17:8 *He will not have regard for the altars, the work of his hands, Nor will he look to that which his fingers have made, Even the Asherim and incense stands.*

Jeremiah 11:13 *For your gods are as many as your cities, O Judah; and as many as the streets of Jerusalem are the altars you have set up to the shameful thing, altars to burn incense to Baal.*

Jeremiah 19:13 *The houses of Jerusalem and the houses of the kings of Judah will be defiled like the place Topheth, because of all the houses on whose rooftops they burned sacrifices to all the heavenly host and poured out drink offerings to other gods.*

Some people believe that because they have a Bible, cross, or other religious artifacts on their altar, that it makes it a divine altar. Some believe that because they complete different practices on their altar in the name of Jesus Christ that their altar is divinely sacred. But God is clear about what he deems as an acceptable altar.

Zephaniah 1:5-7 The Amplified Bible *And those who worship the starry host of the heavens upon their housetops and those who [pretend to] worship the Lord and swear by and to Him and yet swear by and to [the heathen god Molech or] Malcam [their idol king], And those who have drawn back from following the Lord and those who have not sought the Lord nor inquired for, inquired of, and required the Lord [as their first necessity]. [Hush!] Be silent before the Lord God, for the day [of the vengeance] of the Lord is near; for the Lord has prepared a sacrifice, and He has set apart [for His use] those who have accepted His invitation.*

In the New Testament, God's people tore down demonic altars physically and spiritually.

Ephesians 6:12-18 *For we wrestle not against flesh and blood, but against principalities, against powers, against the rulers of the darkness of this world, against spiritual wickedness in high places. Wherefore take unto you the whole armour of God, that ye may be able to withstand in the evil day, and having done all, to stand. Stand therefore, having your loins girt about with truth, and having on the breastplate of righteousness; And your feet shod with the preparation of the gospel of peace; Above all, taking the shield of faith, wherewith ye shall be able to quench all the fiery darts of the wicked. And take the helmet of salvation, and the sword of the Spirit, which is the word of God: Praying always with all prayer and supplication in the Spirit, and watching thereunto with all perseverance and supplication for all saints;*

Sometimes during Intercessory prayer, God may reveal demonic altars that have been created to do harm against a person, place, or thing. God will guide the intercessor to cancel the effects the altar has on that person, place, or thing. God may even require a releasing of his Holy Spirit power and fire to destroy the workings of that altar. Doing this nullifies that altar's work where the assignments from it are being broken off that person, place, or thing.

THIRD EYE
The third eye is the seer operation of opening a gateway or portal within the eye gates, imagination, psyche, and inner realms of the second heaven. The person opens these pathways to receive information illegally through demonic assistance, for the purposes of engaging in witchcraft operations, and to ascend to higher states of consciousness. The third eye is also called the mind's eye or inner eye and is often depicted as being on the forehead between a person's physical eyes. It is mysterious, demonic, and abstruse, in nature because it is an invisible eye that is used for evil purposes, or for perceived good purposes that is rooted in demonic operations. People receive mental images, visions, revelation, and guidance that they believe has some deep spiritual significance, but these insights derive from demonic spirits that have tracked their lives, or that are using familiarity to transmit information, enlightenments, vibes, energies, powers, and sensations from which the person desires to experience. When Satan dealt demons to Eve in the garden, he opened her to a third eye.

Genesis 3:4-7 English Standard Bible *But the serpent said to the woman, "You will not surely die. For God knows that when you eat of it your eyes will be opened, and you will be like God, knowing good and evil." So when the woman saw that the tree was good for food, and that it was a delight to the eyes, and that the tree was to be desired to make one wise, she took of its fruit and ate, and she also gave some to her husband who was with her, and he ate. Then the eyes of both were opened, and they knew that they were naked. And they sewed fig leaves together and made themselves loincloths.*

Satan told eve that the reason God did not want her to eat from the tree was because her eyes would be opened to good and evil and she would be like God. Even just with talking to Satan, Eve began to see the tree as good for food and it became delightful to her eyes. This is the power witchcraft can have on a person. Just considering it can be influential to one's desires and will. The portal was already opening simply by entertaining the greatest demon dealer of all time – Satan. After eating of the tree, the third eye completely opened, and Eve begin to see in ways God had forbidden. She then dealt the food to her husband and opened a third eye in him. There purity and righteousness regarding their identity became tainted where they sowed fig leaves together to hide their nakedness. What once was pure and holy about them had now taken on a form of shame and condemnation. This is what operating through a third eye does. It twists what could be good if God led it and makes it perverted and evil. Or it exposes what we should not engage in altogether and makes it acceptable though God forbids it.

God forbids witchcraft and the third eye.

There is no way to make the third eye godly. God will never be okay with your identity exposed in ways that alters to truth about your ordained blueprint and the truth about him as your God. **SHIFT! SHIFT RIGHT NOW!**

Matthew 4:16 *The people which sat in darkness saw great light; and to them which sat in the region and shadow of death light is sprung up.*

The Amplified Bible *The people who sat (dwelt enveloped) in darkness have seen a great Light, and for those who sat in the land and shadow of death Light has dawned.*

<u>Darkness</u> is *skotos* in Greek and means:
1. shadiness, i.e., obscurity (literally or figuratively): — darkness,
2. darkness of night, darkness of darkened eyesight or blindness,
3. metaph. of ignorance respecting divine things and human duties, and the accompanying ungodliness and immorality, together with their consequent misery in hell persons in whom darkness becomes visible and holds sway.

When we sit in darkness death becomes even more lightened within us. It springs up and becomes a shadow over us. New Agers do not like to hear the truth that God forbids witchcraft and the third eye. This is because they have sat in darkness and their eyes have become darkened and blind to the truth of God, and now death is the light that evokes and provokes them. They are so deceived that they will go to great lengths to prove these forbidden practices have godly merit.

Matthew 6:21-24 *For where your treasure is, there will your heart be also. The light of the body is the eye: if therefore thine eye be single, thy whole body shall be full of light. But if thine eye be evil, thy whole body shall be full of darkness. If therefore the light that is in thee be darkness, how great is that darkness! No man can serve two masters: for either he will hate the one, and love the other; or else he will hold to the one, and despise the other. Ye cannot serve God and mammon.*

The Amplified Bible *For where your treasure is, there will your heart be also. The eye is the lamp of the body. So if your eye is sound, your entire body will be full of light. But if your eye is unsound, your whole body will be full of darkness. If then the very light in you [your conscience] is darkened, how dense is that darkness! No one can serve two masters; for either he will hate the one and love the other, or he will stand by and be devoted to the one and despise and be against the other. You cannot serve God and mammon (deceitful riches, money, possessions, or whatever is trusted in).*

Enlightenment through witchcraft and the third eye is darkness to God.

It is interesting that New Age practitioners speak of enlightenment, but the Bible says opening a third eye makes the conscience dark. The natural or spiritual eyes are no longer sound when a third eye has opened in a person. The treasure of their heart is now rooted in idolatry and what they have exposed themselves to through the third eye has filled them with darkness. Many who still want to hold on to Christian practices and the benefits of serving God, preach that they can serve two masters, three masters, four masters, as they demon deal the lie that there is more than one way to eternal life. But truthfully, they love that they are exposed to through the third eye more than God. For this reason, they have a difficult time relinquishing the treasures they have illegally obtained. God is clear that loving two masters is not possible and that he vomits those who even dare try to live such a life.

Revelation 3:15-16 *I know thy works, that thou art neither cold nor hot: I would thou wert cold or hot. So then because thou art lukewarm, and neither cold nor hot, I will spue (vomit or throw up) thee out of my mouth.*

Other ways a third eye can be opened is through witchcraft and satanic movies, TV shows, commercials, cartoons, music, music videos, video games, media, social media websites, demonic and witchcraft websites, occult board games, occult practices. Some movies, songs, websites, have been dedicated to witchcraft. This is the reason you can watch or read something, and instantly become bound with a migraine, and/or a band like pressure on the eyes or around the head. This bondage can also be felt in some places or around some people that have succumb to witchcraft practices.

God and his Holy Spirit is the only deity that should be guiding us into inner realms or higher states of consciousness. This pursuit is not about us exploring realms and enlightenments to define ourselves or so we can be defined by demonic deities. This consciousness is about receiving truth regarding who God is and who we are as created identities of God.

John 16:13 *When the Spirit of truth comes, he will guide you into all the truth, for he will not speak on his own authority, but whatever he hears he will speak, and he will declare to you the things that are to come.*

Luke 8:10 *He replied, "The knowledge of the mysteries of the kingdom of God has been given to you, but to others I speak in parables, so that, 'Though seeing, they may not see; though hearing, they may not understand.'*

Ephesians 1:18 *The eyes of your understanding being enlightened; that ye may know what is the hope of his calling, and what the riches of the glory of his inheritance in the saints.*

EXTRAORDINARY SIX SENSE (ESP)

ESP is defined as having keen intuitive power to discern things beyond one's natural senses or ordinary perception. Such people usually are clairvoyant and operate as psychics, fortune tellers, mediums, high priests, witches, warlocks, etc. Usually, a third eye has been opened generationally or personally, giving a person ESP ability. Many people can be born with this and assume it is a gift from God, when really it is a gateway that has been passed down through the generational line. A person may very well have a gift of prophecy upon their lives, but if that gift has been exposed to witchcraft or dedicated to demons, then it can be used as ESP rather than what God intended it for. The third eye will have to be closed, the person, generational line, and the gift will need to be rededicated to God and submitted to God before it can be used for the purposes he intended.

ASTRAL PROJECTION

Astral projection is an out-of-body experience, during which one's soul separates from the physical body and traverses the astral plane with the intent of traveling to different places and spheres. An astral plane is a literal road type plane or world that the soul crosses over into for the purposes of astral projecting to different areas.

Ecclesiastes 12:5-7 *Also when they shall be afraid of that which is high, and fears shall be in the way, and the almond tree shall flourish, and the grasshopper shall be a burden, and desire shall fail: because man goeth to his long home, and the mourners go about the streets: Or ever the silver cord be loosed, or the golden bowl be broken, or the pitcher be broken at the fountain, or the wheel broken at the cistern. Then shall the dust return to the earth as it was: and the spirit shall return unto God who gave it.*

New Agers engage in astral projection to "mind trip" which basically means for fun and thrills, for the purposes of engaging in various witchcraft practices, to engage demons for enlightenment or higher consciousness, to maneuver from one place to another, etc.

- Prophet Ezekiel speaks of being taken up or snatched up out of his body by the spirit of God (***Ezekiel 3:14, Ezekiel 8:3, Ezekiel 37:1, Ezekiel 43:5***).
- Apostle Paul speaks of having out of body experiences where he was translated to into heaven (***2Corinthians 12:2-4***).

- Prophet Elijah was taken up to heaven in a whirlwind and never returned (*2Kings 2:3-12*).
- Phillip the eunuch, was snatched away never to be seen again (*Acts 8:39*).

These experiences where not lead by the soul but through the guided translation of the spirit of God – the Holy Spirit. Astral projection is illegal because it is done by the soul and guided by the person or demonic spirits. Sometimes a gateway to this type can be opened in the generational line which will cause a person to astral project without trying. This was my experience. I had to close these witchcraft gateways via generational repentance and intercession to stop my soul from astral projecting as I slept at night.

SHAPESHIFTING & ALTER EGOS
Shapeshifting or alter ego witchcraft is where a practitioner may use a spirit guide to oppress their identity and change their personality or allows a demon to enter them. A practitioner may already have demons that have oppressed or possess them, such that they shift shape into an alternate personality or form. Depending on the level of witchcraft practice a person engages in or offers their lives to, they can shapeshift into animals, artifacts, other manifestations of themselves like an evil alter ego, a man, woman, old person, child, etc., and even look and act like these personalities. They can use demons to change their form to appear as any person living, dead, or fictional. Shapeshifters will enter a person's dream realm and appear innocent, then turn into something evil or vicious, while instilling fear, harm, shock, tragedy, etc. Initially, shapeshifters can initially appear harmless (cats turning into lions and attacking) or even look like someone the dreamer may know. It will then turn into a demon or evil being in the dream and attack the person. Shapeshifters are very subtle in dreams and tend to attack when they get a person to a place of trusting them or thinking he or she is safe and have no reason to be alarmed. Shapeshifters will attempt to draw the person to places in a dream where they will be harmed, attacked, chased, and/or running for their lives.

In the world of psychology, the word "alters" is known as "Dissociative Identity Disorder" or "Multiple Personality Disorder." This disorder is usually a reaction to trauma in which a person's personality splits during a traumatic event in effort to avoid the pain, shock, fear, or the hideous evil that they are experiencing. The personality then becomes two or three personalities due to the trauma. Sometimes people are healed of the trauma. This occurs when their brain, emotions, and soul heal, allowing their personality to mend as one healthy identity. It is my experience in deliverance ministry that sometimes demons enter the person's identity during a traumatic event and take on certain personalities. In these instances, demonic spirits are taking advantage of the trauma that has taken place in the person's life. The demonic spirits live in the person and manifests at different times in the person's life depending on the day and the situation. Delivering and healing the person of the trauma, casting these spirits out the personality, and commanding the identity to become well, is key to mending and healing the person where they operate in a healthy whole identity. Sometimes this takes a processing of wholeness overtime through counseling; sometimes, a deliverance session can bring healing to this issue, while providing the person keys to operating in their new whole identity.

In witchcraft, embracing alters and even allowing demons to enter one's life in order to operate as an alter has become a "cool phenomenon." There are multiple videos online under the hashtags "#alterwitch" or "#alterswitch" where witchcraft practitioners reveal their alters and show others how to evoke an alter. Rather than being healed of trauma, those with dissociative identity disorders are encouraged to embrace their alter personalities, and how to live life with their alters, rather than process in healing so they can be made well in operating in one whole identity. When operating in an altered state, witchcraft practitioners escape responsibility for behaviors while blaming it on the alter. Some witchcraft practitioners like to engage in alters for role play, sexual play, child's play, or to escape knowing what activities they are engaging in during rituals, spell casting, offering sacrifices or being sacrificed, and the like. Some practitioners evoke spiritual guides to come live in and around them and allow these demonic spirits to enter their bodies when they want to engage in certain altered personalities and witchcraft practices. Teenagers who are dabbling in witchcraft embrace this practice. Their parents think they are experiencing normal teenage hormonal changes, but they have opened their lives to alters.

Romans 12:1 *I beseech you therefore, brethren, by the mercies of God, that ye present your bodies a living sacrifice, holy, acceptable unto God, which is your reasonable service.*

1Corinthians 7:17-20 The Amplified Bible *But the person who is united to the Lord becomes one spirit with Him. Shun immorality and all sexual looseness [flee from impurity in thought, word, or deed]. Any other sin which a man commits is one outside the body, but he who commits sexual immorality sins against his own body. Do you not know that your body is the temple (the very sanctuary) of the Holy Spirit Who lives within you, Whom you have received [as a Gift] from God? You are not your own, You were bought with a price [purchased with a preciousness and paid for, made His own]. So then, honor God and bring glory to Him in your body.*

NEW AGE OR INTRINSIC MEDITATION
The founding roots of intrinsic meditation can be found in the following practices: Western culture, Eastern philosophy, mysticism, yoga, Hinduism, and Buddhism. Intrinsic meditation is also an ancient yogic practice where the person seeks to engage in serenity and balance of their emotional and physical center for the purposes of entering realms of higher consciousness. It is said that hippies first began practicing intrinsic meditation which helped it to gain attraction and attention. Meditation SHIFTED further into the mainstream new age movement in the 1960s and 1970s when Christian youth begin to rebel against the lack of truth, righteousness, and effective guidance from their religious systems and leaders.

New Age or Intrinsic Meditation is the art of blanking the mind and releasing oneself from conscious or undesirable thinking. This is done by focusing on a concept or object, while repeatedly chanting a phrase related to what the person desires to be released from or to. When a person blanks the mind, a clearing occurs so that as the person connects to its higher power, enlightenment and/or information can release into them. The problem with this is, often the higher power is a false concept such as the worshipping or connecting to earth, mood, stars, universe, some manmade deity, or a demonic idolatrous god. The Bible does not tell us to blank the mind. It forbids us from communing with false perceptions, demons, and idols. We should be pursuing the mind of Christ, as meditation in and of itself is not bad, but it being used for anything that is not guiding or pursuing God or being guided by God, causes it to be bad.

Joshua 1:8 *This book of the law shall not depart out of thy mouth; but thou shalt meditate therein day and night, that thou mayest observe to do according to all that is written therein: for then thou shalt make thy way prosperous, and then thou shalt have good success.*

Psalm 19:14 *Let the words of my mouth, and the meditation of my heart, be acceptable in thy sight, O LORD, my strength, and my redeemer.*

Psalm 49:3 *My mouth shall speak of wisdom; and the meditation of my heart [shall be] of understanding.*

Psalm 63:6 *When I remember You on my bed, I meditate on You in the night watches.*

Psalm 104:34 *My meditation of him shall be sweet: I will be glad in the LORD.*

Psalm 119:97-99 *O how love I thy law! it is my meditation all the day. Thou through thy commandments hast made me wiser than mine enemies: for they are ever with me. I have more understanding than all my teachers: for thy testimonies are my meditation.*

Isaiah 26:3 *Thou wilt keep [him] in perfect peace, whose mind is stayed on thee: because he trusteth in thee.*

Romans 12:2 *And be not conformed to this world: but be ye transformed by the renewing of your mind, that ye may prove what [is] that good, and acceptable, and perfect, will of God.*

1Peter 1:3 *Wherefore gird up the loins of your mind, be sober, and hope to the end for the grace that is to be brought unto you at the revelation of Jesus Christ.*

Philippians 2:5-11 *Let this mind be in you, which was also in Christ Jesus.*

Philippians 4:8 *Finally, brethren, whatsoever things are true, whatsoever things [are] honest, whatsoever things [are] just, whatsoever things [are] pure, whatsoever things [are] lovely, whatsoever things [are] of good report; if [there be] any virtue, and if [there be] any praise, think on these things.*

VISION (DREAM) BOARDS

Vision boards can be dated to cave man days where the cave paintings were created as mental pictures and prophecies as hunting strategies. Indigenous People and Native Americans also painted mental pictures on caves to record current events, dreams, and insights they received from their gods, and for mental guidance of further endeavors. Cave Men, Indigenous People, and Native Americans believe in many gods – not one god but many gods. They also engaged in rituals, spell work, incantations, for the purposes of encountering their gods and receiving foresight and strategy regarding their lives and circumstances. Basically, their vision boards were the result of witchcraft practices.

In 2006, a book and film entitled, "*The Secret*," SHIFTED vision boards into mainstream popularity. Oprah Winfrey approved the book and it sold 19 million copies. *The Secret* movie features in-depth interviews on self-proclaimed authors, philosophers, and scientists who share secrets of success via visualizing their goals. The movie presentation addressed the idea that the universe responds to our thoughts and feelings - what we think, feel, and focus on - the universe aligns to make sure we get just that. The movie demonstrated this philosophy in such a masterful way that people begin to adopt this concept. The popularity of creating vision boards SHIFTED forth. People implemented the concepts provided in the movie so the universe could align them with their desires for success, fame, and fortune.

A vision board is a collage of images, pictures, markers, and affirmations that encompasses a person's goals, dreams, and desires of places they want to live or visit, their desired careers, dream homes, spouse, children, and family desires, etc. There are some websites and apps such Pinterest that serve as virtual vision boards, where users can pin photos of their dreams, aspirations, and affirmations.

A vision board serves as a source of encouragement, inspiration, and motivation, to the person attaining their dreams. What many may not realize unless they have researched vision boards, is that it is also used as a law of attraction – a witchcraft law - to attain goals. The vision board is the process of taking the ideas in a person's mind and heart, and physically displaying them on a board, where they can engage them and pursue them as the universe guides them. The visual board's intent is to SHIFT the person from just thinking about their desires and dreams to doing and becoming them. This is done by making sure the images are so engrained in their psyche until their daily actions are guided by the images, and the person is drawn into circumstances by the universe to bring their desires to pass. The ideology of the law of attraction asserts that a person's thoughts and feelings can manipulate energy within the environment and upon frequencies and airways, thus giving the person the power needed to manifest their desires through their own will, thoughts, and feelings, they have released into the universe. The premise is that you are a magnet and draw to you what you think and feel. By having the physical board, the theory of the law of attraction guides the mind's eye to the things the person wants to attain, while helping them to imagine their lives becoming what they created on the board. The person is to consistently engage and use the board for visual mediation and affirmation. People are encouraged to spend time with the board. They are encouraged to meditate, daydream, journal and spend significant amounts of time envisioning it. Some people report meditating on their board for hours and receiving visions of how they will SHIFT forth their desires or how circumstances within the universe will align them with their desires. The intent is to create energy power to go after the things they put on the board. Through this guided imaging, the board opens a THIRD EYE – witchcraft portal - that draws the person constantly to images

Let me say it in a way so you totally grasp the concept of sneaky witchcraft.

that remind them of the board, so they can achieve their goals. Many do not realize that in addition to opening a third eye, the constant meditating on the board rather than God can cause the board to become an idol god. The self-driven images on the board and the demons that are operating within the third eye are guiding the person's life, rather than God.

Let's pause and think about that for a moment.

SIGH!

Many famous people equate their success to vision boards. Many of them have testimonies of creating a vision board then meditating on what they desired for hours. As that image is imprinted in their minds, their eyes, life pathways and circumstances begin to attract and draw those things to them. I would encourage you to read the information on copra.com regarding how a vision board works. This crafty activity seems harmless, but it is witchcraft. It is guided imagery, which is witch work.

Because I know so many people have and enjoy their vision boards, I have tried so hard to explore a way that this activity can be salvaged. I even wanted to suggest that if believers were going to do vision boards, they need to seek God for guidance regarding their purpose, destiny, dreams, aspirations, desires, and whether they align with his will and purpose. But because the roots of the vision board are idolatry and witchcraft, there is really no way to salvage it. There is no way to expunge that once created, the intent is to align it with universe – the universe is not GOD. Or to rid the third eye that is opened when a person is receiving encouragement, inspiration, and vision from the board. SIGH!

1Corinthians 3:19 *For the wisdom of this world is foolishness before God. For it is written, "He is the one who catches the wise in their craftiness."*

As Christians we are to write the vision, make it plan, and run with it; for where there is no vision, the people perish.

Habakkuk 2:1-2 *I will stand upon my watch, and set me upon the tower, and will watch to see what he will say unto me, and what I shall answer when I am reproved. And the Lord answered me, and said, Write the vision, and make it plain upon tables, that he may run that readeth it.*

Proverbs 29:18 *Where there is no vision, the people perish: but he that keepeth the law, happy is he.*

Rather than a vision board, I would encourage completing an artsy activity that includes the following:
- Journal YOUR desired dreams, aspirations, needs, and desires.
- Spending time with God asking him what HIS will and purpose is for you; journal what he says.
- Compare your notes to God's notes. Identify the similarities and the differences. Ask God for specifics on the reason he may not approve of something that may be on your

list. Ask for specifics regarding strategies for how to love and align your life with what is on his list.
- Ask God for time frames - what is for now and what is for later. Set goals with God based on what he says.
- Search out scriptures that can encourage to consistently work the strategies and time frames God gives you. Acquire an accountability partner who can keep you focused on what God is speaking.
- If you are a visual person, ask God how to create a scripture affirmation wall that keeps him as head of the vision, and you submitted to him. That way your power source is coming from him and his word, and not some third eye that opens through a random picture or a picture that will have you focused on your desires and not on purpose – not on God who is the supplier of all things. If you must use pictures, ask God if this is okay with him before doing so. Using pictures of yourself or that you have taken may be an option too but ask God and following his leading. He will guide you on how to create your vision plan in a way that is creative, encouraging, pure, and holy.
- Ask God to give you a name for your scripture affirmation wall that is tailor made to you and him and what you all are envisioning.
- Spend time praying to God for further insight on the vision plan and affirmation wall he has given you. Instead of meditating on what you want, meditate on God and his scriptures, and spend time waiting on him to give you visions, daydreams, night dreams, and prophetic revelation on attaining your destiny and calling.

Matthew 6:30-34 Wherefore, if God so clothe the grass of the field, which to day is, and tomorrow is cast into the oven, shall he not much more clothe you, O ye of little faith? Therefore take no thought, saying, What shall we eat? or, What shall we drink? or, Wherewithal shall we be clothed. (For after all these things do the Gentiles seek:) for your heavenly Father knoweth that ye have need of all these things. But seek ye first the kingdom of God, and his righteousness; and all these things shall be added unto you. Take therefore no thought for the morrow: for the morrow shall take thought for the things of itself. Sufficient unto the day is the evil thereof.

Philippians 4:19 But my God shall supply all your need according to his riches in glory by Christ Jesus.

MASTERING MANIFESTATION
I must admit when one of my spiritual daughters mentioned mastering manifestation as a New Age practice, I was appalled this community would use the word, 'manifest" as that is a term used by believers as related to scripture. Within the body of Christ, we believe in manifesting miracles, signs, and wonders – the greater works of God – so that he can get glory.

Mastering manifestation is the concept of a person being a magician in their own lives. "MAGICIAN?" Fix it God. Magician is an illusionist who uses tricks, deception, telepathy, mind control, charms, spells, hexes, incantations, to control and manipulate natural and supernatural forces, beings, and spirits. As we consider the definition, if you are mastering manifestation, you are operating in the demonic activity of witchcraft.

The person becomes a skilled master in being able to think, feel, behave in such a way that they are able release that into the environment and universe to that it can manifest what they desire. Mastering manifestation goes hand and hand with the laws of attraction as it is the results of what the person is attracting. The key to mastering manifestation is to consume enough energy power from the universe to manifest what you want. This is done through clearing blockages via meditation that hinder the person from encountering the universe and a higher level of consciousness, meditating to clear oneself of bad vibrations so that only good vibrations can emanate from the person, developing what is considered a healthy relationship and dialogue with and about what you want so it can be magnetized to you. All of this is witchery and is not of God.

Many people will say that this the reason the church and saints live in poverty or lack the full blessings of God. There is nothing wrong with wanting to be prosperous, successful, or pursuing it. But doing so much be in align with God's biblical principles and what he is saying for our lives. We are to be manifesting the will and purposes of God - his miracles, signs, and wonders - not our own manifestos.

Proverbs 19:21 *There are many devices in a man's heart; nevertheless the counsel of the LORD, that shall stand.*

Proverbs 23:17-19 The Amplified Bible *Let not your heart envy sinners, but continue in the reverent and worshipful fear of the Lord all the day long. For surely there is a latter end [a future and a reward], and your hope and expectation shall not be cut off. Hear, my son, and be wise, and direct your mind in the way [of the Lord].*

We can devise and manifest the greatest of plans, and even appear to be living a blessed life because of all we have accomplished and accumulated. But without God we are still voided of destiny fulfillment and whether in our lifetime or after we die, what we manifested will fall. We also must understand that as we put out vibes and energies of what we want into the universe, it is connecting to demons who will eventually want repayment for what the success they have helped us to gain.

Mark 13:21-23 *Then if anyone says to you, 'Look, here is the Christ!' or 'Look, there he is!' do not believe it. For false christs and false prophets will arise and perform signs and wonders, to lead astray, if possible, the elect. But be on guard; I have told you all things beforehand.*

John 14:12 *Verily, verily, I say unto you, He that believeth on me, the works that I do shall he do also; and greater works than these shall he do; because I go unto my Father.*

1John 4:1-3 *Beloved, believe not every spirit, but try the spirits whether they are of God: because many false prophets are gone out into the world. Hereby know ye the Spirit of God: Every spirit that confesseth that Jesus Christ is come in the flesh is of God: And every spirit that confesseth not that Jesus Christ is come in the flesh is not of God: and this is that spirit of antichrist, whereof ye have heard that it should come; and even now already is it in the world.*

1Thessalonians 2:7-12 *For the mystery of iniquity doth already work: only he who now letteth will let, until he be taken out of the way. And then shall that Wicked be revealed, whom the Lord shall consume with the spirit of his mouth, and shall destroy with the brightness of his coming: Even him, whose coming is after the working of Satan with all power and signs and lying wonders, And with all deceivableness of unrighteousness in them that perish; because they received not the love of the truth, that they might be saved. And for this cause God shall send them strong delusion, that they should believe a lie: That they all might be damned who believed not the truth, but had pleasure in unrighteousness.*

Revelation 16:14 *For they are demonic spirits, performing signs, who go abroad to the kings of the whole world, to assemble them for battle on the great day of God the Almighty.*

There is a manifestation board called, "board of directors." Witches and practitioners place the names and pictures of people they want to be like on this board. The person may be rich, have a certain gift talent, or calling; may have a level of success, influence, or power. The practitioner then spends dedicate consistent time meditating on the person and channeling their energy to acquire an impartation of their identity, success, and abilities. If they want knowledge of how the person became who they are, they meditate and channel their energy consistently until they begin to hear demon spirits - their higher powers - their idol gods - give them revelation regarding how the person flourished the way they did. They then implement this revelation into their lives so they can achieve in the same manner the person did. I heard a famous person who is a known Yoruba witch, share how she had a popular famous preacher's picture on her board, along with some other famous successful people she wanted to be like, and whom she wanted to manifest their wisdom and knowledge. I wondered why she had the popular preacher on their since she worshipped many gods and was not Christian. I discerned how I have seen Christians contact and watch the TV show of this witch for guidance; they assume that because she may mention Jesus Christ or respect any god that a person serves, has so much knowledge and wisdom, and has insight on their religion, that it is okay to receive guidance from her. She also presents as an empower, a preacher, a prophet, a teacher, a reformer, a savior to people's lives and to the world. Christians also tend to believe God can and will use anyone and that the source does not matter, especially if they present a "hint of Jesus." They do not realize that God has boundaries and is not using everyone and everything. They do not realize that this witch's posture appears as good and a helper, but her motivation and drive is to be god, be a god, take the place and voice of god in their lives; not to submit to the one true God. They do not realize that she channels and meditates on the names and energies of famous preachers and receives an impartation of their gifts, talents, knowledge, and wisdom from demons - familiar spirits - who gain insight for her regarding her directors' board, then shares it with her as she yields her mind and spirit to them through meditation and channeling. This is the reason the Bible tells us to believe not every spirit and to test every spirit. The witch is not getting her wisdom from God or her own personal pursuit of God for the purposes of being in relationship with him or preaching his gospel, but channeling the energies of people who serve him. Yet saints highly

Witches do not get their revelation from God. They get it from demons.

regard her wisdom, pursue it, and utilize it in their lives. The other challenge is, often what is being given to them is mixed with other witchcraft and occult practices and impure motives that opens the door to demons and draws believers away from God and into idolatry.

Deuteronomy 13:1-5 *If there arise among you a prophet, or a dreamer of dreams, and giveth thee a sign or a wonder, And the sign or the wonder come to pass, whereof he spake unto thee, saying, Let us go after other gods, which thou hast not known, and let us serve them; Thou shalt not hearken unto the words of that prophet, or that dreamer of dreams: for the LORD your God proveth you, to know whether ye love the LORD your God with all your heart and with all your soul. Ye shall walk after the LORD your God, and fear him, and keep his commandments, and obey his voice, and ye shall serve him, and cleave unto him. And that prophet, or that dreamer of dreams, shall be put to death; because he hath spoken to turn you away from the LORD your God, which brought you out of the land of Egypt, and redeemed you out of the house of bondage, to thrust thee out of the way which the LORD thy God commanded thee to walk in. So shalt thou put the evil away from the midst of thee.*

Deuteronomy 18:14 *For these nations, which thou shalt possess, hearkened unto observers of times, and unto diviners: but as for thee, the LORD thy God hath not suffered thee so to do.*

<u>Diviner</u> is *qâsam* in Hebrew and means:
1. properly, to distribute, i.e., determine by lot or magical scroll; by implication, to divine,
2. divine, diviner, divination, prudent, soothsayer, use (divination),
    a. of diviners of the nations, Balaam,
    b. of false prophets of Israel, prohibited.

Proverbs 14:15 *The simple believeth every word: but the prudent man looketh well to his going.*

Prudent is *ârûm* in Hebrew and means, "*cunning (usually in a bad sense): — crafty, prudent, subtil.*"

Jeremiah 14:14 *Then the LORD said unto me, The prophets prophesy lies in my name: I sent them not, neither have I commanded them, neither spake unto them: they prophesy unto you a false vision and divination, and a thing of nought, and the deceit of their heart.*

Jeremiah 23:16 *This is what the LORD of Hosts says: "Do not listen to the words of the prophets who prophesy to you. They are filling you with false hopes. They speak visions from their own minds, not from the mouth of the LORD.*

Jeremiah 29:8 *For thus saith the LORD of hosts, the God of Israel; Let not your prophets and your diviners, that be in the midst of you, deceive you, neither hearken to your dreams which ye cause to be dreamed. For they prophesy falsely unto you in my name: I have not sent them, saith the LORD.*

1John 1:4 *Beloved, believe not every spirit, but try the spirits whether they are of God: because many false prophets are gone out into the world.*

DIVINATION

Divination is the occult practice of pursuing, having, and foretelling the divine will of a god. A practitioner of divination is called a "diviner." They seek to acquire knowledge, strategies, decisions, answers, clarity, foresight, and to understand the hidden significance or cause for various situations occurring in people's lives, regions, and in society via supernatural powers. Diviner's use meditation, astrology, horoscopes, crystal gazing, tarot cards, manifestation and director boards, Ouija board, rituals, sacrificing, omens, channeling, prayer chanting to gods to acquire their knowledge. Diviners will also study all types of books, doctrines, theories, ideologies, from ancient to present history, medical, economic, societal, and psychological practices, and theories. They do this to gain wisdom and insight on various topics and ways to heal and fix situation, so they can be viewed as extremely wise and needful to resolve matters. They will also channel wise and successful people and folklore to obtain wisdom so they can use it in their practice. They know that knowledge is power. They constantly seek natural and supernatural knowledge so they can impact, control, and gain a foothold into people's lives.

Jeremiah 14:14 Then the LORD said unto me, The prophets prophesy lies in my name: I sent them not, neither have I commanded them, neither spake unto them: they prophesy unto you a false vision and divination, and a thing of nought, and the deceit of their heart.

It is important to note that any knowledge obtained by way of divination or for the purposes of cunning, tricking, manipulating controlling, or demonizing someone is not of God. It does not matter if it is true, came true, appear helpful, is needful. It does not matter if miracles, signs, or wonders follow it. To God it is unlawful if it was obtained illegally via demonic operations or to be used prudently. (**Study Deuteronomy 13, Deuteronomy 18-22, Deuteronomy 29**).

Jeremiah 27:9 But as for you, do not listen to your prophets, your diviners, your dreamers, your soothsayers or your sorcerers who speak to you, saying, 'You will not serve the king of Babylon.'

Jeremiah 29:8-9 For thus says the Lord of hosts, the God of Israel, 'Do not let your prophets who are in your midst and your diviners deceive you, and do not listen to the dreams which they dream. For they prophesy falsely to you in My name; I have not sent them,' declares the Lord.

Ezekiel 12:24 For there will no longer be any false vision or flattering divination within the house of Israel.

Ezekiel 13:6-7 They see falsehood and lying divination who are saying, 'The Lord declares,' when the Lord has not sent them; yet they hope for the fulfillment of their word. Did you not see a false vision and speak a lying divination when you said, 'The Lord declares,' but it is not I who have spoken?"

TELEPATHY

Telepathy is the acclaimed process of knowingly or unknowingly communicating between the minds of people by some means of sensory or demonic perception. It is also the transmitting of information from one person to another without using any known human sensory channels or physical interaction. When done knowingly, the people are seeking to engage one another in pleasures, concepts that SHIFTS them to a place of higher consciousness, or in effort to meet one another in the same place or sphere of higher consciousness. When done unknowingly, the person is often striving to influence, alter, stifle, or control the mind and perception of another person. Either way this behavior is witchcraft and illegal in the eyes of God.

There is no place in the Bible where God tells us to communicate with one another through our minds or to seek to have control or interject information into the minds of others. We are not to have anything governing our minds or exalting in our minds that is not God directed and God inspired. The Bible tell us the following directions when it comes to our minds.

Colossians 3:2 *Set your minds on things that are above, not on things that are on earth.*

Philippians 2:5 *In your relationships with one another, have the same mindset as Christ Jesus.*

Philippians 4:7 *And the peace of God, which transcends all understanding, will guard your hearts and your minds in Christ Jesus.*

Romans 12:2 *Do not conform to the pattern of this world, but be transformed by the renewing of your mind. Then you will be able to test and approve what God's will is—his good, pleasing and perfect will.*

Hebrews 8:10 *This is the covenant I will establish with the people of Israel after that time, declares the Lord. I will put my laws in their minds and write them on their hearts. I will be their God, and they will be my people. (Notice God our creator is placing divine inspiration into us so we can aligned properly in thought and deed to be his people and receive the fruit of him being Lord of our lives).*

Isaiah 26:3 *You will keep in perfect peace those whose minds are steadfast, because they trust in you.*

2Corinthians 10:3-5 *For though we live in the world, we do not wage war as the world does. The weapons we fight with are not the weapons of the world. On the contrary, they have divine power to demolish strongholds. We demolish arguments and every pretension that sets itself up against the knowledge of God, and we take captive every thought to make it obedient to Christ.*

Philippians 4:8 *Finally, brothers and sisters, whatever is true, whatever is noble, whatever is right, whatever is pure, whatever is lovely, whatever is admirable—if anything is excellent or praiseworthy—think about such things.*

I also want to dispel the myth that discernment is telepathy. Discernment is not us putting something in people's minds or entering people's minds to gain revelation about them. Discernment is the Holy Spirit providing us with knowledge, revelation, insight, judgment, distinction, regarding the disposition of a person's spirit, a demonic spirit, or the spirit realm and climate of a sphere we are in. Through this information, the Holy Spirit may reveal the heart, mind, thought, will, and intent of a person but this is done through our spiritual senses and guided by the Holy Spirit. We are not entering inside the minds of a person to gain access to information. To do that is telepathy. This is illegal and dangerous

ASTROLOGY WORSHIP & HOROSCOPES

Astrology is the belief that the alignment of stars and planets affects every individual's mood, personality, and environment, depending on when he was born. New Agers tend to study astrology so they can have insight on when the moon, stars, sun, galaxies, cosmos is at its greatest peak of power and light source, to meditate and receive a transference of that energy to rule in the earth at the highest level possible. They also use astrology to examine their birth charts via horoscopes. Horoscopes are a foretelling of a person's future, generally encompassing a depiction of character, personality and identity traits, and circumstances. This information is obtained based on the distinct positions of the stars and planets at the time of that person's birth. The 12 zodiac signs are Aries, Taurus, Gemini, Cancer, Leo, Virgo, Libra, Scorpio, Sagittarius, Capricorn, Aquarius, and Pisces. People believe that different sun signs of the zodiac present different characteristics and talents. This is witchcraft as such information comes from God and not the aligning of stars and planets.

SPIRIT GUIDES

A spirit guide is a disincarnate spirit which serves as a guide or protector that governs the family line.

Diagram 7.3 Spirit Guides

Names of Spirit Guides			
Archangels	Angels/Helpers	Guardian Angels	Angel Guides
Ancestors	Ascended Masters	Enlightened Beings	Goddesses
Elemental Energies	Spirit Animals	Ancient Ones	Sylphs
Undines	Salamanders	Gnomes	Kids may call them imaginary friends

Source: Baker, 2021

Though many names, spirit guides are demonic spirits that have claimed ownership to the family line. The movie Coco provides keen revelation for how a spirit guide operates in a family line. If you watch the movie, make sure you pray to close any portals that may open the door to demonic spirits, and break the spells that are attached to it as it is full of witchcraft.

Ancestral spirit guides are superior to the living and are revered in the family line. It is perceived that spirit guides provide advice, assistance, and pathways for success. These are just familiar spirits who have tracked the family line and use information to direct those in the family line in the way they desire rather than their God identity and purpose. Many people have altars in their homes where they commune with their spirit guides and cast spells. Some spirit guides are attached to objects in some cultures. For example, when you enter Chinese restaurants and businesses, the animal pictures on the walls are spirit guides. In Mexican culture, many of the sculptures of fantastical creators, are attached to ancient spirit guides. In African culture, ancestors have been long considered spirit guides even before the spread of Christianity. This is one of the reasons Africans and African Americans are rooted in ancestral worship.

There are spirit guide transformational retreats that people can attend. Some of these retreats require a consecration of intense fasting of up to two weeks before the retreat occurs. At the retreat, they spend hours chanting and calling on their spirit guides. Once the demon guides manifest, they commune with them, while receiving what they believe to be healing from blockages, relationship issues, heart and life pains, wisdom and inspiration concerning their lives, strategies, and empowerment to follow through with what the spirit guide tells them.

HERO WORSHIP OR CULT WORSHIP
Hero worship is the excessive admiration of someone. There can also be a presumption that the person is special, perfect, superhuman, a god, or have deity-like qualities. The person can be famous actor, singer, rapper, musician, artist, media influencer, athlete; rich, successful, a close relative or loved one that has a profound impact on the worshipper's life. The person can be a position, or someone holds the same ideologies and beliefs as the worshipper. The person can be a killer as a lot of prisoners who receive news coverage or have unique experiences surrounding their crimes and arrests gain hero worshippers. It is not uncommon for people to become their pen pals and consistently write and visit them in jail, put money on their books and send them gifts, start blogs and online pages in their honor, want to marry them, or mimic their crimes. A hero who is worshipped can be alive or dead, an ancestor, or a historical icon. Some heroes are fictional characters, animated characters, or fantasy characters as people acquire fetishes and worship figures that are computerized, a part of games, or online fantasy sites. A hero person who is worshiped can be a pastor, a spiritual leader, or even an ethnic leader that has an impact on a people in relations to justice or being idolized for overcoming racial and economic barriers to achieve success.

Hero worship is very dangerous because often sins and ungodly behavior is overlooked. The person is presented as an icon regardless of treacherous behavior. With the rise of branding, being an influencer, starting businesses or advertising businesses online, becoming the brand, hero worship has become a popular phenomenon in our society. People are worshipped for their popularity, gifts, cunning - charismatic words or talents, with no regard to whether they really have the education, knowledge, capability, or moral character to be a hero. Many people will brag about the fact that they never asked to be a hero, especially when they engage in unbecoming behavior. They are not held accountable for inappropriate behavior as fame and platform tends to override morality. People who worship heroes tend to relish in the negative behaviors of their idols. They love to brag, drag, gossip, analyze, and make excuses for their behaviors and many become more famous because of their ungodly behaviors rather than being held accountable for them. Many modern idols are self-absorbed and narcissistic. Because it has become a needful part of branding and promoting oneself and product to talk or boast about oneself, narcissists is able to operate in mainstream with no consequences to how their actions impact others, the culture, systems, societies, or their spheres of influence. They are able to rape, rob, abuse, offend, victimize, ridicule, oppress, gaslight, with no regard to what is being violated or impacted by their behavior. Those that worship them are willing to kill, punish, threaten, degrade, cancel, anyone who comes against their hero. The hero can stand behind freedom of speech and incite their worshipers to be violent and offensive with no consequences to their actions. We have created TV shows with titles like, "American Idol" as we see nothing wrong with hero worship. We have an innate need to worship something and when we are not in full convent at with the true and living God, we will make our own golden calves so we can fulfill our need to worship. The word says the following about how society will become due to hero worship:

Isaiah 5:20-23 The Amplified Bible *Woe to those who call evil good and good evil, who put darkness for light and light for darkness, who put bitter for sweet and sweet for bitter! Woe to those who are wise in their own eyes and prudent and shrewd in their own sight! Woe to those who are mighty heroes at drinking wine and men of strength in mixing alcoholic drinks!—Who justify and acquit the guilty for a bribe, but take away the rights of the innocent and righteous from them!*

2Timothy 3:1-7 Worldwide English Bible *Be sure of this. In the last days hard times will come. People will love themselves. They will love money. They will talk about themselves and be proud. They will say wrong things about people. They will not obey their parents. They will not be thankful. They will not keep anything holy. They will have no love. They will not agree with anybody. They will tell lies about people. They will have no self-control. They will beat people. They will not love anything that is good. They cannot be trusted. They will act quickly, without thinking. They are proud of themselves. They love to have fun more than they love God. They act as if they worshipped God, yet they do not let God's power work in their lives. Keep away from people like that. They are the kind who go quietly into people's houses. There they get foolish women to believe them. These women know that they have done many wrong things. And they want to do many kinds of wrong things. They are always trying to learn, but never able to find out what is really true.*

James 4:17 *Therefore to him that knoweth to do good, and doeth it not, to him it is sin.*

I will explore more on this topic in the next section, however, along with many ethnic groupings, Ancient Greek religions also engaged in hero cult worship. They worshipped ancestors or people they deem a god, or idolatrous deities. Such worshippers find it difficult to let go of the practice of hero worship. The ancestral hero worship tends to be generational witch creates a stronghold of ideologies and beliefs within the generational line. The ancestral hero worshippers will pass down the stories and ideologies. They will set up memorial sites in and around their homes and communities to worship the person. They will go to their ancestors' graves and erect altars to worship them. They will engage in necromancy in effort to conjure and commune with their hero's spirit or to embody their spirit so they can be like their hero or keep their hero operative in the earth. It is not uncommon to dig up graves and take remains to keep on altars to worship ancestral heroes or take dirt from in and around the grave and keep it altars as a point of contact in rituals and sacrifices to ancestral heroes. They will provoke their spirit in effort to gain guidance, favor, protection, prosperity, success, life advancement.

Though it is applicable to admire and esteem one another, it is idolatrous to worship one another. We should not exalt anything or anyone above God. He is the only, Lord, savior, and true hero.

Isaiah 45:5 *I am the LORD, and there is none else, there is no God beside me.*

ANCESTRAL WORSHIP

It is important to note that ancestral worship is manmade and not a godly custom. It has been around for centuries, which is the reason people deem it acceptable. They equate its ancient history with revering their ancestral lineage and honoring the legacy they were birthed into. Though ancestral worship can be found in all ethnicities, Indians, Asians, Africans, and Hispanics, possess ancient practices that have been engrained in their cultural identity. Through the New Age movement, the drive to be liberated from racial, spiritual, and culture oppression, and the failure of leaders to truly live through the biblical standards of God, has caused many ethnic groups (especially Africans and Africans who are born in America), and the millennial generation, to embrace ancestral worship as needful for reestablishing and connecting themselves back into their pure roots. The need to reject mainstream Christianity and years of racial oppression as a way of confronting and combating the injustices done against certain ethnic groups and against millennials who have been abused or misused in the church, has been a catalyst for ancestral worship. New Agers are seeking to understand and live through their identity. The challenge is, ancestral worship has nothing to do with identity, especially not God identity. It is rebellious idolatry against God and therefore, can only breed further rebellion and the cultivation of an idolatrous identity.

Ancestral worship is the reverence and homage to deceased relatives or esteem figures of ethnic groups. Ancestors are generally those who have lived a moral life and are able to be a spiritual guide for the family or a mediator between the family and their god. In some families, the people who are immoral or mean are still regarded fear that their spirits will return after death and cause havoc in the lives of those who defy them. Children are valued in cultures where ancestral worship is practice because they can provide for their parents' spirits after death.

Ancestral worship is done for the purposes of:

- Converse with those that have passed on.
- Honor those who have passed on.
- Secure their life in the afterword.
- Secure their reincarnation is blessed.

- Receive blessings, favor, fame, and success to family members deemed to be living a moral life.
- Render curses, judgments, and justices to family members deemed to be living an immoral life.
- Receive guidance and wisdom regarding life endeavors.
- Receive protection from evil and challenging experiences.
- Receive assistance for challenging life situations.
- Rid life and atmospheres of demons and evil.
- Offer sacrifices to idol gods.
- Offer a gateway for the ancestor to commune with the gods on behalf of the worshipper and/or family members.

Diagram 7.4 Methods of Sacrifice

Sacrifices can be offered in the following ways:		
Blood, Water, and Fire Offerings	Essential Oils, Tinctures, Cannabis, and Sage Burning	Crystals and Candles
Wearing of Certain Garments	Food	Water and Other Beverages
Bewitching, Chanting, Prayers, Spells, and Hexes	Altar Sacrifices and Spirit Tablets	Incantations
Murder of Animals or People, Especially Babies and Women	Dance and Rhythmic Ceremonies	Rituals and Customs
Traditions, Feasts, Celebrations, Worship Memories, and Holidays	Necromancy and Spiritual Seances	Grave Visiting and Cleansing for Thank Offerings

Source: Baker, 2021

Losing loved ones, battling grief, and learning to live life without those who have passed can be difficult, but it still does not justify ancestral worship. Especially when God forbids its practices. Though there is an assumption that a person is communing with dead relatives, ancestral worship is the entertaining of familiar demonic spirits.

The dead either goes to heaven or hell. There is no communing with the dead after they die as they exit the natural world. If there are circumstances surrounding this, it should be God led, as seeking out the dead for any purpose is not of God.

Hebrews 9:27 *And just as it is appointed for man to die once, and after that comes judgment.*

2Samuel 12:23 *But now he is dead, wherefore should I fast? can I bring him back again? I shall go to him, but he shall not return to me.*

In ***1Samuel 28***, King Saul enquirers of the witch of Endor to conjure up the spirit of Prophet Samuel so he could receive prophetic direction since God had rejected him and stopped communing with him. When reading this chapter, you will learn that even the witch of Endor knew this was a forbidden practice. She informed King Saul that he had exiled all the mediums out the land, and to engage in such a practice was punishable by death. King Saul had to convince her that she would not be punished for performing this act for him. Even after he assured her, she took careful action to attend to King Saul such that she preserved her life. It is unclear if Prophet Samuel truly appeared, if the witch conjured a familiar spirit, or if she performed some type of deceptive act of witchery. If it was indeed Prophet Samuel, then it was God allowing it for some purpose of enacting a final judgment upon King Saul and was not through any power of the witch. Even if this is the case, God continued to forbid it all throughout the Bible. This lets us know that this is not a practice we should pursue and if we do have such an experience, God should be orchestrating it.

God is Sovereign! God may engage in divine acts that are forbidden to us.

The only mediator between use and God is Jesus Christ. The Bible lets us know that we can boldly approach the throne of grace. Jesus Christ is only mediating to make intercession on our behalf, but we have direct access to God.

Hebrews 4:14-16 *Seeing then that we have a great high priest, that is passed into the heavens, Jesus the Son of God, let us hold fast our profession. For we have not an high priest which cannot be touched with the feeling of our infirmities; but was in all points tempted like as we are, yet without sin. Let us therefore come boldly unto the throne of grace, that we may obtain mercy, and find grace to help in time of need.*

1Timothy 2:5-6 *For there is one God, and there is one mediator between God and men, the man Christ Jesus, who gave himself as a ransom for all, which is the testimony given at the proper time.*

Believing in Jesus Christ as Lord and savior and living a discipled life in covenant relationship with him is the only way to eternal life in heaven. Praying and offering sacrifices to dead ancestors for intervention or to guide your soul will not change this truth. Honoring your dead ancestors as gods or celebrating the gods they served during their lifetime will not change this truth. Creating your own god and deeming it the way to eternal life, will not change this truth.

Leviticus 19:31-32 *Regard not them that have familiar spirits, neither seek after wizards, to be defiled by them: I am the LORD your God. Thou shalt rise up before the hoary (gray) head, and honour the face of the old man, and fear thy God: I am the LORD.*

Leviticus 20:6 English Standard Bible *If a person turns to mediums and necromancers, whoring after them, I will set my face against that person and will cut him off from among his people.*

Leviticus 20:27 *A man or woman who is a medium and has a familiar spirit or is a wizard shall surely be put to death, be stoned with stones; their blood shall be upon them.*

Deuteronomy 18:10-12 *There shall not be found among you any one that maketh his son or his daughter to pass through the fire, or that useth divination, or an observer of times, or an enchanter, or a witch, Or a charmer, or a consulter with familiar spirits, or a wizard, or a necromancer. For all that do these things are an abomination unto the LORD. And because of these abominations the LORD thy God doth drive them out from before thee.*

Jeremiah 27:9-10 The Amplified Bible *So do not listen to your [false] prophets, your diviners, your dreamers [and your dreams, whether your own or others'], your soothsayers, your sorcerers, who say to you, You shall not serve the king of Babylon. For they prophesy a lie to you which will cause you to be removed far from your land; and I will drive you out, and you will perish.*

Jesus Is the Only Way to Heaven.

John 14:6 *Jesus answered, 'I am the way and the truth and the life. No one comes to the Father except through me."*

John 3:36 *Whoever believes in the Son has eternal life; whoever does not obey the Son shall not see life, but the wrath of God remains on him.*

John 3:16 *For God so loved the world, that he gave his only Son, that whoever believes in him should not perish but have eternal life.*

John 10:9 *I am the door. If anyone enters by Me, he will be saved, and will go in and find pasture ... I have come that they may have life, and that they may have it more abundantly.*

John 11:25 *Jesus said to her, "I am the resurrection and the life, he who believes in Me, though he may die, he shall live. And whoever lives and believes in Me shall never die."*

John 17:3 *And this is eternal life, that they know you, the only true God, and Jesus Christ whom you have sent.*

Acts 4:12 *And there is salvation in no one else, for there is no other name under heaven given among men by which we must be saved.*

Romans 10:9 *Because, if you confess with your mouth that Jesus is Lord and believe in your heart that God raised him from the dead, you will be saved.*

Ephesians 4:4 *There is one body and one Spirit ... one Lord, one faith, one baptism, one God and Father of all, who is above all, and through all, and in you all.*

Ecclesiastes 3 states that there is a time to live, a time to die, and a mourn. This lets us know that death is inevitable, and mourning is for a specific time. We were never meant to mourn forever. And though we have an appointed time in our natural life, we get to live in eternity with God. God is adamant about him being the head of our lives and is not holding on to anything that exalts above his position as God and king. God declares in ***Exodus 20:30***, "Thou shalt have no other gods before me." When we engage in ancestral worship, we are engaging in idolatry as that person and what we believe we can receive from them becomes our God.

When we engage in ancestral worship, we are also striving to operate in practices that only belong to God. God is the guide of our lives. Our trust and obedience to him determines our fate, blessing, and success. He is the only one who has power over life and death and control those realms. When we attempt to participate in something God has deemed dead or no longer needful in our lives, we have transgressed into sin.

1Timothy 4:1-2 *Now the Spirit speaketh expressly, that in the latter times some shall depart from the faith, giving heed to seducing spirits, and doctrines of devils; Speaking lies in hypocrisy; having their conscience seared with a hot iron.*

<u>Iron</u> in Greek is *kaustēriazō* and means:
1. to brand ("cauterize"), i.e. (by implication) to render insensitive (figuratively),
2. sear with a hot iron, to mark by branding, to brand, branded with their own consciences,
    a. whose souls are branded with the marks of sin,
    b. who carry about with them the perpetual consciousness of sin,
3. seared; in a medical sense, to cauterize, remover by cautery.

When a person delves into ancestral worship, they brand their own conscience. They become their own God as they begin deciding what is right or wrong through their own desired conduct and motives. They create their own moral and ethical code and what they believe becomes cauterized – seared upon their hearts. This is the reason they can contend what they are doing is God, while declaring God approves of it. They are their own god, so the rules have become whatever they decide to make them.

Because our free will allows it does not mean God approves.

1Corinthians 10:19-23 *What say I then? that the idol is any thing, or that which is offered in sacrifice to idols is any thing? But I say, that the things which the Gentiles sacrifice, they sacrifice to devils, and not to God: and I would not that ye should have fellowship with devils. Ye cannot drink the cup of the Lord, and the cup of devils: ye cannot be partakers of the Lord's table, and of the table of devils. Do we provoke the Lord to jealousy? are we stronger than he? All things are lawful for me, but all things are not expedient: all things are lawful for me, but all things edify not.*

REINCARNATION

Reincarnation is the belief that the soul of a person or animal is reborn after they die. The person or animal may return as themselves, someone else, as an animal even though they were a person, as a reason even though they were an animal. The belief is that a person or animal can reborn multiples times depending on their life's calling or how they lived in their previous lives. There is the belief that if a person passes through enough bodies, while reaching a level of high spiritual enlightenment they can break the cycle of reincarnation and enter eternal bliss. It is also believed that is the person's or animal's soul was guided properly by family members into the afterlife, they can be reborn. If their souls were not guided properly by family members, they cannot return. This is the reason children are so important in certain cultures. It is also the reason customs are revered and obligations to follow the traditions of the family are entrenched in the children with fear or obligation.

Some cultures believe there is another world in the afterlife to which people can be whatever they desire, can be revered based on how they lived in the present life, or based on whether they were a martyr in their present life. There is the belief in gaining great blessings and living prosperously in the afterlife. Such beliefs sound great to those living difficult lives, living in war zones, living a life that is chosen for them. Often a child being wise beyond their years or mimicking the behaviors of an adult is described as *"an old soul that has been here before."* Some people will go as even consider who the person acts like. Sometimes, people will look like those who have passed on years ago. These perceptions are the basis of viewing reincarnation as factual. Many who reject living or know of loved ones who have not lived a life discipled in God on earth, want some type of alternate possibility of what may happen after death. Concepts like reincarnation have been created to give people false hope at a change at for a better life or to live a life of eternity despite a sinful life. When we take on these ideologies, we create alternate pathways regarding afterlife that are not of God. However, the Bible is clear that once we die, we either become present with the Lord or go to hell.

Daniel 12:2 *Multitudes who sleep in the dust of the earth will awake: some to everlasting life, others to shame and everlasting contempt.*

Job 9:12 *As a cloud vanishes and is gone, so one who goes down to the grave does not return.*

Hebrews 9:27 *And just as it is appointed for man to die once, and after that comes judgment.*

Hebrews 78:39 *He remembered that they were but flesh, a passing breeze that does not return.*

2Corinthians 5:1 *For we know that if the earthly tent we live in is destroyed, we have a building from God, an eternal house in heaven, not built by human hands.*

Chapter 8
CURIOUS ARTS
PURIFICATION and ENLIGHTENMENT

This chapter is a continuation of the previous one as many New Age participants believe in purification and enlightenment. They engage in these practices by using various witchcraft practices that includes spells, astral projection, intrinsic meditation to which we discussed in the previous chapter. Many of them will spend hours consecrating themselves, fasting, and praying to their god for purification, enlightenment of mental clarity, peace, peaceful sleep, protection, deliverance, healing, favor, relationships, marriage, children, blessings, prosperity, success. They will use various witchcraft spells, herbal regimens, drugs, gems, and meditation techniques to rid themselves of evil vibes, energies, waves and ascend into idol god consciousness. They will also seek to cast out demons or receive deliverance from ungodly and unhealthy strongholds, behaviors, cycles, and curses. The Bible is clear about how we obtain purification and enlightenment. It is certainly not through these practices.

Mark 9:39-40 And John answered him, saying, Master, we saw one casting out devils in thy name, and he followeth not us: and we forbad him, because he followeth not us. But Jesus said, Forbid him not: for there is no man which shall do a miracle in my name, that can lightly speak evil of me. For he that is not against us is on our part.

Acts 19:13-19 The Amplified Bible Then some of the traveling Jewish exorcists (men who adjure evil spirits) also undertook to call the name of the Lord Jesus over those who had evil spirits, saying, I solemnly implore and charge you by the Jesus Whom Paul preaches! Seven sons of a certain Jewish chief priest named Sceva were doing this. But [one] evil spirit retorted, Jesus I know, and Paul I know about, but who are you? Then the man in whom the evil spirit dwelt leaped upon them, mastering two of them, and was so violent against them that they dashed out of that house [in fear], stripped naked and wounded.

This became known to all who lived in Ephesus, both Jews and Greeks, and alarm and terror fell upon them all; and the name of the Lord Jesus was extolled and magnified. Many also of those who were now believers came making full confession and thoroughly exposing their [former deceptive and evil] practices. And many of those who had practiced curious, magical arts collected their books and [throwing them, book after book, on the pile] burned them in the sight of everybody. When they counted the value of them, they found it amounted to 50,000 pieces of silver (about $9,300). Thus the Word of the Lord [concerning the attainment through Christ of eternal salvation in the kingdom of God] grew and spread and intensified, prevailing mightily.

In *Mark 9*, Jesus welcomes the follower casting out demons in his name. He expressed that those who can perform such miracles were for him rather than against him. In *Acts 19*, the traveling Jewish exorcist was attacked by the demonic person he was trying to cast the demon out of. He was unauthorized as he and the people in this region were engaging in forms of godliness and witchcraft practices to minister, succeed, acquire purification, and enlightenment. They lacked true power and authority through the name, salvation, and covenant relationship of Jesus Christ. They were engaging in strange curious works that made them enemies of Jesus rather than sons of God.

Curious arts in Greek is *periergos* and means:
1. working all around, i.e., officious (meddlesome, neuter plural magic),
2. busybody, curious arts,
3. busy about trifles and neglectful of important matters,
4. esp. busy about other folks' affairs, a busybody,
5. of things: impertinent and superfluous, of magic arts.

It is interesting that the definition deems these workings as that of a busybody. Though we know some people are blatant witches and warlocks, we can discern from this story that when we are not grounded in God, idle or unintentional regarding our relationship with God and our God identity, start to inquire and engage in activities due to curiosity or nosiness, or when we pursue the supernatural, signs, wonders, knowledge without proper guidance of God and good leaders, we can become entangled in all forms of curious works that veer us away from God. These people were meddlesome and got caught up in magical arts – witchcraft. They were drawn into curious through unbridled interest and became an enemy of God. The incident with the traveling Jewish exorcists caused fear and repentance to fall upon them where true deliverance became their portion as they confessed and rid their lives of witchcraft books.

Being curious (or meddlesome) with no God-defined focus is a pathway to becoming a witch.

In the book of Exodus, God told Moses to have the Israelites bring him specific items as an offering. God states that he would provide specific instructions on how to build the sanctuary, what was to be in it and how use the items. He listed specific items that he wanted them to offer unto him and stated clearly that HE WOULD provide pattern regarding these items.

Exodus 25:1-9 *And the LORD spake unto Moses, saying, Speak unto the children of Israel, that they bring me an offering: of every man that giveth it willingly with his heart ye shall take my offering. And this is the offering which ye shall take of them; gold, and silver, and brass, And blue, and purple, and scarlet, and fine linen, and goats' hair, And rams' skins dyed red, and badgers' skins, and shittim wood, Oil for the light, spices for anointing oil, and for sweet incense, Onyx stones, and stones to be set in the ephod, and in the breastplate. And let them make me a sanctuary; that I may dwell among them. According to all that I shew thee, after the pattern of the tabernacle, and the pattern of all the instruments thereof, even so shall ye make it.*

Pattern in Hebrew is *tabniyt* and means:
1. structure; by implication, a model, resemblance,
2. figure, form, likeness, pattern, similitude,
3. construction, image, figure (of an idol).

God was providing the pattern. He knew that the sanctuary was not only for the present purposes of worshiping him but was a prototype of the sanctuary we were to be for him, of how we were to enter his presence, and of Jesus who he would send to save the world. This was a pattern to specifically follow, not to veer from. They were not to offer their own items of sacrifice or patterns for approaching him. These items and patterns were not for the purposes of casting spells, engaging in pagan rituals, ridding evil, engaging in supernatural explorations.

Exodus 35:4-19 And Moses spake unto all the congregation of the children of Israel, saying, This is the thing which the LORD commanded, saying, Take ye from among you an offering unto the LORD: whosoever is of a willing heart, let him bring it, an offering of the LORD; gold, and silver, and brass, And blue, and purple, and scarlet, and fine linen, and goats' hair, And rams' skins dyed red, and badgers' skins, and shittim wood, And oil for the light, and spices for anointing oil, and for the sweet incense, And onyx stones, and stones to be set for the ephod, and for the breastplate. And every wise hearted among you shall come, and make all that the LORD hath commanded; The tabernacle, his tent, and his covering, his taches, and his boards, his bars, his pillars, and his sockets, The ark, and the staves thereof, with the mercy seat, and the vail of the covering, The table, and his staves, and all his vessels, and the shewbread, The candlestick also for the light, and his furniture, and his lamps, with the oil for the light, And the incense altar, and his staves, and the anointing oil, and the sweet incense, and the hanging for the door at the entering in of the tabernacle, The altar of burnt offering, with his brasen grate, his staves, and all his vessels, the laver and his foot, The hangings of the court, his pillars, and their sockets, and the hanging for the door of the court, The pins of the tabernacle, and the pins of the court, and their cords, The cloths of service, to do service in the holy place, the holy garments for Aaron the priest, and the garments of his sons, to minister in the priest's office.

Verse 20-29 And all the congregation of the children of Israel departed from the presence of Moses. And they came, every one whose heart stirred him up, and every one whom his spirit made willing, and they brought the LORD's offering to the work of the tabernacle of the congregation, and for all his service, and for the holy garments. And they came, both men and women, as many as were willing hearted, and brought bracelets, and earrings, and rings, and tablets, all jewels of gold: and every man that offered offered an offering of gold unto the LORD. And every man, with whom was found blue, and purple, and scarlet, and fine linen, and goats' hair, and red skins of rams, and badgers' skins, brought them. Every one that did offer an offering of silver and brass brought the LORD's offering: and every man, with whom was found shittim wood for any work of the service, brought it. And all the women that were wise hearted did spin with their hands, and brought that which they had spun, both of blue, and of purple, and of scarlet, and of fine linen. And all the women whose heart stirred them up in wisdom spun goats' hair. And the rulers brought onyx stones, and stones to be set, for the ephod, and for the breastplate; And spice, and oil for the light, and for the anointing oil, and for the sweet incense. The children of Israel brought a willing offering unto the LORD, every man and woman, whose heart made them willing to bring for all manner of work, which the LORD had commanded to be made by the hand of Moses.

God chose specific **HOLY SPIRIT FILLED** people with specific gifts to assist with helping to build and work in the sanctuary. These people had his Spirit. They did not have the spirit of different gods, believed in, pursued after, or worshiped other gods. Even as he stated that they would do curious works and cunning work, he also stated that **HE** placed these in their heart that **HE** may teach and guide them on how to build and construct the sanctuary. They were not creating on curious and cunning works and certainly were not offering these works as spells, rituals, sacrifices to devils, for person reasons, or to ward off.

Verse 30-35 *And Moses said unto the children of Israel, See, the LORD hath called by name Bezaleel the son of Uri, the son of Hur, of the tribe of Judah; And he hath filled him with the spirit of God, in wisdom, in understanding, and in knowledge, and in all manner of workmanship; And to devise curious works, to work in gold, and in silver, and in brass, And in the cutting of stones, to set them, and in carving of wood, to make any manner of cunning work. And he hath put in his heart that he may teach, both he, and Aholiab, the son of Ahisamach, of the tribe of Dan. Them hath he filled with wisdom of heart, to work all manner of work, of the engraver, and of the cunning workman, and of the embroiderer, in blue, and in purple, in scarlet, and in fine linen, and of the weaver, even of them that do any work, and of those that devise cunning work.*

<u>*Curious* and *Cunning Work* in Hebrew is *maḥăšâbâ* and means:</u>
1. contrivance (plots, schemes, plans),
2. i.e. (concretely) a texture, machine (workings), or (abstractly) intention,
3. plan (whether bad, a plot; or good, advice): — cunning (work), curious work,
4. device(-sed), imagination, invented, means, purpose, thought.

These were curious and cunning workings from the Lord, for the Lord, was his specific design, and was to be treated as pure and holy. They were not for idolatrous or pagan acts, or even for human intent.

Exodus 30:34-38 The Amplified Bible *Then the Lord said to Moses, Take sweet spices— stacte, onycha, and galbanum, sweet spices with pure frankincense, an equal amount of each— And make of them incense, a perfume after the perfumer's art, seasoned with salt and mixed, pure and sacred. You shall beat some of it very small and put some of it before the Testimony in the Tent of Meeting, where I will meet with you; it shall be to you most holy. And the incense which you shall make according to its composition you shall not make for yourselves; it shall be to you holy to the Lord. Whoever makes any like it for perfume shall be cut off from his people.*

In ***Exodus 30:34-38***, God provides specific composition for incense and tells Moses not to veer from the pattern - not to make it for himself. God knew how he wanted the incense to smell and wanted it to be set apart as a holy fragrance unto him. In ***Exodus 30:8-9***, God made it clear that no strange incense shall be offered unto him.

And when Aaron lighteth the lamps at even, he shall burn incense upon it, a perpetual incense before the LORD throughout your generations. Ye shall offer no strange incense thereon, nor burnt sacrifice, nor meat offering; neither shall ye pour drink offering thereon.

<u>*Strange* in Hebrew is *zûr* and means:</u>
1. to turn aside (especially for lodging),

2. hence to be a foreigner, strange, profane,
3. specifically (active participle) to commit adultery,
4. (come from) another (man, place), fanner, go away, (e-)strange (-r, thing, woman),
5. to be strange, be a stranger
    a. (Qal)to become estranged,
    b. strange, another, stranger, foreigner,
    c. an enemy,
    d. (participle)loathsome (of breath),
    e. participle) strange woman, prostitute, harlot (meton),
    f. (Niphal) to be estranged,
    g. (Hophal) to be a stranger, be one alienated.

God viewed any incense burnt on his altar that was NOT his composition as strange, foreign, profane, adulterous. When we offer things up to God that he has not approved of, he says you have become a stranger before him, enemy, loathsome (causing feelings of loathing, disgust, revolting, repulsing), and he has separated from you. Though you may think you are offering a sweet incense to him as a sacrifice, he states that your sacrifice is foreign and going to your lover - your God, but not him. He is not concerned about your motive or intent, but about your obedience. He deems obedience as a heart posture for motive and intent, thus he rejects it because it is not his pattern.

Exodus 31:11 *And the anointing oil, and sweet incense for the holy place: according to all that I have commanded thee shall they do.*

Throughout Exodus God continue to provide a pattern for the construction of the sanctuary and what each item was to be used for. This pattern was followed in the book of Chronicles as Solomon rebuilt the sanctuary for God. God's pattern was deemed holy and the only way. King David longed to rebuild the tabernacle for God, but even as a man after God's own heart, a kingly warrior, God told him he could not build it. David's bloodshed and wars were due to being a soldier for God. Yet his bloodshed was part of the reason God did not want him to rebuild his temple. God stated that David's son would be the one to build him a temple.

- ➢ David could have contended the devil was talking to him and built the tabernacle anyway.
- ➢ David could have decided that because he had done so much for God, he was the right man to build God's temple.
- ➢ David could have become upset because God told him "no" and yielded to sin, rebellion, and went straying after curious works and idol gods.

David resisted strange fire, obeyed God, and honored his desire for Solomon to build the temple (study ***2Samuel 7 and 1Chronicles 17***).

1Chronicles 22:7-10 *And David said to Solomon, My son, as for me, it was in my mind to build an house unto the name of the LORD my God: But the word of the LORD came to me, saying, Thou hast shed blood abundantly, and hast made great wars: thou shalt not build an house unto my name, because thou hast shed much blood upon the earth in my sight. Behold, a son* *shall be born to thee, who shall be a man of rest; and I will give him rest from all his enemies round about: for his name shall be Solomon, and I will give peace and quietness unto Israel in his days. He shall build an house for my name; and he shall be my son, and I will be his father; and I will establish the throne of his kingdom over Israel for ever.*

This passage lets us know that inquiring of God before doing things is important. This keeps us safe and aligned – from being meddlesome. This passage also reveals that our obedience is more important than our thoughts, desires, and intent of our hearts. We may believe we qualify to do certain things that God disqualifies us for. God also disqualifies certain things that we can assume he has qualified. Asking him is the key to knowing his will and his truth. There are certain times I want to attend certain events, even ministry events, and God will say "no," but allow others to attend. There are times when I want to do certain things for God like have certain services and build certain things, God will say "no," but allow others to have and construct them. There are certain times I will want to engage in a certain activity and God will say "no," yet others get to do them. God knows how our calling impacts what is acceptable and lawful in his eyes, how it will impact the earth, and future generations. He knows what is in us and the reason he does not want us doing certain things. We must trust his guidance.

In *Leviticus 10:1*, Nadab and Abihu, sons of Aaron took an incense and offered up strange fire, God killed them on the spot.

Leviticus 10:1-3 And Nadab and Abihu, the sons of Aaron, took either of them his censer, and put fire therein, and put incense thereon, and offered strange fire before the LORD, which he commanded them not. And there went out fire from the LORD, and devoured them, and they died before the LORD. Then Moses said unto Aaron, This is it that the LORD spake, saying, I will be sanctified in them that come nigh me, and before all the people I will be glorified. And Aaron held his peace.

Nadab and Abihu was not sanctified in God's eyes. They also presumed to offer an unauthorized offering. God did not see their acts as glorifying him. He saw them as glorifying themselves and he devoured them. He consumed them as a sacrifice. We can engage in a lot of practices and declare they are for God, but that does not mean that God is receiving what we are offering.

Isaiah 29:13 Wherefore the Lord said, Forasmuch as this people draw near me with their mouth, and with their lips do honour me, but have removed their heart far from me, and their fear toward me is taught by the precept of men.

Matthew 15:7-9 This people draweth nigh unto me with their mouth, and honoureth me with their lips; but their heart is far from me. But in vain they do worship me, teaching for doctrines the commandments of men.

Curious and cunning arts derived from our own heart is vain - of no purpose - fruitless to God. What is being offering God that he is rejecting as strange fire?

INCENSE, CANDLES, PERFUMES, ANOINTING OILS, SPICES & HERBS

- ✓ We can use incense and candles to set the ambiance in an environment and for prayer.
- ✓ We can wear perfume as a fragrance and grooming.
- ✓ We can groom and cook food with our spices and herbs or use them as a healing aid.

But when these items are being used as curious arts and cunning workings, that is witchcraft.

- ✓ When they are used in witchcraft ceremonies, rituals, spells, incantations, sacrifices, to ward off evil and demonic forces, God deems that strange fire.
- ✓ When they are used for the purposes of luring people for personal gain, sexual and demonic reasons, have control over someone's will, cause hurt or harm to people, magical curious arts is the culprit not God.
- ✓ When being used to enter spiritual realms to connect to a deity, to pursue higher levels of consciousness or mysticism, and to engage in supernatural experiences, God does not recognize this pattern; he is not responding.

Incense & Candles
Many religions use incense and candles in worship. In Christendom, incenses symbolize prayer and or worship offering. Candles symbolize the light of God or the light of Jesus Christ. Roman Catholics believe candle burnings signify that prayers are being offered to God long after the prayer was prayed, and the candle was burned. This is not biblical and is strange fire. Prayer is communion between a person and God. We are the conduits of our prayers. There is no item that can carry or ensure our prayers are getting to God.

Some idolatrous religions believe incenses and candles provides a light for their god to engage them, raise vibration levels, draw energy from the sun, draw spirit guides and certain spirits into the atmosphere, dispels evil and demons, brings protection, purifying the person and the atmosphere, stimulate the sexual drive, enhance memory, can be lit as a sacrifice to gods for certain purposes, e.g., for luck, prosperity, love, friendship, wellness. Candle magic is a witchcraft practice that requires nothing more than a candle and a person's intent. The person basically set a clear purpose for what they want to witchcraft to do, imagine that being done during meditation, concentrate on their desired purposes, build a connection between their energy and the candle (this is called dressing the candle), then once the person has entered a particular level of consciousness light the candle to release the spell. Candles can also be dressed in herbs, spices, and oils and it is believed that this provides extra energy. The person can use chanting to also strengthen the spell. They are encouraged to use verbiage that is meaning to them as it contains the most energy and power. Colors are symbolic in witchcraft and are viewed as having their own unique power. A particular color of a candle can be used to associate with the intentions of the spell being released.

Perfumes & Anointing Oils
Apothecary was the name for a person in the Bible who made perfumes, anointing oils, and incense. In the Bible perfumes were used as anointing oils, sanctification, consecration, dedication, cosmetic fragrances, grooming, gifts, healing, and embalming dead bodies. Depending on the scripture, sometimes perfumes were called anointing oils, precious

ointments, incenses, and spices. In modern times we have made greater distinctions between perfumes, anointing oils, and the like. We even call some anointing oils by the name of essential oils or aromatic oils, which are generally oils for healing. There is evidence of essential oils being used as far back as 3500 B.C. There are 33 essential oils mentioned in the Bible and many of them such as myrrh, cinnamon, sweet calamus, cassia, frankincense, olive, was used in the tent of meeting and the tabernacle. Regardless of the type of perfume, these oils were not to be used recklessly or profanely. The first biblical mentioning of perfume was when God told Moses to compound perfume for the tent of meeting.

Exodus 30:22-26 *Moreover the LORD spake unto Moses, saying, Take thou also unto thee principal spices, of pure myrrh five hundred shekels, and of sweet cinnamon half so much, even two hundred and fifty shekels, and of sweet calamus two hundred and fifty shekels, And of cassia five hundred shekels, after the shekel of the sanctuary, and of oil olive an hin: And thou shalt make it an oil of holy ointment, an ointment compound after the art of the apothecary: it shall be an holy anointing oil. And thou shalt anoint the tabernacle of the congregation therewith, and the ark of the testimony,*

Verse 30 – 33 *And thou shalt anoint Aaron and his sons, and consecrate them, that they may minister unto me in the priest's office. And thou shalt speak unto the children of Israel, saying, This shall be an holy anointing oil unto me throughout your generations. Upon man's flesh shall it not be poured, neither shall ye make any other like it, after the composition of it: it is holy, and it shall be holy unto you. Whosoever compoundeth any like it, or whosoever putteth any of it upon a stranger, shall even be cut off from his people.*

God desired his pattern for using the anointing oil to be honored from generation to generation. Strange fire causes a generational deterring from God's principles and ways, making his people strangers to him, and extinct from godly covenant.

Witches call some of their perfumes, fragments, scents, spices, potions, magic perfumes, magic cures, and deadly herbs. They have all types of reasons and concoctions for spell casting their perfumes. Everything means somethings, especially the composition and the smell. Many of their curious concoctions are attached to the constellations, sun, moon, stars, vibrations, energy frequencies and/or demons, to give it further power. Sometimes hair, nails, saliva, blood, urine, feces, plants, trees, dirt, and animal parts are mixed into spells. When a person goes to a witch for a spell, that witch will often ask for some type of item or fluid in connection with the person, the purpose is to make a connection between the inquirer and the target for the spell or potion. Witches are known for collecting items, body fluids, and the like from their prey and using them in spells, rituals, ceremonies, and contact points for altar sacrifices. Depending on the type of witch, it is dedicated and given a name that connects them to a certain deity. Names can reveal a lot about the intent to which a perfume, potion, etc., was made. It is beneficial to study the name of a perfume before buying it as you may be purchasing more than a sweet fragrance. When perfumes, cosmetics, and the like, have names sexual names, spooky, mysterious, demonic or evil names, names after Greek gods, names with the word diva or goddess in it, you can be sure it has some type of witchcraft intent regarding what it is intended to allure or to lure. Though this is forbidden by God, a witchcraft perfume can have the same or similar composition of those that are in the Bible. But when used for ungodly purposes, God deems it strange fire.

Isaiah 57:9 The Amplified Bible *And you went to the king [of foreign lands with gifts] or to Molech [the god] with oil and increased your perfumes and ointments; you sent your messengers far off and debased yourself even to Sheol (Hades) [symbol of an abysmal depth of degradation].*

In **Proverbs 7**, Solomon warns men of strange women. He shares a proverb regarding the luring of a woman with the attire of a harlot. The woman perfumes her bed with myrrh, aloes, and cinnamon for the purposes of making love all night. Though she uses anointing oils to that are in order with those acceptable to God, as they engaged in these sinful pleasures, Solomon describes a slaughtering of the man taking place.

Proverbs 7:15-27 The Amplified Bible *So I came forth to meet you [that you might share with me the feast from my offering]; diligently I sought your face, and I have found you. I have spread my couch with rugs and cushions of tapestry, with striped sheets of fine linen of Egypt. I have perfumed my bed with myrrh, aloes, and cinnamon. Come, let us take our fill of love until morning; let us console and delight ourselves with love. For the man is not at home; he is gone on a long journey; He has taken a bag of money with him and will come home at the day appointed [at the full moon]. With much justifying and enticing argument she persuades him, with the allurements of her lips she leads him [to overcome his conscience and his fears] and forces him along.*

Suddenly he [yields and] follows her reluctantly like an ox moving to the slaughter, like one in fetters going to the correction [to be given] to a fool or like a dog enticed by food to the muzzle Till a dart [of passion] pierces and inflames his vitals; then like a bird fluttering straight into the net [he hastens], not knowing that it will cost him his life. Listen to me now therefore, O you sons, and be attentive to the words of my mouth. Let not your heart incline toward her ways, do not stray into her paths. For she has cast down many wounded; indeed, all her slain are a mighty host. Her house is the way to Sheol (Hades, the place of the dead), going down to the chambers of death.

Even in using anointing oil, if there is an ungodly purpose attached to it, the oil will be unholy and unacceptable to God.

This proverb describes an act of making a bed undefiled or appear godly, by using the holy oils of God. But what is really occurring is a seduction – an alluring and luring through the powers of witchcraft spell work. The woman the man had sex with was comparable to strange fire that God rejects. She was identified as strange. Her motives and intent were ungodly and therefore, the acts that would have been viewed as godly and covenant in marriage, was destructive unto death. The man became a sacrifice unto the bed that was anointed for defiled worship.

Ezekiel 23:40-41 The Amplified Bible *And furthermore, you have sent for men to come from afar, to whom a messenger was sent; and behold, they came—those for whom you washed yourself, painted your eyelids, and decked yourself with ornaments; And you sat upon a stately couch with a table spread before it upon which you set My incense and My oil.*

Amos 6:4-6 The Amplified Bible *Woe to those who lie upon beds of ivory and stretch themselves upon their couches, and eat the lambs out of the flock and the calves out of the midst of the stall, Who sing idle songs to the sound of the harp and invent for themselves instruments of music like David's, Who drink wine in bowls and anoint themselves with the finest oils, but are not grieved and sick at heart over the affliction and ruin of Joseph (Israel)!*

In 2020, a famous singer, Erykah Badu released a perfume for sale at $50 a bottle, called "Badu's Pussy." Upon the initial release, the perfume sold out in 24 hours. It is now selling on eBay and other sites for $100 to $250. Erykah stated her perfume was created by burning her old panties. Yes, you heard correctly. She contends that portions of her old panties are in her perfume composition. In the same year, American actress, Gwyneth Paltrow released a "This Smells Like My Vagina" that quickly sold out for $75 each. Gwyneth's business to which she calls "Goop" is worth over a quarter of a billion dollars, mostly because of her conversing about her vagina. We can only imagine what spells are being released to draw people to her products. Like me you may find these two examples are disgusting. This is not uncommon among those who practice this type of curious art, which is the reason the items sell well and is the reason God has strict boundaries between what is holy and profane.

Proverbs 30:12 *There is a generation that are pure in their own eyes, and yet is not washed from their filthiness.*

The greatest symbolism in the Bible regarding the anointing oil is the promise of Jesus Christ coming as Messiah to deliver the world from sin and death. The Hebrew word Messiah is *Mashiach* and means, *"the one anointed with oil."* Moses tabernacle represented the prototype of Jesus. The anointing oil was representative of Jesus Christ's coming, and how his righteousness, holiness, sanctification, and consecrated life, possessed the anointing to destroy death and hell, while restoring God's people to eternal life with him. God did not want any confusion regarding what the purpose of the coming of the Messiah would be and how it would impact the earth.

Hebrews 2:14-15 *Inasmuch then as the children have partaken of flesh and blood, He Himself likewise shared in the same, that through death He might destroy him who had the power of death, that is, the devil, and release those who through fear of death were all their lifetime subject to bondage.*

Hebrews 8:1-5 *Now of the things which we have spoken this is the sum: We have such an high priest, who is set on the right hand of the throne of the Majesty in the heavens; A minister of the sanctuary, and of the true tabernacle, which the Lord pitched, and not man. For every high priest is ordained to offer gifts and sacrifices: wherefore it is of necessity that this man have somewhat also to offer. For if he were on earth, he should not be a priest, seeing that there are priests that offer gifts according to the law: Who serve unto the example and shadow of* *heavenly things, as Moses was admonished of God when he was about to make the tabernacle: for, See, saith he, that thou make all things according to the pattern shewed to thee in the mount. But now hath he obtained a more excellent ministry, by how much also he is the mediator of a better covenant, which was established upon better promises.*

Jeremiah 23:5-6 *Behold, the days come, saith the LORD, that I will raise unto David a righteous Branch, and a King shall reign and prosper, and shall execute judgment and justice in the earth. In his days Judah shall be saved, and Israel shall dwell safely: and this is his name whereby he shall be called, THE LORD OUR RIGHTEOUSNESS.*

Isaiah 53:4-5 *Surely he hath borne our griefs, and carried our sorrows: yet we did esteem him stricken, smitten of God, and afflicted. But he was wounded for our transgressions, he was bruised for our iniquities: the chastisement of our peace was upon him; and with his stripes we are healed.*

Isaiah 61:1-3 *The Spirit of the Lord GOD is upon me; because the LORD hath anointed me to preach good tidings unto the meek; he hath sent me to bind up the brokenhearted, to proclaim liberty to the captives, and the opening of the prison to them that are bound; To proclaim the acceptable year of the LORD, and the day of vengeance of our God; to comfort all that mourn; To appoint unto them that mourn in Zion, to give unto them beauty for ashes, the oil of joy for mourning, the garment of praise for the spirit of heaviness; that they might be called trees of righteousness, the planting of the LORD, that he might be glorified.*

When we anoint items with oil, we are essentially anointing ourselves with Jesus and his completed work on the cross. This anointing is separating us from that which is profane, oppressive, afflicting, sickly, and deadly. The anointing oil is a representation of the resurrection power of Jesus Christ – our Messiah – who saved the entire world.

Even though the Bible tells us to anoint the sick with oil, and we can use it to anoint our bodies, homes, lands, material possessions, and the like, it does not tell us to anoint anything or anyone to rid of demons.

The Bible tells us to CAST out demons!

The anointing releases an identifiable marking that what we are anointing is now under the blessing and government of God. An affliction or demon, however, leaves when godly commands, judgments, decrees, are released by asserting the blessing and governmental authority of God's anointing power given through the salvation of Jesus Christ.

Acts 10:38 *You know of Jesus of Nazareth, how God anointed Him with the Holy Spirit and with power, and how He went about doing good and healing all who were oppressed by the devil, for God was with Him.*

We can resist the devil, and he will flee.

James 4:7 *Submit yourselves therefore to God. Resist the devil, and he will flee from you.*

We can use the armor of God to stand against and overthrow demons.

Ephesians 6:10-18 *Finally, my brethren, be strong in the Lord, and in the power of his might. Put on the whole armour of God, that ye may be able to stand against the wiles of the devil. For we wrestle not against flesh and blood, but against principalities, against powers, against the rulers of the darkness of this world, against spiritual wickedness in high [places]. Wherefore take unto you the whole armour of God, that ye may be able to withstand in the evil day, and having done all, to stand. Stand therefore, having your loins girt about with truth, and having on the breastplate of righteousness; And your feet shod with the preparation of the gospel of peace; Above all, taking the shield of faith, wherewith ye shall be able to quench all the fiery darts of the wicked. And take the helmet of salvation, and the sword of the Spirit, which is the word of God: Praying always with all prayer and supplication in the Spirit, and watching thereunto with all perseverance and supplication for all saints.*

We cast devils out in Jesus name!

Matthew 10:8 *Heal the sick, cleanse the lepers, raise the dead, cast out devils: freely ye have received, freely give.*

Matthew 12:28 *But if I cast out demons by the Spirit of God, then the kingdom of God has come upon you.*

Luke 10:17 *And the seventy returned again with joy, saying, Lord, even the devils are subject unto us through thy name.*

Mark 16:17 *And these signs will accompany those who believe: in my name they will cast out demons; they will speak in new tongues.*

Luke 4:33-36 *And in the synagogue there was a man, which had a spirit of an unclean devil, and cried out with a loud voice, Saying, Let [us] alone; what have we to do with thee, [thou] Jesus of Nazareth? art thou come to destroy us? I know thee who thou art; the Holy One of God. And Jesus rebuked him, saying, Hold thy peace, and come out of him. And when the devil had thrown him in the midst, he came out of him, and hurt him not. And they were all amazed, and spake among themselves, saying, What a word [is] this! for with authority and power he commandeth the unclean spirits, and they come out.*

Mark 5:1-9 *And they came over unto the other side of the sea, into the country of the Gadarenes. And when he was come out of the ship, immediately there met him out of the tombs a man with an unclean spirit, Who had [his] dwelling among the tombs; and no man could bind him, no, not with chains: Because that he had been often bound with fetters and chains, and the chains had been plucked asunder by him, and the fetters broken in pieces: neither could any [man] tame him. And always, night and day, he was in the mountains, and in the tombs, crying, and cutting himself with stones. But when he saw Jesus afar off, he ran and worshipped him, And cried with a loud voice, and said, What have I to do with thee, Jesus, [thou] Son of the most high God? I adjure thee by God, that thou torment me not. For he said* unto him, Come out of the man, [thou] unclean spirit. And he asked him, What [is] thy name? And he answered, saying, My name [is] Legion: for we are many.

Acts 16:16-18 *As we were going to the place of prayer, we were met by a slave girl who had a spirit of divination and brought her owners much gain by fortune-telling. She followed Paul and us, crying out, "These men are servants of the Most High God, who proclaim to you the way of salvation." And this she kept doing for many days. Paul, having become greatly annoyed, turned and said to the spirit, "I command you in the name of Jesus Christ to come out of her." And it came out that very hour.*

Acts 19:1-3 *Then certain of the vagabond Jews, exorcists, took upon them to call over them which had evil spirits the name of the Lord Jesus, saying, We adjure you by Jesus whom Paul preacheth. And there were seven sons of [one] Sceva, a Jew, [and] chief of the priests, which did so. And the evil spirit answered and said, Jesus I know, and Paul I know; but who are ye? And the man in whom the evil spirit was leaped on them, and overcame them, and prevailed against them, so that they fled out of that house naked and wounded.*

We can rebuke a demon and cast him out. *Rebuke* means to "*charge out, command out, reprove, censure severely, to admonish or charge sharply.*" When rebuking, the demons are responding to the authority of Jesus Christ that is within the person. They are being cast out harshly and charged sharply to leave by the authority of Jesus Christ.

Matthew 17:14-18 *And when they were come to the multitude, there came to him a [certain] man, kneeling down to him, and saying, Lord, have mercy on my son: for he is lunatick, and sore vexed: for ofttimes he falleth into the fire, and oft into the water. And I brought him to thy disciples, and they could not cure him. Then Jesus answered and said, O faithless and perverse generation, how long shall I be with you? how long shall I suffer you? bring him hither to me. And Jesus rebuked the devil; and he departed out of him: and the child was cured from that very hour. Then came the disciples to Jesus apart, and said, Why could not we cast him out? And Jesus said unto them, Because of your unbelief: for verily I say unto you, If ye have faith as a grain of mustard seed, ye shall say unto this mountain, Remove hence to yonder place; and it shall remove; and nothing shall be impossible unto you.*

Some spirits require prayer and fasting to come out. They are still being cast out but through the us being delivered and cleansed via prayer and the person offering themselves through consecration as a sacrifice to Jesus.

Mark 9:29 *And he said unto them, This kind can come forth by nothing, but by prayer and fasting.*

Jesus overcome demons through his precious blood, works of the cross, and resurrection power.

John 10:10 *The thief does not come except to steal, and to kill, and to destroy. I have come that they may have life, and that they may have it more abundantly.*

Galatians 1:4 *Who gave Himself for our sins so that He might rescue us from this present evil age, according to the will of our God and Father.*

1John 3:8 *The one who practices sin is of the devil; for the devil has sinned from the beginning The Son of God appeared for this purpose, to destroy the works of the devil.*

1Peter 18-25 *Forasmuch as ye know that ye were not redeemed with corruptible things, as silver and gold, from your vain conversation received by tradition from your fathers; But with the precious blood of Christ, as of a lamb without blemish and without spot: Who verily was foreordained before the foundation of the world, but was manifest in these last times for you, Who by him do believe in God, that raised him up from the dead, and gave him glory; that your faith and hope might be in God.*

Seeing ye have purified your souls in obeying the truth through the Spirit unto unfeigned love of the brethren, see that ye love one another with a pure heart fervently: Being born again, not of corruptible seed, but of incorruptible, by the word of God, which liveth and abideth for ever. For all flesh is as grass, and all the glory of man as the flower of grass. The grass withereth, and the flower thereof falleth away: But the word of the Lord endureth for ever. And this is the word which by the gospel is preached unto you.

Revelation 1:17-18 *And when I saw him, I fell at his feet as dead. And he laid his right hand upon me, saying unto me, Fear not; I am the first and the last: -- I am he that liveth, and was dead; and, behold, I am alive for evermore, Amen; and have the keys of hell and of death.*

Revelation 12:11 *And they overcame him by the blood of the Lamb, and by the word of their testimony; and they loved not their lives unto the death.*

God protects us from evil!

Psalm 20:1-2 *The LORD hear thee in the day of trouble; the name of the God of Jacob defend thee; Send thee help from the sanctuary, and strengthen thee out of Zion.*

Psalm 34:19-22 *Many are the afflictions of the righteous: but the LORD delivereth him out of them all. He keepeth all his bones: not one of them is broken. Evil shall slay the wicked: and they that hate the righteous shall be desolate. The LORD redeemeth the soul of his servants: and none of them that trust in him shall be desolate.*

Isaiah 40:10 *Fear thou not; for I [am] with thee: be not dismayed; for I [am] thy God: I will strengthen thee; yea, I will help thee; yea, I will uphold thee with the right hand of my righteousness.*

2Thessalonians 3:3 *But the Lord is faithful, who shall stablish you, and keep you from evil.*

The anointing oil was for the purposes identifying what was holy, consecrate it, and set it apart unto the Lord. This practice was to be generational as God desired holiness to be an eternal part of our lineage.

Exodus 30:22-32 *Moreover the LORD spake unto Moses, saying, Take thou also unto thee principal spices, of pure myrrh five hundred shekels, and of sweet cinnamon half so much, even two hundred and fifty shekels, and of sweet calamus two hundred and fifty shekels, And of cassia five hundred shekels, after the shekel of the sanctuary, and of oil olive an hin: And thou shalt make it an oil of holy ointment, an ointment compound after the art of the apothecary: it shall be an holy anointing oil. And thou shalt anoint the tabernacle of the congregation therewith, and the ark of the testimony, And the table and all his vessels, and the candlestick and his vessels, and the altar of incense, And the altar of burnt offering with all his vessels, and the laver and his foot. And thou shalt sanctify them, that they may be most holy: whatsoever toucheth them shall be holy. And thou shalt anoint Aaron and his sons, and consecrate them, that they may minister unto me in the priest's office. And thou shalt speak unto the children of Israel, saying, This shall be an holy anointing oil unto me throughout your generations.*

> We must appropriately apply God's pattern so that we do not lend ourselves and our generations to strange fire.

There is a grave difference between anointing your bodies or homes and commanding demons to go in Jesus name and casting spells, burning incense and candles, for the purposes of dispelling demons. We must appropriately apply God's pattern so that we do not lend our lives and generations to strange fire.

Spices, Herbs

Biblically, spices were used primarily for purposes relative to the composition of incense. There is a scripture referencing spice being used to flavor wine in Songs of Solomon.

Songs of Solomon 8:2 *I would lead thee, and bring thee into my mother's house, who would instruct me: I would cause thee to drink of spiced wine of the juice of my pomegranate.*

Biblically, herbs were used daily as medicine, cosmetic ointments, aromatic oils, perfumes, fumigation, religious rituals, cooking, and embalming. Herbs were viewed as a balm which means *"distillation, medicine, salve."* There are a host of scriptures referencing spices and herbs, referencing them by name.

Genesis 37:25 *And they sat down to eat bread: and they lifted up their eyes and looked, and, behold, a company of Ishmeelites came from Gilead with their camels bearing spicery and balm and myrrh, going to carry it down to Egypt.*

Jeremiah 8:22 *Is there no balm in Gilead; is there no physician there? Why then is not the health of the daughter of my people recovered?*

Jeremiah 46:11 *Go up into Gilead, and take balm, O virgin, the daughter of Egypt: in vain shalt thou use many medicines; for thou shalt not be cured.*

Jeremiah 51:8 *Babylon is suddenly fallen and destroyed: howl for her; take balm for her pain, if so be she may be healed.*

Ezekiel 27:17 *Judah, and the land of Israel, they were thy merchants: they traded in thy market wheat of Minnith, and Pannag, and honey, and oil, and balm.*

Herbalism is one of the most ancient medical systems in the earth and can be correlated with the history of medicine. Also known as phytotherapy or botanical medicine, herbalism entails the practice of making or prescribing plant based herbal remedies for medical conditions. Practitioners can be licensed or unlicensed as most herb medications are not recognized by the Food and Drug Administration. The Food and Drug Administration is responsible for making sure the medicines, foods, cosmetics, and products that emit radiation are safe. Though herbalism has a history of medical benefits, until recently as exposure to some of the operations of Big Pharma, there has been a straying away from plant-based medication. Many people must become self-taught to use herbs for medical purposes and at times pursue herbalist practitioners or converse with employees at herb stores for information.

There are herbalists who do not engage in witchcraft, then there are others who do not just compound medicines but are witches. Herbal witches engage in herbal magic and plant magic. Such workings are for the purposes casting spells on people, places, or things, and are like the curious arts we have already discussed (love, relationships, luck, success, control people, etc.). Those who deem themselves healers, may compound medicines then perform spell work on it or dedicate it to a demon or deity, as the belief is this increase its healing power. For this reason, it is beneficial be careful about where you purchase your herbs, spices, and vitamins; pray and break any spells off them just to keep yourself safe from curious workings. Finding true Christian herbalists who do not dabble in witchcraft would be great as well. Ministries would be wise to educate their congregations in the use of herbs, vitamins, spices, and essential oils. With the increase in health issues and the expense of health care, learning how God has provided these healing aides in addition to his power to heal, is key to improving the wellness of people, and identifying those who can become herbalists. We need believers to rise and take their place in the earth so we can close the ranks on being subjected to curious arts.

Sage Workings
Sage is a primary herb used by New Age practitioners. Godly believers, particularly Africans and African American swear by the power of sage. It is an ancient practice that has been passed down from generation to generation. Sage practices are such a stronghold, that many will refuse to relinquish their curious workings.

The root Latin word for *sage* is "*salvia*," also known as saliva, and means "*to heal.*" Additionally, *sage* means, "*to bring wisdom, clarity, and definition.*" If a person is using sage to assist with health issues or cooking, then this is a natural practice and is not witchcraft. Though not medically proven, Homeopathic and Herbal medicine believes that what you extract from sage can help a person heal. It purifies and protects against allergens such as pet dander, pollution, dust, and mold. It is also said to have antimicrobial properties which aides in fending off infection, bacteria, and fungus. It is believed that sage benefits people with allergies, asthma, bronchitis, and respiratory issues. Burning sage can be harmful but it is believed that once the smoke clears, these people can be helped and healed by what is released after the burning sage is in the air. We already discussed that God does give us herbs to heal, but there is nothing about burning herbs in the Bible.

Genesis 1:29-31 *And God said, Behold, I have given you every herb bearing seed, which is upon the face of all the earth, and every tree, in the which is the fruit of a tree yielding seed; to you it shall be for meat. And to every beast of the earth, and to every fowl of the air, and to every thing that creepeth upon the earth, wherein there is life, I have given every green herb for meat: and it was so. And God saw every thing that he had made, and, behold, it was very good. And the evening and the morning were the sixth day.*

If you are burning sage or using it to ride of evil spirits, then that is witchcraft and NOT OF GOD. This witchcraft practice came about through the Native Americans and other indigenous peoples (our wise ancestors). Your grandma, great grandma, and other ancestors may have engaged in it, but it is still a witchcraft practice created by the Native Americans and other ancestors. They burned sage for centuries as part of a spiritual ritual to cleanse a person or space, and to promote healing and wisdom. This is their ancient ritual practice known as *smudging*. They believe that some herbs have spirits in them, and sage was one of the herbs they believed this about. They believe that when you burn sage you are invoking those spirits to help dispel evil out of a person, place, or thing. When smudging, a person is invoking demons and calling more demons into their life, rather than casting them out. When smudging you are burning the sage in corners, and in hidden or hiding places so the spirits can come to the center and then be cast out by the spirits in sage.

Matthew 12:26 *And if Satan cast out Satan, he is divided against himself?*

This scripture asks us to search out if a demon can cast out a demon. And how doing so would cause that kingdom to be divided against itself. Truth is the demons may appear to work contrary with one another but really, they are all working for one common goal, and that is to bind, oppress, or possess you or what is of you. They may fight for territory because they want to inhabit a person, place, or thing, but they cannot bring cleansing or purification. Demons defile. They also come to kill, steal, and destroy. So, when you use sage demons to rid your life, you are releasing more opportunity to be bound and destroyed rather than to be free. The spirits may no longer manifest in the manner of those you claim to be cleaning your home of, but now they are manifesting in other ways. Let us also note that you must constantly engage in this practice because the initial demons never went anywhere. They just lay dormant in your home and atmosphere, give the new demons a time of wreaking havoc in your life, then reappear later so you can smudge again - engage in witchcraft again.

Scriptures Used to Justify Burning Sage

Exodus 35:8 *And oil for the light, and spices for anointing oil, and for the sweet incense,*

2Chronicles 13:11 *And they burn unto the Lord every morning and every evening burnt sacrifices and sweet incense: the shewbread also set they in order upon the pure table; and the candlestick of gold with the lamps thereof, to burn every evening: for we keep the charge of the Lord our God; but ye have forsaken him.*

Malachi 1:11 *For from the rising of the sun even unto the going down of the same my name shall be great among the Gentiles; and in every place incense shall be offered unto my name, and a pure offering: for my name shall be great among the heathen, saith the Lord of hosts.*

Isaiah 45:7 *I form the light, and create darkness: I make peace, and create evil: I the Lord do all these things.*

None of these scriptures truly justify the use of sage. We already discussed how incense was burned as a symbolism of prayer, worship, and what God deemed as an acceptable fragrance. Sage burning has no powers against demons. Only the authority of Jesus Christ within us have power to dispel demons. God did not want us to know evil. When Adam and Eve ate of the tree of the knowledge of good and evil, God was challenged that they knew. And he would not have us engaging in ungodly practices to rid evil.

Genesis 3:22 The Amplified Bible *And the Lord God said, Behold, the man has become like one of Us [the Father, Son, and Holy Spirit], to know [how to distinguish between] good and evil and blessing and calamity; and now, lest he put forth his hand and take also from the tree of life and eat, and live forever.*

It is okay for us to recognize that our ancestors engaged in some curious and cunning arts, and God is revealing truth to us so we can deliver our lineage from strange fire. We are not dishonoring our ancestors by doing this. Our defiance is not against them, but against sin and the demons sin expose us to. We must reject sin and demonic oppression no matter who deals it to us as it is better to be obedient to God rather than man.

One revelation I gathered is many people believe the demons they dispel are going to attack them if they relinquish sage practices. They also equate the resistance of demons leaving to their ancestors punishing them for no longer engaging in sage rituals. I will admit that sometimes these demons will not want to leave because they have been in the generational line so long, they believe they own the lineage. Therefore, they may be initially resistant to leaving without a spiritual battle. But PLEASE know God is greater. He will give you the strategy and the power to war against these strongholds and cast them out your life and generations.

WARDING

Warding is when witchcraft practitioners engage in certain rituals and spell casting to cleanse their atmosphere and space of negative energies forces. Sometimes the Native American practice of smudging can be used in warding, but other spell casting rituals are also used. Practitioners offer up sacrifices, conduct rituals, prayers and chants, while inviting their higher power, spirit guides, demon spirits, to protect them or their space. They use these practices in effort to ward off spirits they deem harmful or evil, ward off bad luck, hardship, and evil from coming to them or cleanse the atmosphere of oppressive and unwanted energies, feelings, sensations, or possessions. Essentially, they are collaborating with demons to protect them or bring them a false sense of peace and purity. They do not realize that the protection, tranquility, and purification come with a cost. They are cohabiting with demons. Moreover, if they do not continue to offer themselves, their lives, and atmospheres to the demons, these demons turn on them and begin to oppress them. They may also open the door for other demons to come in and attack their lives. There is no such thing as a good demonic spirit. All demons are bad. The only spirit that is good is the Holy Spirit which is God's spirit. The Holy Spirit can be invited into our lives and space to take up residence and help bring protection, peace, wellness, and purity to our lives. So can God's angels, his governments Kingdom, his saving blood, his glory, and the fruit of his spirit. Witchcraft does not cleanse or ward off; it defiles. It will always be a perverse twisted illegal act that is against God and his kingdom. If your desire to cleanse your home of evil spirits and SHIFT in the kingdom of presence of God, I recommend purchasing my ebook called "Spiritual House Cleansing," at Kingdomshiftingbooks.com.

BLOOD RITUALS
Some professed Christian witches use the partaking of the Lord's supper as a justification for drinking and engaging in blood sacrifices. They claim that when we partake of wine or grape juice, bread, or crackers, as remembrance of the shedding of Jesus blood, and dying on the cross for our sins, we are engaging in a blood ritual. THIS IS A FLAT-OUT LIE. The following scripture has been used to justify this LIE.

Mark 14:22-25 And as they were eating, he took bread, and after blessing it broke it and gave it to them, and said, "Take; this is my body." And he took a cup, and when he had given thanks he gave it to them, and they all drank of it. And he said to them, "This is my blood of the covenant, which is poured out for many. Truly, I say to you, I will not drink again of the fruit of the vine until that day when I drink it new in the kingdom of God."

This scripture is a symbolizing of remembrance but is not a literal act of drinking blood or eating body parts, whether Jesus or otherwise. Many witches drink real blood - whether animal blood, their blood, or human blood. Some extreme witches kill animals, babies, women, and people in general, so they can offer sacrifices and blood sacrifices to their god and ancestors. Jesus is not requiring us to drink literal blood. Jesus is not requiring us to kill or make a sacrifice offering. When animals were offered as sacrifices in the Old Testament, it was a way for God's people to atone for their sins, while drawing in prayer and worship unto him.

Leviticus 15:15-16 Then shall he kill the goat of the sin offering, that is for the people, and bring his blood within the vail, and do with that blood as he did with the blood of the bullock, and sprinkle it upon the mercy seat, and before the mercy seat: And he shall make an atonement for the holy place, because of the uncleanness of the children of Israel, and because of their transgressions in all their sins: and so shall he do for the tabernacle of the congregation, that remaineth among them in the midst of their uncleanness.

This was a temporary act that was a foreshadowing symbolism of how Jesus Christ would sacrifice his life for the sins of the world.

Jesus' blood was shed and mentioned seven times in the Bible:
1. His body sweating blood in the Garden of Gethsemane. (*Luke 22:44*)

2. His beard, cheeks, and face. (*Isaiah 50:6*)
3. His head from the crown of thorns. (*Matthew 27:29*)
4. His back beaten. (*Matthew 27:26*)
5. His hands nailed to the cross. (*Psalm 22:16*)
6. His feet nailed to the cross (*Psalm 22:16*)
7. His side pierced. (*John 19:34*)

Animal sacrificing was no longer necessary after Jesus Christ died and rose again on the cross. Moreover, any other sacrificing was considered a sin. In the Old Testament, God had his leaders destroy high places and drive out witches and diviners who offered sacrifices to idol gods and engaged in curious workings.

Remembrance is just that - to recall how he delivered, healed, and saved us; how his body was sacrificed, and his blood was shed to set us free. This remembrance draws us to him and the blessings that come with him being our God, which serves as communion with him. Not with demons, the universe, other gods, enlightenment, but it him. Sometimes people are healed because of the truth they embody regarding Jesus works on the cross or through how remembering draws them into his delivering power. Also, Jesus told us to participate in this ritual, so it is acceptable.

Matthew 26:26-29 And as they were eating, Jesus took bread, and blessed it, and brake it, and gave it to the disciples, and said, Take, eat; this is my body. And he took the cup, and gave thanks, and gave it to them, saying, Drink ye all of it; For this is my blood of the new testament, which is shed for many for the remission of sins. But I say unto you, I will not drink henceforth of this fruit of the vine, until that day when I drink it new with you in my Father's kingdom.

Mark 14:22-25 And as they did eat, Jesus took bread, and blessed, and brake it, and gave to them, and said, Take, eat: this is my body. And he took the cup, and when he had given thanks, he gave it to them: and they all drank of it. And he said unto them, This is my blood of the new testament, which is shed for many. Verily I say unto you, I will drink no more of the fruit of the vine, until that day that I drink it new in the kingdom of God.

John 6:53-59 Then Jesus said unto them, Verily, verily, I say unto you, Except ye eat the flesh of the Son of man, and drink his blood, ye have no life in you. Whoso eateth my flesh, and drinketh my blood, hath eternal life; and I will raise him up at the last day. For my flesh is meat indeed, and my blood is drink indeed. He that eateth my flesh, and drinketh my blood, dwelleth in me, and I in him. As the living Father hath sent me, and I live by the Father: so he that eateth me, even he shall live by me. This is that bread which came down from heaven: not as your fathers did eat manna, and are dead: he that eateth of this bread shall live for ever. These things said he in the synagogue, as he taught in Capernaum.

1Corinthians 11:23-27 For I have received of the Lord that which also I delivered unto you, That the Lord Jesus the same night in which he was betrayed took bread: And when he had given thanks, he brake it, and said, Take, eat: this is my body, which is broken for you: this do in remembrance of me. After the same manner also he took the cup, when he had supped, saying, This cup is the new testament in my blood: this do ye, as oft as ye drink it, in remembrance of me.

For as often as ye eat this bread, and drink this cup, ye do shew the Lord's death till he come. Wherefore whosoever shall eat this bread, and drink this cup of the Lord, unworthily, shall be guilty of the body and blood of the Lord. But let a man examine himself, and so let him eat of that bread, and drink of that cup. For he that eateth and drinketh unworthily, eateth and drinketh damnation to himself, not discerning the Lord's body. For this cause many are weak and sickly among you, and many sleep. For if we would judge ourselves, we should not be judged. But when we are judged, we are chastened of the Lord, that we should not be condemned with the world.

Exodus 12:12-14 *For I will pass through the land of Egypt this night, and will smite all the firstborn in the land of Egypt, both man and beast; and against all the gods of Egypt I will execute judgment: I am the LORD. And the blood shall be to you for a token upon the houses where ye are: and when I see the blood, I will pass over you, and the plague shall not be upon you to destroy you, when I smite the land of Egypt. And this day shall be unto you for a memorial; and ye shall keep it a feast to the LORD throughout your generations; ye shall keep it a feast by an ordinance for ever.*

Hebrews 9:11-12 *But Christ being come an high priest of good things to come, by a greater and more perfect tabernacle, not made with hands, that is to say, not of this building; Neither by the blood of goats and calves, but by his own blood he entered in once into the holy place, having obtained eternal redemption for us.*

In **Exodus 12**, God has Israelites using blood to mark their home. Pharaoh refused to let the Hebrew Israelites free from slavery. God commissioned Moses as a deliverer to lead the Israelites out of Egypt into the promise land. Moses approached Pharaoh multiple times regarding freeing the slaves but with each interaction, his heart became hardened and God released plagues upon him and the nation of Egypt as judgment. The final plague was the death of the firstborn of all households. God told the Hebrew Israelites to sacrifice an unblemished lamb and brush its blood on the lintel and doorposts of their homes. The death angel would then pass over these homes and spare their firstborn - instituting the Passover.

This act was a foreshadowing of the coming of Jesus Christ. In **1Corinthians 5:7**, the Amplified Bible states, "*Purge (clean out) the old leaven that you may be fresh (new) dough, still uncontaminated [as you are], for Christ, our Passover [Lamb], has been sacrificed.*" This is the reason believers pray applying the blood of Jesus, decreeing a blood line over their home, or declaring their home be passed over from evil. Because Jesus died as the ultimate sacrifice, believers now verbally pray that the blood of Jesus is being applied to whatever they are praying for, but they are not using literal blood for this application. There are other scriptures that reveal God applying the blood of Jesus to a believer's life.

Romans 3:25 *Whom God hath set forth to be a propitiation through faith in his blood, to declare his righteousness for the remission of sins that are past, through the forbearance of God.*

Hebrews. *9:22 And almost all things are by the law purged with blood; and without shedding of blood is no remission.*

Ephesians 1:6-7 *To the praise of the glory of his grace, wherein he hath made us accepted in the beloved. In whom we have redemption through his blood, the forgiveness of sins, according to the riches of his grace.*

The blood is applied through the posture of faith, salvation, and covenant with Jesus Christ. This disposition is what produces the authority, remission, and redemption of the blood of Jesus. Aside from the blood sacrifices God directed in the Old Testament for atonement, and the sacrifice of Jesus Christ in the New Testament, God was against any other blood sacrifices - the eating or drinking of any blood of animals and people.

Genesis 9:4-5 *But you must not eat meat that has its lifeblood still in it. And for your lifeblood I will surely demand an accounting. I will demand an accounting from every animal. And from each human being, too, I will demand an accounting for the life of another human being.*

Deuteronomy 12:23 *Only be sure not to eat the blood, because the blood is the life, and you must not eat the life with the meat.*

Ezekiel 23:36-39 *The LORD said moreover unto me; Son of man, wilt thou judge Aholah and Aholibah? yea, declare unto them their abominations; That they have committed adultery, and blood is in their hands, and with their idols have they committed adultery, and have also caused their sons, whom they bare unto me, to pass for them through the fire, to devour them. Moreover this they have done unto me: they have defiled my sanctuary in the same day, and have profaned my sabbaths. For when they had slain their children to their idols, then they came the same day into my sanctuary to profane it; and, lo, thus have they done in the midst of mine house.*

Acts 15:19-21 *It is my judgment, therefore, that we should not make it difficult for the Gentiles who are turning to God. Instead we should write to them, telling them to abstain from food polluted by idols, from sexual immorality, from the meat of strangled animals and from blood. For the law of Moses has been preached in every city from the earliest times and is read in the synagogues on every Sabbath."*

Acts 15:28-29 *For it seemed good to the Holy Ghost, and to us, to lay upon you no greater burden than these necessary things; That ye abstain from meats offered to idols, and from blood, and from things strangled, and from fornication: from which if ye keep yourselves, ye shall do well. Fare ye well.*

Jesus blood SHIFTED the believer into eternal life with God. There is no comparison between Jesus who sacrificed his life for the saving of the world, and demonic drinking and eating of blood to idols.

CRYSTALS & STONES

Crystals and stones practitioners claim they have healing and protection powers, although there is no scientific evidence to support this theory. The claim is that they have unique mystical healing powers that cure ailments protect against illness, disease, and injury, provide mental and emotional wellness, balance, and stability, promotes creativity, and awakens spiritual consciousness. The use of these talismans and amulets dates to the Sumerians in 4500-5000 BC. The ancient Egyptians mined for crystals and used them for jewelry, as healing aides, wellness, success, to attract love, protection, burials, etc. Crystals and stones are positioned on various parts of the body, in correspondence to chakras. Chakras are focal points used in many ancient meditation practices, such as Tantra or Hinduism. The crystal and stone placement are in effort to create an energy grid to draw healing energy from the crystals and stones into the body and draw various negative energies out of the body into the stones. There is also the belief that certain physical properties—e.g., shape, color, and markings—determine the ailments that a stone can heal. Most people who promote crystal and stone healing are involved in occult activity.

Exodus 28:17-19 *This chestpiece will be made of two folds of cloth, forming a pouch nine inches square. Four rows of gemstones will be attached to it. The first row will contain a red carnelian, a chrysolite, and an emerald. The second row will contain a turquoise, a sapphire, and a white moonstone. The third row will contain a jacinth, an agate, and an amethyst. The fourth row will contain a beryl, and onyx, and a jasper. All of these stones will be set in gold.*

Exodus 28:30 *Insert into the pocket of the chestpiece the Urim and Thummim, to be carried over the heart when the priests goes into the Lord's presence.*

Revelation 21:11 *Having the glory of God: and her light was like unto a stone most precious, even like a jasper stone, clear as crystal.*

Verse 18-21 *And the building of the wall of it was of jasper: and the city was pure gold, like unto clear glass. And the foundations of the wall of the city were garnished with all manner of precious stones. The first foundation was jasper; the second, sapphire; the third, a chalcedony; the fourth, an emerald; The fifth, sardonyx; the sixth, sardius; the seventh, chrysolite; the eighth, beryl; the ninth, a topaz; the tenth, a chrysoprasus; the eleventh, a jacinth; the twelfth, an amethyst. And the twelve gates were twelve pearls; every several gate was of one pearl: and the street of the city was pure gold, as it were transparent glass.*

Though crystals and stones are mentioned in the Bible, there is no scriptures to support them as God's healing talismans and amulets. They appear more for adorning and symbolism. These practices were common among paganism to which God warns not to engage in. In this modern day of crystal and stone healing, the practitioners regard it as white magic, which is magic used for good, selfless purposes, especially to counteract evil. Black magic is used for evil purposes, to release and provoke evil. Since the practitioner deem it white magic, they convey that even if not biblical, it is only intended to bring good so what harm is it doing. This perspective takes us back to everything that we perceive good is not lawful or acceptable in God's eyes. When we make something our source of attention when we should be going to God, it becomes sinful and idolatrous behavior.

In the Bible, there are several instances where people did what they believed was lawful with various objects, even those God gave to them, and it provoked God's wrath and or judgment.

In *Leviticus 10:1-2* Aaron's sons offered incense unto God on their own accord, God deemed their offering strange fire and struck them dead. The incense was part of holy customs that God put in place but was only to be used for those purposes and at his leading.

In *Numbers 20:11* Moses struck the Rock with his Staff that God gave him as a miracle rod for leading the people. Out of anger when God told him to speak to it. It still produced water, but God's anger was kindled because of his disobedience. It cost him entering the promise land.

At the people's request, God made Saul king. As long, he had great authority, but obedience was essential to his success. In *1Samuel 15*, he did not follow the word to kill and destroy everything and everyone from the Amalekites, to who he won a war against. He kept what he deemed to be the best from their lands and kept the king alive. He claimed to be offering the best items up to God as a sacrifice, but God wanted no parts of it. As a result, Saul's kingdom was snatched for him and given to King David.

PHARMAKEIA

Pharmakeia is an ancient and New Age witchcraft practice that releases the spirit of pharmakeia into the lives of people through its workings.

Revelation 18:23-24 *And the light of a candle shall shine no more at all in thee; and the voice of the bridegroom and of the bride shall be heard no more at all in thee: for thy merchants were the great men of the earth; for by thy sorceries were all nations deceived. And in her was found the blood of prophets, and of saints, and of all that were slain upon the earth.*

<u>*Sorcerers* in Greek is *pharmakeia* and means:</u>
1. medication ("pharmacy"), i.e. (by extension) magic (literally or figuratively),
2. sorcery, witchcraft,
3. the use or the administering of drugs, poisoning,
4. sorcery, magical arts, often found in connection with idolatry and fostered by it,
5. metaph. the deceptions and seductions of idolatry.

This passage of scripture is referring to Babylon and how it engages in magical arts, witchcraft practices, and the administering of witchcraft in the form of drugs that poison and destroy people's minds, souls, and bodies. God was judging this deceptive, seducing, idolatrous behavior, and revealing how it was not only killing nations, but his prophets and saints.

America is the modern-day Babylon. Pharmakeia is where we derive our English word "*pharmacy*." Pharmacy is a well-organized and professionalized system, known as Big Pharma Industry, that administers drugs in America. Many of the drugs have more side effects than they have health benefits. The side effects alter the mood, mind, and perception of individuals, suppress symptoms rather than heal them, give the illusion of healing yet never really making the mind, soul, and body well, while stealing countless dollars from people due to the high cost of doctor's visits and medication treatments. Many of the true cures and beneficial medical treatments, tend to be withheld and only utilized for wealthy groups, or those who can find the way to afford them. There is also a conspiracy in America by "Big Pharma Theorists," that treatments are withheld to make more money from people purchasing pharmakeia medications, thus spreading and increasing diseases for further financial gain. Healthcare is a crisis dilemma in America. While healthcare is free in most nations, it is costly and expensive in America; the average American is unable to afford good health services. When the pharmaceutical companies are questioned regarding these practices, they contend the expense is due to lab experiments to ensure medications and treatments are sufficient.

Many people, including believers are addicted to these drugs. The average person in America, including saints, digest some type of medication daily for stress, anxiety, ailments, and pain. These prescription drugs cause intoxication, a euphoric high, or hallucinations, while opening a person's life to the spirit of pharmakeia.

Opioids & Prescription Drugs
The most commonly used opioids are oxycodone, oxymorphone, morphine, methadone, codeine, fentanyl, oxy, blues, zanny bars, OC.

Unlike the street drugs above, these drugs are created and sold by Big Pharma. The addiction to these drugs has increased over the years and can result in more addictive drug use such as heroine. People usually take opioids to kill pain. *Drugabuse.gov* states the following: *Opioids bind to and activate opioid receptors on cells located in many areas of the brain, spinal cord, and other organs in the body, especially those involved in feelings of pain and pleasure. When opioids attach to these receptors, they block pain signals sent from the brain to the body and release large amounts of dopamine throughout the body. This release can strongly reinforce the act of taking the drug, making the user want to repeat the experience.*

Amphetamines
Other prescription drugs for central nervous system depressants are barbiturates and benzodiazepines are sedatives and tranquilizers prescribed for anxiety and sleep problems. And stimulant prescription drugs are generally for mental health issues such as depression, ADHD, the sleep disorder narcolepsy, and obesity, known as amphetamines. These are dangerous habit-forming drugs that can be purchased illegality or prescribed by a doctor. While making people feel energetic, confidently social, productive, and successful, and intensely energetic, they speed up the brain, while causing severe depression, anxiety, and mental issues.

Methamphetamine
meth, crystal, crystal meth, speed, crank, blue, ice, chalk

The is addictive recreational drug is generally in the form of a pill or white power that can be odorless and bitter-tasting substance that can be dissolved in water or a drink. This drug damages the central nervous symptom. This drug causes a person to be energetic, talkative, suppresses the appetite, confident, elated, while causing a euphoric high. Since it is classified as a stimulant by the U.S. Drug Enforcement Administration, it is considered a legal drug that is available through a nonrefillable prescription. It also is produced in the labs of foreign countries for illegal use.

People will misuse the way they are to take these medications, take the medications in a way to produce a high effect, or take someone else's medication. Some people will sell their prescription drugs on the street or steal other people's prescription medication for this purpose. The withdrawal and dependence on these medications cause by horrific which causes people to use street drugs due to not being able to handle the side effects.

Alcohol
Though highly addictive, alcohol is not generally viewed as a drug. It is most available due to being legal and have the most dangerous withdrawals of all drugs. Some people are functioning alcoholics and therefore do not believe they are addicted.

Drugabuse.gov reports the following: *"2017, about 18 million people, 12 and older, misused prescription drugs. This site also reports that the National Survey on Drug use reports that about 2 million Americans misuse pain killers, one million misused prescription stimulants, 1.5 million misused tranquilizers, and 271,000 misused sedatives for the first time."*

Some prescription medications are so addicting the pharmaceutical companies have been exposed for their practices, thus having to place restrictions on the dosage, usage, and purchasing of some drugs.

Though the Bible is not against medication or doctors, it does warn us against sorcerers and their pharmakeia practices, as much of what is being cooked up by these pharmakeia scientists and served as medicines is really the demon dealing of the spirit of pharmakeia. Let us address the spirit of pharmakeia a bit more, as we also see this spirit operating in street drugs. Many pharmaceutical scientists are witch doctors serving us the spirit of pharmakeia which is the reason we do not become well yet are addicted to the medication because of its hallucinogenic side effects or dependent on the medication due to its suppression of systems. The Bible declares that God is our healer. We should be seeking him regarding healing and on what doctors are best for us, what medications we should agree to take, and protection against pharmakeia. We should study herbs, essential oils, and other health and medical benefits that come from God, and that will bless rather than poison our minds, souls, and bodies.

Some New Agers make their own pharmakeia drugs and are addicted to pharmakeia drugs that have hallucinogenic affects. Those who make their drugs are known as cooking witches, voodoo priests, voodoo or medicine doctors, herbalists, or diviners. Not all herbalists are witches or warlocks, but a significant percentage are pharmakeia demon dealers. Drug dealers and drug cartels have increased with making their own street drugs. They may hire a chemist to head their labs or to formulate them as drugs. They may get drug ingredients from the international and use regular people they hire to work in their makeshift lab houses. Some drug cartels engaged in Haitian Voodoo, Cuban Santeria, Narco Saints, and Mexican witchcraft to be more powerful where they can have supernatural protection from the police, be the biggest drug lords in their spheres of influence, and where their drugs can make people so addicted, they can keep making money from them. Some drug cartels hire voodoo priests to work for them.

These voodoo priests consistently cast spells and offer up sacrifices on behalf of the drug cartel leader so they can control people and their sphere of influence. The voodoo priest may also continuously offer sacrifices to idol gods on behalf of the drug lord leader so that they can be endowed with supernatural powers from demons that enable them to be unexplainably strong and terrifying, where others will fear them, are loyal and subservient to them, and so that they are financially successful and powerful as a drug pin. It has become common for police to find shines and altars in drug labs, smuggling rings, trafficking houses, drug dealing night clubs, etc. Many spells are cast against law enforcement, such that they fear arresting and prosecuting these drug lords, due to succumbing to tragedies inflicted by demons that work with these cartels. Law enforcement and the people within communities need prayer to break free from the witchcraft that is tied to drug usage and from exposing and prosecuting drug lords. This is one of the main reasons it is so difficult for people to be delivered from drug addiction, and for people to reveal who their dealers are. They are under witchcraft spells that keep them addicted and bound in false loyalty even when they want to be free. This is how the spirit of pharmakeia operates. It makes commands that you serve it for serving you. It demands that you remain bound to it, even when you no longer want to.

No doubt the spirit of pharmakeia opens a third eye that alters consciousness and cause all types of delusions, hallucinations, astral projections, ecstasy and euphoric experiences, and demonic supernatural encounters. Along with witchcraft, it is the number one reason people are addicted to street drugs and prescription drugs that yield these types of mind trips. People are addicted to leaving their stressful day-to-day reality, and entering a spiritual sphere that provides escape, fantasy, delusional bliss, with the consequences of entertaining demonic spirits who for payment of this experience, now own and oppress their lives.

A series called the "Queen's Gambit," on Netflix provides a clear insight on how the spirit of pharmakeia operates. This series offers a clear portray of how the spirit of pharmakeia operates. The series is about a young girl, age nine, name Beth, who goes to live in an orphanage after her mother kills herself in a car crash. Though awkward, introverted, sullen, Beth is very smart and resilient. The orphanage gives her and the other children what they are told are tranquilizers to keep them calm. Beth becomes addicted to the tranquilizers because they help her sleep, and she likes the way they make her feel. She realizes that if she cheeks the pills, stockpile them, and take a couple at one time, her high sensations and experiences increase. Beth learns how to play chest from the janitor, and finds that when she takes the pills, a portal opens her consciousness to the spirit world, and she can see the chest on the ceiling above her and can calculate certain movements that she can make to help her beat her opponents. She becomes a master chest player through this method. Though a chest master, she grows up addicted to these pills, dysfunctional in her personal life, while needing them to function in life and to play during her chest tournaments.

The movie literally shows how the pills opens a portal in Beth when she takes them, and how the spirit of pharmakeia takes over her. In one scene, after consumption, a huge dark eerie looking chest piece overshadows Beth as she ascends into higher consciousness. Though the movie does not state. It is obvious that a spirit guide is directing Beth when the portals open, which makes her dependent on the pills and the spirit rather than the fact that she truly has a pure masterful gift of playing chest. This is how witchcraft operates. It steals a person's natural god identity, gifts, and purpose, while interjecting spirits and demonic pathways that alter and steal destiny.

Years later, Beth is not only addicted to these pills but also alcohol. She is very dysfunctional to a point where it begins to interfere with her ability to win chest matches. A friend tries to help her get sober to which she conquers for a while, but due to this open door in her life, she cannot maintain her sobriety. She enters a downward spiral and must dig her way out of a pit of self-sabotage, spiritual natural death, and despair. At the end, I love that this movie enables her to do just that and even shows her wining chest matches while having a prophetic vision of how to beat her opponent but without drugs or a demon guiding her. She stops drinking and taking the pills, comes into the realization of who she is and the gift she possesses, and this enables her to tap into the purity of her chess gift and seer gift from her God identity.

Of course, this series is not spiritual and that is just my spiritual interpretation of what occurred, but many who use street and pharmaceutical drugs for a euphoric high, have these same demonic encounters and do not realize that are open portals and engaging demons. Those that are striving to enter a level of higher consciousness will claim they are engaging God, deities, their higher self, the universe, but it is demons they are communing with. The hallucinations, delusions, even those that appear to be presenting something good like with Beth, is all a facade that will cost a person their destiny. While succeeding in one area, the person is spiritually and naturally dying and deteriorating in other areas of their lives. This is because demons require a sacrifice of your soul for the high that they are giving to you and the success that you receive from engaging them. The true and living God is never going to have you engaging in an activity that compromises your health, safety, emotional well-being, and the eternity of your soul. This is the work of demons - spirits of pharmakeia that want to make you feel good but with a price - you are the price. You are the sacrifice.

God has declared an eternal judgement on these demon dealers and those who succumb to them.

Revelation 21:8 *But the fearful, and unbelieving, and the abominable, and murderers, and whoremongers, and sorcerers, and idolaters, and all liars, shall have their part in the lake which burneth with fire and brimstone: which is the second death.*

Revelation 22:14-15 The Amplified Bible *Blessed (happy and to be envied) are those who cleanse their garments, that they may have the authority and right to [approach] the tree of life and to enter through the gates into the city. [But] without are the dogs and those who practice sorceries (magic arts) and impurity [the lewd, adulterers] and the murderers and idolaters and everyone who loves and deals in falsehood (untruth, error, deception, cheating).*

Below are some of the street drugs people use to enter higher consciousness, thus succumbing to the spirit of pharmakeia.

Marijuana
weed, pot, hash, green, hemp, Mary Jane, herb, kush, purple haze.

Marijuana is a gateway drug that leads to other addictions. After plateauing from the experience of marijuana, people will seek a stronger drug for a greater euphoric experience. We will discuss marijuana in detail later in this chapter.

Synthetic Cannabinoids
synthetic marijuana, Spice, K2, black mamba, genie, salvia, Scooby Snax.

These are unpredictable drugs that can have horrible side effects when smoked, vaped, or ingested. Due to their makeup, there is no way to know how a person will respond, which makes these drugs extremely dangerous.

Cocaine
crack, coke, blow, snow, dust

Cocaine is snorted, inhaled as smoke, or dissolved and injected into a person's veins. It generally starts out as a recreational drug then a people become addicted due to its strong stimulating high that makes a person feel extremely relaxed, confident, happy, sexually aroused, edgy which is really agitation, and out of touch with reality. This drug can cause severe damage to the body and to one's life and success.

Heroin
dope, smack, black tar, mud, China white, dragon

Though heroin is used for pain in other nations, it is illegal in the United States because it is extremely addictive; especially when a person has abused abusing prescription opioids and start taking this drug to obtain a similar euphoric high.

MDMA
ecstasy, molly, E, X, rolls, happy pill.

This is a pill form, synthetic club drug, used to increase euphoria. Sometimes this drug is laced with other drugs without the user's knowledge.

Mushrooms
shrooms, caps, boomers, liberties, magics.

This drug looks like an actual mushroom. It causes sorcery, euphoria, and hallucinations.

MARIJUANA
Many New Agers use marijuana and other drugs to assist them with enter realms of consciousness, engage in acts of ecstasy, as an aphrodisiac, to connect to spirit guides, as a

healing medication, journaling experiences during meditation, to employ spell work, and to engage in witchcraft rituals and sacrifices. New Agers also smoke marijuana for the purposes cloud gazing, sparking creative energy, depth perception and intensity of an experience, to quiet the mind to focus more on inner contemplative thoughts or voices from outside forces. These experiences occur because of the altered state of consciousness that is opened through the spirit of pharmakeia. With marijuana becoming legal in some states as a healing aide known as CBD oil, some Christians justify its use without recognizing the spiritual ramifications.

Cannabidiol aka CBD oil is the natural cannabinoid chemicals derived from the marijuana plant. Due to its extraction from the plant, CBF does not provide the complete a "high" effect or any form of intoxication that is caused by another cannabinoid, known as THC found in the marijuana plant. CBD oil can make a person very relaxed and depending on who compounded the oil, a level of high and intoxication does occur. It is also important to note that there is now way to fully extract all the THC from the CBD oil.

People enjoy how marijuana makes them feel; how it heightens their senses, and as they relax and meditate, how it causes them to ascend into inner realms of consciousness. Some people believe it helps them to enter deeper realms of mediation; people report leaving their body and even astral projecting into these realms.

Many people use the following scripture to justify their marijuana and CBD oil usage:

Genesis 9:3 *Every moving thing that liveth shall be meat for you; even as the green herb have I given you all things.*

There are no definitive scriptures where God tells us to smoke for any reason less known to draw near to him. Many attempts to make smoking marijuana biblical stretched the scriptures, biblical history, and word interpretations of the Greek, Hebrew, and other biblical languages. Even the practice of incense was a representation of offering an acceptable sacrifice and was only done when God permitted. It was not an act that could just be given up to the Lord. It was unlawful to burn incense without God's permission, thus just as unlawful to smoke marijuana and try to make it a godly practice.

Leviticus 10:1-2 The Amplified Bible *And Nadab and Abihu, the sons of Aaron, each took his censer and put fire in it, and put incense on it, and offered strange and unholy fire before the Lord, as He had not commanded them. And there came forth fire from before the Lord and killed them, and they died before the Lord.*

1Samuel 15:22 *Samuel said, "Has the Lord as much delight in burnt offerings and sacrifices As in obeying the voice of the Lord? Behold, to obey is better than sacrifice, And to heed than the fat of rams.*

John 5:30 *I can of mine own self do nothing: as I hear, I judge: and my judgment is just; because I seek not mine own will, but the will of the Father which hath sent me.*

> *Anything that takes our spirit out of the realm of the Holy Spirit's jurisdiction is forbidden.*

If marijuana SHIFTS you from within the authority of the Holy Spirit, thus causing you to access another spirit that is not the Holy Spirit, it is error. Marijuana also takes us into spiritual realms through mind consciousness. The Bible never tells us to engage our mind in such a practice. In fact, we are to trade our "mind" for the mind of Christ. God's mind should be our pursuit because it is rooted in biblical principles and draw us into practices that are acceptable to him.

Romans 12:2 *And be not conformed to this world: but be ye transformed by the renewing of your mind, that ye may prove what [is] that good, and acceptable, and perfect, will of God.*

When people have given testimonies of experiencing the true and living God while high or intoxicated, the spirit of conviction that they are sinning through the Holy Spirit or the spirit of condemnation from their inner selves emanating feelings shame and guilt for smoking and sinning, overtakes them. Unlike those who claim marijuana smoking draws them to a higher level of consciousness with God, the encounters of conviction and condemnation pricked people who truly experienced the "real" God, to recognizing their behavior is wrong. The sin of smoking drugs and mind tripping was highlighted before God, not glorified before him. I know this to be true in my own life. Before I gave my life to God, I smoked marijuana. Nothing about how it made me feel - the elation, ecstasy, the thoughts I experience, or what I did while smoking it was godly, or drew me to God. I would enter an altered state of consciousness. I did not meditate or attempt to enter realms, the marijuana in and of itself would SHIFT me there. The more I would relax, the deeper into spiritual realms I went. Even though I was raised in the church and though a backslidden sinner during this time, I consistently read my Bible, prayed, and listened to church music, I never encountered God. What would come over me is the spirit of condemnation. Nothing about the condemnation I experienced was God. It was my own inner man becoming aware that I was transgressing against God. I knew better so I would often become condemned and start to preach about how we were going to hell for our sins. Though I loved the high feeling marijuana gave me, I hated the mind trip it took me on. Due to being already sensitive to the spirit realm, I would have the craziest visions, and encounter all kinds of demonic realms and beings. Depending on how high I was, the worse my mind trip was in accordance with the high. Sleeping high only confounded matters as I would encounter witches, warlocks, shapeshifting demons, in my dreams. I have these same types of experiences when I take certain prescription medications that doctors have prescribed me. It is the number one reason I tend to reject taking medications when they are prescribed.

Proverbs 6:16-19 *These six things doth the Lord hate: yea, seven are an abomination unto him: A proud look, a lying tongue, and hands that shed innocent blood, An heart that deviseth wicked imaginations, feet that be swift in running to mischief, A false witness that speaketh lies, and he that soweth discord among brethren.*

People who smoke marijuana or any drugs, especially those who are seeking a God conscious experience, display most if not all these attributes. If a person were really experiencing God, they would be pricked to self-examination of these sin issues as they would run into the spirit of truth regarding their sin issues. If you are truly encountering God, his presence or even the thought of him, the spirit of truth will make you not want to smoke because you would know you are sinning. God would never glorify sin or any activity that is against his word. If you are experiencing glorification of smoking marijuana, you did not encounter God. That was a devil. A deceiving demon. Any revelation you received, no matter how enlightening it appears, came from a demon and not Jesus. Jesus runs you to the redemption of the cross not away from it.

John 14:6 *Jesus saith unto him, I am the way, the truth, and the life: no man cometh unto the Father, but by me.*

- The word *way* means journey or a course of conduct.
- The word *truth* means truth, in reality, in fact, certainly what is true in things appertaining to God and the duties of man, moral and religious truth; truth as a personal excellence; that candor of mind, which is free from affection, pretense, simulation, falsehood, deceit.
- The word *life* means, life, vitality, and souls devoted to God and his logos word; a real and genuine, active, and vigorous, life devoted to God, blessed, trusting, and consummated by the resurrection of Christ.

If you are encountering God, deception for mind consciousness should be replaced with his way, truth, and life.

MAGIC
Magic is deception, strong delusion and doctrine of devils utilizing trickery and illumination to make people believe something supernatural is happening. It is the art of something appearing real, but it is deception altering a person's sense, so they will believe something happened that never truly occurred.

Different types of magic practices:
- **Black Magic** - Supernatural powers or magic used for evil, malicious, vindictive, and selfish purposes.
- **White Magic** - Supernatural powers or magic used for good, kind, selfless purposes: usually with an intent to healing, blessings, helping, and advancing others.
- **Spoken Magic** - Foundation of all magic; cast spells through invoking specific words and voice inflection.
- **Gesture Magic** - Due to growth in one's craft, speaking the spell is no longer needed: simply working the spell invoked its power. In this rand of words are spoken it strengthens the power and impact of the spell.
- **Thought Magic** - highest and most dangerous level of magic. Spells and gesturing are rarely used as the person has gained supernatural powers and energies to think the spell and invoke its power upon a person, place, or thing.

- **Levitation** – an illusion where a magician appears to defy gravity by making a person or object float in the air. It appears as if the person is not being assisted by anything or anyone, but clever paranormal workings accompany levitation. Demonic spirits either possess the person or object, which enables the levitation or is part of the experience by holding the person or object in the air. When possessed, the magician sometimes appears in a trance like state during levitation. There are also instances where magicians have acquired a level of supernatural power and energy force from demonic spirits via meditation, rituals, sacrificing themselves to idol gods, where they no longer appear in a trance; the demonic spirit/s has become the identity of them. They can engage and perform their magic through the higher powers of the demonic spirit/s that rule them. Since demons are supernatural beings, they may not appear to the human eye without discernment of demonic realms. This is the reason people do not see the demon that is holding an object or a person. The spirit, however, is indeed present, and is in cohorts with the magician to trick and deceive the onlookers into believing levitation is occurring without assistance. Trickery, hypnosis, psychic workings, secret trap boxes and wirings, stage, and hand maneuvering tricks, can also be used to make people believe they are watching magic tricks, or a person levitate. The magician uses spells and psychic powers on those watching to put them in a state of experiencing what he wants them to see. Because people are so intrigued and vulnerable, they come under the subjection of the magician's spells and powers, thus experiencing, and believing the illusion. The magician can also manipulate the atmosphere with spells and magical workings to make it appear as he desires. People believe they are experiencing magical tricks and levitations but have succumbed to witchcraft powers controlled by the magician.

Many New Agers try to equate magic to the miracle working power found in the Bible. However, miracles are the true supernatural power and compassion of Jesus Christ working through the presence of his Holy Spirit. There is nothing trickery or illuminating occurring through miracles. Miracles are God supernatural interventions and causing what could not occur by natural means to physically manifest concerning a person or matter. The person or situation is supernaturally changed and transformed by God's miracle working powers. With magic, nothing is changed as only delusion and masterful deceit is occurring through secretive formulas and arts, designed to yield the illusion of a happening that is not really occurring or occurring through demonic intervention.

In *Exodus* we have Moses performing supernatural workings through the power of God and Pharaoh's magicians mimicking him using divination.

Exodus 7:9-13 When Pharaoh shall speak unto you, saying, Shew a miracle for you: then thou shalt say unto Aaron, Take thy rod, and cast it before Pharaoh, and it shall become a serpent. And Moses and Aaron went in unto Pharaoh, and they did so as the LORD had commanded: and Aaron cast down his rod before Pharaoh, and before his servants, and it became a serpent. Then Pharaoh also called the wise men and the sorcerers: now the magicians of Egypt, they also did in like manner with their enchantments. For they cast down every man his rod, and they became serpents: but Aaron's rod swallowed up their rods. And he hardened Pharaoh's heart, that he hearkened not unto them; as the LORD had said.

Magic is man- and demon-created. Miracles are God created!

Pharaoh had wise men (skillful and prudent), sorcerers (whispering spell workers and diviner's), and magicians (those who operate with horoscopes as drawing magical lines or circles), magic, divining, astrologer engravers, occult workers), who all cast their rod down as Aaron did. Though they were able to perform the same act, their power was a form of godliness, rooted in craft, cunningness, and deception, and not greater than God's power, thus we see Aaron's rod swallowing up their rods.

INCANTATIONS, CHARMS, & SPELLS

An incantation, a spell, a charm, an enchantment or a bewitchery, are magical formulas or workings intended to incite a magical effect on a person or objects. The formula or workings can be spoken, sung, chanted, created in a potion, and can be used in rituals and prayers.

- An **incantation** can also be performed during ceremonial rituals or prayers with the intent to create a box type binding around a person, place, or thing, that makes them subject to the formula or working that is being released. Incantations can cause physical, emotional, mental stifling, affliction, turmoil, tragedy, and death to its prey. Incantations often must be broken for the person, place, or thing to be free from its binding.

- A **charm** is a ritual utterance or potion used for the purposes of attracting, magnetizing, or connecting, to a desired person, object, or experience. Often the acts of charming manipulates the senses and actions of others where they are bound by the magical powers of the charmer, also can be known as enchanter. Charming is used to break up relations, draw a desired mate to a person, cause a preferred happening to occur, draw success, fame, fortune. Demonic spirits are attached to these acts and is the catalysts for binding its prey to the charmer or the person, place, or thing, that desires the connection.

- A **spell** is a strong wish, desire, motive, intent, or compilation of words rooted in magical powers that can be worked by simply pointing a finger, meditating, and willing a situation to occur, performing a ritual using various tools, herbs, and crystals, or drawing from energies, vibrations, and demonic powers to complete its workings. Interesting the ***Luke 11:20***, states, *But if I with the finger of God cast out devils, no doubt the kingdom of God is come upon you."* This is not a spell working but the power of God working in a believer through the Holy Spirit, to command demons to be cast out of a person's life. Just like the Holy Spirit, a person can be bound by a demon, that causes them to inflict spells simply by the commanding of workings while using their finger. Words have power. ***Proverbs 18:21*** lets us know that, *"Death and life are in the power of the tongue: and they that love it shall eat the fruit thereof."*

- **Emoji Spell Casting** – I was shaken when I learned about emoji spell casting. Google this topic so you can be shaken, too. Or check out hashtags #emojispell or

#spellcasting on Instagram. I continue to express how the internet entail real spiritual realms. That we are operating in spheres and spiritual airways within the heavenlies, therefore, it is important to be mindful of demonic and witchcraft activity, as demons, witches, and warlocks have claimed these realms and spheres since the beginning of time; they are housed here and know how to operate to control the territory and negatively influence people's lives and regions. Modern witches have created emoji spell casting for various reasons (e.g. to impact political leaders, political parties, laws, discredit and divide religious sects, dismantle the impact God's people and their ministries and destines, have on the world, shutdown activities they do not approve of, etc. They release good and bad spells to people and situations, control and manipulate people, places, and things for their favor, draw people into their witchcraft practices, etc. In traditional witchcraft handmade talisman and sigil magic are used to cast such spells. Talismans are stones, rings, or other objects, engraved with figures or characters, worn as an amulet or charm, that are perceived to possess spell casting occult powers. Sigil magic use occult symbols and numbers that have meanings of certain spirits attached to them which aide in casting spells. Emoji magic is similar. Witches use emoji symbols, along with chants, rituals, and spells spoken over the emojis they choose to release their cunning works. When sent, the charge of the spell is said to become more powerful. So much that even if the witch does not send it to someone else, they will message, email, or text it to themselves. In this manner it is released into the spirit realm to connect to energy frequencies and demonic spirits, to ensure its working is strategically fulfilled. This is taught online on Pinterest, in private groups, and the like, and therefore has become popular among teenagers. Help us Lord.

- **Hashtags -** Witchcraft hashtags have become an increased phenomenon. Using the hashtags, witchcraft and occult practitioners can cast spells on the hashtag itself to release divination or to utilize algorithms to unify so they can gather physically and online to engage in witchcraft practices for a common purpose. This has become so popular that the hashtags allow them to operate like an organization or even a church. They use the hashtags to get the word out of unifying for the purposes of fasting together, pray witchcraft spells, spell casting, offering sacrifices, attending certain groups, and meeting places online so they can strategize together on how to unify and what practices to use to fulfill their agenda. They respect order, rank, and experience so this enables them to have more success in fulfilling their purposes and following the guidelines and rules that are given to them. Practitioners also cast spells and perform rituals on their videos to sharing information and releasing divination. TikTok algorithms have made the app a safe haven for those interested in witchcrafts and the occult. The interest becomes increasingly popular daily, and as people unit on this app, they branch out and unify on other social media platforms. Using hashtags increases the ability to unify and even allow those interested to cast spells and strengthen their unity in casting spells together to give them more power in whatever it is they are seeking to influence or control. Popular witchcraft practices against the President, the election, to influence laws and social issues are common themes. The hashtag #WitchesForBLM - Black Lives Matter - is immensely popular and serves as a meeting place for practicing witches who desire to be trained and operate in how to cast protection spells, draw occult sigils, hex police, influence laws, and social issues. After being utilized for just five days, this hashtag garnered 10 million views on the TikTok app and continues to be popular in gathering like-minded occult practitioners and casting spells. The Black Lives Matter co-founder Patrisse Cullors openly practices the occult religion "Ifa," an African "system of divinization" that is also known as voodoo. Other hashtags like #Witch has over 584 million views. To date, there are multitudes of witchcraft hashtags on TikTok and other apps and social media platforms with over a million views. While the church is busy trying to recreate their personal church online with minimal unity among the body of Christ itself, witchcraft practitioners are building an empire. Hashtags and emojis are just the tip of the scale regarding digital witchcraft. We have not even discussed how such witchcraft is ingrained in online TV, media, music and music videos, online commercials, ads, and the like. Believers must come out of their little personal kingdoms and begin to unify for global impact as this is the level witchcraft practitioners are operating. We need one another! We need a kingdom SHIFT and manifold collaboration to catch up to and overtake what the witchcraft practitioners have already established.

- Many of the viral challenges, ads, gaming, Avatars, horoscope, mating, marriage, destiny, giftings, callings, and identity predicting and personality questionnaire quizzes on social media sites are connected to marketing strategies, but also to witchcraft practices; they are gateways for marketers and witches to obtain personal information about the user and track them online and in life. Witches cast spells and release demonic activity and entities into people's lives, while marketers personalize the person's internet searches and experiences in efforts to sell the items related to their answers and personalities. Anyone can create a challenge or a questionnaire quiz. This is the reason witches and random people seek the opportunity to utilize them. Some of the warfare believers are having via the internet is becomes of these activities.

DAYS OF THE WEEK IN WITCHCRAFT

In paganism and many witchcraft practices, each day of the week is important in magical spell casting. It is believed that each day contains healing properties that are essential to witchcraft practices - to people receiving answers, guidance, wellness, prosperity, success, and divine enlightenment through a higher level of consciousness. Many practitioners use ritual guides to assist them with working witchcraft according to the days of the week. They will keep a journal of what day and time they spell cast, sacrifice, conduct rituals, as this provides further insight or further spell casting that is needed to make sure their desires come to past. There is an impression that depending on a person's birthdate and month, certain days of the week, month, or year are luckier and present more opportunity for success than others. The days of the week are associated with certain colors that are key for working crystal magic or engaging certain demon gods, elements in the earth, astrology, and the universe. This is one of the reasons it is important for believers to be careful when engaging in pagan holidays. Many of these holidays are connected to witchcraft practices and have been dedicated to idol gods. While we think we are just celebrating, witches and warlocks are offering up sacrifices, rituals, and spell casting to idol gods, and using our ignorance to strengthen their wicked and dishonorable workings against the true and living God. Our Lord and savior definitely owns every day of the week, but he did not invent or approve any pagan or witchcraft workings that have been connected to them. We must resist approving and engaging in these workings, while making sure we are dedicating our days to God.

CHAKRAS

Chakras is ancient energy system that originated in India. It is a religious construct of Hinduism and Buddhism and has become well known among New Agers with the use of yoga and new age philosophies. In Sanskrit, the Root Chakra is known as the Mooladhara Chakra. This root is said to define a person's relationship with Mother Earth. The belief is that chakra influences a person's passion, creativity, youthfulness, vitality, and their basic survival instincts.

Chakra (cakra in Sanskrit) means "wheel" and refers to energy points in a soul and what is known as the Subtle body. Presumably, the chakras reside along one of two central energy channels within a person called a Sushumna. The Sushumna is perceived to be the initial Nadi, or channel, that flows throughout a person's body to deliver life energies called Prana, or subtle winds. Chakras are thought to be spinning disks of energy that should remain "open" and aligned, as they correspond to a cluster of nerves, major organs, and areas of a person's energetic body that impact a person's emotional and physical well-being. It is believed that are 114 different chakras, and that seven main chakras run along a person's spine. Each of the seven main chakras correspond to a number, name, color, along the spine from the sacrum to the crown of the head and has a specific health focus. The concept is if a specific area of the chakra is blocked, then it can cause a certain illness or ailment to occur. Usually, these illnesses or ailments can be traced to life issues that impacts the person's emotional, physical, and spiritual well-being, thus causing blockages of chakras in the body. When the chakra is unblocked, the person can be healed, and enter a sense of well-being where they can embrace and resolve life issues in a wise and appropriate manner.

Chakras are essential to Kundalini, a meditation technique associated with the goddess that possess the same name. Kundalini is a female energy serpent spirit that lies coiled at the base of the spine – along the seven chakras. It is said to live at the base of a person's spine and requires awakening to migrate to the head of that person, so that it can release spiritual awareness through mystical higher conscious type experiences. The Kundalini spirit opens a third eye on the seven chakra points, so that demons can gain access to a person's life to make them believe they are being healed and emotionally balanced yet being drawn into the dark world of witchcraft arts. Because the Kundalini spirit has migrated to the head of a person, it has become their god, which makes it difficult for the person to receive that chakras, yoga, acupuncture, and other forms of witchcraft practices are ungodly and not beneficial to their wellbeing. The goddess serpent spirit – Kundalini has beguiled them and through meditation, they have entered cunning wisdom and knowledge that overrides the ability to hear truth as many New Agers, even Christians, believe chakras is good for them and they can put a Christian twist on these practices and contend they are of God.

Diagram 8.0 Yoga

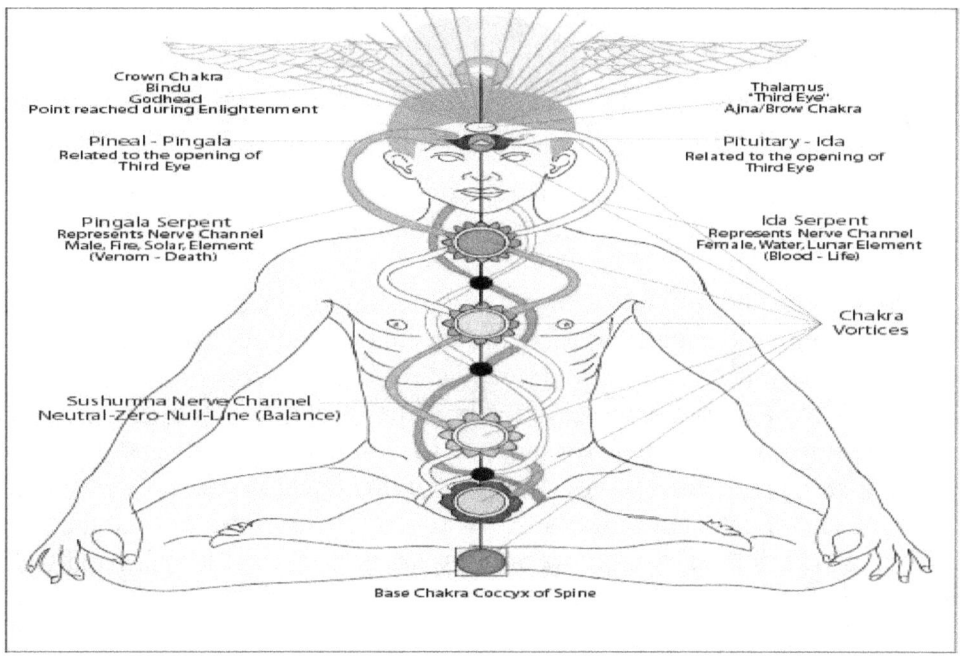

Source: Fractional Enlightenment Website, 2021

Yoga, Christian Yoga – Yoga is rooted in Hinduism and Spiritualism. Yoga practitioners encourage a person to meditate while emptying their mind to enter to a place the Hindu theology calls "a blank mind." Meditation in and of itself is not wrong or idolatrous. However, meditation that is not centered on God or his word can be dangerous, especially when a person is so relaxed, they enter spiritual realms or spheres of unconsciousness or subconsciousness within their brain and spiritual realms. As one is ascending into higher consciousness, having a blank mind exposes a person to all types of demonic and manmade infestations that is operating in the spiritual realms they are engaging in. God tells us to mediate on him and his word day and night, and to fill our mind and Spirit with him, so we are girded in our mind, are renewed in our mind, and can have his mind. Being filled pushes out anything that is ungodly and unhealthy in our mind. Hindu meditation also requires a person to center their mind, body, and spirit where they are focused on themselves. The focus becomes the person, their issues, their desires, their will, instead of being centered on God, allowing God to be the center and mindset, and allowing him to guide them in what to deal with regarding themselves and their mediation time.

Psalm 1:2 *But his delight is in the law of the LORD, And in His law he meditates day and night.*

Romans 12:2 *And be not conformed to this world: but be ye transformed by the renewing of your mind, that ye may prove what is that good, and acceptable, and perfect, will of God.*

Ephesians 4:23 *And be renewed in the spirit of your mind.*

***Philippians* 2:5** *Let this mind be in you, which was also in Christ Jesus.*

***Philippians* 4:8** *Finally, brethren, whatsoever things are true, whatsoever things are honest, whatsoever things are just, whatsoever things are pure, whatsoever things are lovely, whatsoever things are of good report; if there be any virtue, and if there be any praise, think on these things.*

1Peter 1:13 *Wherefore gird up the loins of your mind, be sober, and hope to the end for the grace that is to be brought unto you at the revelation of Jesus Christ.*

The breathing techniques in yoga is pranayama breathing. Prana is the Hindu word for life force, which is the same concept as the word tai chi in some martial arts. Tai Chi relies on the manipulation of mythical energies to draw power and ability for completing different martial art movements. As a person is utilizing the breathing techniques they are participating "an emptying of the mind," which can cause a person to leave their body and engage in astral projection. Astral projection is a voluntary out of body experience. It is illegal without the leading of the Holy Spirit and is deemed as witchcraft when done without the direction of God. When we are not led by God, we are trespassing in the spirit realm and yielding to divination and witchcraft.

Even if a person contends that they are meditating on God, the yoga stretching positions declare that they are bowing to a Hindu God. Every yoga pose has symbolism that is tied to mysticism, idol gods and demonic spirits. The quest of yoga is to be able to reach a height of meditation where a person can perform unexplainable supernatural poses that demonstrate how energy forces of peace, light, enlightenment, and power have overtaken their body, spirit, and life. What really has happened is demonic spirits have entered their body through mediation and surrender into spiritual realms and has given the person formation power to do such unique poses. It is no way to make yoga godly because its source is from demonic realms. If a person is utilizing the practices of yoga to obtain a word from God, they are engaging in witchcraft. The source of the word is not Jesus Christ but is whatever god they have exposed themselves to as they meditate and engage in the pose's techniques.

There are 33 million idol gods in Hinduism. They have an idol god for everything that a person may need or desire. When a person is engaging in yoga, they are offering up a sacrifice upon an idolatrous altar as that is the main purpose of the practice, the meditations, and the positions. Therefore, the person is drawing enlightenment, peace, strength, relief, and healing, from whatever it is they are needing and desiring in their lives at that time from these idol gods, as all sacrifices produce a transference from the person to the god and vice versa. This peace and enlightenment are more of escape and atmospheric manipulation than really entering the pure glory realms and tranquil peace of God. As when a person is guided into spiritual realms by their own will and by demons, they are having second heaven experiences and not kingdom of heaven – third heaven experiences. While engaging the second heaven, that idol god and energy from that spiritual realm enters the person's atmosphere, mind, spirit, and body, and create an illusion of peace. A major truth we must understand about God is just because we think we are engaging him; does not mean he is engaging us. God does not accept strange fire no matter how we package it. He may not strike us dead like he did people in the Old Testament times, but he still will not receive an offering from the altar of idolatry.

The main stronghold spirit of yoga is the Kundalini demon which is often discerned in ministry events, especially during high times of worship and crowded altar calls. The Kundalini demon in yoga is a female energy serpent type spirit that lies coiled at the base of the spine. It comes in through yoga practices and even practices of mediation that open demonic realms rather than realms of God. Often people are so addicted to the feeling of worship itself that it has become God in their life. They are not having encounters with God, but with how the atmosphere and presence of the glory make them feel. When worship itself becomes their God, it SHIFTS a person into vain imaginations where they begin to have encounters in realms that they think are heaven or heavenly, or of God, but are spiritual realms that are free access to anyone. Because they are in a vulnerable state of worship and are not discerning, they encounter demonic spirits who pose as angels of light and thus open the door to kundalini and all types of other spirits. Spirits of Pharmakeia operate in these realms which is the reason many people will appear intoxicated or high during and after worship but reveal no true transformation, and no real encounter of revelations with the spirit of God. **Though not always the case,** they only tend to speak about how great the encounter was, with no reverence or fear of the Lord, no download of word, strategy, knowledge, or revelation, deliverance, healing, or no tangible change in their lives. Even days after such a major encounter, they do not seem to have any revelation from God for what the purpose was and what changed in them. I am not saying that you should always have revelation, but when you are having such encounters all the time with no word or transformation to SHIFT your life, you are just smoking glory – similar to a person smoking crack, marijuana or using prescription drugs to get high. Such experiences are yoga-like practices that open your spirit and life to witchcraft practices and demonization. Sadly, many are not even aware that they are bound because these acts occurred during ministry events.

- Moses received his purpose of delivering the Israelites after the burning bush, his face would be white as snow that it brought fear and reverence to the Israelites when he left the glory of God, and he wrote the Ten Commandments when encountering God (***Exodus 34:29-35***).
- Isaiah was saying "woe is me" after his awe striking encounter in the glory; he was full of repentance and fear of the Lord (***Isaiah 6***).
- Ezekiel received prophecies while being in the spirit realm with the Lord (**Ezekiel 3:24, 37:1-14**).
- Paul did not know if he was in the body or out of it, but he received such powerful revelation that God buffeted him to keep him humbled (***2Corinthians 12:3***).

It is important to make sure your divine visitations and encounters are being God led, God-focused, and producing of God revelation, enlightenment, strategy, transformation, etc. Make sure you have the fruit and spirit of God that attest to the visitations that you contend are of God. Many believers have taken the principles of yoga and added a God focused thus calling it Christian yoga. I would encourage believers not to use the word "yoga" at all, because yoga is a Hindu practice. If you are using God center meditation and stretching, then ask God for a new creative name to call your exercise technique or class. This way, you are not giving people the impression that yoga is okay. But you are drawing them into a new paradigm of God centered mediation and stretching their bodies in ways that truly draw them to God and into his revelation, divine peace, and true healing.

SOUND BOWLS

Tibetan Singing Bowls or Himalayan Bowls is an ancient Chinese sound therapy technic that dates back over 6000 years. It is a type of mediation and chanting technic to which a bell that vibrates produces rich, deep tones that are said to release healing vibrations and frequencies into the body to produce relaxation, physical harmony, relieve stress, emotional balance, personal enlightenment, spiritual alignment, healing of ailments. These bowls have been used by Buddhist monks and wellness practitioners such as musical therapists, massage therapists, and yoga therapists. This technique is tied to the kundalini spirit that we discuss in the yoga section. As the sound bowls is making music, it is offering up homage to the spirit of the kundalini which wraps itself around the chakras within the body, thus creating and illusion of wellness and peace. As you engage in this practice, you invite the kundalini spirit – a snake like spirit - to live along spine, thus becoming to god of your life.

MANIFESTATION & MOOD RINGS

Manifestation rings are jewelry pieces made by witches to be worn on the fingers for the purposes of connecting people to energy demons of love, attraction, favor, prosperity, abundance, higher consciousness, emotional calmness, healing, etc. These rings have been sacrificed to idol gods; rituals and spells have been cast over them so that the laws of attraction can operate on behalf of the wearer, and so that whatever else they need in the areas of healing, stress relief, relaxation, divine connections to the universe or higher consciousness can manifest. These rings are sold in witchcraft shops, on the internet and people can have a ring personally handcrafted to their liking, with specific spells and rituals performed in relations to what they desire to manifest in their lives.

Mood rings, created in 1975, contains liquid crystal called thermochromic element, that changes color based on a person's temperature and emotional mood within their finger. A color chart may accompany the mood ring to indicate a description of the mood the person is in based on the color of the ring at that time. Though the mood ring is not 100% accurate, because the ring is scientifically designed to reflect the temperature of your mood, the mood ring is not going to tell you anything about your mood and emotions that you already would not know simply by identifying and gaging your emotions. However, some people use these results of the ring to engage in other witchcraft practices which then opens the door to demonic activity. Some witches and new age practitioners make their own mood rings and speak spells and rituals over it to connect it to chakras and the kundalini spirit. People then claim to experience supernatural healing, peace, favor, attraction, prosperity, when wearing the ring.

REIKI

Reiki is an energy-healing practice developed by Mikao Usui, a Japanese Buddhist, in 1922. The word can be broken down into two meanings. "Rei" means God's wisdom or higher power. "Ki" is the life force energy. When combined, Reiki is the spiritually guided life force energy. Reiki practitioners use their hands to massage the body and operate through specific verbal mantras and blessings they speak out loud to clear negative energy from the body for the perceived purposes of raising a person's vibration, bringing harmony and balance to one's mind, open and balance energy Kundalini chakras, bringing mental, emotional, and spiritual healing and balance. This is not like the laying on of hands in the Bible or touching someone and praying for healing or deliverance. Reiki is rooted in demonic and idolatrous practices and its source is demons, not God and his Holy Spirit.

ACUPUNCTURE

Acupuncture was founded in the 1600s by the Chinese culture. It was widely used at that time, then the Chinese strayed from its use, yet in recent years, it has become a common practice of Chinese medicine, herbalists, and New Agers who embrace its principal roots in energy forces, and with people seeking alternative medical forms of healing.

Though a Chinese healing technique that many claims has been helpful in their wellness process, especially among substance abuse, the foundation of acupuncture is not based in biblical principles. Acupuncture is founded in the philosophical system of Taoism evolved by Lao-tzu and Chuang-tzu. Most devout Taoists believe in polytheism (belief in many gods) and in ancestral worship in the form of offering food and burning paper money as a sacrifice to ancestral gods. Taoists believe that a life of complete simplicity, naturalness, and non-interference with the course of natural events, is necessary to attain an existence in harmony with the Tao. Tao means *"road, path, way,"* and is a cosmic life-force of energy from the universe that Taoists contend flows and impacts all things. When reading this Tao sounds a lot like an idol god, which basically it is, yet many Taoists claim is it just a way of thought. At any rate, the concept is that Tao is guiding a person's life, so this is in opposition to a person being guided by the true and living God – our Lord and savior Jesus Christ. This makes Taoism and anything rooted in it, divination, and idolatry. This comic life-force Tao operates as two opposing forces, Yin and Yang or Chi and Qi (chee), which they believe circulates in special channels (meridians) throughout the body. In acupuncture, meridian is any of the pathways in the body along which vital energy flows, essentially the central area of chakras and is connected to chakra beliefs and the Kundalini spirit.

- Yin or Chi - is negative, dark, and feminine.
- Yang or Qi -positive, bright, and masculine.

It is believed that the interaction of these two forces is the guiding influence for the destinies, progress, and success, of all creatures, and that balance between the two is essential to releasing harmony into the body so that a person can maintain healing, wellness, and destiny success. The philosophy contends that when the Yin and Yang is imbalance, disease, mental instability, misguided and inappropriate behavior enters the body, causing sickness, disease, and behaviors, that alter destiny.

The four types of acupuncture techniques are:

- *Acupressure* - the use of blunt pressure, without puncture, over the same points,
- *Laser Acupuncture* - use of lasers on the same points,
- *Electroacupuncture* - using electric current,
- *Moxibustion* - various substances are burnt on the skin at the acupuncture points.

Through the insertion of needles into specific points along the energy pathways (meridians), acupuncture is intended to balance the Yin and Yang, thus bringing complete harmony to the body. The only force that the Bible states is to live in us is the Holy Spirit. And the Holy Spirit comes to live in us when we accept Jesus Christ as our personal savior (**John 3:5, John 16:13 15, Acts 1:8, Acts 2:38-39, Romans 8:26**). We do not need to engage in idolatry or divination to receive balance, truth, healing, or anything else from the Holy Spirit. We do not need to align with the universe or stick our bodies with needles to receive from the Holy Spirit. All we need to do is commune with the Holy Spirit, and as we are guided into all truth concerning the works of Jesus Christ and who he is as our Father, Lord, and Savior, he will release his power into us such that we are well and made whole, physically, emotionally, mentally, and spiritually.

When acupuncture is performed, there is the perception that the universe is helping to align the Tao in a person's body; they are receiving the energy power they need from the universe to balance the Tao within them. The needles are focal points to specific parts of the body that the universe uses to transfer energy power the person need in their bodies to bring that alignment and balance. When that alignment and balance occurs, healing and wellness occurs. Since the universe is not God nor is God an energy force, there is no telling what is being transferred into the person and who is doing the transferring. We have already discussed how demonic spirits operate in these realms to influence peoples' lives. The fact that acupuncture is rooted in Taoism, which is atheistic and idolatrous, demons along with whatever the practitioner believes and is tapping into through these energy portals, is being transferred and utilized in these practices. There is the mindset that since acupuncture been viewed by science as having some healing benefits, then it can be separated from a person's spirituality. Even if there is healing occurring via acupuncture, it is not from God and science does not make it be godly or acceptable. There is no way to profess to know God yet deal people a practice that is against who God is in all his sovereignty, who he signifies, and what his word says is of him and not of him.

HENNA TATTOOS
Originating from ancient India, henna tattoos are decorative designs created on a person's body, using paste and powdered dry leaves of the henna plant. They are generally applied to dye the skin of a person's fingernails, hands, and feet. Henna can also be dyed to silk, wool, and leather fabric, and henna designs have made their way into new age color books for adults and children.

Henna has been practiced in Pakistan, India, Africa, and the Middle East for over 5000 years. Mehndi pictures are what is considered when completing henna skin art. Sanskrit Dictionary,

Mehndi is from the word "mendhikā," which defines plants commonly used to make temporary coloring. Hindu Vedic customs reveal that henna tattoos were used to "awaken one's inner light," which is a portal opening within the person so they can enter higher consciousness and connect to gods that are connected to the sun.

Biblically henna tattoos were used by Babylonians, Assyrians, Sumerians, Semites, Ugaritics and Canaanites. These groups were known for engaging in pagan and idolatrous practices. They would use henna tattoos for adornment of brides and for special events of women. In ancient Egyptian times, mummies wore henna designs, and it is documented that Cleopatra used henna for decorative purposes. Indian tradition also use henna for Hindu weddings, Namboordiri weddings, and Hindu festivals. For about three thousand years, Henna has been used in erotic rituals in China and is associated with their ancient Goddess cultures. Iran, Iraq, Egypt, and Palestine use henna tattoos on their Arabic prostitutes to draw men for services. Henna tattoos are also used in sex trafficking and brothels around the world, for this purpose.

Henna became a trend in the western culture, especially the United States, because celebrities such as Madonna, Gwen Stefami, Yasmin Beethoven, Rihanna, Erika Badu, Prince, Vanessa Huygens, Xena, Beyoncé, and Liv Tyler, began wearing them in their movies, videos, concerts, events, and personal lives. This popularity has provoked teenagers to want henna tattoos and their parents have been approving the wearing of them. People will acquire henna tattoos at festivals, fairs, community gatherings, and even church events. In addition to hands and feet, westerners have henna tattoos applied to their backs, their bellies during pregnancy, and cancer patients tend to have them applied to cover their bald head or scars. People deem henna tattoos harmless because they are temporary tattoos that fade after a while, are painless, and they are ignorant to the pagan roots. Henna tattoos infiltrating the church is baffling. The henna symbols and designs are links to idol gods, and witchcraft and idolatrous practices. Many of these include incantation circles that are basically portals linked to universe ideologies and gods connected to astrology and the cosmos. This is not God's art and it is not harmless. The person's body has just become a fashion statement for witchcraft and demons, and a door opener to demonic activity.

BLEACHING
Skin bleaching is the practice of using chemical substances to lighten, whiten, or reduce the melanin in the skin. Many of these substances are toxic, cause blood poisoning, cancer, and have long term effects on the skin, body system, organs, and a person's emotional wellbeing. Though people are known to use the household product of bleach to lighten their skin, bleaching products, e.g., pills, creams, soaps, injections, have become extremely popular because the perception among celebrities, societies, and racial groups who have been oppressed by the "white superior race," that lighter skin is beautiful and more acceptable. These products still have major side effects on the body because of the chemicals that are in them. Due to the ramifications, bleaching has been deemed a public health crisis. Many countries are working on banning its use and some have already banned hydroquinone, which is a skin bleaching agent used in most products.

Skin bleaching historically started in the Victorian era, but is widely practiced everywhere, including Ghana, Africa, The Caribbean Islands, Southwest Asia, India, and the United States. During the Victorian era women were using lead paint to bleach their skin because whiteness was associated with purity. In countries like Africa, darker melanin helps protect from sun damage. When the body stops generating melanin, health implications can ensue.

The World Health Organization (WHO), reports:

- 77% of women in Nigeria use skin lightening products, the world's highest percentage,
- 60% of India bleach their skin,
- 40% of Asians bleach their skin,
- 40% of Africans bleach their skin,
- The statistical analysis of bleaching in the United States is difficult to assess due to the shaming and stigmas surrounding using bleaching. However, skin bleaching is quite common and is evident among celebrities, African American groups, and women with darker skin,
- It is estimated that by 2027, the global skin whitening industry is projected to be worth over $24 billion and $31.2 billion by the year 2024.

It is claimed that bleaching promotes independence, individuality, builds confidence, self-esteem, and positively impact mental health. Many bleach users SHIFT to believing they are a different race and deny their ethnic identity completely. There is the perception that the lighter a person is the more power, privilege, opportunities, and success they will have. Some people engage in skin bleaching to a point of losing their entire identity. Such practices are rooted in identity issues of self-hatred, hatred for God and how he created them, self-rejection, despising of ethnicity and skin color, a need for approval, validation, and acceptance.

Skin bleaching is not just a personal, but a society issue since the concepts around beauty and race and is factor. Other areas such as using chemicals to straighten one's hair, contouring using lighter make up products, Botox, plastic surgery, also need to be addressed by society, as they are all related to white supremacy approval issues.

ADORNMENT
- Contouring
- Make-up
- Permanent Make-up Tattooing
- Eyebrow Microblading and Microshading
- Eyelashes
- Hair coloring
- Cutting and Shaving Hair
- Perfume
- Body piercings
- Wigs
- Weaves and Hair Extensions
- Body Tattoos

- Clothing Styles and Fashions

With the rise of adornment to a point such that perfecting one's appearance and ability to 'brand' oneself has become a new age practice of necessity, along with maintaining the current trends and styles, it is important to explore the above areas in one's relationship with God. I encourage the reader and those they minister to, to study the scripture references in these areas and let God speak to you regarding what he was stating at the time of the text was written and is speaking to you now regarding them. Let him examine your identity, motives, personal and generational propensities, and lead you in what he believes is best for you.

One of the destiny guidelines I teach in my ministry is knowing God's standard for one's life and living that standard regardless to what others believe or do not believe - do or do not do. God's standard keeps believers rooted in God identity, from crossing boundaries where our soul may be stolen, and help us sustain in a destiny lifestyle with him. God's standard for you may be different for someone else. For example, I. wear makeup, and I color my hair. I often ask God is this something he wants me to stop doing. He lets me know that he is fine with these areas. I believe because I check with him and am willing to give them up if he says so that he recognizes that my desire is to please him, and my identity is rooted in him. Then there are other areas where God has said those things are not for you. For example, I do not wear perfume, I do not have tattoos or body piercings. These are areas that God has told me 'no." That they would become open doors to the demonic realm for me. But others may ask God and he may be okay with it.

Anything that overtakes our identity, becomes excessive, or something we feel we cannot live without, should be a caution to really go before God and see if deliverance and healing is needed. If you are contouring, wearing makeup, wigs, eye lashes, etc., to a degree that you look like an entirely different person than your original self, cannot go in public or around people without them, do not feel confident with them, then that should be a pause for self-examination with the Lord. If you are continuously getting tattoos and it has covered your entire face and body, this is something to examine with the Lord. You want to make sure you have not opened a door somewhere or crossed a boundary that does not honor God, or that he is not pleased with. As you would study the scriptures in these areas, you will find how adornment was used perversely, was driven by pride, lust, trends, and worldly desires, was an idol among some, and was idol worship, among others. These are the boundaries you want to be cautious about and to check yourself with before God. He will let you know what is best for you and your covenant with him. And anything he has you to relinquish will come with greater recompense than anything you must give up.

YORUBA WAIST BEADS
History of Yoruba waist beads dates to the fifteenth century and were initially popularly among the Nigeria tribe and African women. Yoruba waist beads are also called Ileke, Jigida, and Lagidigba. They are worn mostly by females of all ages and have various meanings within the Yoruba religion. Yoruba waste beads are handmade and comes in all forms, colors, shapes, and sizes. Traditionally waist beads were worn hidden underneath the clothes, unless being used as part of a costume for dance performances, for marriage ceremonies, or to allure desired

attention. Depending on the creator, they may serve as witchcraft charms as the stones and colors have significant meanings and serve as rights of passages for different types or purposes, symbolizes, and messages. Those who make the beads may perform rituals and spells on the beads as they are intended to attract male attention, release lustful and sexual advances, incite deep emotional responses from onlookers, invoke healing, provide protection from spirit guides, promote fertility, and protect the baby during pregnancy, increase the likelihood of twin birth, ward off demonic water type spirits, promote weight loss and the maintaining of a curvy waste. Yoruba women are known to wear waste beads that cause them to be irresistible to men and can also be considered African lingerie. Some men give waste beads to their wives or suitors as claim to them. In some African cultures, when a girl gets her period, the Yoruba waste beads are worn as a rite of passage into womanhood. Why a woman would want to display such a SHIFT to the world I will never know. Depending on how a woman wears the waste beads and walks, they can display whether the woman is chaste or provocative. Women may wear beads simply because they find them fashionable, feel beautiful, sensuous, sexy, are more aware of stomach and posture which helps maintain weight and figure, feel a sense of African heritage or pride. If you are going to wear such beads, due to not knowing whether those who made them performed a ritual or cast a spell on them, it would probably be best to make your own or purchase them from a trusted seller. Though I do not wear waste beads, I love jewelry. As a precaution, I pray to break any witchcraft off any clothing, jewelry, that I purchase. I highly suggest this. I also do not buy and throw away anything the Holy Spirit highlights to me as possibly being dedicated, incapable of being cleansed, and is just downright idolatrous and does not need to be in my house or on my body.

HYPNOTISM, MESMERISM, & THE NEW WITCHCRAFT (HYPNOSIS & ALTERED STATES OF CONSCIOUSNESS)

According to dictionary.com, *hypnosis* is *"the induction of a state of consciousness in which a person apparently loses the power of voluntary action and is highly responsive to suggestion or direction. Its use in therapy, typically to recover suppressed memories or to allow modification of behavior by suggestion, has been revived but is still controversial.* Memories can be accessed all the way back to birth until the present age.

In the New Age Movement, many people engage in self-hypnosis and hypnotize one another. They believe they can access their spiritual core or greater self, and some may be able to communicate with their spirit guides and other beings on the Other Side. The Other Side can be heaven or other perspectives of life after death, depending on the person's beliefs.

TAROT CARDS

Tarot cards (78 deck of cards) was created in the 15th century Europe as a regular card game like bridge called *trionfi*, and later named *tarocchi* or *tarock*. It became a witchcraft practice of divination, fortune telling, and tarot card readings, in the 17th century when occult decks were created for these reasons. Many participated in this witchcraft practice at that time, however, Frenchman Jean-Baptise Alliette published the first definitive guide to tarot card reading. His guide provided information for utilizing beliefs in astronomy and the four elements to read people's lives. In 1909, Rider-Waite deck, updated the cards and including information on the meaning of each card and how to read them. Rider-Waite deck was updated again in 1970 with a guide revision by Stephen Kaplan. Psychic, mystic, and occult demon dealers provided a tool of divination that unlock the future of people's lives through occult practices.

The tarot reading begins with the demon dealer engaging in questioning conversation to gain entail on their prey. The pack of cords are cut or touched then spread face down on a table in a spread pattern. A card is chosen then the demon dealer begins to construct information based on the entail they have gathered during the conversation and the familiar spirits, frequencies, and airways, they are connecting with through their third eye into the second heavens.

Some psychics deem themselves Christians as claim God uses them to foretell the future with these cards. Some declared Christians have created altered versions of tarot cards. They use them in their ministries under the guise of evangelism, prophecy, and providing enlightenment or encouragement to individuals.

Foretelling the future is biblical and is known as prophecy. Enlightenment and encouragement are also part of the prophetic gift and can be used for evangelism and discipleship. However, prophecy should come from God and his ordained prophets and what is spoken is not derived through Tatar card readings, third eyes, divination, psychic powers, or witchery. The Bible tells us not to be anxious for anything, particularly about the future for God will take care of us. He also provides guidance for those who are in relationship with him.

Many psychics operate in clairvoyance and telepathy. Some psychics may have prophetic callings, but unless they repent, leave this lifestyle, and live for God, they are not of him. They are receiving their revelation from the second heaven and from the questions they are asking the person they are providing services too. This information is more soulish and clever manipulation accompanied with witchcraft tactics tied to demons who assist to bring situations to pass so that people will believe in its workings and keep paying money to acquire psychic readings. Demons have also gained access to the person's life and now are operating in other ways to stronghold the person to the demonic kingdom and keep them bound in witchcraft practices. Some believers have resulted in calling themselves psychic Christians and are even being accepted in some Christian ministries. Psychic workings will never be accepted by God and is not a practice of prophecy or any of the gifts of the spirit listed in 1Corinthians 12 or offices of fivefold ministry as found in *Ephesians 4*.

Galatians 6:7 *Be not deceived; God is not mocked: for whatsoever a man soweth, that shall he also reap.*

<u>Deceit</u> is *planaō* in Greek and means:

1. to (properly, cause to) roam (from safety, truth, or virtue),
2. go astray, deceive, err, seduce, wander, be out of the way,
3. to cause to stray, to lead astray, lead aside from the right way, to go astray, wander, roam about,

4. metaph.
    1. to lead away from the truth,
    2. to lead into error,
    3. to deceive, to be led into error, to be led aside from the path of virtue, to go astray, sin,
    4. to sever or fall away from the truth, of heretics,
    5. to be led away into error and sin.

I use this scripture because we like to think that we can sow to the demonic realm or sow in witchcraft and reap God benefits, but this is deception and leads us away from God. It mocks God and his kingdom; to resist being mocked, God blatantly rejects these operations. There is no way around reaping witchcraft and demon oppression when engaging in witchcraft. It may appear to produce good and godly results, but it is wickedness rooted in vain idolatry.

CLAIRVOYANCE
Clairvoyance is the supernatural ability to gain information from an object, person, location, or physical event and to know a thing by way of a divine or mystical power. This knowledge is beyond one's sensory perception or natural intellect. Operators of this practice are known as clairvoyant, which means "one who sees clearly." Despite this ideology, the person is seeing through a third eye using imagery, hearing from the second heaven, which is controlled by demonic forces, or is seeing and hearing through their natural senses.

CHAIN LETTERS
A chain letter is a message that strives to convince the recipient to make several copies or to pass along a certain number of the messages to recipients for the purposes of receiving good luck, favor, love, success, fortune, protection, a specific desired item, or venture. These chain letters are sent via mail, email, spam mail, website add-ons, text messages, private messenger, etc. It is perceived that if the chain letter is not adhered to, then a curse will ensure upon the person not obeying the message. With the rise of social media and an effort to spread the gospel, or to get people who are devout Christians to succumb to witchcraft mixture, a spiritual twist is now being added to the chain letter. An example of a chain letter would be as followed, "send this to ten people and you will be blessed." The person who started the chain letter is often a witch who perceives themselves to be a good witch or an evil witch wants to soul tie people to them and their idol gods. Either way, witches pray what they call "good spells or good luck fortune telling" over chain letters and tarot cards. The blessings attached to the affirmations and perceived good prayers written on those messages, cards, posts, letters, ads, are completed by perceived good spirits who are demonic spirits that want access to a person's life, so they draw and bind other demons and demonic assignments to them. These demons work together to release challenging situations into a person's life such that the person must keep relying on these psychic powers for "luck" and "blessings." Those who participate are usually ignorant to the fact that the chain letter is not a harmless practice and that by participating, they just released a witchcraft spell into the person's life they sent it too. No matter how much it uses the word pray or blessings, its root is not God, it is demons. And

there is no such thing as good witch, good witchcraft, or a good demon. The only good spirit is the Holy Spirit of God. Every other demon is an imposter and have a demonic plan of attack beyond a person's "pray this prayer over ten people and you will get a new car" witchcraft blessing. It is deception – witchcraft deception that sacrifices the person and their life to idol gods.

PALM READING

Palm reading is fortune telling through the study and utilization of the palm. Palm practitioners can be called palmists, hand readers, hand analysts, or chorologists. They believe they can tell the fortune, success, and further through the reading of the lines, bumps, and marks on a person's hand. Palm reading is a pagan practice rooted in Greek methodology and is considered divination. Much of its practice is rooted in deception and channeling of demonic spirits through psychic powers, while providing vague interpretations by generalizing, and reading a person's emotions and body languages.

DOLLS

Often connect to Haitian and Louisiana voodoo priest, Juju Dolls - Voodoo Dolls - Lucky Dolls - Hoodoo Dolls - Poppy Dolls – Poppet Dolls (also known as popping, moppet, mommet, or pippy), are generally used in folk magic and dark witchcraft, but New Agers have increased in this practice. These dolls are generally made to represent a person and are oftentimes fashioned to look like makeshift dummies of a person. Sometimes an item, body fluid, hair, etc. from that person is collect, often unbeknownst to the person, and pinned to the doll as a point of contact. Spells and rituals are cast via sympathetic magic and incantations; pins are stuck in the doll to solidify the spell or inflict pain, control, enticement, to a particular body part or to the person in general. Some witches make a living making these dolls and selling them to others. The doll can be made from carved root, grain or corn shafts, fruit, paper, wax, potatoes, clay, branches, or clothes stuffed with herbs. It is not uncommon for people to find these dolls on their property, particularly their chimney, hidden in bushes, or if there is a blatant offense where the witch wants the person to know they are being bewitched, at the front or back door. These dolls are extremely dangerous because high level witchcraft and dark magic is attached to their workings. People can feel the pains and overpowering that is occurring through them. Often the curse must be broken before the person can be from of the control of these witchcraft attacks.

NUMEROLOGY

Numerology is any concept that there is a divine or mystical connection, relationship, message, confirmation, or revelation between a number, coinciding events, and a divine power. Numerology is also the study of the numerical value of the letters in words, names, and ideas. Numerology has been a widespread practice in Africa, Asia, and America since ancient times. Some believers use numerology to predict the present and future of their own lives or the lives of others, reveal or confirm prayers, dreams, visions, inquiries, or prophecies, receive stock, trade, and numbers for business and investment endeavors, or to decode the Bible. Some believers will take numbers and match them to Bible chapters and verses and use them as a sign that God is speaking a message through that scripture. Many times, they are using this method at their own leading and not through the direction of God. Many believers will use the number of the day, of the month, or the year to speak a message for prophecy they claim is from God. Some will see repetitive times on a clock, be awaken or alerted at certain times of the day, see the same numbers over and over in the same or different locations, and contend God is speaking a message to them. Some believers practice numerology called Enneagram, which is an ancient occult practice depicting nine possible personality types using a numerical typology classification grid.

Diagram 8.1 Personality Styles

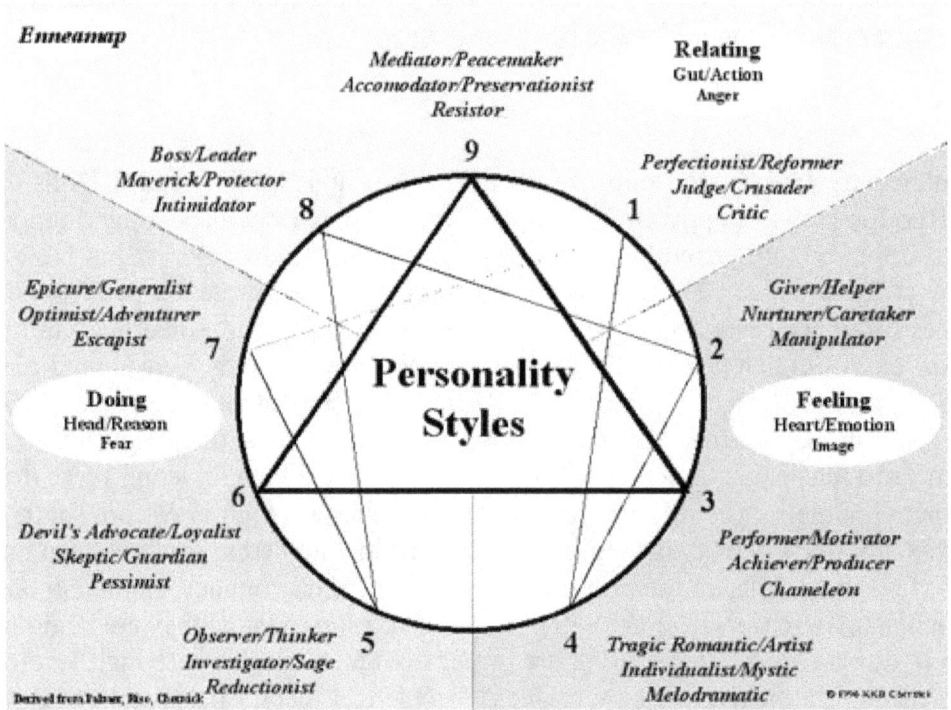

Source: Google Images, 2021

If God can speak through a donkey (Numbers 22:21), he can surely speak through Numbers. We have a host of scriptures where God is speaking through numbers. Generally, when numbers were used in the Bible wasn't it symbolic? The main point was to point to God or Jesus Christ as a type of shadow of the coming Messiah. For instance, the significance of "3" was the foretelling of Jesus rising from the grave. We also find that there is a foundational biblical connection between God and numbers and even colors that can be verified in the Bible. However, when this becomes to only or main way God speaks to a believer, there should be some exploration as to whether they have yielded to numerology, which is witchcraft divination, rather than hearing from God.

One consideration I noticed is that many believers who rely on numerology as the main method for hearing God,

- Have open doors to witchcraft.
- Engage in other witchcraft practices that they have justified as God.
- Have trouble hearing the voice of God.
- May equate every or most things as a sign from God and use numbers to further confirm this fact.
- Are constantly seeking confirmation of what God has already said because they do not fully trust their ability to hear him.
- May be insecure in their identity and relationship with God. Sometimes their insecurity manifest as pride, especially when they are striving to get you to believe that what they are presenting is of God.
- May worry and stress a lot about life experiences and is constantly seeking ways to avoid challenges while striving to get ahead of these issues.

Numerology tends to be used to provide a comfort that really is more vain or deceitful. It produces a dependence to use numerology to prove more that God is speaking rather than to seek God personally for revelation.

Zechariah 10:2 *For the teraphim (household idols) have spoken vanity (emptiness, falsity, and futility) and the diviners have seen a lie and the dreamers have told false dreams; they comfort in vain. Therefore the people go their way like sheep; they are afflicted and hurt because there is no shepherd.*

I encourage a strong relationship and practice with hearing and experiencing God without any dependence on anything outside his voice, his presence, and his scriptures. Let these three avenues be the way that you hear him and other ways be at his leading.

ANGEL NUMBERS

In numerology, seeing a consecutive sequence of numbers like 555, 999, 5:55pm, 3:33pm seeing the same time consecutively, being awakened at the same time repetitiously, is called Angel numbers. Numerologists and witchcraft practitioners believe each number is connected to vibrational energy or frequency that is providing a sign, insight, or direction from the universe or some other higher power. There is a grid that contains the meaning of each number that a numerologist or witchcraft practitioner uses to interpret the message that is being sent to the person. In addition to these numbers appearing as demonic forces aka high powers manifest them in a person's life, people can also meditate, offer sacrifices, or wish for numbers from their higher power. This is the reason it is so important for believers to make sure they are not just assuming sequences of numbers are a sign from God. Unless God is actually directing this act, a person could be receiving information from demons and not from God. A person could be directing their lives, the lives of others, and entire ministries, from the guidance of demons rather than God.

SUN & MOON WORSHIP (SUNBATHING)
Witchcraft theology holds the idea that sunlight can be used to increase one's energy infusion and enter a state of greater vibration upon frequencies and higher light of consciousness. There is also the presumption that there are codes in the sun and the moon to cause divine or mystical awakening, divine intelligence, or that the sun and the moon are gods within themselves that should be worshipped. There is a custom in witchcraft called sunbathing where a person spends a specific amount of time in the sunshine to commune with the sun and receive energy and enlightenment. This is also the reason that ancient and devoted yoga practitioners tend to have their classes or engage in yoga at different times of the day. They believe that as they engage in yoga, it is offering up worship through the different techniques unto the sun to evoke enlightenment, higher levels of consciousness, ascending into increased dimensions of mastery related to the practice, produce healing, health, wellness, wealth, supernatural powers, protection, etc. though the sun does have some health benefits, worship of the sun itself is idolatrous and forbidden in the Bible.

The theology of moon worship is centered on the concept that the rhythm of time embodies the cycle and operation of the moon and reveals specific messages, enlightenment of higher consciousness, energy, and protection. There is also a perception that the moon symbolizes immortality, eternity, enlightenment, or dark dimensions of living and wickedness, and is its own deity that should be worshiped for these purposes. Like sun worship, moon worship is also forbidden by God and should not be practiced.

Ezekiel 8:16-18 And he brought me into the inner court of the LORD's house, and, behold, at the door of the temple of the LORD, between the porch and the altar, were about five and twenty men, with their backs toward the temple of the LORD, and their faces toward the east; and they worshipped the sun toward the east. Then he said unto me, Hast thou seen this, O son of man? Is it a light thing to the house of Judah that they commit the abominations which they commit here? for they have filled the land with violence, and have returned to provoke me to anger: and, lo, they put the branch to their nose. Therefore will I also deal in fury: mine eye shall not spare, neither will I have pity: and though they cry in mine ears with a loud voice, yet will I not hear them.

Deuteronomy 4:19 And beware not to lift up your eyes to heaven and see the sun and the moon and the stars, all the host of heaven, and be drawn away and worship them and serve them, those which the Lord your God has allotted to all the peoples under the whole heaven.

Deuteronomy 17:2-5 "If there is found in your midst, in any of your towns, which the Lord your God is giving you, a man or a woman who does what is evil in the sight of the Lord your God, by transgressing His covenant, and has gone and served other gods and worshiped them, or the sun or the moon or any of the heavenly host, which I have not commanded, and if it is told you and you have heard of it, then you shall inquire thoroughly. Behold, if it is true and the thing certain that this detestable thing has been done in Israel, read more.

Job 31:26-28 If I have looked at the sun when it shone or the moon going in splendor, and my heart became secretly enticed, and my hand threw a kiss from my mouth, that too would have been an iniquity calling for judgment, for I would have denied God above.

2Kings 23:5-11 *He did away with the idolatrous priests whom the kings of Judah had appointed to burn incense in the high places in the cities of Judah and in the surrounding area of Jerusalem, also those who burned incense to Baal, to the sun and to the moon and to the constellations and to all the host of heaven. He brought out the Asherah from the house of the Lord outside Jerusalem to the brook Kidron, and burned it at the brook Kidron, and ground it to dust, and threw its dust on the graves of the common people. He also broke down the houses of the male cult prostitutes which were in the house of the Lord, where the women were weaving hangings for the Asherah.read more.*

Jeremiah 8:1-2 *"At that time," declares the Lord, "they will bring out the bones of the kings of Judah and the bones of its princes, and the bones of the priests and the bones of the prophets, and the bones of the inhabitants of Jerusalem from their graves. They will spread them out to the sun, the moon and to all the host of heaven, which they have loved and which they have served, and which they have gone after and which they have sought, and which they have worshiped. They will not be gathered or buried; they will be as dung on the face of the ground.*

It is time to mature and overthrow the true enemies of God. Especially those that would release doctrines upon the wind that would SHIFT people from the truth of God.

TRANSCENDENTAL MEDITATION (TM) Transcendental Meditation movement was created by Maharishi Mahesh Yogi in India in the mid-1950s. It is reported to be one of the most widely practiced and widely research meditation techniques. Transcendental Meditation refers to a specialized type of silent mantra meditation that enables a person to achieve a state of perfect stillness and consciousness. A mantra is a word, phrase, or formula, chanted, sung, or meditated on as an incantation or prayer. A mantra can also serve as mastering manifestation where through higher consciousness the person gains the strategy and confidence to produce forth whatever it is that they are meditating on. The practitioners sit in silence with eyes closed, for 15-20 minutes a day to perfect their skill of peace, while achieving higher dimensions of silence and consciousness through one's own self-awareness. The focus is self as it relates to the mantra that is meditated on, the person is engaging with their own ideologies and those that are opened through a third eye in their higher consciousness rather than focusing on God and him providing a focus for peace, stillness, strategy, and manifestation.

ALCHEMY
Alchemy is an ancient Egyptian practice that was sort of a forerunner of science and chemistry. In ancient times, alchemists would attempt to turn metal and lead into gold. They would also strive to create jewelry, potions, perfumes, medicines, and embalming substances. Alchemists were not necessarily scientists or chemists but were witches, sorcerers, magicians, and mystics. They used witchcraft practices founded in the occult wisdom, paganism, and sorcery, along with inventions and science like activities to produce their products and methodologies. Their witchcraft was rooted in complex spiritual ideologies of astrology, numerology, hermeticism which pagans viewed as the world's most ancient, sacred, and desirable wisdom. Kabbalah, which is a pagan occult organization, believes knowledge is received from God only by a

select few. Rosicrucianism is wisdom rooted in a mixture of religious doctrines and occult practices. They believed in a universal spirit, that all metal was alive, grew inside the earth, and had certain potentials and powers. Alchemists also believed that metals that were of lesser value were a spiritual or physical immature form of higher valued metals such as gold; and that medals had the potential to grow into spiritual maturity and value.

In addition to metal workings, alchemists practiced striving to purify people's spirit using techniques of higher consciousness through dreams and visions to encounter and gain divine wisdom from their universal spirit. They operated on the premise of experiencing dimensions of consciousness SHIFTING the lead or immature value of people into spiritual maturity and value by turning it into gold. This ideology assumes that only people who have attained higher consciousness possess the knowledge of the universe to transform earthly things into gold, into another form, while awarding the practitioner with immortality, supreme enlightenment, and perfectionism as fine gold. As they attain this knowledge, they receive enlightenment to create the ultimate object of alchemy called the "philosopher's stone," "the tincture," or "the powder." The philosopher's stone is said to be a mythical substance that possesses the ability to change any metal into gold or silver and, according to some practitioners, to cure all diseases and prolong life indefinitely. Alchemy has resurfaced in modern times with the rise of the new age movement. Modern alchemists are focused on operating in magical powers to turn one thing into another. And even to turn themselves into another form. They are committed to learning and practicing the ancient ideologies along with new methods to attain dimensions of consciousness that enables them to the operate in magic and sorcery with supernatural power and manifestation.

POTION & SALVES
In mythology, potions are generally made by a magician, witch, or fairy, and contains magical properties. Potions is the Latin word *potus* which means to "drink or drinking." The potions are used to cause people to fall in love, to lure or cause attraction, to produce luck, success, healing of the sick, for changing someone's appearance, even to the point of making them beautiful, more desirable, ugly, less desirable, prolonging life, cause immortality, etc. Potions can also be made with the intent to incite harm, such as to poison someone, cause bad luck, to oppress or possess someone. Potions are often used in voodoo and Santeria witchcraft, root working, and incantations.

The making of the potions involves alchemy and, in the professional world, is viewed as science in this modern day and age. We see alchemy utilized in the making of medicines, skin care cosmetics, and perfumes. Many of these products are created with the intention to lure customers, and to provide some form of impression, presumption, need, change, healing, cure, to make them feel connected and even dependent on the product so they will keep purchasing it. The key is knowing what properties to use utilizing the correct effective ingredients to produce the perfect intended potion.

Many potions created in households are not created by scientists. These magicians, witches, or fairies have taken it upon themselves to hone their craft. For health, safety, and biblical reasons, potions should not be considered a substance that believers partake of or give to others. Such potions can be extremely dangerous due to the ingredients and the spells and rituals that are cast upon them. Throughout history some ingredients include Spanish fly, the nightshade plant, cannabis, and opium, herbs, plants, food, household products, elements from the earth, medals, body fluids, and particles from the practitioners, customer, or the victim is sometimes used along with many other unknown substances. Not to mention, you may think you are receiving a great smelling perfume or medicine but can be ingesting a demonic and physically dangerous potion.

ROOT WORKERS OF ROOT DOCTORS
Roots give support to plants from the ground. They must be watered and nurtured to sustain their productivity. In witchcraft, root means to assert control over someone or something. Root working originated between the seventeenth and eighteenth century in South Africa and was brought to the South of the United States via those who were part of the slave trade. Practitioners of root workings are called root workers or root doctors. They are known among the African American culture as traditional healers and conjurers who live in the rural, black South parts of America. They use herbs, plants, potions, spells, magic rituals, black magic, white magic, voodoo, voodoo dolls, hoodoo, smudging, dirt from graveyards which is called goofer or goober dust, animals, animal parts, to aide or to harm recipients depending on what they or their customers desire. Through these practices, they seek to heal, cure, provide protection, eradicate injustices, control their prey, break poverty, produce success, business advancement, obtain money, property, favor, commune with the dead, attract and seduce love and lovers, etc. When seeking to do harm the phrase "put a root on you," was used. It meant a spell, ritual, or curse was going to be released using supernatural powers. Often an item or something from that person is used in the root working. This can be a piece of hair, fingernail, unwashed clothing, bodily fluids, skin particles along with herbs and other substances alchemized together with the supernatural ritual, curse, spell, to form a root. Sometimes making sure the root is placed in the person's home, office, property, etc., is needful for it to be a point of contact for the root doctor to continue spell casting and sending workings and demonic forces to bind the recipient. Also burying the roots at specific crossroads and locations is part of the root working effectiveness.

Some indications that a root may be put on you:

- Being attracted to someone that is not your husband or wife that is not good for you or appear to have power over you.
- When the relationship is totally sexual, and you cannot get enough of the person.
- Being control by your husband or wife and no matter what you do, you cannot break their powers over you.
- When you seem to not be able to make decisions without the person's opinion and often it is to their benefit and is drawing you of your time, finances, energy, emotions, identity.
- When you dream realm constantly evolve around the person.
- Having constant bad luck even in situations that were in your favor.
- Constantly obtaining money and material goods but losing it whether to poor habits, bad investments, or unforeseen circumstances.

- Constantly feeling like something is following you or watching you.
- When there seems to be a dark presence abound you and your atmosphere for no apparent reason and that you cannot seem to get rid of.
- When you have constant dreams of dying or even encounters of near-death experiences.
- Ailments that feel like prickings and stabbings - that have no underlying root cause.
- Finding salt incantations and ley lines, animals or animal parts, voodoo dolls, potions, ritual sites, in and around your property.

POLTERGEISTS

Poltergeist is a demonic spirit that haunts people and locations, causes physical disturbances, and incites fear and terror. These demonic spirits can also operate as familiar spirits where they appear looking like family members, loved ones, or familiar persons. They will attempt to commune with people so they can gain access to their lives or even haunt them. Poltergeists spirits are known to follow people around, appear and disappear, move things around, make messes, pinch, hit, punch, trip, harass, and torment people. They may constantly cause disturbing or tormenting sounds like knocking, banging, start fires, turn lights on and off, shake beds and furniture, open and close doors, and windows, make impressions on walls, furniture to demonstrate they are a true manifestation, appear as a mist or ghostly type figure to scar its victims. Sometimes open doors to witchcraft, sin issues, generational curses, dedications, and covenants, ancestral worship, not properly grieving and letting go of loved ones who have passed on, root workings, astral projectors and open doors in the dream and sleep realm, allow poltergeists spirits access to one's life.

A location can be dedicated or may have been used in pagan, occult, witchcraft, sadistic, murderous, or extreme ungodly practices which can cause poltergeists spirits to assert authority over the land and atmosphere. Sometimes poltergeists' spirits will attack those who are called to witchcraft and occult realms of ministry. They will attempt to weary, drain, terrorize, make fearful, and cause psychological warfare, to run the person out of their purpose and calling. It is important for those called to this level of ministry to be discerning and learn and operate in their authority over these poltergeists where they assert dominion in the realms and spheres God has called them to govern as it relates to principalities and powers. Any open doors in people's lives and generations, a cleansing of the land by breaking curses, dedications and covenants, and casting poltergeists out of people's lives and the land is vital to freeing people and spheres of these demons. We have power over all the power of the enemy and have authority to put the devil out, while SHIFTING in the freedom and kingdom of God.

Psalm 23:4 Even though I walk through the valley of the shadow of death, I will fear no evil, for You are with me; Your rod and Your staff, they comfort me.

Psalm 91:5-6 Thou shalt not be afraid for the terror by night; nor for the arrow that flieth by day; nor for the pestilence that walketh in darkness; nor for the destruction that wasteth at noonday.

Matthew 18:18-20 Verily I say unto you, Whatsoever ye shall bind on earth shall be bound in heaven: and whatsoever ye shall loose on earth shall be loosed in heaven.

Luke 10:19 *Behold, I give unto you power to tread on serpents and scorpions, and over all the power of the enemy: and nothing shall by any means hurt you.*

Ephesians 6:12 *For we wrestle not against flesh and blood, but against principalities, against powers, against the rulers of the darkness of this world, against spiritual wickedness in high places.*

An example of wizardry is the "Harry Potter Series." Harry Potter is a series of seven novels turned into movies written by J.K. Rowling. Harry Potter is about a young boy who learns on his eleventh birthday that he is the orphaned son of two powerful wizards and possesses unique magical powers of his own. He enters a life of wizardry by being summons from his life as an unwanted child to become a student at Hogwarts, an English boarding school for wizards. He becomes friends with several students who help him use his magical powers to discover the truth about his parents' mysterious deaths. Those series have been key to ushering wizardry in the lives of our youth and cultivating a fascination with magic, sorcery, and divination.

IDOLATROUS RATIONALE
People will quote ***Titus 1:15***, *Unto the pure all things are pure: but unto them that are defiled and unbelieving is nothing pure; but even their mind and conscience is defiled,* to defend these curious art practices. This scripture does not mean we can take something God has deem sinful, idolatrous, and witchery, and purify it. Let us explore the entire context to which this scripture is written.

Titus 1:10-16 *For there are many unruly and vain talkers and deceivers, specially they of the circumcision: Whose mouths must be stopped, who subvert whole houses, teaching things which they ought not, for filthy lucre's sake. One of themselves, even a prophet of their own, said, The Cretians are alway liars, evil beasts, slow bellies. This witness is true. Wherefore rebuke them sharply, that they may be sound in the faith; Not giving heed to Jewish fables, and commandments of men, that turn from the truth. Unto the pure all things are pure: but unto them that are defiled and unbelieving is nothing pure; but even their mind and conscience is defiled. They profess that they know God; but in works they deny him, being abominable, and disobedient, and unto every good work reprobate.*

What are you professing with your mouth, but your actions state otherwise? What we are contending is pure because we want to hold onto it, are oppressed by the spirits attached to it, or we have convinced ourselves we can purify it, God is strict in declaring it is abominable, disobedient, and lending us to being reprobate. I rather relinquish a practice than to risk being reprobate. When we enter a reprobate stage, God gives us over to our own will and desires. We know longer experience the conviction of his spirit and believe, because we have no conviction, God approves of what we are doing. But really, God has left us to our own demise, and is no longer warning us of our actions.

Witchcraft will be released at an enormous rate in the coming days. There will be divination and dimensions of witchcraft unveiled that the earth has not seen yet. There is an increase of people becoming witches and warlocks and this is becoming a norm. There is and will continue to be an increase of people declaring they are Christian witches and warlocks; this will be received as the lines of biblical standards become blurred, devalued, and outlawed. Vain hope will sway you if you cannot discern or know the truth regarding witchcraft. It is time out for fearing witchcraft, witches, warlocks, and scared to confront and overthrow it.

Ephesians 4:14 *That we henceforth be no more children, tossed to and fro, and carried about with every wind of doctrine, by the sleight of men, and cunning craftiness, whereby they lie in wait to deceive.*

The Amplified Bible *So that we are no longer children [spiritually immature], tossed back and forth [like ships on a stormy sea] and carried about by every wind of [shifting] doctrine, by the cunning and trickery of [unscrupulous] men, by the deceitful scheming of people ready to do anything [for personal profit].*

Chapter 9

THE ETHNICITY OF JESUS

I admit that I am so in love with Jesus Christ, he could be blue green, and I would still be yelling "JESUS IS MY MESSIAH." In my encounters with Jesus Christ, he is blazing with such glory and light, I only see a silhouette of his human image. This does not mean ethnicity is not important. Ethnicity is particularly valuable; especially to the Millennials, Generation Z, and New Agers, who have taken a rebel cause to expose the church of generational sins and errored teachings. They are tired of being dealt a Christianity that is rarely lived by those who have proceeded them, and that is full of obvious falsehoods used to brainwash and suppress generations of people, particularly minority people.

Ethnicity is particularly important because it aids in expressing our unique God identity. I love that God made us all different races and shades, yet said we were ALL created in his image.

Genesis 1:26-27 *And God said, Let us make man in our image, after our likeness: and let them have dominion over the fish of the sea, and over the fowl of the air, and over the cattle, and over all the earth, and over every creeping thing that creepeth upon the earth. So God created man in his own image, in the image of God created he him; male and female created he them.*

God not only made us ALL in his image, but he also made us ALL equal to one another.

Acts 17:25-28 *Neither is worshipped with men's hands, as though he needed any thing, seeing he giveth to all life, and breath, and all things; And hath made of one blood all nations of men for to dwell on all the face of the earth, and hath determined the times before appointed, and the bounds of their habitation; That they should seek the Lord, if haply they might feel after him, and find him, though he be not far from every one of us: For in him we live, and move, and have our being; as certain also of your own poets have said, For we are also his offspring.*

We are all God's offspring. Everything about us resides in his likeness and demonstrates an intricate part of him. For this reason, we should be able to embrace Jesus Christ as Lord and savior no matter what color he is. However, for the purposes of correcting erred teaching that has been commercialized for centuries. And has a vast of people rejecting him altogether or creating their own image of him, we must acknowledge truth, and teach truth to right this wrong.

For centuries, the western cultures have depicted Jesus Christ as a good looking, blue eyed, fair-skinned, bearded white man with long wavy light brown or blond hair. This image emerged in the Fourth century A.D. The concept derived from the influence of Greek and Roman gods, one significantly being the Greek god of Zeus. Though Greek and Roman methodology is rooted in idolatry, at that time, the focus was merely to demonstrate Jesus in his sovereignty as Lord and savior who sat on his heavenly throne after resurrecting from the cross. Over the years, this image has taken on different perspectives, one being used to deal a white Jesus to the world, while yielding the impressing that white is pure, supreme, and the best.

The Bible does not give a definitive description of the exact appearance of Jesus, but from what it does reveal, this portrayal is a facade - a falsehood - lie. Even in the last few years of the younger generation and new agers publicly denouncing this depiction, I have witnessed Caucasian Christians be appalled at the thought that Jesus is anything other than white. Others adamantly state that they know Jesus looks this way because they have had visitations of him. One person was an artist who have photographed and painted many pictures of the blue-eyed Jesus and thus, was refusing to consider that she may NOT have been encountering the true Jesus Christ.

2Corinthians 11:14 *And no marvel; for Satan himself is transformed into an angel of light.*

2Corinthians 11:4 *New Living Translation You happily put up with whatever anyone tells you, even if they preach a different Jesus than the one we preach, or a different kind of Spirit than the one you received, or a different kind of gospel than the one you believed.*

Demons mascaraing as God and revealing themselves in visions to saints. Hmmmm???

Saints believing the lie of white Jesus thus being deal an "other Jesus." Hmmmm???

Another possibility of the reason Jesus revealed himself to her in this manner is because that is what she was familiar with or could handle about him. Paul made the following confession which I believe reveals the heart of Jesus Christ that was within him.

1Corinthians 9:19:23 *Though I am free and belong to no one, I have made myself a slave to everyone, to win as many as possible. To the Jews I became like a Jew, to win the Jews. To those under the law I became like one under the law (though I myself am not under the law), so as to win those under the law. To those not having the law I became like one not having the law (though I am not free from God's law but am under Christ's law), so as to win those not having the law. To the weak I became weak, to win the weak. I have become all things to all people so that by all possible means I might save some. I do all this for the sake of the gospel, that I may share in its blessings.*

God did not put any emphasis on Jesus' appearance so to think that people would see and experience him in a form that resembles themselves is not farfetched. Especially as we consider how we were made in his image. *Isaiah 53:2* states the following about Jesus.

For he shall grow up before him as a tender plant, and as a root out of a dry ground: he hath no form nor comeliness; and when we shall see him, there is no beauty that we should desire him.

There was nothing unique or eccentrics about Jesus's natural appearance. I believe he was created this way so that man would not look on or be drawn in by his natural beauty but by his spirit man. God wanted people to be saved because they loved Jesus, not because of his looks.

History reveals that Jesus was a Palestinian Jewish man living in Galilee in the first century, so he would look more like a Jewish Galilean. Even as we would consider other scriptures that describe Jesus, they are more in relations to his heavenly form after he rose from the dead, than his natural manmade appearance.

Daniel 7:9 *As I looked, "thrones were set in place, and the Ancient of Days took his seat. His clothing was as white as snow; the hair of his head was white like wool.*

Revelation 1:14-18 *The hair on his head was white like wool, as white as snow, and his eyes were like blazing fire. His feet were like bronze glowing in a furnace, and his voice was like the sound of rushing waters. In his right hand he held seven stars, and coming out of his mouth was a sharp, double-edged sword. His face was like the sun shining in all its brilliance. When I saw him, I fell at his feet as though dead. Then he placed his right hand on me and said: "Do not be afraid. I am the First and the Last. I am the Living One; I was dead, and now look, I am alive for ever and ever! And I hold the keys of death and Hades.*

If we considered these heavenly perspectives as the natural appearance of Jesus, though his hair was white, the passages do not state Jesus was white. Neither does it say he was black. Jesus' hair was like wool. If we were to consider humans with wool hair, then Jesus hair could be that of an African ethnicity. Yet because it was white wool and Jesus was a young man, not an old man, this seems to be describing a more heavenly state than an ethnicity. Jesus' feet were bronze which would suggest a brown hue or sun-tanned type skin color. This could also be denoting a golden glory illusion. All of this is just a thought for searching.

Though we can debate whether these passages mean Jesus was Black, and even whether this was a divine depiction of Jesus and not a human illustration of him, we know he was not white. Based on Jesus' birthplace and generational heritage, he was most likely a brown-skinned, Middle Eastern Jew. He could have been anywhere from light to dark brown in skin color.

The most challenging issue regarding this insight is the refusal of it being embraced because of color. Africans and other ethnicities have worshipped, lived for, been martyred for Jesus Christ despite the false depiction they have been dealt for centuries. Yet, when asked to embrace a clear possible biblical reality that the white Jesus is a lie, and that Jesus may have been of a brown color, the concept is met with disgust, rejection, and the utilization of white supremacy and privilege to disregard this lie, the oppression, suppression, enslavement, abuse, and murder of African and other minority people through this lie, and the need for repentance and doctrinal correction regarding this false ideology. It is okay for the Black person to serve a blue-eyed Jesus, but not okay for a White person to embrace a Black Jesus. The other challenge is that some Africans, lie the Hebrew Israelites believe that Jesus is Black and only came to save those of Black descent, yet, the Bible clearly states that Jesus came to save world, which includes ALL mankind.

John 3:16 *For God so loved the world, that he gave his only begotten Son, that whosoever believeth in him should not perish, but have everlasting life.*

The fact is that the body of Christ must get to a point where truth is all they desire. Truth in their inward parts. And even with truth, they do not care if Jesus is a white with blue eyes or Black with a wool headed; they just want him - want to live in eternal covenant with him.

As we consider the rejection of him based on color, and the disregard of people based on color, Both Black and White Christians must explore whether they have created a gospel that depicts Jesus for what they have cultivated as their truth, rather than living divine truth in and through him. If this is the case, then we have created a Black and White idol called Jesus Christ. The commercialized images have become a gold cache that we refuse to destroy and will have consequences of change does not occur.

Deuteronomy 7:25 *The graven images of their gods you are to burn with fire; you shall not covet the silver or the gold that is on them, nor take it for yourselves, or you will be snared by it, for it is an abomination to the Lord your God.*

I would encourage White Christians to seek God regarding how to address this issue with their congregations and communities to bring true repentance concerning this issue into the body of Christ and their regions. As there is a humbling, acknowledging, and turning of the wrong that has been done regarding this false image, Black people will begin to heal and denounce the ideologies of Jesus only coming to save them versus all mankind. We must want to restore one another more than we want to hold on to a lie. The impact of white supremacy, privilege, slavery, and generational injustices that are rooted in Christianity and the usage of scriptures must be dealt with if we want to restore a new age generation to Jesus Christ.

Psalm 141:5 New King James Bible *Let the righteous strike me; It shall be a kindness. And let him rebuke me; It shall be as excellent oil; Let my head not refuse it. For still my prayer is against the deeds of the wicked.*

Galatians 6:1-2 *Brethren, if a man be overtaken in a fault, ye which are spiritual, restore such a one in the spirit of meekness; considering thyself, lest thou also be tempted. Bear ye one another's burdens, and so fulfil the law of Christ.*

Hebrews 12:13 *Make straight paths for your feet, so that the lame may not be debilitated, but rather healed.*

Decreeing this chapter provokes healing in the body of Christ and world at large. **SHIFT! SHIFT RIGHT NOW!**

Chapter 10
DEMON DEALING ORGANIZATIONS

OCCULTISM
Occultism involves different ideologies and practices surrounding beliefs, knowledge, and use of supernatural forces or beings, magic, divination, witchcraft, and alchemy. Occult practices include the ability to manipulate natural laws with the intent to navigate life experiences, produce luck, favor, fame, fortune, impact someone else's life, engage in wicked or evil practices. People form cults on all levels of society. On an extreme scale there are witchcraft occults that teach their practices, train people to be witches and warlocks, engage in witchcraft rituals, prayers, and operations. These groups may operate in secret creeds and codes that makes it difficult for people to leave for fear of retribution. Retribution can be fear of being hurt due to the violence and spells the cult participates in, as many cult leaders threaten the lives of their members. There is also the impression that spell work will be done towards the person to make their lives miserable and full of demonic opposition. People feel a sense of loss of self, innocence, trust, destiny, and community and fear of integrating back into mainstream society and family and relational structures. They experience guilt and shame regarding the belief systems and acts they have committed. Often people must be deprogrammed due to the dependence and inordinate dedication they have been groomed to have to the cult. They may experience post-traumatic stress disorder and other mental anxieties and disorders due to the trauma of being in the cult and leaving the cult. Intense counseling is needed to help such people be reintegrated into normal life and society.

Children and teenagers learn how to form pacts and cults via movies, cartoon, TV shows, media, music, videos, video games, books, websites, social media, online groups, influence of their peers, and even parents and loved ones. They will reenact incantations, rituals, and spells, that they learned from these platforms. They will cut one another and make blood covenants that can include sexual, pregnancy, suicide, and death. They will engage in self-injurious cutting and offer sacrifices to demons, idol gods, goddesses, the universe, and even their favorite Hollywood idols. Some children and teens have gone as far as being violent towards one another and even murder. They are often unsupervised in these practices, so it makes it easier for demonic forces to influence and overtake them. The lack of biblical principles and practices governing the home, leave children and teens vulnerable to exploring alternative pathways to understanding their existence and connecting to a higher power. As the New Age movement grows, the body of Christ will need to educate themselves on how occults operate and how to deliver and heal those involved in these practices.

SATANISM, IDOLATRY, & ATHEISM
Satanism entails a group of religious ideologies and philosophical beliefs based on Satan. These practices are designed to worship, serve, live, and build the kingdom of Satan. Satan is a fallen angel that God kicked out of heaven because he pridefully exalted himself above God, thus wanting to be God (***Ezekiel 28:1-26, Isaiah 14:2, John 12:31***). Satan has a host of other demons, fallen angels working with him, and people who revere his adverse, evils and wicked plans (***Jude 1:6, Revelation 12:1-17***). The Hebrew word for Satan is, "*adversary.*" Satan and

his disciples are against God, his people, and his principles. Once kicked out of heaven, he roams the earth seeking to kill, destroy, and devour the plans and purposes of God and God's people.

Job 1:6-7 Now there was a day when the sons of God came to present themselves before the LORD, and Satan came also among them. And the LORD said unto Satan, Whence comest thou? Then Satan answered the LORD, and said, From going to and fro in the earth, and from walking up and down in it.

John 10:10 The thief does not come except to steal, and to kill, and to destroy. I have come that they may have life, and that they may have it more abundantly.

John 8:44 You are of your father the devil, and your will is to do your father's desires. He was a murderer from the beginning, and has nothing to do with the truth, because there is no truth in him. When he lies, he speaks out of his own character, for he is a liar and the father of lies.

2Corinthians 4:4 In whom the god of this world hath blinded the minds of them which believe not, lest the light of the glorious gospel of Christ, who is the image of God, should shine unto them.

There are Satanist churches in various parts of the nation and the world, with the initial public church of Satan being founded in 1966 by Anton Lavey. Before this, Satanists practiced in private undisclosed settings or witchcraft covens as they were not considered an organized religion. The leaders of these sects call themselves high priests. Some extreme Satanists are dangerous, as they are into very dark witchcraft and magic that includes animal, baby, and human sacrificing, and wicked behaviors. Some Satanists may just be ordinary people. Some of them claim not to worship Satan at all, yet are atheistic, agnostic, or deistic, as they do not believe in a higher god or any religious doctrines. Those that do gather, claim to attend the church of Satan due to its ability to allow them to be free thinkers who desire to find their own way in life. The church of Satan has their own bible, religious creeds, and doctrines. They claim not to promote evil but humanistic values that empower self-assertion, extreme individualism and egoism, rebellion against unjust authority, vital existence that reject the concept of heaven, and undefiled wisdom that is not impacted by societal or religious doctrines. They host seminars and rituals such as the Black Mass, satanic weddings, and funerals. They are anti-Christ in nature, and whether extremists, or subtle followers, they are against God.

Matthew 12:30 He who is not with Me is against Me, and he who does not gather with Me scatters abroad.

The founder, LaVey, who died in 1997, was a notorious Satanist. One of his most famous publicized rituals was the satanic baptism of his daughter Zeneca Schreck in 1967. She was three years old at the time. LaVey cast spells over her, while dedicating her to Satan. There is a lot of controversy around the practices of LaVey and the church of Satan. However, there is no doubt that there is a group of extreme Satanists that engage in satanic ritual abuse that dates all the way back to the Bible days. Satanic ritual abuse includes the abduction and breeding of children for human sacrifice, pornography, and prostitution. Women can also be chosen, groomed, abducted for this reason, while also being used in satanic altar rituals that are usually sexual and sadistic in natural. Women and children are viewed as the purist and most powerful sacrifices offered to Satan. Extreme high priest will even kill them as sacrifices unto Satan in exchange for power, fame, and fortune.

New Agers will reject these premises as though they want to be part of the Satanists movement, they do not want to be associate with the extreme workings of this demonic religion. However, there is no way around its roots and practices and how they are anti-God and evil. On the surface the ideologies can appear harmless but the more involved a person becomes, the darker the ideologies and practices are.

GOTH AND EMO MOVEMENT

Since the culture of Goths have changed since its origination in the 18th century, I am only going to address the modern-day subculture. Goth subculture began in the United Kingdom in the late 1980s by Gothic rock fans and began to spread to other parts of the world, especially the United States. The music styles of goth include, gothic rock, death rock, post-punk, cold wave, dark wave, and ethereal wave. Goth culture also draw ideologies and dark concepts from B movies, Gothic literature, horror films, vampire cults and traditional mythology. Their culture has taken on cultural and doctrinal mythologies from Celtic mythology, Christian mythology, Egyptian mythology and their gods, some traditional paganism, and witchcraft practices. Such mixture makes it difficult to pinpoint what Goths believe. Many Goths form their own belief systems from these mythologies and tailor make what their Goth ideologies to their personal identities.

Generally, Goths are drawn to the dark and mysterious people, places, things, and spheres. They tend to wear black clothing, make up, accessories, fingernail polish, and hair color. This style of clothing is usually punk, new wave, or New Romantic fashion that take on the likeness of Victorian, Edwardian, and Belle Époque eras of time. It is not uncommon for men to dress more androgynous such that they are gender blending fashions of clothing, women accessories, make up, and skirts. Women may dress very sexy, utilizing short skirts, lingerie type attire, fishnet stockings, and corsets. There tends to be a resistance against conventional gender roles in behavior and style and have a greater openness to homosexual activities, courting roles, and lifestyles. Initially, traditional Goths were into bizarre and deviant sexual practices such as polyamorous, bondage acts, sadomasochism, and queer activities, but as Goths have evolved, these practices have been rejected by many new age goths.

Goths are drawn to dark comedy, movies, writings, mystic activities, and video games. Goths are often intelligent, unique, artistic, realists, romantics, and do not fit into mainstream groups. They possess great leadership and genius level qualities, yet there need for love and belonging, cause them to be drawn to other Goths and likeminded individuals. The dark practices they are drawn too and difficulty fitting into popular culture tends to be the reason they experience gloominess, depression, sadness, and loneliness.

Emo culture is a coming of age, millennial New age mythology that surfaced with the population of social media are 2015. It is sparked by Emo music that emphasizes loud, boisterous, highly emotional, or personal turbulence, behaviors, attitudes, and values. Themes is the emo culture include despair, depression, heart break, sensitivity and easily triggered, introversion, and self-loathing. Emos tend to be drawn to extreme violence, hardcore punk rock, goth like culture, beliefs, and fashion. Usually, emo practitioners have a strong dislike, hatred, and distrust for humankind; are angry at society, at someone, or about life issues; are rebelling against laws, rules, and regulations that they believe violate how they feel, think, or believe. Such emotional and soul wound issues cause a major gravitation to emo culture, to darkness, emotional instability, self-harming, and suicidal tendencies.

Though some Goths and Emos worship the devil or engage in activities that are dark, demonic, and full of witchcraft, many of them are not necessarily seeking to be devil worshipper. Most Goths and Emos, especially youth, confused or searching for who they truly are. They are intrigued by goth culture and could also be experiencing a demonic oppression that is using their life challenges to lure them into such dark practices. Generally, there is an unmet need, void, or desire for personal clarity, and they are seeking fulfill it. Patience is key when ministering and seeking to reach someone who is into or interested in goth as being overly judgmental, pushy, controlling, will draw them further into the culture. Being there for them, seeking to understand and identify their desires, needs, and voids, seeking to understand their interest in Goth, emo, and dark concepts, creating opportunities and a support system that makes them feel loved, valued, and included. Pray and ask God to reveal the open doors that are drawing them to dark things and to socializing with these cultures. There could be a generational propensity to witchcraft, pagan, and idolatrous practices. There could be a generational curse, destiny killing spirit, or dark oppressive spirit at work. There could be an open door due to the music, movies, video games, online and social influences and relationships the person is engaging in. These areas need to be dealt with in consistent prayer via intercession and spiritual warfare before addressing the person directly. Trying to engage in prayer and imposing biblical views on the person without a godly strategy will most likely make the person resistant, guarded, and closed off. They will be more willing to engage in these practices if you live before them, accept them as they are, and allow them to be drawn to the light that is within you. Spend time studying the scriptures below and asking God how dismantle darkness in Goths and Emos. Ask him how you can be light among those who are draw to darkness. Practice what he says as a lifestyle.

John 1:4-5 *The Word gave life to everything that was created, and his life brought light to everyone. The light shines in the darkness, and the darkness can never extinguish it.*

John 3:19-20 *And the judgment is based on this fact: God's light came into the world, but people loved the darkness more than the light, for their actions were evil. All who do evil hate the light and refuse to go near it for fear their sins will be exposed.*

Isaiah 5:20 How *horrible it will be for those who call evil good and good evil, who turn darkness into light and light into darkness, who turn what is bitter into something sweet and what is sweet into something bitter.*

1John 1:6 *If we claim that we have fellowship with him but keep living in darkness, we are lying and not practicing the truth.*

Ephesians 5:11 *Have nothing to do with the fruitless deeds of darkness, but rather expose them.*

RASTAFARIANISM

Rastafarians use marijuana as a religious ritual. They do not consider marijuana a drug, but a medium to open the mind to higher consciousness that creates opportunity for spiritual awareness. Rastafarianism is a pro-African movement that started in Jamaica in the 20th century by Leonard Howell and Marcus Garvey. Singer Bob Marley helped to make the religion famous. Rastafarianism was established with the intent to empower African people. Their leaders taught that Africans were superior, while encouraging the hatred of Europeans and other cultures that suppress African people. They believe the world system is rooted in a Babylon system and resist living in the ways and customs of this system. Rastafarians believe in the Judeo-Christian God, where they believe the Old Testament covenant supersedes the Jewish covenant, and instead of Jews, they are God's superior race. They believe in the Old Testament laws, and esteem prophets like Elijah and Moses. They reject much of the New Testament but regard some allegories of the book of Revelation. They refer to God as Jah, worship him as the divine, and believe Christ came to earth as a divine manifestation of Jah. Some Rastafarians believe that Christ was Black, while others focus on Emperor Haile Selassie of Ethiopia as the Black messiah and rebirth of Christ. They believe they are immortal, do not believe in the afterlife, refer to Africa as "Zion, "and believe it is heaven on earth. Rastafarians say a prayer to their god Jah before smoking Marijuana. As they connect to Jah, while smoking, they believe he draws them into higher self-awareness and enlightenment.

Rastafarians have strict religious views about their bodies as temples. They are health conscious, do not drink alcohol or eat none nourishing foods. They wear their hair in dreadlocks and allow them to grow long as a symbol of strength and Jah identity. This custom derived from Sampson in the Old Testament. Sampson was a chosen Nazarite from birth, who was not permitted to cut his hair, because it embodied his supernatural strength and power. Men dominate this religion. They are called kings and call women queens. Women are not called to be Rastafarians, only become part of the religion via marriage, and must adhere to strict religious rules that are centered on honoring and caring for her husband. Though many of their views regarding their disciplined life are taken from the bible, this religion is rooted in idolatrous practices. They believe that these disciplines provoke purity and power, is essential to a higher level of consciousness, enabling them to reign in their superiority as the chosen people of Jah.

THE BLACK HEBREW ISRAELITES

There is a sector of the "STAY WOKE" community that identify as the Black Hebrew Israelites. Here is a list of information regarding this group.

- The Hebrew Israelites date back to the 19th Century. They have no association with Beit Yisrael and Falahas which are Ethiopian Jewish groups from the 1930s to the 1960s.

- They were founded by Frank Cherry and William Saunders Crowdy. In 1886, Cherry established the "Church of the Living God, the Pillar Ground for All Nations," and Crowdy established the "Church of God and Saints of Christ.

- The modern day Black Hebrew Israelites now have various sectors throughout the United States, with a host of branches splitting into their own groups, due to leadership disputes and theological differences.

- The Black Hebrew Israelites are deeply passionate. Some sects can be volatile, confrontational, and intimidating, in their preaching style and stance regarding their beliefs. This has caused some sects to be categorized as racists hate group.

- Some of the teachings can be extremely hateful, suppressive to Caucasians, Jews, and other ethnic groups, while making the Black Hebrew Israelites racially superior.

- They believe they are descendants of Jacob from the Twelve Tribes of Israel - known to them as the "lost tribes," and people of color.

- The Lost tribe of Israel include Blacks, Hispanics, and Native Indians. They do not believe all people of these ethnic groups are part of the lost tribe nor are they all God's chosen people. Especially those who they deemed to be brainwashed by the religious and social jargons of society. Those who embrace consciousness and enlightenment are the true Black Hebrew Israelites who must stand for the identity of God and their right to be his chosen people.

- They believe **Deuteronomy 28:29** is a prophecy to the reason the trans-Atlantic slave trade occurred, thus relocating Africans to America. They believe this curse was because the Black Hebrew Israelites were disobedient to God's word to remain pure in their race and religious practices and did not reign properly in the earth. They believe this disobedience can only be cured through their ideology.

- They believe the Jews are not God's chosen people. They believe they are God's chosen, are the only race that will go to heaven, and will one day be given dominion by God to rule the earth.

- They believe every other race is subject to them as they contend that they are the first race created on earth and all races derived from them. This concept flips the switch, making them the superior race. Biblically all mankind is created in God's image and equal to one another. There is no superior race (**Genesis 1:26-28, Deuteronomy 10:17, Galatians 3:28**).

- They mainly incorporate beliefs from Christianity and Judaism. Their philosophies are rooted in the biblical chapter of Exodus, along with African American Religion,

Pentecostal Christianity, The Holiness Religion, Freemasonry, the Anglo-Israelites movement, Judaism, Theosophy, Mind Power, and the occult.

- They equate their uprising to reclaiming the people of the lost tribe of Israel and taking their rightful place in the earth so they can reign when God returns to restore their rulership.

- They utilize the King James Version of the Bible as their faith and practice but do not acknowledge all books as true to their identity or to mankind. Especially those portions that appear to suppress their people and make them slaves. They do not regard Paul's writings for this reason and believe his teachings were written to give white slave masters authority over them as a people.

- Many Black Hebrew Israelites reject the deity of Christ and believe Jesus was just another prophet or teacher of the faith. This is problematic because it denies Jesus as the Messiah and the only way to eternal life.

- They believe God is the supreme being of the universe and that they can pursue him through the powers of the universe for consciousness, enlightenment, power, reclaimed dominion, and God identity. They refer to God as Yahawashi, Yahawah, YHWH, or Yahweh.

- Black Hebrew Israelites reject the images of a white Jesus and believe these images were created to steal their ordained identity. They believe Jesus is a Black man according to ***Revelation 1:15***.

- Black Hebrew Israelites reject Christian and pagan holidays regard them as idolatrous and demonic. They celebrate the Passover but have adopted their ideologies regarding many biblical symbols, feasts, and celebrations.

- Some sects view Caucasian people as Satanic. They believe Caucasian's are the descendants of Esau the twin of Jacob. They refer to them as Edomites. Esau is described as red and ugly and Jacob is described as dark skinned.

- Within the prison culture of religion, non-Blacks are welcome to become a Hebrew Israelite but with acceptance of standards of their faith that uphold the cultural beliefs and practices.

- They have dishonorable views towards the Jewish community and base their theories from ***Revelation 3:9***.

With the upheaval of racial injustices, falling Christian leaders, and painful church experiences, African Americans are embracing the teachings of Black Hebrew Israelites at a rapid pace. The over imprisonment of African Americans has also caused a drawing to this sect, as it is popular within the prison system. Social media sites have also enabled the Black Hebrew Israelites to spread their beliefs and recruit souls to their sects. Even if people do not join, the re-preach the beliefs, thus spreading the mixed ideologies. The ancient trauma that African Americans have endured makes it easy to consider the ideologies as needful truths. Many African Americans find them empowering and liberating, while SHIFTING them in a position of superiority over their suppressors. As long as this trauma goes unaddressed in the African American community, African American church, and body of Christ at large, the Black Hebrew Israelites will become larger in numbers and raging passion. Christians must want to take the time to truly heal people.

YORUBA RELIGION
I want to note that when it comes to the traditions of Africans, religion in and of itself cannot be separated from culture, society, environment, family dynamics, and ancestral history. It is a way of life where the spiritual aspect of their identity is the guiding force of life and eternity. This is the reason music, dance, clothing style, traditions, rituals, beliefs, family, political, social systems are all intertwined in spirituality. For the traditional African beliefs system, they are one and the same.

Yoruba religion is the basis for several religions, notably Santeria, Umbanda, Trinidad Orisha, Haitian Vodou, and Candomblé. The Yoruba's religious history, known as Ita encompasses the traditional religious, spiritual, and ancestral concepts and practices of the Yoruba people. The Itan includes a complexity of songs, poetries, histories, stories, and other cultural ideologies. It is rooted in necromancy, witchcraft, divination, sorcery, magic, charms, consulting with familiar spirits, and occultism. Yoruba's religious homeland is in Southwestern Nigeria and the adjoining parts of Benin and Togo, a region that is called has Yorubaland. Due to the slave trade, there is also a host of Yoruba people in America and surrounding parts of the world, who consider themselves Christian, Muslim, or Catholic, but have not relinquished their traditional Yoruba roots. Initially these practices have been maintained in secret because slave owners forbid Africans to practice their religion, therefore, they were secretly fostered and passed down from generation to generation, while mixing in more accepted public forms of religion and worship. Presently (year 2010 onward), with the rise of new age concepts, a drive to restore African identity, rebellion against racial injustice and systematic slavery, many African Americans, and Africans in general, are returning to Yoruba religion. They deem this to be acceptable since Yoruba people and their religion are over thousands of years old and have been in existence before Christianity or Muslim religions. Many also believe the only way for Africans to truly rid themselves of slave systems, religions, and identities, is to embrace their original ancestral culture and roots.

The traditional Yoruba religion believes in a non-gender supreme being who lives in the sky, called Olodumare. Olodumare is a distant all-powerful god of the universe who utilizes spirits call Orishas to handle daily issues, needs, desires, and interventions for people; to guide them in how to live and be successful on Aiye which means earth. Orishas are spiritual beings that already existed in the spirit world at creation, who become incarnated beings that live on earth. It is also believed that ancestors also become Orishas after dying and being reincarnated as a reward for an exceptional life on earth. Yoruba high priest can also become possessed by Orishas for the purposes of helping to guide, heal, and assist the lives of humans. Followers can also be possessed by Orishas. Possession is often done via a ritual where Orishas are evoked with prayer like chanting, rituals, and drumbeats. Once a priest or follower is possessed, they take on the spirit of the Orisha.

It is said that when an African is born, they are accompanied by an Orisha governing head, a spirit guide that is a protector of the person's life. It is not uncommon for followers to physically see their Orisha and know exactly what they look like and how they operate. In the United States, Latin America, and the Caribbean, there are a host of significant Orishas known to be in operation that are referred to as "The Seven African Powers." Their names are Eleggua, Obatala, Yemaya, Oya, Oshun, Shango, and Ogun. There is the belief that the Yoruba followers share common traits with their Orisha, who aided them in a pathway of destiny and success. If followers are not aware of who their Orisha is, they can seek a high priest who completes rituals to help them reveal their Orisha.

In addition to being protectors and guides, Orishas can be invoked through rituals and divination to aide with specific life purposes and issues. One of the most beloved and powerful Orisha deities is called Oshun. Oshun is viewed as a mother goddess and a river goddess that tends to be associated with water, purity, fertility, love, sensuality, beauty, healing, destiny, success, and divination. Oshun is a mother: It is said that het waters were central to the creation of humanity, and that she is the protector and guide for babies and small children. Oshun is considered queen of witches who empowers and equips her followers with the education of mysticism and the ability to do magic, sorcery, and divination. Followers engage in bath rituals for love, spell casting for beauty, love, and attraction, rituals offerings for fertility, ritual offerings, and spell casting for prosperity, etc. They use candles, food, herbs, plants, flowers, etc., along with a representation of the goddess Oshun, to complete rituals and spells. The artist Beyoncé invoked the goddess Oshun in several of her musical and movie projects. She sings the following lyrics in her song "Mood4Eva" on her "Black Is King" album:

I am Beyoncé Giselle Knowles-Carter
I am the Nala, sister of Yoruba
Oshun, Queen Sheba, I am the mother
Ankh on my gold chain, ice on my whole chain
I be like soul food, I am a whole mood

Beyoncé also compares herself to Oshun throughout the movie "*Black Is King*" and in her visual imagery album entitled "Lemonade." Like Beyonce, many women are intrigued by this spirit being because of what it represents and produces, and its ability to hide within a person, while taking on the likeness and power of a woman's natural femininity. However, let us not forget that this is a demon. There is indeed a price for having her guide or possess your life.

Yoruba religion believes in Atunwa, which is reincarnation within the family. Many believe when a baby is born and resembles a dead relative, he or she is the reincarnation of that person.

Yoruba practitioners believe that there are negative or evil beings called Ajogun who cause hardship, sickness, disease, accidents, calamities, death, etc. to people. A person who is possessed or oppressed by a Ajogun usually visited a high priest for deliverance.

Yoruba practitioners also believe in an eternal energy life force called Ashe. Ashe is supernatural energy that comes from Olodumare. It is manifested through Olodumare, their supreme deity who rules the heavens, is associated with the sun, and possess the power to bring about good or bad change.

Ifa divination is practiced among Yoruba. Ifa refers to the mystical being Ifa or Orunmila, regarded as the deity of wisdom and intellectual development. Ifa divination is held in high regard as it is viewed as significant in guiding a person's destiny and life outcomes. Ifa divination encompasses a multiplex system of signs, compiled in a literary corpus, and mathematical formulas, that are interpreted by a diviner to guide followers to important personal or collective life decisions. The literary corpus is a treasury of knowledge concerning Yoruba history, philosophy, medicine, and mythology.

Babalawos (priest fathers of secrets or Iyanifas (priest mothers of secrets), are trained from their youth and viewed as masters of Ifa wisdom. They use either the divining chain known as Opele, or the sacred palm or kola nuts called Ikin, on the wooden divination tray called Opon Ifá. During the divination session, the priest places a powder called iyerosun over the tray and draws it into nine sections, each representing an ancient being. The priest praises and honors each ancient being before asking questions and casting sacred palm or kola-nuts across the tray to see answers. The carved face on the tray represents an Orisha, Esu, a messenger from the deities. As the session progresses, the open Ifa is used to communicate with the deity Ifa, who provides revelation, insights, and solutions to the issues at hand, while claiming to restore peace and harmony to the person's life through the ancient spirit beings.

As I have studied African culture and even Yoruba religion, it will be important for leaders of Jesus Christ to find non idolatrous and anti-witchcraft ways to empower and impose value in their African American and African members, that affirms their heritage, identity, and culture. This can be done by having events that educate, celebrate, and promote, the positive aspects of African history and culture. Having events that address the enslavements and colonization of the African people, how this impacted their culture and identity, and bringing personal and generational healing regarding these issues. Such affirmation will instill God identity and value in a way that honors the race without dishonoring the principles and standards of God.

SANGOMAS
Sangomas are highly respected healers, shamans, priests, herbalists, witch doctors, and cultural prophets in some African cultures. Particularly southern Africans who tend to diagnose, prescribe, and perform rituals, sacrifices, and spells that are thought to produce physical, mental, emotional, or spiritual healing. Though an ingenious and traditional practice, the ways of Sangoma are becoming a modern practice among Africans and African Americans.

FREE MASONRY
Freemasonry was founded in between the 1500s and 1700s in England and
Scotland. Freemasonry is exclusive to men and is the oldest, and largest worldwide secret

society. It has an estimated 3 million members around the world, including 1 million in the United States. Freemasonry made its way to the United States in the 1800s with the formation of the country, and its investment of business, social, political, and economic undertakings. The first president of the United States, George Washington, was a master freemason, which the highest rank in the organization. Freemasonry is rooted in the very fiber and foundation of the nation as many other American revolution leaders were free masons. Masonic rites were witnessed at various national and political events such as the presidential inauguration and the building of the United States Capital, while Masonic symbols can be found on governmental buildings and one-dollar bill. Many other presidents and Supreme Court chief justices have affiliations with Freemasonry. These idolatrous roots must be dealt with to restore the purity of the nation unto the heart and worship of the true and living God.

There are several sects within Freemasonry such as the Shriners (known formally as the Ancient Arabic Order Nobles of the Mystic Shriners, they are also required to be Masons). The masons meet at a local site they call the lodge, which is overseen at the regional level, yet there is also a national governance called the Grand Lodge. Freemasonry operates like a religion, has a host of ceremonies and rituals, but it is far from being religious. It is an idolatrous organization, where some Christians believers, even pastors and major ministry leaders, and religious theologies such as Baptist religions, celebrate and advocate for being part of the organization. Though Freemasonry encourages and supports charitable activities, it contains both multi-religious and inclusive teachings which means a person does not have to believe in the one true and living God. They only have to believe in a supernatural being, can believe in several gods, and can be simultaneously a Christian, a Muslim, and a Hindu. This ideology is not Christian and is idolatrous in nature, as biblically there is only one God.

Deuteronomy 4:35 *You were shown these things so that you would know that the LORD is God; there is no other besides Him.*

Deuteronomy 32:39 *See now that I am He; there is no God besides Me. I bring death and I give life; I wound and I heal, and there is no one who can deliver from My hand.*

Psalm 18:31 *For who is God besides the LORD? And who is the rock except our God?*

Isaiah 43:10 *"You are My witnesses," declares the LORD, "and My servant whom I have chosen, so that you may know and believe Me and understand that I am He. Before Me, no god was formed, and none will come after Me.*

Freemasonry also believes in the Great Architect of the Universe which they essentially refer to as the unknown God or a neutral deity. They view Jesus as more of a prophet even though biblically Jesus is the savior and the only way to salvation.

Acts 4:12 *And there is salvation in no one else, for there is no other name under heaven given among men by which we must be saved.*

Applicants must be male adults with good character, that believe in the existence of a supreme being and in the immortality of the soul. Freemasons are from different backgrounds, religious, and ethnic groups. Freemasons believe all people will eventually go to heaven which is a universalist theology. They are about unifying for the good and common causes and empowering one another to be successful in society.

Becoming a Freemason requires achieving three ceremonial stages called degrees, which have their roots in medieval craftsmanship of apprentice, fellow craft, and master Mason. These degrees symbolize the "three stages of human development: youth, manhood, and age." The ceremonies, rituals and covenants made are secret and only known to Freemasonry members. It is a violation to share this information and doing so results in excommunication.

EASTERN STARS

The Eastern Stars, founded in the mid-1800s in the United States, began as a group of women who were related to the male Freemasons, but now admits both men and women into the organization. It has similar beliefs as the Freemasonry and focuses on Charitable, Educational, Fraternal and Scientific community endeavors. Many Christians join because of these causes and assume it is Christian because of their community works, morals, values, and strivings of goodwill and acts of love and kindness. However, the organization is rooted in non-Christian beliefs that I spoke of above regarding the Free Masonry.

GREEK ORGANIZATIONS

The decision to join Greek Organizations (Sororities and Fraternities) is often posed in college as, youth enter young adulthood and seek to find their identity and their own way of life. The challenge with this is they should already have clarity about their identity and direction in what pathways and standards they need to live to progress and sustain in a healthy identity and in their destiny. The failure to instill this in youth before college causes them to pursue activities and organizations that are more experimental and detrimental to their identity and wellbeing where they must learn from their mistakes, while also testing with their parents have instilled in them, rather than building on a solid foundation that can positively advance them in life. It is essential that we begin identifying and raising our youth in God identity from the womb, so that they will not have wait until college to find out who they are and who they are not. Especially at the expense of their innocence, integrity, and relationship with God. I highly recommend the book, *Cultivating Destiny from The Womb*, authored by myself and Shannon White. It provides essential keys for in this area so that your child grows up in the ordain purpose and calling of God.

Greek Organizations are rooted in Free Masonry, Greek philosophy, and occult ideologies. They were founded by Free Masonry and Easter Star members and are rooted in Masonic rituals, chants, ceremonies, and customs. Greek Philosophy was surfaced in 6th century B.C. and was focused on how to examine the world in a non-religious way. Greek Philosophy progressed throughout the Hellenistic period and the period in which Ancient Greece was part of the Roman Empire. The Greek Organization letters and new Greek names given to members, derived from Egyptian and Babylonian culture with ties to mythology and idolatry. In Acts 9:29, we find Apostle Paul boldly debating with the Hellenistic Jews who were considering slaying him for his biblical insights.

The Amplified Bible *Preaching freely and confidently and boldly in the name of the Lord. And he spoke and discussed with and disputed against the Hellenists (the Grecian Jews), but they were seeking to slay him.*

Like Free Masonry, Greek organizations disguise themselves as beneficial to acquiring improved college status, having public service acts on resumes, and connecting to future members for employment opportunities and economic advancement, but this is at the expense of giving one's soul over to idol gods, sworn devotions that idolize founders, other members, and the organization in and of itself; the exaltation of secret creeds, passwords, homages, mottos, passwords, demonic and blood covenants, hazing, and shameful, perverted, sexual, and sometimes violent practices. The idolatrous worship and blindfold confessions at demonic altars.

Many try to maintain some sense of biblical and spiritual connection with the one true living God; however, Greek Organizations are full of partying, lascivious behavior, and lawlessness, that draws youth from God rather than to him. Because being a believer is not shunned, and many proclaimed Christians are part of Greek Organizations, people think they can do both without it hindering their relationship with God; this is delusion and unbiblical. There is also the combining of Greek methodology and symbols with scripture which makes people believe the organization is morally correct, righteous, and virtuous. Later in life, many proclaimed believers are no longer partying and engaging extreme worldly acts, but wholehearted hold on to their Greek organization membership and status. They use this to justify it being harmless and more for the community, social and economic benefits, yet there is no way around these organizations being rooted in idolatry, secret ventures, and forbidden biblical practices. God is clear about us coming out of the world and loving not the things of the world.

Matthew 6:24 *No man can serve two masters: for either he will hate the one, and love the other; or else he will hold to the one, and despise the other. Ye cannot serve God and mammon.*

1John 2:15-16 *Love not the world, neither the things that are in the world. If any man love the world, the love of the Father is not in him. For all that is in the world, the lust of the flesh, and the lust of the eyes, and the pride of life, is not of the Father, but is of the world.*

1Corinthians 10:21-22 *Ye cannot drink the cup of the Lord, and the cup of devils: ye cannot be partakers of the Lord's table, and of the table of devils. Do we provoke the Lord to jealousy? are we stronger than he?"*

1Peter 4:3 *For the time past of our life may suffice us to have wrought the will of the Gentiles, when we walked in lasciviousness, lusts, excess of wine, revellings, banquetings, and abominable idolatries.*

James 4:4 *Ye adulterers and adulteresses, know ye not that the friendship of the world is enmity with God? whosoever therefore will be a friend of the world is the enemy of God.*

Colossians 2:8 New Living Bible *Don't let anyone capture you with empty philosophies and high-sounding nonsense that come from human thinking and from the spiritual powers of this world, rather than from Christ.*

Youth need to be educated before they go to college on the idolatrous nature of Greek organizations. Parents and believers need to repent, renounce, break covenants and vows, and receive deliverance from demons and idolatrous acts related to these organizations so they can cleanse their generational lines and the foundations of the church in these areas. Believers need to come all the way out of these groups so we can really demonstrate a separation between God's church and the world, and truly be positioned to save souls for his glory.

FEMINIST MOVEMENT

Dictionary.com defines feminism as:
1. the doctrine advocating social, political, and all other rights of women equal to those of men,
2. an organized movement for the attainment of such rights for women.

The feminist movement focuses on the empowerment of women, while ensuring that women are treated equal to men and have the right to make independent personal decisions about their lives, bodies, political, economic, and societal issues. Their priorities and purpose may vary depending on the nation, the community, and the reason for women advocacy. The feminist's movement encompasses various political campaigns to ensure woman have the following rights, advocacies, and protections:

- Reproductive rights
- Domestic violence
- Maternity leave
- Equal pay
- Equal Opportunity
- Voting rights
- Sexuality
- Sexual harassment
- Sexual violence
- Sexual control
- Body mutilation

The movement can be dated back to early era of civilization. It is often viewed in waves:

1. First wave (19th and 20th Century - contending for property rights and the right to vote.
2. Second wave (1960s) - contending for equality, anti-discrimination, sexuality, and reproductive rights.
3. Third wave (1990s) - contending for equality for not just white privileged strait women but all women - women of color, lesbians, and other gender related desires of women.

4. Fourth wave (2012 to present) - contending for women's empowerment, the use of internet tools, and the challenges of how the overlapping of various social identities, as race, gender, sexuality, and class, contributes to certain systemic oppression and discrimination. The fourth wave advocates greater gender equality by focusing on gendered norms and marginalization of women in society.

This Fourth wave modern day feminist movement, has fought for language equality where they want words that reference men to be changed where it references women or just a person. For example, saying "chairperson" instead of "chairman," or having the right to say "chairwoman" should a woman hold that position, "Amen" and "Awoman" at the end of a prayer. They also advocate for rights of redefining gender equality. Gender equality is the concept that both genders - male and female - share the same civil rights, have the same access to social goods and opportunities, and bear the same obligations. It is the premise that all people regardless of gender are allowed the same legal rights and are regarded by society as being equals. Neither gender is valued less or subjected to the other. Such ideologies can be challenging when we consider the abilities and capabilities between genders. There will always innately be somethings that one gender can do that the other cannot do or will require assistance or some type of additional intervention or invention to accomplish certain tasks. This should be viewed as understandable and necessary because women and men are innately different.

Within the modern-day movement, there is a more radical group of feminists who have actively sought to overthrow any glimmer of male dominance or governance in society. This is where the feminist movement can become sketchy where its original intent for good regarding safety, protection, care, and equal rights for women, is now being used in a negative way that contaminates the positive impact it can have in the earth. There is this ideology that it is about equality and fairness, but there is a whole other agenda that is more about emasculating men, dehumanizing men, dismantling the need and importance of men, thus making women superior and dominating over men. When there is a focus to emasculate and disempower men and SHIFT them out of their role as the biblical and needful headship of marriages, families, and communities, the feminist agenda becomes demonic, sinful, and unscriptural. This is where godly believers and women in general, must be careful in what they are supporting and making sure it is aligning with God's word and purpose for making us distinctly male and female, and the roles he gave us one to another, and in the earth, in marriage and family.

There is no doubt that though God made man first, put him as head of the garden, made woman from the rib of man, put man as head of the woman and of the family, he made both equal in worth and God identity.

Genesis 1:27 *So God created man in his own image, in the image of God he created him; male and female he created them.*

Galatians 3:28-29 *There is neither Jew nor Greek, there is neither slave nor free, there is no male and female, for you are all one in Christ Jesus. And if you are Christ's, then you are Abraham's offspring, heirs according to promise.*

Ephesians 5:22-28 *Wives, submit yourselves unto your own husbands, as unto the Lord. For the husband is the head of the wife, even as Christ is the head of the church: and he is the saviour of the body. Therefore as the church is subject unto Christ, so let the wives be to their own husbands in every thing. Husbands, love your wives, even as Christ also loved the church, and gave himself for it; That he might sanctify and cleanse it with the washing of water by the word, That he might present it to himself a glorious church, not having spot, or wrinkle, or any such thing; but that it should be holy and without blemish. So ought men to love their wives as their own bodies. He that loveth his wife loveth himself.*

The roles of men and women compliment, complete, uphold, and support one another (Study ***Genesis 1-3***). However, God placed man as the head. Having a head is not for the intention of oppressing and controlling others. Having a head provides leadership, governance, protection, guidance, vision, initiative, responsibility, and accountability. These are divine qualities that are needful for advancing lives, families, generations, community, and society.

Within the premise of gender equality, in effort to make gender neutrality legal in society, people groups like homosexual males, the transgender community, and parents or advocates of youth that believe they are opposite sex, have supported and partnered with feminist movements for the purposes of receiving legal equality. The ideology has been that they should legally be whatever sex they desire, they should be able to marry and have equal rights as heterosexual marriages, they should be able compete, use public facilities, be imprisoned, based on their preferred gender, and they should be safe in circles where their sexual preferences has caused them to be ridiculed, abused, and mistreated. Though providing certain rights are essential, the overreach in what is appropriate and practical has now compromised the safety and equal practices of women.

- Laws are being lobbied and implemented stripping parents of rights to make decisions for their youth regarding their sexuality.
- People who veer with the opposite sex are being allowed to use the same bathroom of their sex preference, thus putting woman and girls at risk of their safety.
- Transgendered males are being allowed to compete as women, thus breaking records that were held by women competing against those born of their same gender.
- Businesses and organizations are being made to take biological gender titles off bathrooms; they are making bathrooms equally available despite gender and sexual preferences which gives rapists and pedophiles an opportunity to prey on women and youth.
- Christians are being made to go against their spiritual beliefs, thus regarding same sex marriages, providing services to gay couples; they risk imprisonment and being sued for preaching and refusing services to homosexual couples.
- Men and those who speak against the unsafety of these laws are being viewed as homophobic and heartless regarding the experiences of the homosexual community, thus voiding them of a realistic voice to provide rational and balanced dialog that is safe and applicable for all parties involved.

This is just some of the ways the radical modern feminist movement has impacted our current society. For the most part, women are generally embracing of gay men, and many of them have them as friends. Even women who are believers have gay friends. This may play a factor in there being more gay men in church than masculine men. There are generally more women in church. Many gay men feel comfortable and embraced around women, and they tend to gravitate to places where there is no judgment or judgment would be viewed as a lack of godly love or insensitive. Such men are put in ministry positions and allowed to lead without any questioning of whether they are living a life conductive to biblical standards regarding sexual preferences and activities. In some ministries, masculine men have been viewed as homophobic or religious due to their lack of tolerance for effeminate men. Historically, masculine men have been the leaders of the church. Some of these men have made women subservient to women to the point of disempowering their identity and using the biblical word and scriptures of men as the head of women, families, and the church, to mishandle, control, and oppress women. Recently there has been a rise in female leadership. Many women have had to contend for their right to be used in ministry and leadership. This has caused them to be viewed as Jezebels rather than strong confident female women who have a calling on their lives. The lack of balanced in this area has caused a divide, competition, and contention between women and men.

Also, as society has progressed, men in general have focused more on being providers, leading their homes, and advancing their lives, than attending church. Men having to contend for their right to be men in society, in their communities, in their homes, and the lack of fathers in homes, has caused a disconnect of men regarding marriage and the biblical standard for family as important in their lives. Also, the empowerment of women, has allowed for women to be able to work many jobs that men would have and has made it more challenging for men to feel like they are the bread winners or are the providers, protectors, gatekeepers, and leaders of society, communities, and families. Accompany this with a movement that is for silencing, usurping, and overthrowing the voice and presence of men, and we have a dangerous challenge on our hands. We truly need balance in how to continue empowering men, but also respecting the advancement and needful destiny of women in our society. We truly need a balance in how to aide in the safety, protection, and legal rights of the Lesbian, Gay, Bisexual Transgender, Queer, and Gender Neutrality community, while also making sure we regard the realities about our gender differences, roles, and how key and vital they are to our society, communities, and families. This is a very sensitive topic that believers need to study and even have dialog about so that they can implement goals and strategies to bring biblical balance and wellness to the interactions and empowerment of genders. There also needs to be strategy on how to advocate for women but not promote extreme feminist ideologies that can be detrimental on society.

GODDESS MOVEMENT – GODDESS WORSHIP
Goddess means "female deity." It also means female who possess great charm and can arouse others with her beauty and adoration. The Latin word "diva" also means goddess. Some believers use these words to describe themselves, not realizing that they have an idolatrous nature to them. Goddess movement or Goddess worship is the Pagan polytheistic practice that includes spiritual beliefs, and worship of different goddesses and gods from various religions. The origin of goddess worship is Africa. Many proclaimed Christians have converted to goddess worship. They have added witchcraft and pagan customs, beliefs, and rituals to their Christian doctrines and practices. They will have ministries that have Christian names and

themes, use Christian worship music, scriptures, biblical principles and teachings in their practices, but will mix it with new age meditation, spell casting, divination, sacrificing, rituals, root working, astrology, necromancy, horoscopes, candle magic, tarot card reading, worshiping of other gods and the elements, etc. They will contend these practices are godly and needful to a complete spiritual experience. There is a feminist component to it. The goddess believe they are a god and are equal in power and rank to male gods and men in general. They worship other female gods and seek to draw enlightenment, wisdom, and power from them. As the feminist movement has resurfaced in this modern time, being a goddess has become commonplace. Expect self-proclaimed goddesses and goddess worship to continue to increase as many rebel against the religious system of the church, leave ministries hurt, while seeking to use their gifts and give themselves a voice that they deem was silenced, disregarded, or manipulated, in the religious sector. It will take divine truth, patience, and love to draw these goddesses out of their demonic ministries and practices. Many of them have built their own idolatry and truly believe what they are doing is of God, approved of God, needful in the earth, and necessary to draw others from mainstream religion into what they deem as spiritual freedom.

WHITE SUPREMACY
It is important to note that the left-wing is characterized by an emphasis on "ideas such as freedom, equality, fraternity, rights, progress, reform and internationalism." The right-wing is characterized by an emphasis on "notions such as authority, hierarchy, order, duty, tradition, reaction and nationalism."

Many Americans, especially white supremacist deem themselves "patriots." A patriot is a person who vigorously supports their country and is prepared to defend it against enemies or detractors. There is nothing wrong with loving and wanting to defend your country. But when your actions are violent, provokes violence, cause division, threatens the safety of others, ostracize and genocide other people and ethnic groups, you have SHIFTED from patriot to terrorist. A terrorist is a person who unlawfully uses violence, intimidation, extreme rhetoric, and measures, particularly against civilians to make a statement, incite fear, draw others to their stance, or to fulfill political, religious, ethnic, ideological, or social, self-willed ambitions. There are no explanations around white supremacists being terroristic in nature. Their concepts are not about patriotism but control, rule, and power. They deem anyone that is harmed as a sacrifice for the common good of their ideologies. Often those harmed are innocent, good standing citizens, who did not deserve to be a victim of their carnage.

With the rise of exposure of racism, privilege, and racial injustices, it is essential that believers are educated so they can pray and advocate against all forms of White Supremacy. Though White supremacy is an age-old hate ideology, there have been many groups forms in the last five years, especially around the time the first African American, Barack Obama took office. This speaks volumes to what has been hidden and seething in our nation regarding slavery, racism, privilege, and white power, still being a severe issue in our nation and even the world at large. It would be beneficial to research your region and learn what White supremacy groups are in your area, what they stand for, and how they operate within your sphere. Many white people need to reach themselves as they research and break free from any conscious and unconscious ideologies they may have regarding white supremacy, white power, and privilege. It will take a desire to acknowledge the entitled privileges that come with your race and being willing to relinquish them, to truly disconnect, reject, and advocate against these demonic organizations. Without an acknowledgement of truth and dismantling the false superiorities come with it, these groups are strengthened in their ideologies and use the soul ties and commonality of being white to further fortify and advance their agenda to oppress and murder other races.

White supremacy is the ideology and belief that "white" or "lighter-skinned" human race are superior to all other ethnic groups. White supremacists tend to be racist, fascist and have an extreme devotion to their causes and their nation. They believe they are the guardians of the nation and need to protect it from other racial groups they deem less superior. Violence and aggressive tactics are often used to achieve their goals and uphold their doctrinal beliefs. Though white supremacy is deemed as terrorism, there are no laws that make the groups illegal. Generally, when there are arrests against them, it is when they are caught or thought to have broken the law. However, the groups within themselves, is not systematically viewed as illegal. This should be a grave concern and injustice that needs to be changed in our nation and the world at large. Here are a few White supremacists' groups to be aware of.

Ku Klux Klan

Ku Klux Klan (KKK) dates all the way back to the 1800s. During the 1800s they were the main resistance against the Republican Party constitutionally establishing political and economic rights to African Americans. They are an American white supremacist hate group who primarily target African Americans. Lesser enemies of the KKK include Jews, immigrants, leftists, homosexuals, Muslims and, until recently, Catholics. They advocate for white supremacy, white nationalism, complete separation of racial groups, and are anti-immigration. The KKK are known for terrorism, extreme violence, and murder. They have a history of terrorizing, intimidating, beating, lynching, and murdering African Americans, especially if they believe their power and position of reigning is threatened. It is not uncommon for them to engage in bombings, burning crosses, rallies, parades, and marches, to intimidate and cause harm to their intended targets.

Neo-Nazis

Neo-Nazis is a global movement with many networks operating in various countries. Its far-right wing politics and right-wing extremists' ideologies are rooted in Nazi doctrine that idolizes Adolf Hitler and other Nazis. It encompasses ultranationalism, racism, xenophobia, ableism, homophobia, anti-Romanyism, antisemitism, anti-communism and initiating the Fourth Reich. Neo-Nazis consists of post-World War II militant, social or political movements seeking to revive and implement the ideology of Nazism. Neo-Nazis also promote hatred and attack racial and ethnic minorities, employ white supremacy, while striving to create a governmental system led by a dictator having complete power that oppresses, suppresses, and criticizes these minority races. A lot of their paraphernalia and symbols have been banned in many countries as they are considered dangerous terrorists. It is difficult to identify who is an affiliated with the Neo-Nazi; they are generally part of the political, law enforcement, and military system. Those designed to protect and serve ALL people, are generally part of a group that only regard "white people" and who they deem to be the "elite." This makes them dangerous and makes trusting these systems difficult, especially for minority groups. It is important for believers to study the character and rhetoric of Neo-Nazis so they can be discerning of how it operates, and can identify, expose, and advocate against it when it occurs.

White Powered - Racist Skinheads
The original skinheads of the 1960s was not based in race or white supremacy. They originated in the United Kingdom, most likely London or Southeast England, and where working class you who wanted a space and group to express their uniqueness and altered ideologies regarding working class pride and being value for their contribution to society. An offshoot of this group formed in the 1980s within the United States, is now nationwide, and has become a global movement that terrorize communities worldwide. Racist Skinheads is a very hateful, dangerous, violent, criminal, Neo-Nazis driven, white supremacy group. Their ideologies are rooted in racism and white power, where they are governed by Neo-Nazi beliefs about Jews, blacks, immigrants, LGBT people and other groups they deem beneath them. Racist skinheads usually appear as head shaving, combat boots, Dr. Marten laced boots, blue jeans, bomber jackets, red suspenders, distinct Neo-Nazi and white power tattoos and symbols on their clothing and skin. They mobilize in small groups or individually, which makes their workings are difficult for law enforcement to detect and prosecute. They can be rowdy and antagonistic, especially when drinking, and are known for seeking to kick a few skulls in when under the influence.

Proud Boys
The Proud Boys was established during the 2016 presidential election by VICE Media co-founder Gavin McInnes. The Proud Boys are self-described "western chauvinists" who believe their group is superior, dominant, virtuous, valiant, and absolute in power, compared to other similar supremacy groups and all racial groups. They will work alongside of other white supremacy groups but believe they need them and that they are stronger than them. The proud boys operate as a far-right, neo-fascist, and male-only political organization that promotes and engages in extreme political violence in the United States and Canada. They are misogynistic in nature, egocentric, narcissistic, transphobic, Islamophobia, anti-Muslim, advocate for white supremacy, and white power. Their ideologies have elements of genocide and conspiracy; they tend to view everyone else as objects to oppress and use for their advantage and expendable. The Proud Boys organization has been banned by Facebook, Instagram, Twitter, and YouTube due to the hateful and violent rhetoric. The Proud Boys resolutely reject any connection to the racist "alt-right," insisting they are simply a fraternal group spreading an "anti-political correctness" and "anti-white guilt" agenda.

Alt-Right
Alt-right (alternative right) term surfaced in 2008 by Richard Bertrand Spencer, who heads the white nationalist think tank known as the National Policy Institute. Alt-right

is right-wing political movement founded in 2017, who believes their white identity is under attack by many cultural and racial organizations and agendas using "political correctness" and "social justice" to undermine and oppress white people and "their" civilization. They also advocate against multiculturalism, immigration, and feminism. Though they organize events and rally behind political parties to further their agenda, they utilize a lot of social media and online memes to influence and "correct" the cultural thinking of white people in hopes that they understand they are the superior race and should assert their right of supremacy and white power. These memes tend to oppress and reject the power, authority, and equality of all other races, especially and leaders who seek to empower and advocate for justice and liberation of minority ethnic groups.

Antifa
Antifa is a secretive anti-fascist political protest movement in America and a few other countries, that gained notoriety in 2017's Charlottesville, VA rally. They arrived on the scene with the inauguration of President Donald Trump in 2017 and has been highlighted as a terrorist group who is on the national watch list. This is mainly due to President Trump affiliating them with the Democratic Party and marking them as violent lawless rebels. Though the media has run with these claims and continuously release fearful and false rhetoric that presents Antifa in a negative light, none of it has been substantiated.

The Democratic Party continues to reject and condone all affiliations, actions, and ideologies of Antifa. Antifa claims no ties to the Democratic Party, has no national leader, however, does have some loosely national organizers that rally them together for common causes and events. Antifa includes a host of autonomous organizations that are affiliated by their militant opposition to fascism, capitalism, nationalism, far-right ideologies, white supremacy, authoritarianism, racism, homophobia, and xenophobia. They sometimes work around and rally with movements like Black Lives Matter or the Occupy Movement though they are their own distinct group and ideology. Misinformation about Antifa often pegs them as extremely violent, and many acts done by violent white supremacy groups or people looking to create trouble at peaceful protests are often blamed on them. Though some members can be extreme in advocating for their beliefs, most members are nonviolent; they are for peace, unity, and justice. They usually attend events of this nature, and unless provoked or standing up for those who are being physically threatened or violated, this is generally their posture at public events. Antifa activists often wear top-to-toe black and face coverings during public demonstrations. This increases the opportunity to be viewed as wired, suspicious, and violent.

BLACK SUPREMACY
Black supremacy is the belief that black people are superior to people of other races. People who maintain this belief often believe this superiority is innate and is a position given by a higher power or a god. Some people who operate through this premise believe this is the reason White people strive to oppress and assert control over Black people. They believe it

ensures that the Black race will not rise and walk in their right to rule and have dominion in the earth. Some people who operate through this ideology are bound by generational, personal, social, legal, economic, and systematic trauma of racism that may be dating all the back to slavery itself. Being unhealed from such wounds and reliving racism over through life experiences causes anger and hatred to the White races and other ethnic groups that seek to oppress Black people. Though racism needs to be addressed and dismantled in every area of our lives and within society, engaging in the extremity of Black supremacy just reverses the racism and cause more problems in striving to eradicate it. No racism or supremacy is justifiable no matter who is engaging in it. There must be a mindset of equality for all people and empowering this theology over all others. This will ensure that all people are valued, honored, and regard regardless of racial and cultural differences.

BLACK LIVES MATTER
Some of this information is from my manual, Eradicating the Powers of Racism.

Many people equate "Black Lives Matter," movement with the organization formed in the summer of 2013, by three radical Black organizers — Alicia Garza, Patrisse Cullors, and Opal Tometi - after George Zimmerman's acquittal for the shooting death of Trayvon Martin. The movement and the organization are two quite different visions. "BLACK LIVES MATTER," became the hashtag among social media platforms when people felt the acquittal was unjust. An organization was formed to help combat the injustices of race against Black people and other victimized groups. Its mission is to eradicate white supremacy and build local power to intervene on injustices and violence inflicted on Black people and Black communities by the justice, social, and political systems and groups. It has become a member led global organization with over 40 chapters spreading from the United States, United Kingdom, and Canada. In addition to being a Black liberation organization, Black Lives Matter also advocates for queer and transgender individuals, the disabled, undocumented populations, people with criminal records, and women. The network centers on helping those who have marginalized within Black liberation movements. Because of this broad mission challenges many individuals' religious and political beliefs, there is an extreme resistance in advocating for the organization, though many affirm the "Black Lives Movement." Those who do not know that there is a difference tend to rally against the movement, while engaging in heartless rhetoric and behavior that strengthen the need for reform around slavery and racial injustice. Many companies financially support the "Black Lives Matter" network without knowing the full agency. Millions of dollars have been poured into this organization; there has been minimal evidence of where the money is going and how it is funding racial injustice. This factor has also complicated the ability to truly rally and produce for racial reform. Such challenges cause people to view the Black Lives Matter movement as a farce. The agenda presents as being more for financial gain at the expense of a controversial and emotional challenge that truly needs be rectified in society and the world at large. There is no doubt that this issue needs to be addressed and the financial dollars given to the organization need to be accounted for and utilized for the purposes of reforming and eradicating racial injustices. All other mission agendas should be separated, and specific vision quests should be available to the public, explained on the website, and significantly distinguish, so that people can trust the mission and the vision to which it was originally founded.

The Black Lives Matter movement is essential to racial reform and enlightening the public on racial injustices. The movement is not designed to exclude other races, but to emphasize the lack of necessary action and attention brought to the systematic racism and violence Black people are enduring. In no way is the movement meant to take away from the importance of human life of any other race, sexuality, ethnicity, age, or gender.

Most people who are declaring, "BLACK LIVES MATTER," are proclaiming it as truth, due to the racial injustices, and not because they are part of this organization. It is important for White people, believers of Jesus Christ, and people in general, to resist getting caught up in rhetoric, that they miss the intent and purpose of needing to eradicate racism and racial injustices.

It is also important not to take the declaration as a negation against one's own identity or race. We are all important. We are not in a competition with one another. We are not inferior of one another. People are not highlighting one race or person over another.

ALL PEOPLE ARE IMPORTANT!

ALL PEOPLE DESERVE JUSTICE!

ALL PEOPLE DESERVE EQUALITY!

This is the sole purpose of saying loudly and proudly,

BLACK LIVES MATTER!

"ALL LIVES MATTER" is often used at the wrong time and is generally used when there is a need to acknowledge the lives of Black people. It is important for White people, believers of Jesus Christ, and people in general, to search themselves when they feel a need to respond with "ALL LIVES MATTER."

EXAMINE YOURSELF ON THIS MATTER!

WE NEED YOU ADVOCATING - NOT FEELING INFERIOR!

Some Reasons People Say, "ALL LIVES MATTER."

Hatred of Black People
We need to be honest that some people truly do not care about Black people so saying, "ALL LIVES MATTER," is there way of deadening the need to support, honor, and protect the Black race from racial injustices. They are on assignment to murder and sacrifice the lives of Black people through their hatred of them.

Inferiority Complex
There are people who are prideful, haughty, heartless, and operate in a superiority complex towards others. This complex is rooted in their sense of inferiority. They present as if they are confident, but truthfully, they feel subservient regarding who they are, so they operate through a well of comparison, and performance. When someone else appears to be spotlighted, even for a righteous or justified cause, it triggers their inferiority. Degrading others to a standard or rank they can handle or that makes them feel superior over that person. Psychology calls this "The Inferiority Complex." These people tend to be self-absorbed due to their issues of inadequacy, low self-esteem, low self-worth. They need to always feel validated in their identity and at all cost. Until they get delivered from this complex, they will be demonic sacrifices of Black people and the injustices they ensue by declaring, "ALL LIVES MATTER."

False Grace and Love Agendas
Some people think they are keeping the peace by contending, "ALL LIVES MATTER." They dread conflict, especially any conflict that place them in a negative light, cause drama or upheaval, or disrupt peace and unity. They would rather have false peace and pretend unity than confrontation and open dialog, as they view it as division and strife. They hate when trouble and challenges manifest around them. They often operate in a "grace" or "let's just love one another," model. But even the grace and love model are rooted in unrealistic, false, surface, superficial, pseudo interaction, rather than the true embodiment of real engagement, support, and drive to have in-depth relationship, equality, and justice for all. Often due to a grace and love agenda, such persons are unable to accept constructive criticism, where they would be required to examine themselves concern their heartless "ALL LIVES MATTER," banter. They are convinced they love everyone with the unconditional love of Jesus. It often takes a lot of dismantling their vain imaginations regarding grace and love for them to change.

Inclusion Methodology
Some people use the "ALL LIVES MATTER" concept, because they want everyone to feel included, even as they understand that "BLACK LIVES MATTER." They recognize the need for Black people to be the focus of current racial injustices or regarding the eradication of racism, but it is easier to approach the agenda from an "ALL LIVES MATTER" slant. They are not striving to negate Black people and their struggle. They understand it clearly, but recognize that for who is in their sphere, including everyone is the best approach to get people to unite for a common cause; or to get people to acknowledge that racial injustices of Black people need to be examined, supported, and rectified. This does not make using the slogan correct, but sometimes, the circumstance and other factors, are taken into consideration. I recommend that when such a posture is needful, that at some point, the education of the racism

and Black injustices is implemented. Also discussing the underlying issues for having to use the inclusion factor need to be confronted, so that the hidden roots of racism can be exposed and uprooted.

Ignorance and Lack of Knowledge
The Bible speaks of ignorant people and of being destroyed for a lack of knowledge. Some people are ignorant and unknowledgeable. Instead of seeking knowledge, they strive to make peace by saying stupid stuff that makes matters worse - that destroys others and interfere with the justice that needs to prevail. "ALL LIVES MATTER," is an ignorant and unknowledgeable comment to express when someone has just endured an injustice - especially one where someone's life is unnecessarily lost. It is important to educate oneself during these times before speaking fruitlessly. It is important not to add to the problem, but to be a solution to the problem. Education concerning the challenges of Black people is vital in understanding the declaration, "BLACK LIVES MATTER." Speaking aimlessly tears Black people down, rather than empowers them, and build them up. Decreeing a SHIFT to being educated, knowledgeable, and a change agent in the earth!

Proverbs 19:2 *Desire without knowledge is not good, and whoever makes haste with his feet misses his way.*

Hosea 4:6 *My people are destroyed for lack of knowledge: because thou hast rejected knowledge, I will also reject thee, that thou shalt be no priest to me: seeing thou hast forgotten the law of thy God, I will also forget thy children.*

Self-Hatred
Some Black people who contend ALL LIVES MATTER, suffer from self-hatred. Self-hatred is a horrible complex in any race or regarding any person who battles with it. Some other races of people can hate themselves, thus hating others. The Bible tells us to esteem others higher than ourselves. We cannot esteem others if we are not first esteeming ourselves. We cannot love others if we do not love ourselves.

Philippians 2:3-5 *Let nothing be done through strife or vainglory; but in lowliness of mind let each esteem other better than themselves. Look not every man on his own things, but every man also on the things of others. Let this mind be in you, which was also in Christ Jesus.*

Mark 12:31 *The second is this: 'You shall love your neighbor as yourself.' There is no other commandment greater than these."*

Self-hatred is the concept of having an intense dislike, disdain, loathing, repugnance, ill will, detestation, extreme aversion, self-resentment, self-rejection, or hostility towards self.

Some people may hate themselves for the things they have done or endured. They cannot forgive themselves or others. This causes bitterness, and bitterness breeds self-hatred.

Self-hatred is the inability to see one's self in a positive likeness. The person hates themselves to a point where they change themselves and live behind a façade. Or they totally reject themselves where they can no long see themselves or they see someone else when they look at themselves. Often when a person enters this dimension of self-hatred, a demonic spirit has overtaken their eyesight, perception of self, and their identity. They also may have split personalities where they fluctuate between seeing their true self and seeing their alternate personality of who they want to be. The person can also become possessed by the spirit where they no longer see themselves. They take on the alternate personality and begin to live through that personality. When this occurs, they will not identify with anyone or anything that is associated with their identity. They will speak against it with acrimony, bitterness, hostility, revulsion, abhorrence, disfavor, dread, horror. This is because the alternate identity has caused enmity between the person and their identity (We are to have enmity against the devil, not against ourselves or one another).   The person has rejected God's ordained identity, focused on recreating their identity, thus become their own God and creator. God then gives them over to their own heart's desires, thus becoming their own creation.

Psalms 81:12 *So I gave them up unto their own hearts' lust: and they walked in their own counsels.*

Romans 1:24 *Wherefore God also gave them up to uncleanness through the lusts of their own hearts, to dishonor their own bodies between themselves.*

1Corinthians 6:19-20 *Or do you not know that your body is a temple of the Holy Spirit within you, whom you have from God? You are not your own, for you were bought with a price. So glorify God in your body.*

Ephesians 5:29 *For no man ever yet hated his own flesh; but nourisheth and cherisheth it, even as the Lord the church: For we are members of his body, of his flesh, and of his bones.*

Psalms 16:8-11 *I have set the Lord always before me; because he is at my right hand, I shall not be shaken. Therefore my heart is glad, and my whole being rejoices; my flesh also dwells secure. For you will not abandon my soul to Sheol, or let your holy one see corruption. You make known to me the path of life; in your presence there is fullness of joy; at your right hand are pleasures forevermore.*

When a person's life and perceptions are not set in and before God, they are subject to enter dimensions of hell even as they live on earth that can grip their soul, thus, changing the trajectory of their identity and journey with him. There are people who hate themselves so much that they will change their gender, reject their race while claiming to be another ethnicity, bleach their skin, have cosmetic surgery, engage in bulimic and anorexic behavior, slander and reject those who are of their identity. They believe in the exalted persona and campaign that has stronghold them and will defend it with no regard to how their actions impact others. Such persons have become self-absorbed, self-indulged, and self-promoting. Their intent is to get people to see and accept the created them and to only love what they have become and what they believe is worth loving. This behavior is idolatry. When considering the scriptures above, such idolatry can cause God to turn a person over to themselves. The more a person engage a self-hatred identity, the greater they yield to narcissism. Narcissists tend to have an excessive need for admiration, disregard for others' feelings and struggles, an inability to handle any criticism, and a sense of entitlement. They always play the victim and blame others for the conflicts they create and for the reason others do not like them.

Self-hatred can be the posture of someone who is contending, "ALL LIVES MATTER," as if it is their life's campaign slogan. They hate themselves, so they are incapable of loving someone else. These are the worst kind of "ALL LIVES MATTER," blasters. They will enrage others with their need to be right and need to kill the identity of Black people and people in general.

Counterattacking "ALL LIVES MATTER."
The best way to counterattack the "ALL LIVES MATTER," banter, is to continue to declare that "BLACK LIVES MATTER." Confronting the person, may sometimes bring deliverance, but even if it does not, the fight is not with these people. The true war is with the institutionalize system of racism that must be dismantled and eradicated. Stay focused on the true fight and do not get weary contending with rhetoric battles that distract your purpose. The Bible is full of antagonists. They always lose in the end.

Jeremiah 29:11 *For I know the thoughts that I think toward you, saith the LORD, thoughts of peace, and not of evil, to give you an expected end.*

Isaiah 59:19 *So shall they fear the name of the Lord from the west, and his glory from the rising of the sun. When the enemy shall come in like a flood, the Spirit of the Lord shall lift up a standard against him.*

John 16:33 *These things I have spoken unto you, that in me ye might have peace. In the world ye shall have tribulation: but be of good cheer; I have overcome the world.*

1John 4:4 *Ye are of God, little children, and have overcome them: because greater is he that is in you, than he that is in the world.*

1John 5:4 *For whatsoever is born of God overcometh the world: and this is the victory that overcometh the world, [even] our faith.*

1Corinthians 15:57 *But thanks [be] to God, which giveth us the victory through our Lord Jesus Christ.*

Romans 8:37 *Nay, in all these things we are more than conquerors through him that loved us.*

NAACP
If Black people and people of any race are going to support a Black activist movement, I highly recommend the NAACP (National Association for the Advancement of Colored People). They were founded in 1909 and have actively and consistently advocated against violence and injustices of Black people. The NAACP has 2,200 units and branches across the United States, and over 2M activists. Their mission is to secure and empower the political, educational, social, and economic rights and equality of people and communities to extinguish racial discrimination. Through this vision they can empower and fortify the health, well-being,

and identity of the people they help. Get your family, ministry, business, or organization involved with the NAACP and fight for equality and injustices of all people.

SCIENTOLOGY

Scientology was founded in 1953 by science fiction author L. Ron Hubbard and has gained popularity due to some Hollywood celebrities who have embraced it. Hubbard describes scientology as the Western Anglicized continuance of many earlier forms of wisdom," and cites the teachings of Jesus among belief systems of those "earlier forms". Jesus is recognized in Scientology as part of its "religious heritage," and "is seen as only one of many good teachers."

Contradicting the Christian concept of Jesus' "atonement of mankind's sins" through his death on the cross, Hubbard states in the *Volunteer Ministers Handbook* that "Man is basically good, but he could not attain expression of this until now. Nobody but the individual could die for his own sins – to arrange things otherwise was to keep man in chains."

Hubbard became a multi-millionaire because of creating Scientology. In fact, one of the most common criticisms of Scientology is that it is nothing more than a complex money-making scheme. Members who have exposed the money scheme of Scientology report that Scientology's motto is to 'make money, make money, and more money," at the expense of the self-care, physical health, emotional wellness, balance with family relationships and social activities.

1Timothy 4:1-2 *Now the Spirit speaketh expressly, that in the latter times some shall depart from the faith, giving heed to seducing spirits, and doctrines of devils; Speaking lies in hypocrisy; having their conscience seared with a hot iron.*

Chapter 11

WITCHES AND WARLOCKS

Types of Witches:

1. **Cosmic or Star Witch** – Utilizes energy from the planets in solar system, constellations, galaxies, supernovas, stars, asteroids, black holes, and meteors in their practices. Practices Astrology, Zodiac Signs, Horoscopes Celestial Energy.

2. **Traditional Witch** – Study and practice historical and old crafts of witchcraft. They honor the traditional practices and teach and train on the importance of regarding the historical roots and customs of witchcraft.

3. **Hereditary Witch** - Are born into witchcraft. The witchcraft practices are viewed as their lineage and inheritance. They may be dedicated in the womb, at birth or at a young age and taught how to operate in witchcraft at an early age. It is perceived that their powers are stronger due to the generational heritage that they are born into. Some children are given a choice while others are groomed and even forced to embrace witchcraft practices.

4. **Kitchen Witch – Sorcery Witches** - Practice Spell Cooker, Bewitching Spell Recipes, Magic, Charmer, Home Routines, Homemade Offerings, Cleansing, Protection Spells.

5. **Divination Witch** – Psychics, Fortune Tellers, Mediums, Oracles, Magic Workers, seeking to predict the future. Practices Tarot Cards, I Ching, Palmistry, Tasseography.

6. **Green Witch** – Connected to Mother Earth and the energy it possessed, the natural world, and utilizing herbs, plants, and flowers as worship and spell witchery. They love nature and anything green. They practice Herbalism, Botany, Folk Magic, Essential Oils.

7. **Hedge Witch** – Operate in earth magic and herbs, and engage in hedge jumping by communicating, sending messages, and astral projecting into different realms and spheres, while communing and working with demonic and spirit beings.

8. **Sea Witch** – Water witches that works the elements of the water and the demonic forces under the water. Worship Oceans, Lakes, Lunar Magic, Weather Magic, and Mystical Energy.

9. **Elemental Witch** – Such witches study and practice witchcraft connected to the four elements of earth, air, wind, and fire. Their magical practices are rooted in honoring the elements then manipulating them through the casting spell work, incantations, prayers, and rituals.

10. **Secular Witch** – These witches are not necessarily attached to their practice even though they engage in casting spells, using crystals and stones, oils, herbs, and candles. They are non-religious as they do not worship a deity and they are not part of any sects.

11. **Dianic Witch** – Goddess witch full of feminine energy and power. The most feminist operations of all witchcraft practices. Cult followers of the Goddess Diana and her three concepts: The Maiden, The Mother and The Crone, and Dianne Witchcraft worship and the embracing of the Goddess and all her customs. Practices witchcraft that is connected to the moon and its cycles, while seeking to produce witchcraft that produces freedom, independence, healing, and creativity. This form of witchcraft is connected to the feminist movement, emasculating men, and making women superior beings of divinity.

12. **Solitary Witch** – Witch is not connected to a group or coven. Practices alone and are thought to be reincarnated witches who have been trained since puberty, skilled in their craft and are awakened in their witchcraft powers.

13. **Ceremonial Witch** – Operate in ceremonial magic, rituals, and spell work. Work with specific spiritual forces and beings to help complete their workings.

14. **Electric Witch** – Eclectic Witches are not confined to any particular brand of witchcraft. They make their own rules concerning their practices, dabble in different areas, and combine practices based on what they and those they perform witchcraft for need and desire.

15. **Wiccan** – Modern day witches who practice traditional and new age witchcraft. They may be regular people who are not part of a coven, are individually trained, or dabble in witchcraft due to curiosity, personal reasons, or enlightenment. They may form their own groups or covens as they initiate others into witchcraft practices or join established covens for training and community. *"Father of Wicca,"* Gerald Gardner, founded Gardnerian Wicca Witchcraft in 1950. Gardnerian Wicca is an initiated only witchcraft practices that focuses on private rituals and practices privy only to members. They believe and practice rituals to two specific deities, the Horned God and Mother Goddess. They engage in customs connected to nature and the earth, seek to impact and challenge societal norms and laws through their lives and witchcraft practices and rituals.

Alex and Maxine Sanders founded Alexandrian Wicca in 1960. They were students of Gardnerian but where more eclectic in nature as they used ceremonial magic and Qalabalah mysticism in their practices. They believed in utilizing whatever witchcraft that works but maintained an order regarding having to be initiated into the practice and needing to achieve degrees and levels of witchcraft expertise to increase in rank within their practice.

The most widely used Wicca practice in this time is Carrellian Wicca, founded by Caroline High Corell. She was a skilled Arcadian, eclectic, self-initiatory, universal, hereditary witch, groomed from a lineage of psychics, spiritual healers, and herbalists. She launched what is now known as Cornell Mother Temple in Danville, Illinois in 1879 and was its leader unto dying in 1940. She was known as a "Nativist" traditionalist. Her practice was acknowledged as Wiccan in 1970 and is a trending wicca practice in this New Age Movement.

Types of Warlocks:
Warlock is the name for a male witch. The definition of the word warlock is "path breaker, deceiver, traitor, liar. These definitions derived from historical acts of foundational warlocks making a pact with the devil, while separating from God and religious practices. I would contend that warlocks are lockers. They lock their prey down and hold them in bondage with their clever powers. Warlocks are very militant and learn and operate in their craft in a very military type of system. The way they learn their trade and operate in their craft requires them to become a master and obtain certain ranks until they reach a level of mastery. As they train and SHIFT through the ranks, they are required to memorize their rituals and spells, thus embodying the works, such that they become the identity of the magic and witchcraft powers they are studying. The intent is to SHIFT to the highest rank of thought magic where they can control and manipulate everything and anything through supernatural powers.

Warlocks craft in the dark arts (manic and spell work used to harm, control, or kill their victim), magic, sorcery, conjuring and necromancy. They are generally called necromancers, pit servers, high priests, with doctors, shaman, and witches. Extreme warlocks operate in high level witchcraft that include altar worship and rituals, ceremonies, cosmic energy practices, spell casting, astral projection and communing with demonic forces and being in realms and spheres, communing and covenanting with Satan, animal and human blood sacrificing, and sexual and sadistic rituals. The average warlock is overly self-absorbed, egotistical, and some are narcissistic. They pride themselves on being supreme and individualistic in their ideologies and behaviors, and many view those around them as subservient and opportunities to work their craft for the purposes increasing their warlock rank. Some warlocks are so possessed by demons, they may manifest demonic traits, exhibit inhuman strength, and supernatural behaviors. High level warlocks and witches can operate as shape shifters where they can change their physical form at will or adapt behaviorally to any situation.

A wizard tends to be a male, who operates in skillfully magic, mysticism, magical and mystical practices, or wizardry. Wizards tend to work as illusionists or in positions that allow them to perform acts of trickery and deception on people. Some of them make pacts with demons to perform their wizardry as they aim to be the best at their craft and engage in illusions that present them as masters of their craft. They rarely share their techniques with others because the more individualistic they are, the greater the fame, success, and fortune of their craft.

Chapter 12

COSMIC MEDITATION AND CELESTIAL ACTIVITY

Cosmic meditation is a type of meditation that is designed to heighten and enhance a person's awareness of their connection to the universe. The premise is that cosmic meditation causes heighten spiritual awareness, divine consciousness, and awakening by receiving energy, enlightenment, and spiritual and natural power from different regions, spheres, and properties (e.g., sun, moon, stars, galaxies), in the universe. Such enlightenment, power, and strength are used to assert authority over one's life, people, situations, systems, laws, ideologies, spheres, regions, and the world at large. The utilizes guided meditation techniques and postures to empty their mind so that their soul can astral project and ascend to the highest level of consciousness where they are connecting and communing with the universe to receive transformation, answers, strategies, assistance, protection, and provision for whatever it is they are meditating about. Essentially, they are performing prayer meditation but not to God, to the universe itself.

People who operate in cosmic meditation tend to study astrology so they can have insight on when the moon, stars, sun, galaxies, cosmos is at its greatest peak of power and light source, whey they can meditate and receive a transference of that energy to rule in the earth at the highest level possible.

Astrology is the belief that the alignment of stars and planets affects every individual's mood, personality, and environment, depending on when he was born.

God was the first astrologer.

Genesis 1:14-18 New Living Bible *And God said, "Let there be lights in the vault of the sky to separate the day from the night, and let them serve as signs to mark sacred times, and days and years, and let them be lights in the vault of the sky to give light on the earth." And it was so. God made two great lights—the greater light to govern the day and the lesser light to govern the night. He also made the stars. God set them in the vault of the sky to give light on the earth, to govern the day and the night, and to separate light from darkness. And God saw that it was good.*

Astrology in and of itself is not bad or sinful, but when engaged as a god, it is idolatrous.

Cosmic meditators also engage in various witchcraft and sacrifices to further provoke the "universe" to on their behalf. The Bible warns us of this activity.

Deuteronomy 4:14-20 The Amplified Bible *And the Lord commanded me at that time to teach you the statutes and precepts, that you might do them in the land which you are going over to possess. Therefore take good heed to yourselves, since you saw no form of Him on the day the Lord spoke to you on Horeb out of the midst of the fire, Beware lest you become corrupt by making for yourselves [to worship] a graven image in the form of any figure, the likeness of male or female, The likeness of any beast that is on the earth, or of any winged fowl that flies in the air, The likeness of anything that creeps on the ground, or of any fish that is in the* *waters beneath the earth. And beware lest you lift up your eyes to the heavens, and when you see the sun, moon, and stars, even all the host of the heavens, you be drawn away and worship them and serve them, things which the Lord your God has allotted to all nations under the whole heaven. But the Lord has taken you and brought you forth out of the iron furnace, out of Egypt, to be to Him a people of His own possession, as you are this day.*

Isaiah 40:25:26 *To whom then will ye liken me, or shall I be equal? saith the Holy One. Lift up your eyes on high, and behold who hath created these things, that bringeth out their host by number: he calleth them all by names by the greatness of his might, for that he is strong in power; not one faileth.*

Isaiah 44:20 *He feeds on ashes. His deluded heart has led him astray, and he cannot deliver himself or say, "Is not this thing in my right hand a lie?"*

Jeremiah 10:14 *Everyone is senseless and devoid of knowledge. Every goldsmith is put to shame by his idols. For his molten images are a fraud; they have no breath in them.*

Jeremiah 13:25 *This is your lot, the portion I have measured to you," declares the LORD, "because you have forgotten Me and trusted in falsehood.*

Jeremiah 16:19 *O LORD, my strength and my fortress, my refuge in the day of distress, the nations will come to You from the ends of the earth, and they will say, "Our fathers inherited nothing but lies, worthless idols of no benefit at all."*

Romans 1:25 *Christian Standard Bible They exchanged the truth of God for a lie, and worshiped and served what has been created instead of the Creator, who is praised forever. Amen. (Study Romans 1)*

Many cosmic meditators like to use the Bible story of the wisemen following the star of Jesus to find him, as justification for cosmic meditation and other witchcraft practices. The star, however, was use as a sign by God to direct them to Jesus. They did not worship the star or strive to draw knowledge, energy, or power from it. They followed it so they could come worship Jesus.

Matthew 2:1-2 *Now when Jesus was born in Bethlehem of Judaea in the days of Herod the king, behold, there came wise men from the east to Jerusalem, Saying, Where is he that is born King of the Jews? for we have seen his star in the east, and are come to worship him.*

Cosmic mediators are embracing demons and either know it but do not care or do not know it. Many who know it channel demons for greater power and engagement in their life desires, needs, and activities. Many are often deceived by the ideologies they have studied, operate in extremely vain pride and entitlement, and present as very intellectual and knowledgeable, yet what they speak often is ignorant, foolish, a mixture of truths and falsehoods, grandiose, and full of gaslighting. They prey on people who lack identity, are insecure, need quick answers, help, assistance, are lawless, wounded, and are easily manipulated and controlled. They use these people to build a cult following and as proof that what they are speaking is the way; they contend that their ideologies work because these people's lives are now being transformed through self-consciousness. The followers, however, are awakened to channel their fears, insecurities, needs, anger, and trauma, as a cause to rally against anyone who would inquire or disprove of their practices and lifestyle. When they can disempower people and systems by their bold stance, prudent ideologies, rationales of injustices which generally have a measure of truth to them, they become even more prideful and convinced that their way is the only way and is the authority of ruling in life and destiny.

Cosmic meditators understand the power of agreement when meditating together. With the rise of internet and social media, these cosmic meditators have been able to form groups and networks with other of like-minded diviners. They collaborate days and times of unified cosmos meditation to pray to the universe for various purposes. It is not unusually to come across a flier, post, or email, inviting cosmic meditators to join groups to meditate to the universe regarding the weather, laws, politics, world events, etc. Other witchcraft practitioners will join these events or align with the times of these events, and cast spells, rituals, and sacrifices to idol gods or the universe concerning the meditation focus. Such events mimic the prayer gatherings of ministries but is not to God. It is to the universe. As believers, we know the power of agreement.

Matthew 18:19 *Again I say to you, that if two of you agree on earth about anything that they may ask, it shall be done for them by My Father who is in heaven.*

The activating of this principle is not provoking God to work on their behalf. They know this yet believe that their prayers are manipulating and changing the universe to work in their favor. However, their cunning workings are provoking demons to work these cosmic meditations, which then makes them indebted and connected to these demonic agents.

Believers must be discerning, realistic, and concerned that these activities are occurring and be proactive in governing realms and spheres, and situations that are occurring in society, so that God through us can be the ruling voice that governs and influence the earth and everything that concerns it. Here are some prayer strategies for countering attacking the curious workings of cosmic mediation:

- Consistently, declare the Lordship of Jesus above every other demonic Idol. Spend time establishing him fully over the entire earth - entire universe, your regions, nations, and spheres of influence (***Philippians 2:9-11, Ephesians 6:12***).

- Shut down every united confederate coming together in human form, demonic systems, demonic agents (demons used to complete assignments), and through principalities, powers, and territorial spirts. Use the blood of Jesus to break their soul ties and ley lines and dismantle their abilities to unify and produce power through the covenant of unity (***Amos 3:3, Ecclesiastes 4:9-12***). Ley lines are magical and supernatural power lines of energy that crisscross the planet. They would put you in mind of highways intersecting and crisscrossing but only they are in the spirit realm. They are used by witches, warlocks, cosmic meditators, demons, to communicate, unify and work together for a common cause, send spell workings, translate to different territories and spheres, travel via soul astral projection.

- Shut off every demonic way the moon, stars, sun, galaxies, astrology, cosmos, and astral portals, are being used demonically to provoke and infuse demonic spirits with lightening power to impact the earth. As even if it appears for the good, summoning demons always come with a cost. They will require something of the person as demons demand payment for their workings. Also, too much power light from these regions causes alterations in the earth, chemical and mental imbalances in our bodies, and infect the earth with radiation and toxins. That is the reason the sun, moon, stars, operate the way they do. We cannot handle the full impact of them releasing light, energy, and power at full capacity everyday all day. So, we do not need to be channeling energy, light, and power, from them illegally and demonically (*Samuel 15:23, 2Chronicles 33:6*).

- Cancel the transference of power to cosmic meditators through astral light from the moon, stars, sun, galaxies, astrology, and cosmos. Render them powerless and their impact null and void on the earth, on the systems and issues of this world, lands, regions, on people, generations, and in general. Decree their witchcraft spells and unions will have no authority in the earth. Assert dominion through *Generation 1:26-28, Matthew 6:10, and Revelation 11:11-15* to release Jesus Christ's will and plan one the earth.

- Declare out and call forth a SHIFT for the kingdom of God to come and for the kingdoms of the world to become the kingdoms of our Lord - Jesus Christ, as we position ourselves to draw people out of these kingdoms into his kingdom.

- Consistently, repent for these idolatrous activists and for the sins of our nation and world at large. Ask the only true living God - Jesus Christ - to shine upon us with deliverance and healing of death, premature death, Coronavirus, plagues, famine, and any other hardship in the earth (*2Chronicles 7:14*).

- Spend consistent personal and congregational time prophesying, decreeing, and blessings the earth, your nation and region, the world at large, the people.

Chapter 13

CHURCH WITCHES AND WARLOCKS

How Churches Create Witches

The body of Christ talks a good game about the supernatural but fear it more than they embrace it. For this reason, they have created witches and warlocks for the dark side. For this reason, they have driven supernatural kingdom people into the hands of the devil.

Some saints are now rogue witches and warlocks because they were not taught how to steward their gifts and powers of the prophetic, seed, etc. in the church or in life. They go to the dark side where they can at least walk in their calling even if it is not for the true and living God. The strength of who we are is in our identity. When we cannot be who we were created to be, it weakens, burdens, baffles, confuse, and crush us. We live more days dreading our birth than blessing the day we were born. David knew this truth so well that he declared, *"If I make my bed in hell, you are there."*

Psalm 139:1-18 *O LORD, thou hast searched me, and known me. Thou knowest my downsitting and mine uprising, thou understandest my thought afar off. Thou compassest my path and my lying down, and art acquainted with all my ways. For there is not a word in my tongue, but, lo, O LORD, thou knowest it altogether. Thou hast beset me behind and before, and laid thine hand upon me.*

Such knowledge is too wonderful for me; it is high, I cannot attain unto it. Whither shall I go from thy spirit? or whither shall I flee from thy presence? If I ascend up into heaven, thou art there: if I make my bed in hell, behold, thou art there. If I take the wings of the morning, and dwell in the uttermost parts of the sea; Even there shall thy hand lead me, and thy right hand shall hold me.

If I say, Surely the darkness shall cover me; even the night shall be light about me. Yea, the darkness hideth not from thee; but the night shineth as the day: the darkness and the light are both alike to thee. For thou hast possessed my reins: thou hast covered me in my mother's womb. I will praise thee; for I am fearfully and wonderfully made: marvellous are thy works; and that my soul knoweth right well. My substance was not hid from thee, when I was made in secret, and curiously wrought in the lowest parts of the earth.

Thine eyes did see my substance, yet being unperfect; and in thy book all my members were written, which in continuance were fashioned, when as yet there was none of them. How precious also are thy thoughts unto me, O God! how great is the sum of them! If I should count them, they are more in number than the sand: when I awake, I am still with thee.

When utilized, a person's gift will make room for them whether in the kingdom of God or the kingdom of darkness. Much of what the enemy does is counterfeit, stolen, or perverted. He wanted to be God so his kingdom mimics God while also releasing evil into the world. He took over realms and spheres that belong to us – God's people. We are to be seated in kingdom operation within these realms, and though we have claimed to have taken our seat, we live from the earth instead of heavenly places.

Ephesians 2:6 *And hath raised us up together, and made us sit together in heavenly places in Christ Jesus:*

We claim to fight principalities and powers but shun those who can discern and see these demonic spirits and systems; those who have been given giftings and authority to lead us in the fight. Lack of teaching and training of translating and traveling in spiritual realms for ministry and warfare purposes, and prophetic and supernatural dreams and encounters, cause people to find their own interpretation and education in these areas. Done void of Holy Ghost direction, they open their lives to spirit guides and demon activity that turn them in Christian witches and warlocks. Those that have not yielded to the dark side, are labeled as weird, spooky, silenced in the church, on psych medications, locked up in psychiatric wards. Such labels drive them further into demonic oppression and witchcraft tendencies. Our inability to train and even govern these people, their gifts, and heavenly realms, confound matters for the body of Christ and expose us to being infiltrated by witches and warlocks who the devil send to steal, kill, and destroy people and ministries.

1Samuel 15:23 *For rebellion is as the sin of witchcraft, and stubbornness is as iniquity and idolatry. Because thou hast rejected the word of the LORD, he hath also rejected thee from being king.*

<u>Rebellion</u> is *qesem* in the Hebrew and means:
1. divination (including its fee), oracle.
2. (reward of) divination, divine sentence, witchcraft.
3. witchcraft of the nations, Balaam of false prophets.

When rebellion operates in members and ministries, it opens the door to witchcraft. Rebellious believers,

- Are the people's choice and choose the people's choice. They want leaders who will cater to their fleshly and sinful desires, who they can control and manipulate for their own purposes.
- Hear the word, but implement it how they see fit, according to their own desires, what benefits them and those they are aiming to please.
- Only please or serve God in measure. They make excuses for the reason they are not fully committed or obedient to what God purposes them to do.
- Train just enough to get a position or present as godly, but not enough to sustain in their daily living, destiny, or calling.
- Are interested in position, leadership, rulership, but not submission or honor to God or leadership.
- Implement witchcraft tactics to continue advancing in what they have built in their own strength and will, and to appease those who are flattered by their witchery.
- Operate in mixture, but claim their sinful, idolatrous, and witchcraft practices are of God.
- Utilize witchcraft practices in effort to foretell the future or to hear from God once stops speaking to them.

- Tend to act first, then repent, pray, and seek to hear God after they realized they have disobeyed him, and is risking the repercussions of their actions.
- Seek to manipulate, use, and kill God's chosen leaders due to jealousy and fear that they will be replaced.
- Will continue in their position unrepentant to save face with the people while knowing God has rejected them.

Many ministries do not want to rattle the rebellious, especially if they have been part of, encouraged, tolerated, and benefited from their giftings and callings. The rebellious will become passively and blatantly aggressive when holiness and obedience is encouraged. They will use any information they have against the leaders to silence them and make them feel helpless in addressing the rebellion. The leader become subject to the witches and warlocks, and their vision begins to run the ministry rather than God. Leaders ether resort to complying or risk being exposed for any rebellious acts they have engaged in. The entire ministry and its leaders appear godly, but really is just a form and fashion. They are under the rebellious sin of witchcraft which is breeding through the ministry.

Unresolved hurt and wounds from the world and church can be a factor in converting people into witches and warlocks. Also, a lack of true deliverance and healing cause people to seek alternatives to rid evil, mental torment, soul trauma, sicknesses, disease. Failure to really bring physical and emotional wellness, deal with life issues, admit and heal church issues, has caused a disbelief and mistrust in God and the church. People yield to personal, community, family or ethnic traditions and customs, alternative medicines, or turn to blatant witchcraft practices for relief. When these options provide false hope, they live in mixture and witchery, thus becoming church witches and warlocks who preach Christ, while practicing sorcery.

Failure to address slavery, racial injustices, white privilege, white supremacy, suppression of ethnic cultures, and how the Bible has been used to enslave and oppress races, especially the African American race, has caused them to leave the church at alarming rates, while embracing witchcraft and new age practices. African Americans are becoming witches and warlocks as they embrace Yoruba religion, Santeria, voodoo practices, emoji spell casting,

People feel justified because they are broken. Being taught a gospel void of power fuels their anger and justification. They begin to demand showdowns between the witchcraft they engage in and the form or mediocre power their leaders and ministries operate in. Failure to fully demonstrate the raw power of God, aides the continuation of witchcraft practices.

Witches Infiltrating the Church
It would be beneficial for every leader to study the life and characteristics of Jezebel and Delilah and how they operate. Jezebel and Delilah can be in the ministry already or can infiltrate the ministry. Also study the witch of Endor in ***1Samuel 28*** and the diviner that followed Apostle Paul around in ***Acts 16***.

Witches infiltrate the church to control, manipulate, seduce, gain entail, destroy, or negatively influence the lives of the members or the church. They use flattery, opportunity, generosity, willingness to volunteer and work hard and long hours, to gain favor, while infiltrating organizations within the church. The witches are seeking to get close to the main pastor and their key leaders, so they can gain entail to further control, manipulate, seduce, and wreak havoc. There main desire is to be the leader or close to the leader, for they love the thrill of tricking, deceiving, and overseeing saints. They are sent to cause devastation and/or bewitchment to the leader and the members, cause the ministry to shut down or a ministry split, cause members to leave due to hurt, gain entail to report back to their witchcraft coven or demonic camp. Some witches infiltrate churches to oppress the leader or people with demons. They will join the intercessory team, altar prayer ministry or worship team for this purpose. In addition to willingly volunteering, they wait for the opportune time to shine in their gifting so that people will think they are for the good and will seek to use them again.

I heard a testimony of a converted witch who infiltrated the church for the purposes of oppressing the members with demons. This was her assignment as she stated she would go from church to church doing this. One day she watched the altar workers be unsuccessful in casting out a demon that intensely manifesting and causing a scene. She went to the altar and asked if she could help. They allowed her, she prayed, and it appeared that she cast the demon out. But what she really did was bring the demon into her because she wanted the demon's powers. The altar workers were so impressed they begin to use the witch weekly. While being used she would either take within her the demonic powers for her own purposes, while oppressing the members with other demons that would wreak havoc in the church and the people's lives. The leaders and altar call members where none the wiser. Once the demons she cast into the people begin to really cause discord, she would abruptly leave and go to her next church and do the same thing. She said it was easy to infiltrate churches because church people are impressed with works and giftings rather than the character or nature of a person. They also cannot discern false works from the true works of God.

At a church I use to attend, we would have witches that would only show up when we had significant spiritual moves within the ministry, or during major conferences. One of the witches came consistently for years, would sit on the front row, and speak words that appeared to be spiritual, but would disturb the service. When I became leader of the altar call, I asked the Lord what the woman was doing. He said she was not speaking spiritual words but word curses. She was spell casting within the atmosphere of the church to stop the magnitude of what was to occur within the service and from the impartation of the speakers, so that it would not further overtake the members and the atmosphere of the region. I initially remember telling my leaders and others she was a witch, but they knew the witch as she was a former member, so they were not open to what I was sharing. God told me that since I was a major leader in the church and a watchman, I could counterattack the witch in the spirit and that is what I did. I begin to pray against her tactics to counterattack her works and she would go silent in the services. She eventually stopped coming to the services altogether.

As a watchman, I had to learn to be okay that I would see and discern the activity of demons and devils that others did not see and to be okay with doing what God led me to do even if they did not agree, rejected, or did not want to deal with what was occurring. I remember there was another demonized person that would only come to our services during major events and contend she wanted to be delivered. The altar workers and even speakers would spend a significant time focusing on her to be delivered, but she never would get free and only would show a glimpse of deliverance. She would return the next day severely bound again and the routine continued. Then after the major event she would disappear and only show up for the next one. Never seeking to be a member but only seeking to disrupt major moves the ministry was experiencing. I learned that information from God. I also learned that her reason for showing up during that time was to distract other faithful members from the opportunity to be delivered and set free and to fully grow and mature at those significant times of SHIFTING and elevation. By the time the attention was off her, there was limited time to focus on others. Often that time was rushed, done corporately, or did not occur at all.

During these types of experiences, you will have members say the event was great, but I was left wanting. It was because they knew the level of outpouring that was to occur but did nothing to experience that level of refreshing and breakthrough due to distractions like this. For this reason and others, I added what I called "watchmen" to our altar call team. Every service, watchmen were stationed at specific places within the room before service, during high levels of deliverance, healing, and worship within the service, and at altar calls. Their goal was not to personally pray for people, but to pray for the atmosphere to be pliable for deliverance healing, to pray protection prayers as the ministry was going forth, pray and encourage those God revealed to come to the altar for salvation, baptism, and prayer, and to watch, pray, and intervene regarding suspicious activity within the pews and at the altar. Initially the team were resistant to the Watchman's position but after they begin to catch people doing various ungodly or disorderly things in the pews and saw the increase of God's miraculous power operating in the pews and at the altar, they understood the necessity for having watchmen ton the wall.

Witches love to use altar time to release their spells by acting like they are singing to songs or praising and worshipping God, but they are chanting spells and incantations, directing spell workings that they have already cooked up and released into the spirit realms, and evoking demons into the atmosphere to hinder the works of God that is going forth and so that people leave more bound than they came. They also use this time to prey on the innocent people who are left unattended to in the audience or who have been prayed for and are not slain under the spirit at the altar or spending more time with God in deliverance, healing, and worship.

I remember attending a conference; myself and my spiritual daughter was upfront worshiping, and an altar call broke out. The speaker was laying hands on people and they were dropping like flies from the weightiness of the glory. The glory was so heavy upon the speaker that three or more people was holding him up and multiple people were following trying to catch the people before they fall. Then there were a few more altar workers covering those that fell but no one was watching those fallen. They were exposed to the witches. I watched one witch target a teenager. She got an altar cover and covered the teen. This made it look like she was attending to the girl and as if she was part of the altar call team. She then began to dance around the teen as she lay on the floor. She was conducting an incantation circle so she could cast her spell. I went and stood right by the teen and pray to break the incantation spell. The witch realized what I was doing but knew I was not a worker. She then leaned down by the girl and started to speak spells over her. But I got on the floor leaned over the young lady and begin to pray and worship over her. I straddled her with my arms so the witch could not get to her. She eventually stopped trying to bewitch the teen and saw that I was watching her, so she stood in place doing nothing for the rest of the service. This type of activity goes on all the times at services. At the altar and in the pews. But the saints have shunned or neglected their watchmen, so they are not on the wall. The watchmen are so bitter from being rejected that they resist getting on the wall despite what others think about their gifts and callings. The watchmen must be healed from rejection within and outside the church, and from mental health stigmas that have plagued their gifts. The then must be trained and position so the church can position themselves to take over every realm due them, while dismantling principalities, territorial spirits, powers, and ungodly systems, for God's glory.

Characteristics of a Church Witch
- Strives to get close to leaders so they can acquire inside information, become a leader themselves, be in position to control others, and usurp authority to fulfill their purpose.
- Is an accuser of the brethren - a betrayer - will gather others to accuse and betray along with her?
- Is not interested in unity, fellowship, togetherness, but utilize these methods to gain the favor of people, to infiltrate groups and become a lead voice over people.
- Controlling, manipulative, seductive, jealous – envious.
- Subtle but cunning and conniving.
- Prideful and haughty; overly self-confident, convincing others of their gifts and callings.
- Overemphasis their importance and the importance of their skills and abilities.
- Self-absorbed, preoccupied with self; idolatrous in being one's own god.
- Rebellious, anti-submissive, insubordinate.
- Hate authority, hate those who question or expose them; hate those they want to be or be like, hate those in their position, or those they desire to usurp.
- Need to be the center of attention - thrives and craves attention - will throw a tantrum when not the center - feel rejected and punishes others for rejecting them or when they are not the center of their world.
- Displays little girl or little boy behaviors and tantrums; people are either appalled or empathize with their behavior. Either way, they use it to play the victim.
- Wants their victims all to themselves - will sow seeds of discord and mistrust to kill relationships that their victims are in - strives to isolate their victims into being the main voice and companion in their lives to control them - is jealous and will punish victim if they adhere or consider the voice of others, especially those that in authority, those with great wisdom, those who can bless them, or those who have the potential to draw the victim from under their spell.
- Dramatic; exaggerated everything especially their accomplishments or life trials.
- A convincing liar - can lie with a straight face; lie and turn people against one another.
- Projecting an illusion or perception of extreme power even though they operate in a form of godliness or use demons and sorcery to get their work done.
- Lives and operates through a world of fantasy and distortion. Seeks to draw everyone into their false reality; people become confuse as they are bewitched and can no longer tell their reality from the witch's reality.
- Vindictive especially when their needs and desires are not met, when they do not get their way, when feeling threatened, when feeling like they lost as it is always about winning for them.

- Can be charming and nice one minute and murderous the next, all while possessing a killer instinct.
- Very presumptuous, pushy, determined to the point of overstepping boundaries and justifying their actions.
- Hates boundaries and will manipulate and seduce to get pass them - seeks to be in the inside circle for personal gain.
- Will use undermining tactics to get their way; especially towards leadership and those they are seeking to control.
- Aggressive and passive aggressive but always aggressive nonetheless; can be physically abusive.
- Used silence as a punishment.
- Withhold love, attention, rewards, accolades, and emotions to control the emotional interactions of the relationship or as punishment.
- Emotional abuse and will manipulate emotions through psychological games and mindsets to abuse and get their way.
- Twists words, even truths and use them as ammunition against leadership and their victims.
- Studies and collects entail in their victims so they can use it as ammunition later - especially personal information that may lend to inferences, be open to interpretation or cause questioning of truth and one's integrity.
- Will strike with personal information when relationships end.
- Intimates their victims and makes them feel powerless - does this with words and actions - makes them feel they are helpless without their or that they cannot contend, confront, or overthrow them.
- Instills fear and terror in their victims; also releases it in the atmosphere to subdue their environment and surroundings under their control.
- Chants and use manipulative prayers to control people and the atmosphere of the ministry.
- Sows seeds of damaging and murderous discord without any regard for actions - feels justified regarding these actions and even considers is judgment and due punishment.
- Loves to correct, rebuke, and chastise others, but hates being corrected, rebuked, or chastised - can be driven by this and have a lustful thirst for it.
- Will follow the rules for a time, then will strike at an appointed time.
- Double minded and unstable in thoughts and emotions.
- May have a mental disorder of narcissism, bipolar, schizophrenia, or multiple personality disorder which accounts for time is stability and times of extreme ungodly behavior.
- Often does not accept responsibility for one's actions - has motive if responsibility is taken or has a perceived justifiable excuse for wrongdoing.
- Blames others - it always the other persons fault - will go to extremes to prove one's point or position and to acquire perceived justice.
- Will blame and contend others are witches to cast off the fact that they are one.
- Possessive - possessive in love - sees everything as property - wants ownership of what it is seeking to control.
- Due to rejection issues, the witch can never be fulfilled - the more you feed them love, attention, yourself, the more they will want - are a bottomless pit that cannot be fulfilled.
- Have its victims performing to prove their love, but the victim will never obtain an Oscar because this is a role that cannot be achieved.

- Will sacrifice ANYONE or ANYTHING for personal gain - driven in accomplishing their will and purpose at the expense of anything or anyone.
- Often turns its victims into witches as they end up engaging in rebellious tactics to contend with this witch or to avoid being bewitched in other relationships.
- Will portray themselves as innocent even though guilty - will take on the spirit of the martyr even though they are the killer.
- Does not relinquish power easily - will use charm and manipulation to make their victim think they are making the wrong decision or doing them wrong - will seek ways to regain power and/or position.
- Will have the victim second guess their actions - psychological warfare will be constant because of all the webbing a witch does to hook their victim - when they break free from them, the messages, hooks, traps, webbings, will activate one's mind, soul, heart, social settings, atmospheres, in effort to draw and keep them hooked in and even to considering whether they should return to relations with a witch - all these areas must be broken or cleansed out to totally rid of a witch.

Warlocks Infiltrating the Church

Warlocks groom their women using their spiritual charisma. They appear spiritual as they use their works to seduce women into their web. Most warlocks do not have an intimate relationship with God and are surface in their walk with God. Saints, especially women, tend to look at their religious acts or fall for their seductive spiritual jargon when God looks on the heart.

Characteristics of a Church Warlock
- Can be a believer or non-believer.
- Handsome or distinct, unique, and interesting in physical appearance, demeanor, and character.
- Seductively drawing, alluring, mesmerizing.
- Cunning and crafty.
- Use trickery and deception to lure their victim.
- Prey on the innocence and purity of others.
- Seek to steal one's purity and virtuous standing with God.
- Prey on women who desire marriage, insecure in their identity, and anxious in their ability to wait for a mate.
- Some hide amongst the members and search out his or her prey, while others use religious works to draw prey to himself.
- Rushes relationships, to hook his prey.
- Studies their prey so they can war successfully to lock down their soul.
- Use words to curse, lure, cast spells on his prey.
- Gives gifts to flatter and draw prey unto himself.
- Covenant breakers and lack true commitment though may speak otherwise.
- Not truly submitted to leadership, the vision of the ministry, the fellowship, or to people in general; very individualistic in his ideologies and works; uses this to draw victim into secret encounters and sinful behaviors.
- Self-absorbed but makes other interested in pleasing and engaging him.

- Tend to have two or more personalities; can be charming one minute, angry, violent, and controlling the next.
- Enrages when feels threatened in his manhood.
- Tends to use verbal intimidation, belittling, manipulation, aggression, to steal the victim's identity and self-confidence.
- Poor communicator; insecure, while appearing prideful and overly self-confident; will become aggressive and belittling when misunderstood or when insecurity is exposed.
- Blames inappropriate behaviors on the victim; presents himself as the victim even though he is the offender.
- Soul ties his victim to him then use shame, blame, guilt, false promises, and prophecies to keep her locked to him.
- After grooming his victim, isolates them from loved ones, ministry purposes, and the fellowship.
- Victim will begin to experience spiritual, emotional, physical, and financial decline due to being locked down by the warlock, and him draining them of the fruit of their identity and purpose.
- May try to make the victim financially dependent on him or may become financially dependent on the victim, while claim what is theirs as his, and demanding or manipulating the victim to care for him.
- May come from an unhealthy family or life background; is unhealed of these wounds.
- Controlling, very jealous, accusatory, constantly questioning and demanding answers regarding people, whereabouts, and actions.
- Once sex is involved, it soul ties the warlock to the victim. This makes deliverance more difficult. It also further locks the victim in where they have challenges making decisions for themselves.
- Withhold love, sex, communication as punishment or to further lock victim into his control.
- Embarrasses victim in front of others; may contend it was a joke, a misunderstanding, or deserved.
- Makes victim feel as if they are losing their mind and do not trust themselves anymore; victim has lost self and can only be restored until the relationship is severed or the warlock receives personal deliverance and healing.
- May become physically aggressive; will be nice one minute and engaged as if he is another person the next.
- Will refuse intervention from leaders, parents, authority figures; will claim challenges handled without outside interference; this only further isolates the victim and promotes helplessness and hopelessness with breaking free.
- Is bound by the demonic spirits that oppress or possess the warlock since their soul is tied to his; must be free from these spirits to be totally delivered from the warlock experience.

Chapter 14

BABYLONIAN CHRISTIANITY

Babylon is the spirit of the world, of this age. Babylonians are worldly, manmade, and demonic systems with self-focused and idolatrous agendas. They present a false sense of godliness, liberty, and freedom, but truthfully Babylon is idolatrous, oppressive, and evil. The focus is fame, fortune, pleasure, and success. These achievements are done at the expense of sacrificing god identity, oneself, loved ones, the body of Christ, people they deem expendable or a threat, and the remnant that is divinely attached to a person's life's purpose.

Biblically, Babylonian is a Canaanite goddess idol of fortune and happiness, the supposed consort of Baal and her images. Historically, Nimrod the son of Cush, a descendant of Noah's son Ham, founded the Kingdom of Babel. According to Strong's Concordance, Babel means "confusion, by mixing." There were a group of people in the bible who desired to build a tower from earth to heaven. God confounded, confused them and their languages so they could not understand one another, and scattered them to deter this operation. The city was named Babel (**Genesis 10-11**).

Babylon derived from this place as being the city of rebellion against God. In **Revelation 17:5**, Babylon is referred to as the chief seat of idolatry and is called the great mother of prostitutes and the earth's abominations.

And upon her forehead was a name written, MYSTERY, BABYLON THE GREAT, THE MOTHER OF HARLOTS AND ABOMINATIONS OF THE EARTH.

A harlot is one who one who yields themselves to defilement for the sake of gain or indulge in unlawful sexual intercourse and other relations whether for gain or for lust. Abominations pertain to detestable, abominable, idolatrous things and workings. Babylon is its own kingdom set up directly against and in rebellion to the Kingdom of God. In scripture, not only did they have their own demonic altars and treasures, but they often defiled God's altars, temples, and treasures, and used them for their own idolatry practices. Babylon wants to rule and reign within its own kingdom of the world, as well as defile and overtake God's kingdom. It desires to overtake the people who are of God's kingdom and defile their temple which belongs to God; and persuade godly people to come under its customs and idolatry.

The world serves Babylon. It is a kingdom contrary to God's kingdom and seeks to govern the people, land, and region with its own self focused systems and principles.

Babylon is rooted in pride, idolatry, self-idolatry, sin, murder-ungodly bloodshed, demonic sacrifices, greed, anti-Christ, evil world system, rebellion, drunkenness, sexual sin & immorality, mixture, polytheism, blasphemy, perversion, inordinacy, lust, magic, witchcraft, sorcery, mediums, psychics, false authority, violence, the harlot, fornication-indulge in unlawful lust, practice idolatry, prostituting of the body to the lust of another, and the giving over to unlawful intercourse, due to being given over to idolatry and serving these principalities. It is strongly rooted in the mindset of people, in the land, and regions. Even those who serve God, have some Babylonian ways and tendencies that need to be rooted out of their mindsets and behaviors. They tend to lust after fame, success, fortune, while claiming what they are pursuing and receiving through Babylonian ways and systems are of God. Their followers perceive these things as the fruit of God, which creates a lust for Babylon in them. Character and the standard of holiness become secondary to the prides of Babylon.

1John 2:15-17 The Amplified Bible *Do not love or cherish the world or the things that are in the world. If anyone loves the world, love for the Father is not in him. For all that is in the world—the lust of the flesh [craving for sensual gratification] and the lust of the eyes [greedy longings of the mind] and the pride of life [assurance in one's own resources or in the stability of earthly things]—these do not come from the Father but are from the world [itself]. And the world passes away and disappears, and with it the forbidden cravings (the passionate desires, the lust) of it; but he who does the will of God and carries out His purposes in his life abides (remains) forever.*

If we do not check ourselves, God will eventually do the checking for us.

Consistently check in with God, being willing to search oneself and deny, denounce, or quit anything that even resembles Babylon, having strong accountability that can speak truth to you, and constantly humbling oneself under the rule and reverential fear of the Lord is vital to avoiding the subjection of the Babylonian system. Without these attributes, it is easy to get sucked into the practices that appear godly but do not have his fruit, his nature, or his approval. It is easy to hear an idea and think it is God. It is so easy to start with God, acquire success, and think that everything you do is the hand of God because it is still producing success and wealth. It is easy to begin exalting materialistic things flaunting them as God when they may not necessarily be God or testifying of them in the place of God. It is consequently easy to take on the world's tactics, use them in your God vision, and because it produces, you claim its God. It is therefore easy to work a biblical principle and experience results, but God is not in covenant with you. We hear celebrities speak of tithing and how it has blessed their lives, yet what they do and who they are is far from God, his character, and his nature. We hear people claim God opened the door, yet the door they have entered is full of idolatry and lawlessness. We have watch great men and women of God reach great prosperity statuses and platforms, then are exposed by scandal and fallen lifestyles. If we do not check ourselves, God eventually checks us. Or he leaves us to our own demise and Babylon, who is not our friend, ultimately exposes us.

When I consider the Babylonians building the tower of Baal, I hear one word, "driven." I just see a people so driven by what they were doing, that they did even stop to explore if it was a God idea – did it have God's approval. And if so, what was the purpose – what kingdom purpose did it serve. It was obvious that this project was serving them. Being driven means to strive vigorously or compulsively toward a goal or objective. As believers we are not to be driven by anything. We are to be guided by the Holy Spirit as he guides the vision through us.

John 16:13 *When the Spirit of truth comes, he will guide you into all truth. He will not speak on his own but will tell you what he has heard. He will tell you about the future.*

Often saints will contend that "God is getting glory or will get the glory," out of what they are doing. It is important to really know what it means for God to get the glory.

Psalm 29:1-2 *Give unto the LORD, O ye mighty, give unto the LORD glory and strength. Give unto the LORD the glory due unto his name; worship the LORD in the beauty of holiness.*

The Amplified Bible *ASCRIBE TO the Lord, O sons of the mighty, ascribe to the Lord glory and strength. Give to the Lord the glory due to His name; worship the Lord in the beauty of holiness or in holy array.*

Because "glory" is an actual substance that has the character, nature, identity, weight, and authority of God, ascribing God glory is more than just attributing something to Him or attaching his name to an experience, item, or testimony. When we are ascribing glory, we are literally giving people the presence of God. They are receiving his "weight, reputation, honor, splendor, reverence, abundance, riches, and dignity" as this is the definition of *Kabod*, the Hebrew word for glory. What we do in life should ascribe *Kabod* to God as the sustain economic of *Kabod* should radiate from within us. We cannot contend that God is receiving glory when his substance is not evident in what we are doing. We can claim our working are God all we want, but only the true fruit of what we are doing ascribes the fruit of *Kabod*.

John 15:5-7 *I am the vine, ye are the branches: He that abideth in me, and I in him, the same bringeth forth much fruit: for without me ye can do nothing. If a man abide not in me, he is cast forth as a branch, and is withered; and men gather them, and cast them into the fire, and they are burned. If ye abide in me, and my words abide in you, ye shall ask what ye will, and it shall be done unto you.*

Matthew 7:15-20 *Beware of false prophets, which come to you in sheep's clothing, but inwardly they are ravening wolves. Ye shall know them by their fruits. Do men gather grapes of thorns, or figs of thistles? Even so every good tree bringeth forth good fruit; but a corrupt tree bringeth forth evil fruit. A good tree cannot bring forth evil fruit, neither can a corrupt tree bring forth good fruit. Every tree that bringeth not forth good fruit is hewn down, and cast into the fire. Wherefore by their fruits ye shall know them.*

This scripture is referring to a prophet, minister, believer who is a pretender, imposter, or actor. When we are false in our ministry and walk with God, we become ungenuine, unauthentic, and untrue. We are not from the claimed, pretended, or proper source of God and his written word. We are a counterfeit. We become a sheep that is dressed and operating like one of God's vessel, but really, we are a robber, extortioner, predator, who preys on others for greed and advancement. A tree can last for years and have long roots which represents generational ties of godly or corrupt fruit. When we ascribe something as or to God that lacks his fruit, it is a curious art deserving of destruction. God wants it cut down and burned up, so that it no longer exists in our lives or lineage.

Babylonian Christians become breeders of the fruit that produce. They usually operate in the following manner:

- Vision may not be God or may start off with God's design, but slowly becomes more about prosperity and maintaining status, platform, and wealth, and less about God.
- Vision has a God twist but he is not the main agenda. God is used to bewitch people into buying and soul-tying into the agenda.
- Sacrifice themselves, loved ones, and other Christians for favor, fortune, worldly pleasures, success, and privilege with the ruling government, Hollywood, Hollywood mentality, media, social media, platforms, entertainment, unholy business alliances, other famous or platform ministers, and any other person or system that benefits their lives and agenda.
- Cast their agenda or product as God. Perform witchery and charismatic witchcraft in effort to get people to yield to their agenda or buy their product. Their actions literally appear as spell casting and spiritual foolery with a Jesus twist added to it. They will batter their agenda and products with repetitious decrees and chanting prayers that appear biblical but are witchcraft spells intended to incant people into their agenda.
- Connect sowing and money to most everything. Sometimes uses the scriptures or attach the word of God to the sowing tactic so people will give, which is basically the purchasing of the word or prophecy.
- Use swindling, controlling, bullying, manipulating, guilt driven, and seducing tactics, to hustle people into giving. Have no regard that people maybe poor and have minimal or nothing to give.
- Guilt people into giving or make them believe the only way to be blessed is to give or sow their way out. The problem with this is many who are giving may need education in budgeting, assistance with repairing credit, training in stewardship. They are giving more out of a hustling mentality or through being hustled by a biblical truth, yet do not possess the revelation or skills where the principles work for them. Such tactics are witchery which cause the people to respond with witchery.
- Give half of God's word and then encourage people to sow for the rest of the word. Set up groups, partnerships, private and even free webinars that are pitched as no hassle opportunities then after providing a measure of the product, word, or revelation, manipulate people into sowing. Sometimes receiving the rest of the product, word or revelation is dependent on sowing. Will pitch this as godly and appropriate since it is a marketing strategy since it is used in the secular world, but really is a strategic business scheme.
- Present and make prosperity, fame, and flashiness, be the catalyst for a successful ministry.
- Present their designer clothes and luxurious lifestyle as God when much of it is due to hustling schemes and sacrificing themselves and others to demonic systems and idol god.
- Tell people they are not flourishing because they are not sowing or not sowing into the right people or ministries.
- Use and mimic worldly systems, ideas, pyramids, tactics, and schemes with a spiritual twist to increase wealth. Then contend the wealth and success is from God when it is really from the source they utilized.
- Minimal to no conviction for how their actions impact others or present God. Are so desensitized that they believe it is God and use scripture to justify their actions.

- Must keep hustling and gimmicking to maintain the financial status they have presented and accumulated.
- Promote people that are their idols, famous, have successful public platforms as godly, yet the people lack the character, nature, integrity, or biblical standards of God. The intent is to gain favor, blessing, success, or to maintain certain privileges that are connected to their Babylonian product or agenda.
- Rarely give anything back to the people who are sowing into them, and if they do it is for show, make a point, or is attached to a gimmick, self-imposed pitch, or scheme.

Chapter 15

COMMUNING WITH DECEASED RELATIVES
Overcoming Grief and Loss

Because grief is difficult to deal with, familiar spirits find it easy to prey on people's pain so they can insert themselves in people's lives. When relatives die, loved ones speak of encountering the dead person's spirit. They will contend they felt/feel their presence, or a ghostly form of the person comes and converse with them. They will report seeing them in and around the home or a familiar setting, hear noises, doors opening and closing, knocking, lights going on and off, strong winds coming in the room, creeks and voices in attics, closets, rooms. They will equate these experiences as the dead trying to tell them they are there. Because the presence feels familiar, they will contend it was their deceased relative, but the word states the following regarding the dead.

Ecclesiastes 9:5 *For the living know that they will die, but the dead know nothing; and they have no more reward [here], for the memory of them is forgotten.*

Ecclesiastes 9:10 *Whatever your hand finds to do, do it with all your might, for there is no work or device or knowledge or wisdom in Sheol (the place of the dead), where you are going.*

Isaiah 26:4 *They are dead, they shall not live; they are deceased, they shall not rise: therefore hast thou visited and destroyed them.*

In many ethnic groups and cultures, it is a generational custom to see and embrace familiar spirits. We will hear old wives' tale stories of family members receiving messages, empowerment, and having encounters with deceased relatives. Loved ones will even make statements of deceased relatives being in the room after something unusual occurs in the atmosphere. Just because grandma, grandpa, auntie, shared these stories or said these experiences where happening, does not make them true as being the spirit of the deceased relative. We regard theses customs and their voice in our lives out of false loyalty and honor to who they are in the family line. We also have embraced these practices as being needful to our identity and heritage and have entered covenant with them. Please know that your relatives are entertaining demons and have you doing it too. They are passing along customs that are not in alignment with the biblical word of God. These practices must be cleansed out of the family line as they keep the generations bound to witchcraft and aide familiar spirits in being able to operate from generation to generation.

Isaiah 8:19-22 *When someone tells you to consult mediums and spiritists, who whisper and mutter, should not a people inquire of their God? Why consult the dead on behalf of the living? Consult God's instruction and the testimony of warning. If anyone does not speak according to this word, they have no light of dawn. Distressed and hungry, they will roam through the land; when they are famished, they will become enraged and, looking upward, will curse their king and their God. Then they will look toward the earth and see only distress and darkness and fearful gloom, and they will be thrust into utter darkness.*

Isaiah 57:3-4 *But draw near hither, ye sons of the sorceress, the seed of the adulterer and the whore. Against whom do ye sport yourselves? against whom make ye a wide mouth, and draw out the tongue? are ye not children of transgression, a seed of falsehood,*

Isaiah 57:3-12 The Amplified Bible *But come close, you sons of a sorceress [nursed in witchcraft and superstition], you offspring of an adulterer and a harlot. Against whom do you make sport and take your delight? Against whom do you open wide your mouth and put out your tongue? Are you not yourselves the children of transgression, the offspring of deceit—You who burn with lust [inflaming yourselves with idols] among the oaks, under every green tree, you who slay the children [in sacrifice] in the valleys under the clefts of the rocks?*

Among the smooth stones of the valley is your portion; they, they [the idols] are your lot; to them you have poured out a drink offering, you have offered a cereal offering. Should I be quiet in spite of all these things [and leave them unpunished—bearing them with patience]? Upon a lofty and high mountain you have openly and shamelessly set your [idolatrous and adulterous] bed; even there you went up to offer sacrifice [in spiritual unfaithfulness to your divine Husband]. Behind the door and the doorpost you have set up your [idol] symbol [as a substitute for the Scripture text God ordered]. Deserting Me, you have uncovered and ascended and enlarged your bed; and you have made a [fresh] bargain for yourself with [the adulterers], and you loved their bed, where you saw [a beckoning hand or a passion-inflaming image].

And you went to the king [of foreign lands with gifts] or to Molech [the god] with oil and increased your perfumes and ointments; you sent your messengers far off and debased yourself even to Sheol (Hades) [symbol of an abysmal depth of degradation]. You were wearied with the length of your way [in trying to find rest and satisfaction in alliances apart from the true God], yet you did not say, There is no result or profit. You found quickened strength; therefore you were not faint or heartsick [or penitent]. Of whom have you been so afraid and in dread that you lied and were treacherous and did not [seriously] remember Me, did not even give Me a thought? Have I not been silent, even for a long time, and so you do not fear Me? I will expose your [pretended] righteousness and your doings, but they will not help you.

Colossians 2:8 See to it that no one takes you captive through philosophy and empty deception, according to the tradition of men, according to the elementary principles of the world, rather than according to Christ.

Some people have dreams with dead relatives in it. This is tricky because dreams need to be interpreted with the direction of the Holy Spirit. Most of these dreams include familiar spirits or shape shifting demons. Familiar spirits are spirits are often tied to the family line and have been in the generational line for years.

- The familiar spirit maybe a spirit guide to someone in the family line.
- The familiar spirit maybe a demon that oppressed or possessed someone in the family line, therefore, they are familiar with everyone in the family.

- The familiar spirit gains intel so they can find an open door to remain connected to the family line where they can become the spirit guide, oppress, or possess someone else within the family when the person they previously were tied to has died or is delivered from demonic spirits.
- Family spirits may hang out in the homes and atmospheres of families and assert their right to be the spirit guide of that family through legal open doors to unrepentant generational or present witchcraft.

The Bible speaks of the demonic operation of demons.

Luke 11:24-26 The Amplified Bible *When the unclean spirit has gone out of a person, it roams through waterless places in search [of a place] of rest (release, refreshment, ease); and finding none it says, I will go back to my house from which I came. And when it arrives, it finds [the place] swept and put in order and furnished and decorated. And it goes and brings other spirits, seven [of them], more evil than itself, and they enter in, settle down, and dwell there; and the last state of that person is worse than the first.*

Demon spirits will pursue a place to dwell. They will look for people to live in and around and generally do not like to be cast out of the families, people, and regions, they are used to possessing. Often when they are ejected whether by deliverance or death, they look for a new dwelling place, and often they return to look in and around the familiar person or sphere of influence from whence they came. If they find it, they may go get other demons to cohabitate with them in that person's life, family, home, and region. This is because demons tend to work together and need each other to fulfill their plans in and around that person's life, family, or sphere of influence. Jesus spoke about how Satan's kingdom works together. And how demons will not cast out demons, or a demonic person cannot cast a demon out of a demonic person, because Satan's kingdom works together to oppress and possess. Only the spirit of God cast out demons because it is against Satan's kingdom.

Luke 11:14-22 The Amplified Bible *Now Jesus was driving out a demon that was dumb; and it occurred that when the demon had gone out, the dumb man spoke. And the crowds marveled. But some of them said, He drives out demons [because He is in league with and] by Beelzebub, the prince of demons, While others, to try and test and tempt Him, demanded a sign of Him from heaven. But He, [well] aware of their intent and purpose, said to them, Every kingdom split up against itself is doomed and brought to desolation, and so house falls upon house. [The disunited household will collapse.] And if Satan also is divided against himself, how will his kingdom last? For you say that I expel demons with the help of and by Beelzebub.*

Now if I expel demons with the help of and by Beelzebub, with whose help and by whom do your sons drive them out? Therefore they shall be your judges. But if I drive out the demons by the finger of God, then the kingdom of God has [already] come upon you. When the strong man, fully armed, [from his courtyard] guards his own dwelling, his belongings are undisturbed [his property is at peace and is secure]. But when one stronger than he attacks him and conquers him, he robs him of his whole armor on which he had relied and divides up and distributes all his goods as plunder (spoil).

Familiar spirits will also become connected to people's lives through open doors from horoscope readings, psychic readings, tarot card readings, astral projection, soothsaying. When people engage in these practices, the practitioner utilizes demons to help bring forth the foretelling acts that they claim to be occurring in people's lives, or to produce the luck, prosperity, success, love, etc. that the person desires. The person does not realize that the word from the witchcraft practitioner is coming to pass through demonic assistance. As they read and received readings and agree with what is being stated, demon spirits gain legal ground to operate and bring forth what is agreed with. These demons have access to people's lives through these workings, become familiar with their lifestyles, loved ones, needs, desires, likes, dislikes. They become familiar spirits that can mimic the personality and behavior of the person they are tied to and to their loved ones. It is nothing for them take advantage of the grief of a person by mimicking the behavior of a dead relative so that person can become connected and dependent on their presence and want them to remain close for comfort and to ease the grief of their dead relative.

Sometimes people engage in practices of conjuring up dead relatives. This is called necromancy - the communing with the dead. People think they are engaging with dead relatives, but it is familiar spirits they are interacting with. The Bible lets us know that there is a defilement, darkened, and consequences that occur when communing with the dead.

Leviticus 19:31 *Do not turn to mediums or spiritists; do not seek them out to be defiled by them. I am the Lord your God.*

Deuteronomy 18:10-12 *There shall not be found among you anyone who makes his son or his daughter pass through the fire, one who uses divination, one who practices witchcraft, or one who interprets omens, or a sorcerer, or one who casts a spell, or a medium, or a spiritist, or one who calls up the dead. For whoever does these things is detestable to the Lord; and because of these detestable things the Lord your God will drive them out before you.*

Isaiah 8:19-22 The Amplified Bible *And when the people [instead of putting their trust in God] shall say to you, Consult for direction mediums and wizards who chirp and mutter, should not a people seek and consult their God? Should they consult the dead on behalf of the living? [Direct such people] to the teaching and to the testimony! If their teachings are not in accord with this word, it is surely because there is no dawn and no morning for them. And they [who consult mediums and wizards] shall pass through [the land] sorely distressed and hungry; and when they are hungry, they will fret, and will curse by their king and their God; and whether they look upward Or look to the earth, they will behold only distress and darkness, the gloom of anguish, and into thick darkness and widespread, obscure night they shall be driven away.*

Isaiah 19:2-4 *And I will set the Egyptians against the Egyptians: and they shall fight every one against his brother, and every one against his neighbour; city against city, and kingdom against kingdom. And the spirit of Egypt shall fail in the midst thereof; and I will destroy the counsel thereof: and they shall seek to the idols, and to the charmers, and to them that have familiar spirits, and to the wizards. And the Egyptians will I give over into the hand of a cruel lord; and a fierce king shall rule over them, saith the Lord, the LORD of hosts.*

2Corinthians 11:13-15 The Amplified Bible *For such men are false apostles [spurious, counterfeits], deceitful workmen, masquerading as apostles (special messengers) of Christ (the Messiah). And it is no wonder, for Satan himself masquerades as an angel of light; So it is not surprising if his servants also masquerade as ministers of righteousness. [But] their end will correspond with their deeds.*

In ***1Samuel 28*** we have King Saul consulting a medium to conjure up the spirit of Prophet Samuel for revelation. There is a biblical debate on whether this was Samuel or a familiar spirit acting as Samuel. However, there are a few truths that are clear regarding this Bible story that we can learn from and that is:

- What King Saul was asking the witch to do was idolatrous and forbidden. He had exiled all the witches and magician, but when God would not answer him in prayer, he inquired of a witch to conjure up a familiar spirit knowing it was forbidden.
- Even the witch of Endor that King Saul sought knew that divining was unlawful, stated this to King Saul. She was horrified that he was attempting to trick her into engaging in it as she knew the law, and she knew he was king, and could have her killed.
- The witch made King Saul promise she would be safe if she conjured up Prophet Samuel for him. This gives further insight that she knew this was not a godly act or one God allowed those in the nation he was over to operate in.
- God rejected Saul for his disobedience, rebellion, and participation in divination. ***1Chronicles 10:13-14*** *So Saul died for his transgression which he committed against the LORD, even against the word of the LORD, which he kept not, and also for asking counsel of one that had a familiar spirit, to enquire of it; And enquired not of the LORD: therefore he slew him, and turned the kingdom unto David the son of Jesse.*

This story lets us know that anything that is not God lead or God approved is unacceptable. It does not matter if it is the person's spirit or not. The question should be, **"IS THIS THE WILL OF GOD?" SHIFT!**

Often familiars can be identified in dreams because they do not have the full characteristics or nature of the person they are acting like. They will have some characteristics but often the personality of that spirit will present some characteristics that are contrary to the nature of the person. Shape shifting demons are spirits that appear one way in the dream, generally as someone you know or are familiar with, and once they have you in their grasp, they will turn into something else and attack you. People tend to be confused as to the reason the loved one would act like that in a dream, but it is not their love one but a shape shifter on assignment to attack with intimidation, control, fear, suspicion, confusion, afflict, infirm, violence, tragedy, where you are now questioning that person or yourself.

We must understand that dreams are real realms. Though our body is sleep, our spirit is active and awake. Our spirit lives and operate from supernatural realms. Depending on how we govern our lives when we are awake, our spirit and consciousness can be subject to godly and ungodly activity. Demons also use the night season to attack people because they know people's guards are down, they have not learned to govern their night season and their spiritual realms, so they will enter the dream and sleep realms and attack. They will seek to plant and engage in oppressions and bondages or to disrupt the sleep pattern, so people are not refreshed when they awake. The Bible speaks of spirits that attack while we are sleep and in our dreams.

Demonic spirits, ungodly or demonic dreams, and baffling wicked experiences occur at night to cause fear, dread, depression, grief, isolation, loneliness, gloom.
Proverbs 3:24-26 - When thou liest down, thou shalt not be afraid: yea, thou shalt lie down, and thy sleep shall be sweet. Be not afraid of sudden fear, neither of the desolation of the wicked, when it cometh. For the Lord shall be thy confidence, and shall keep thy foot from being taken.

Demonic spirits and experiences of terror, pesty demons and agitation, and arrows sent as ungodly assignments attack, during the night season and in dreams.
Psalm 91:5 Thou shalt not be afraid for the terror by night; nor for the arrow that flieth by day; Nor for the pestilence that walketh in darkness; nor for the destruction that wasteth at noonday.

Spirit came to impact suspicion and questioning so Job's friend Eliphaz would mistrust and doubt him.
Job 4:12-17 The Amplified Bible Now a thing was secretly brought to me, and my ear received a whisper of it. In thoughts from the visions of the night, when deep sleep falls on men, Fear came upon me and trembling, which made all my bones shake. Then a spirit passed before my face; the hair of my flesh stood up! [The spirit] stood still, but I could not discern the appearance of it. A form was before my eyes; there was silence, and then I heard a voice, saying, Can mortal man be just before God, or be more right than He is? Can a man be pure before his Maker, or be more cleansed than He is?

Some people choose to remain in the grief process so they can keep encountering the dead. They think if they move on to being healed and happy, the encounters will stop. When healed, most likely these encounters will stop because much of the time the people are having souls wound dreams due to locked up grief and trauma rather than experiencing God lead dreams. Such dreams keep people bound to the dead or coffin spirits. Their souls have entered Sheol and is soul tied to this realm; they are communing in the realm of death and hell rather than in the reality of real life. King David speaks of Sheol in the Bible:

Psalm 86:13 *For great is thy mercy toward me: and thou hast delivered my soul from the lowest hell.*

Psalm 16:10 *For You will not abandon my soul to Sheol; Nor will You allow Your Holy One to undergo decay.*

Psalm 23 *The LORD is my shepherd; I shall not want. He makes me lie down in green pastures. He leads me beside still waters. He restores my soul. He leads me in paths of righteousness for his name's sake. Even though I walk through the valley of the shadow of death, I will fear no evil, for you are with me; your rod and your staff, they comfort me. You* *prepare a table before me in the presence of my enemies; you anoint my head with oil; my cup overflows. Surely goodness and mercy shall follow me all the days of my life, and I shall dwell in the house of the LORD forever.*

The Amplified Bible *Yes, though I walk through the [deep, sunless] valley of the shadow of death, I will fear or dread no evil, for You are with me; Your rod [to protect] and Your staff [to guide], they comfort me.*

Psalm 30:3 *O LORD, You have brought up my soul from Sheol; You have kept me alive, that I would not go down to the pit.*

Psalm 56:13 *For You have delivered my soul from death, Indeed my feet from stumbling, So that I may walk before God In the light of the living.*

David did not remain in these realms. When he recognized his soul was there, he sought the Lord for deliverance and then praised God for setting him free. We must do the same as David. We must recognize that we do not have to remain bound to grief, doom, gloom, or realms of death and hell. We can remember and pay tribute to loved ones. However, we do not have to remain in the shadow of our loved ones dying, feeling helpless to overcome their passing, or constantly having encounters with familiar spirits that want to keep up focusing and communing with the dead. This is not God's design for grief. It is also not his way of us remaining connected to those that have passed on. God's desire is for us to be comforted, well, have abundantly life and to consistently live in the present and newness of what he is doing in our lives. Anything that takes away from this stance is not of God.

Isaiah 53:4 *Surely he has borne our griefs and carried our sorrows; yet we esteemed him stricken, smitten by God, and afflicted.*

Psalm 34:18 *The Lord is near to the brokenhearted and saves the crushed in spirit.*

Matthew 5:4 *Blessed are those who mourn, for they shall be comforted.*

Luke 6:21 *Blessed are you who are hungry now, for you shall be satisfied. Blessed are you who weep now, for you shall laugh.*

John 10:10 *The thief cometh not, but for to steal, and to kill, and to destroy: I am come that they might have life, and that they might have it more abundantly.*

2Corinthians 5:17 *Therefore if any man be in Christ, he is a new creature: old things are passed away; behold, all things are become new.*

2Timothy 1:10 *But now has been revealed by the appearing of our Savior Christ Jesus, who abolished death and brought life and immortality to light through the gospel.*

Revelation 21:4 *He will wipe away every tear from their eyes, and death shall be no more, neither shall there be mourning, nor crying, nor pain anymore, for the former things have passed away.*

All dreams must be interpreted through the guidance of the Holy Spirit; he will tell you what reasons you are seeing deceased relatives in your dream and whether this is of him or the devil. I will state that if God is allowing it, it is not to keep you bound in grief or dependent on encounters with your dead relative. It is to reveal to you the state of your soul, to reveal a message that is needful for your life so a dead relative was used to help you pay attention to what God is trying to convey, or to help you move on through the grief process to being healed and set free.

I will give you an example. I had a childhood friend die of cancer. We were so close, we called each other "twin," rather than by our real names. Due to the nature and issues surrounding her death, I was depressed for two years after her passing. I could not get beyond why God did not heal her with all the praying we were doing, and with how some other matters unfolded surrounding her last days of life. I was grief stricken, would have times of severe crying day and night, to the point that I would wake up out of my sleep crying in agony. One night, I had a dream that included her. The dream was at an old church we use to attend together as kids. She looked incredibly sad but beautiful. I begin to cry in real life when seeing her, so I begin to wake up from my dream. As I was waking up, I heard my friend say, "Let me go twin, let me go." I asked, "Why do you look so sad." She said, "I am sad because you are sad, let me go twin let me go." I just begin to cry harder as I said, "I let you go."

This dream broke the spirit of depression and grief from me and I was able to begin to deal with my unforgiveness of God taking her and the circumstances surrounding her death. I had another dream after that where I saw her in heaven. She was happy, healed, and enjoying her life. I believe God was allowing me these dreams so I would move on. My dreams we about accepting her date and accepting where I was and needed to be in continuing to advance in life. They were not about me communing with her and keeping her around to lessen my grief, but never allowing me to move beyond the pain of her being gone.

The general stages of grief are as followed:

1. Shock and Denial.
2. Trauma - Some people experience trauma depending on the reason for death and the depth of the relationship.
3. Pain & Guilt.
4. Anger, Scapegoating, and Bargaining - Even being angry at God.
5. Depression, Despair, Loneliness.
6. Reflection, Focusing on Deliverance and Healing.
7. Reconstruction & Working Through Grief.
8. Embracing the Healing.
9. Acceptance & Hope.

Ecclesiastes 3:4 declares that there is, "A time to weep, and a time to laugh; a time to mourn, and a time to dance." This lets us know that when someone dies, that is the time to mourn. That mourning is part of our seasons of life. But this scripture also lets us know that we cannot and should not remain in the mourning season. Though how long we mourn differs from person to person, we should not stay in this season too long and should not live in the experience of mourning. Though we will most likely experience all the thoughts and emotions of the grief process, it is important to have a focus and desire of navigating through the grief process and wanting to regard that a loved one has passed on so that accept their fate and let them go. Most of the time people refuse to move on, are too grief stricken to move on, or make statements or vows that cause them to not be able to move on. They will state that they will never be the same without the person, never be happy without that person, cannot, will not, or do not know how they are going to live without that person, loved the person too much to let them go. Such vows cause people to become stuck in stages of grief, stuck in trauma and pain, or to experience ungodly grief where demons begin to oppress them and cause all types of major depression, time release curses of depression, suicidal ideation, etc. The grief becomes a wound in the person's soul, thus opening a door for familiar spirits to enter and operate as loved ones.

Proverbs 18:21 *Death and life are in the power of the tongue: and they that love it shall eat the fruit thereof.*

Proverbs 21:23 *He who guards his mouth and tongue keeps his soul from distress.*

Psalm 30:2 Lord, my God, I cried out to you for help, and you healed me.

Psalm 147:3 *He healeth the broken in heart,*
and bindeth up their wounds.

Jeremiah 30:17 *For I will restore health unto thee, and I will heal thee of thy wounds, saith the LORD; because they called thee an Outcast, saying, This is Zion, whom no man seeketh after.*

Dictionary.com defines grief as, "keen mental suffering, sharp sorrow, pain, painful regret, or distress over affliction or loss. Grief can be one of the worst feelings and difficult to navigate. This is because we as people hate losing anything, especially when we know it cannot be replaced or will never return. Also, sudden death, premature death, and any experiences of tragedy, further confounds the grief we experienced. Additionally, we tend to live as if we are never going to die. We live as if we have time. Many people rarely live with a posture of living on and in purpose, knowing that at some point death will be part of our process. However, time never ceases, and death is inevitable. The eternal life that God promised us is not on earth but in heaven with him. So, though we are saved from eternal death unto salvation according to ***John 3:16***, we will still die and then be SHIFTED into living in eternal life with God.
As I have experienced loved ones dying in the last seven years, I had to change how I view death. I had to stop thinking I could not ask God questions. Though God is sovereign, this is not biblical, is not true covenant relationship, and it is not God's will that we do not know his

heart and purpose. The Bible says that God's thoughts and ways are above ours, but it is God's heart that we seek him to know his mysteries and we seek to be enlightened by his thoughts and ways. Such explorations draw us into greater intimacy and covenant truth with God.

Deuteronomy 29:29 *The secret things belong to the Lord our God, but the things revealed belong to us and to our sons forever, that we may observe all the words of this law.*

Jeremiah 33:3 *Call to Me and I will answer you, and I will tell you great and mighty things, which you do not know.*

Proverbs 25:2 *It is the glory of God to conceal a matter, But the glory of kings is to search out a matter.*

Psalm 25:14 *The secret of the LORD is with them that fear him; and he will shew them his covenant.*

Daniel 2:22 *He reveals the deep and hidden things; He knows what lies in darkness, and light dwells with Him.*

Matthew 13:11 *He answered and said unto them, Because it is given unto you to know the mysteries of the kingdom of heaven, but to them it is not given.*

Mark 4:11 The Amplified Bible *And He said to them, To you has been entrusted the mystery of the kingdom of God [that is, the secret counsels of God which are hidden from the ungodly]; but for those outside [of our circle] everything becomes a parable.*

Luke 8:17 *For nothing is hidden that will not become evident, nor anything secret that will not be known and come to light.*

Romans 11:25 *For I would not, brethren, that ye should be ignorant of this mystery, lest ye should be wise in your own conceits; that blindness in part is happened to Israel, until the fulness of the Gentiles be come in.*

Romans 11:25 *For I would not, brethren, that ye should be ignorant of this mystery, lest ye should be wise in your own conceits; that blindness in part is happened to Israel, until the fulness of the Gentiles be come in.*

Ephesians 6:19 *And for me, that utterance may be given unto me, that I may open my mouth boldly, to make known the mystery of the gospel.*

Colossians 1:27 *To whom God would make known what [is] the riches of the glory of this mystery among the Gentiles; which is Christ in you, the hope of glory.*

Colossians 2:2 *That their hearts might be comforted, being knit together in love, and unto all riches of the full assurance of understanding, to the acknowledgment of the mystery of God, and of the Father, and of Christ.*

Colossians 4:3 *Withal praying also for us, that God would open unto us a door of utterance, to speak the mystery of Christ, for which I am also in bonds.*

Death is a mystery that we really cannot understand without God's guidance and revelation. Especially when we are not prepared to lose a loved one. I began engaging God in conversations regarding loved ones dying:

- Whether a loved one will die.
- The reason a loved one had to die.
- The reason it is/was their time to die.
- Was this his permissive (because of their choice or other people's choices) or perfect (of God's purpose) will.

These conversations with God have helped me to understand and navigate death experiences more efficiently. It has helped me to work through the grief process with God where I allow him to comfort and heal me so I can move on. Where I can accept the truth and/or the sovereignty of God, such that I am no longer angry with God, angry about the situation, or stuck in questioning why a loved one died. Being oppressed in this place would ordinarily cause me to remain too long in a season of mourning where I am living in grief - living in the shadow of death that we discussed earlier. There have been times that I have not always liked what God reveals to me. I have had to ask him to give me the supernatural ability to accept it. I then continuously share with God how I feel and spend continuous time communing with him throughout the day when I need it and maintain consistent in times of prayer so I can receive his comfort and love - where I can exchange my sorrow for laughter.

God is not going to leave us without comfort when loved ones die, but he has a plan for the grief process.

John 14:18 says, "I will not leave you comfortless: I will come to you." God will not leave us comfortless, wants to comfort us, and wants to help us process through seasons of morning. We must understand that relationships, even our relationships with God, have their times of needing to work out frustrations, misunderstandings, and challenges. We must draw near to him even in our times of being challenged with him, receive him as comforter and have conversations with him regarding exactly how we are feeling. We must be willing to ask the hard questions so that we can understand him, understand our experiences, and so that he can help us process through the grief and pains of life. We must also receive his comfort and the comfort of others. We must be willing to embrace comfort from him and others and want to be made well from grief.

Psalm 30:11 *Thou hast turned for me my mourning into dancing: thou hast put off my sackcloth, and girded me with gladness;*

Psalm 94:19 *In the multitude of my thoughts within me thy comforts delight my soul.*

Psalm 118:5 *I called upon the Lord in distress: the Lord answered me, and set me in a large place.*

Psalm 119:28 *My soul melteth for heaviness: strengthen thou me according unto thy word.*

Isaiah 40:29 *He giveth power to the faint; and to them that have no might he increaseth strength.*

Isaiah 51:12 *I, even I, am he that comforteth you: who art thou, that thou shouldest be afraid of a man that shall die, and of the son of man which shall be made as grass.*

Matthew 5:4 *Blessed are they that mourn: for they shall be comforted.*

John 16:13 *Howbeit when he, the Spirit of truth, is come, he will guide you into all truth: for he shall not speak of himself; but whatsoever he shall hear, that shall he speak: and he will shew you things to come.*

John 14:26 *But the Comforter, which is the Holy Ghost, whom the Father will send in my name, he shall teach you all things, and bring all things to your remembrance, whatsoever I have said unto you.*

Philippians 3:13-14 *Brethren, I count not myself to have apprehended: but this one thing I do, forgetting those things which are behind, and reaching forth unto those things which are before, I press toward the mark for the prize of the high calling of God in Christ Jesus.*

2Corinthians 1:3-4 *Blessed be God, even the Father of our Lord Jesus Christ, the Father of mercies, and the God of all comfort; Who comforteth us in all our tribulation, that we may be able to comfort them which are in any trouble, by the comfort wherewith we ourselves are comforted of God.*

Now that you have receive some truths of how to heal from grief, let us explore how to close doors to familiar spirits.

- Repent for communing with familiar spirits, spirits of the dead, coffin spirits, and shape shifting spirits. Coffin spirits are spirits that literally cause you to live in a coffin type state even though you or alive. Or they cause your soul to be locked in the coffin with the person that died as you died the day they died. Spirits of the dead can be vampire spirits, doom and gloom spirits, spirits of dead and tragedy, grave spirits, mourning spirits that work with depression - spirits connected to death that come to drain and steal your life and keep you living in Sheol - living in the shadow of death and hell.
- Repent for all personal and generational forms of witchcraft. Break dedications, covenants, vows, and oaths surrounding these idolatrous acts.
- Break soul ties with your deceased relatives.
- Break soul ties with coffin spirits, spirits of the dead, familiar spirits, and shape shifting spirits. Command these spirits to loosen away from your life. Command their legal rights and assignments to be broken off your life and generational line.

- Break covenants with Sheol and command your mind, heart, soul to SHiFT up out of Sheol, to be returned to your body in the land of the living.
- Command all familiar spirits tied to your life and generational line, operating in your home and sphere of influence, and operating in your dream realm and night season, to leave eternally in the name of Jesus never to return. Sometimes spirits will manifest to cower or weary you as they do not want to leave. You may have to war and contend to overcome them but please know you have the authority to command them to leave. Assert your right to be free and get others who are skilled in deliverance ministry and spiritual warfare to help you pray.
- Using the blood of Jesus, eternally close demonic portals in and around your home, your life, and in your dream realm and night season that gives these spirits access to you. These portals are invisible to the natural eyes as demons operate through spiritual realms and spheres. They can enter our lives through gateways in these realms. Close these portals so that demons can no longer enter in and out of your life and sphere through them.
- Command all spirits of grief, depression, heaviness, loneliness, anger, rage, unforgiveness, denial, confusion, pain, agony, excessive crying, etc., to leave your life in the name of Jesus.
- Break every time release curse of grief and loss, and every way it has you stuck in the day and season that loved one passed.
- Break any vows you made regarding never getting over death, never letting them go, or never living without the person that died.
- Search out with God if you need to get rid of any items of the deceased person that is keeping you bound in morning. If he allows you to keep it, pray over the items and break any spirits and powers of grief, depression, and memory recall off them. Memory recall causes you to continuously relive situations as if they are occurring such that you relive the pain and agony of them. Cleanse your memory with the blood of Jesus and command triggers of pain to come out of your memories, brain, and body.
- Soak yourself, your home, and sphere of influence in the blood of Jesus and the glory of God. Consistently maintain an atmosphere of heavenly glory in your midst and regularly cleanse your home and sphere of demonic activity.
- Invite the angels to live in and around you to protect you and to fight for you.
- Resist in engaging in witchcraft practices and entertaining demons.
- Seek counseling when you need help processing through grief. Give yourself the opportunity to be free and made well.

Decreeing your healing from the spirit of grief and breakthrough from familiar spirits, in Jesus name. SHIFT!

Prayer for Grief: Holy Spirit, take the person who is reading this prayer and bring comfort to replace the pain. Bring peace to replace turmoil. Bring hope in exchange for despair. Let their eyes open to the plans you have for them and show them that you are always and forever in control of their steps. You kept your word and did not leave or forsake them (Hebrews 13:5). Speak to their spirit with your Spirit and whisper in their soul that you are their peace, both now and forever. In Jesus' name.

Chapter 16

CHARISMATIC WITCHCRAFT

Charisma an alluring, magnetizing, dazzling, glamorous, drawing spiritual power, personal quality, and distinct physical disposition, that gives an individual the ability to charm, attract, influence, or have authority, over people, ministries, businesses, organizations, regions, or spheres. It is a special ability or function, that places a person in a position, office, platform, or leadership, where they are revered with worthiness and veneration. Though not all ways the case, the special influence and honor is not necessarily because God placed the individual in that space, or they deserve to be there. Charisma in and of itself can catapult a person to this place. There are also those individuals who have charisma but have also worked their gift and life purpose to obtain the influence and position they have. Charisma affords them further open doors, special favors, and reverence, that would not ordinarily be given to someone else who do not possess this special quality or spiritual drawing power.

Some people are naturally charismatic, and others fashion themselves into charismatic beings. The world considers charisma a person's brand or niche. I would contend that divine charisma could be a person's god identity – the unique blueprint of God that is on their life. Many in the church would contend that charisma is the Holy Spirit and his gifts operating in and through a person. However, when people are being negatively influenced by charisma, e.g., controlled, manipulated, seduced, charmed, defrauded, extorted, deceived, it is a person's will, natural personality, and the magical powers of their charisma at work, not the Holy Spirit. They are experiencing prophetic flattery, soulish tickling of the ears, personal heart desires, fears, abuse, slave tactics, mixed with witchery prayers and utterances. The charismatic person's words, charisma, and the manner to which they utilize the scriptures and principles of God, operate like witchcraft spells to woo and subdue people under their powers, while building their personal kingdoms.

1Corinthians 6:7-13 Now therefore there is utterly a fault among you, because ye go to law one with another. Why do ye not rather take wrong? why do ye not rather suffer yourselves to be defrauded? Nay, ye do wrong, and defraud, and that your brethren. -- Know ye not that the unrighteous shall not inherit the kingdom of God? Be not deceived: neither fornicators, nor idolaters, nor adulterers, nor effeminate, nor abusers of themselves with mankind, Nor thieves, nor covetous, nor drunkards, nor revilers, nor extortioners, shall inherit the kingdom of God. And such were some of you: but ye are washed, but ye are sanctified, but ye are justified in the name of the Lord Jesus, and by the Spirit of our God. All things are lawful unto me, but all things are not expedient: all things are lawful for me, but I will not be brought under the power of any. Meats for the belly, and the belly for meats: but God shall destroy both it and them.

With charismatic people and movements, there is also a lot of emotional hype involved that is credited to the Holy Spirit but is not the character and nature of the Holy Spirit, and often does not align with biblical principles. The Pentecost experience in *Acts 2* where the 120 were filled with the Holy Spirit to the point of being mistaken as drunk, and *1Corinthians 1:27* where the foolish things are used to compound the wise, is often used to justify emotional hype and to silence anyone who would call such encounters personal excitement or sacrilegious. Often there is no true deliverance and healing, and a false sense of peace and wellness.

Jeremiah 8:11-12 *For they have healed the hurt of the daughter of my people slightly, saying, Peace, peace; when there is no peace. Were they ashamed when they had committed abomination? nay, they were not at all ashamed, neither could they blush: therefore shall they fall among them that fall: in the time of their visitation they shall be cast down, saith the LORD.*

There is also no sustaining miracles, signs, wonders, prophecy, visions, and dreams, or salvation that follow these movements. Just a bunch of hyped people stealing the glory and focus from God by doing weird things and calling it God. True is their flesh cannot handle the glory of God, or they are experiencing a form of godliness and not true power of the Holy Spirit.

1Corinthians 1:29-31 *That no flesh should glory in his presence. But of him are ye in Christ Jesus, who of God is made unto us wisdom, and righteousness, and sanctification, and redemption: That, according as it is written, He that glorieth, let him glory in the Lord.*

2Timothy 3:1-7 *This know also, that in the last days perilous times shall come. For men shall be lovers of their own selves, covetous, boasters, proud, blasphemers, disobedient to parents, unthankful, unholy, Without natural affection, trucebreakers, false accusers, incontinent, fierce, despisers of those that are good, Traitors, heady, highminded, lovers of pleasures more than lovers of God; Having a form of godliness, but denying the power thereof: from such turn away. For of this sort are they which creep into houses, and lead captive silly women laden with sins, led away with divers lusts, Ever learning, and never able to come to the knowledge of the truth.*

King Saul was charismatic. Though the people had God as king, they wanted a natural king. They were not content with covenant with God and constantly rejected him. God chose them the best possible candidate for a king that was among them. The people took one look at Saul's charismatic appearance and received him as king.

1Samuel 9:2 *And he had a son, whose name was Saul, a choice young man, and goodly: and there was not among the children of Israel a goodlier person than he: from his shoulders and upward he was higher than any of the people.*

1Samuel 10:17-19 *And Samuel called the people together unto the LORD to Mizpeh; And said unto the children of Israel, Thus saith the LORD God of Israel, I brought up Israel out of Egypt, and delivered you out of the hand of the Egyptians, and out of the hand of all kingdoms, and of them that oppressed you: And ye have this day rejected your God, who himself saved you out of all your adversities and your tribulations; and ye have said unto him, Nay, but set a king over us. Now therefore present yourselves before the LORD by your tribes, and by your thousands.*

Verse 23-24 *And they ran and fetched him thence: and when he stood among the people, he was higher than any of the people from his shoulders and upward. And Samuel said to all the people, See ye him whom the LORD hath chosen, that there is none like him among all the people? And all the people shouted, and said, God save the king.*

Saul was not trying to be charismatic. This was simply part of his identity. For a time, God was trying to work with Saul. God anointed Saul, changed his heart, and was able to use him as king in *1Samuel 10*. The Holy Spirit upon Saul increased his charisma. However, Saul was more focused on pleasing the people and the perks that came with being king, that he defied God and was rejected as king. Like many who are promoted because of charisma or who SHIFT into using their charisma for personal gain rather than for God's purpose, Saul began to operate in his flesh and will, rather than being led by the Spirit and heart of God. Such actions lead to witchcraft and eventually being demonically stronghold. Such persons will claim their workings are of God but are charismatically influencing people with the rebellion of witchcraft powers.

1Samuel 15:22-24 And Samuel said, Hath the LORD as great delight in burnt offerings and sacrifices, as in obeying the voice of the LORD? Behold, to obey is better than sacrifice, and to hearken than the fat of rams. For rebellion is as the sin of witchcraft, and stubbornness is as iniquity and idolatry. Because thou hast rejected the word of the LORD, he hath also rejected thee from being king. And Saul said unto Samuel, I have sinned: for I have transgressed the commandment of the LORD, and thy words: because I feared the people, and obeyed their voice.

Those operating in charismatic witchcraft like to save face in the eyes of the people. Even with being judged and rejected by God, they will ask for grace just so the people will not realize they are no longer walking with the Lord. They want a pass to operate in the works and principles that display a form or fashion of godliness even though their heart and character is far from God.

Verse 30 Then he said, I have sinned: yet honour me now, I pray thee, before the elders of my people, and before Israel, and turn again with me, that I may worship the LORD thy God. So Samuel turned again after Saul; and Saul worshipped the LORD.

This is one of the main reasons people are not discerning of charismatic witchcraft. The people are deceived by acts and not discerning of character and godly fruit. The people are also bewitched by the magical powers and personalities of the charismatic person. The people also operate in the schemes of the charismatic person and take them on as being God ordained. If you read Saul's story, you will realize how he used those around him to defraud others and even plot the killing of David, his predecessor. The people were so bewitched by Saul's charisma that they ignored the fact an evil spirit would oppress him at times, cause him to operate in evil and hideous ways; they covered up his mental illness, and aided him in his terrorist attacks. These people will defend the charismatic leader with their lives. They invest and sacrifice their time, finances, giftings, callings into serving this person. They do not realize that they are not living in fullness or true covenant with God as the charismatic leader is their god. They have a difficult time receiving truth and being delivered from their magical powers. They will destroy anyone or anything who attempts to control the truth regarding the bewitchment they are under.

With the rise of social media ministry, we have a lot of people, especially believers, under charismatic witchcraft powers. Since the loyalty to these leaders is so strong, the best attack against charismatic witchcraft is for God's true leaders to come forth and be a pure example of

God's character, nature, and identity. We need godly influencers to SHIFT into Their rightful place in the kingdom. If front liners resist taking their place, these imposters will step into our position and claim to be God's design and God directed. I have always been charismatic. Even as a young girl, I had my own unique style, disposition, mature wisdom, and leadership qualities that caused people to be drawn to me. As a minister I have often dreaded being called charismatic because I do not want to be clumped in with those who engage in charismatic witchcraft. Rejecting the influence upon my life is not going to change the truth about who I am. Making sure I submit my charisma to God is vital to it not becoming god in my life. Being careful not to take God's place in people's lives, not allowing them to make me a god, and not casting myself as God is also key to dismantling charismatic witchcraft. The church shows what it really means to be separated from the world and to be filled and living through the fullness of the Holy Spirit. We must want to be the holy representatives of God, that show forth his true purpose and glory.

Chapter 17

CHRISTIAN GIMMICKS

I had a dream of a well-known prophet showing a baby that would manifest as a reptile to an audience of people. We were at a hotel of some sort and the well-known prophet was showing it outside at a service to a huge crowd of people. People where everywhere and engaged in what the well-known prophet was speaking and showing them. The baby would be still and then suddenly it would manifest into this creature - sometimes the baby would be still on the ground then manifest into a reptile. I was too baffled and was more cautious and hesitant to receive what the prophet was saying and showing, so I decided to leave the service. The prophet saw me walking off and started following me with the baby. The prophet kept calling my name and saying, "It's my niece that turns into a reptile." I proceeding to my room and the well-known prophet kept trying to explain to me as if what they were saying and doing was okay, and as if they wanted my affirmation and agreement. It was not like the prophet was explaining where they wanted me to do something about it, but more so in a way that they wanted me to accept their niece and the fact that it had this manifestation. But I continued toward my room without much conversation.

To get to my room, I had to go up some steps then climb out a window after moving several things from around the window, then climb across a ledge and up a wall to my room. The well-known prophet could not follow me to this dimension. They therefore kept shouting out the information as I proceeded UP to my room. As I was climbing the wall, I told the prophet I was going to my room to pray about their niece and would get back to them. The dream kept replaying this entire scenario over and over like a continual looping, until I woke up.

In one scene I heard God say that I was going into spiritual high places in the heavenlies above principalities and powers and the well-known prophet could not follow me their which is the reason they were telling me the information yet lagging in being able to follow me.

<u>Dictionary.com defines *reptile* as:</u>
any cold-blooded vertebrate of the class Reptilia, comprising the turtles, snakes, lizards, crocodilians, amphisbaenians, tuatara, and various extinct members including the dinosaurs.
1. (loosely) any of various animals that crawl or creep,
2. a groveling, mean, or despicable person,
3. of or resembling a reptile; creeping or crawling,
4. groveling, mean, or despicable,
5. a person who is very dishonest.

Diagram 17.0 Synonyms for Reptile

Thesaurus Words for Reptile			
Cheater	Heel	Rascal	Snake
Coward	Informer	Scoundrel	Toad
Cur	Louse	Skunk	Weasel
Wretch	Con artist	Snake in grass	Dastardly or Sneak

Source: Baker, 2021

Dream Interpretation

This well-known prophet was presenting the people with a gospel that looked innocent but was really witchcraft - a snake, a con, disguised as God. Everyone was fascinated with it and receptive to it; out of all these people, I was the only one questioning and not viewing this gospel as God (that is sad because it was multitudes of people).

The prophet was challenged by my lack of receptivity. When seeing me leave the event they followed in effort to convince me that it was God so I could come into agreement with what was being presented as God. But I was not having it and continued to a high place in God where my truth could be fortified. I was not willing to affirm, agree, or even have a dialog where my truth would be questioned or lend to confusion or consideration that what the well-known prophet was presenting was God, and not a snake or con. No matter how much the prophet followed me they could not catch up to me or even go where I went inside the high places with God. They could only speak their words and hope that I came down to their level and agree and approve their actions. I had no compromise, even to the point of going through windows and taking my secret passage to my safe place inside God.

This is how people, especially God's people need to be in this hour. We need to be discerners who protect our truth and stand in God at all cost. We cannot see a snake - a reptile - a con - and act like it is God when Holy Spirit is clearly showing us it is not of him. We must resist the popular word of well-known leaders over God's truth. We must be willing to be the only one in the room that see truth and separate ourselves from the new age witchcraft, gimmicks, and idolatry, that is being presented to us by platform prophets, apostles, teachers, pastors, evangelists, ministers of this day. No matter how innocent it is presented, we must be willing to stand in truth, go higher in truth, and do whatever is necessary to stand inside the truth of God.

These types of experiences are already before us and will become even more popular in the coming days. The prophet with reputation will know you but will you know truth or want the well-known prophet's accolades, attention, and acknowledgment? They are not acknowledging you because of who you are. They need your agreement, so you will not sound the alarm on their reptile.

Isaiah 5:20 *Woe unto them that call evil good, and good evil; that put darkness for light, and light for darkness; that put bitter for sweet, and sweet for bitter!*

<u>Evil</u> in Hebrew is *ra'* and means:
1. bad or evil (natural or moral), adversity, affliction, calamity displease(-ure), malignant, distress, grief(-vous), harm, heavy,
2. hurt(-ful), ill (favored), mark, mischief(-vous), misery naught(-ty), noisome, not please, sad, sore, sorrow,
3. trouble, vex, wicked, worse, wretchedness, wrong.

<u>Good</u> in Hebrew is *tôḇ* and means:
1. a good thing, a good man or woman; the good, goods,
2. beautiful, best, better, bountiful, cheerful, at ease, fair,
3. (be in) favor, fine, glad, good deed, graciously, joyful, kindly, kindness, liketh (best), loving, merry,
4. most, pleasant, pleaseth, pleasure, precious, prosperity, ready, sweet, wealth, welfare, (be) well,
5. agreeable, excellent, prosperous, happy, ethically right, of benefit, appropriate, becoming, rich, valuable in estimation.

<u>Darkness</u> in Hebrew is *ḥšeḵ* and means:
1. the dark; hence (literally) darkness; figuratively, misery, destruction, death, ignorance, sorrow, wickedness,
2. dark(-ness), night, obscurity, secret place.

<u>Light</u> in Hebrew is *ôr* and means:
1. illumination or (concrete) luminary (in every sense, including lightning, happiness, etc.),
2. bright, clear,
3. day, light (-ning), morning, sun, star
   a. lightening
   b. light of lamp
   c. light of life
   d. light of prosperity
   e. light of instruction
   f. light of face (fig.)
   g. Jehovah as Israel's light

Unless you are drawing people to God, saving souls, helping people be discipled, transformed, trained, equipped, guided into divine truth and revelation, it is a gimmick and entertainment. You can call it God all you want, but God is not in the tricks and hustle. God is where souls are saved and changed for his glory.

Diagram 17.1 Opposition to Believers

Say No and Run from:			
False	New Age	Profane	Con & Con Artist
Counterfeit	Witchcraft	Unholy	Wolf
Godlessness	Wizardry	Confusion	Demonic
Godliness	Magic and Illusion	Scandal	Dark
Forms & Fashions	Delusional	Demonic & Manmade Hustle	Evil
Idolatry	Mixture	Snake	Perverse

Source: Baker, 2021

Run from The Lustful
Lust of The Flesh, Lust of The Eyes, Prides of Life

Run from Alternative Plan B
The Permissive That Is Not the Perfect Will of God

2Timothy 2:22 *Now flee from youthful lusts and pursue righteousness, faith, love, and peace, with those who call on the Lord from a pure heart.*

In my dream it was believers - **SAINTS** - that were not discerning of this false gospel.

Galatians 3:1 *O foolish Galatians, who hath bewitched you, that ye should not obey the truth, before whose eyes Jesus Christ hath been evidently set forth, crucified among you?*

Bewitched is *baskainō* in Greek and means:
1. to malign, i.e. (by extension) to fascinate (by false representations),
2. to speak ill of one, to slander, traduce him,
3. to bring evil on one by feigning praise or an evil eye to charm, to bewitch.

Dictionary.com defines *bewitch* as "*to affect by witchcraft or magic; cast a spell over, to enchant; charm; fascinate.*"

Believers need to understand that they are followers of Christ not man. As Christ followers, anything that is not aligning with God and his word is error or false. It does not matter who it is coming from. The popular prophet in my dream was willing to leave the multitude to chase me for conversion. We must understand that Satan and his imps are soul hunters even as we are seeking to draw souls unto salvation with Jesus.

Exodus 13:18-20 *And say, Thus saith the Lord GOD; Woe to the women that sew pillows to all armholes, and make kerchiefs upon the head of every stature to hunt souls! Will ye hunt the souls of my people, and will ye save the souls alive that come unto you? And will ye pollute me among my people for handfuls of barley and for pieces of bread, to slay the souls that should not die, and to save the souls alive that should not live, by your lying to my people that hear your lies? Wherefore thus saith the Lord GOD; Behold, I am against your pillows, wherewith ye there hunt the souls to make them fly, and I will tear them from your arms, and will let the souls go, even the souls that ye hunt to make them fly.*

The popular prophet appeared to want to connect with me but really wanted to convert me so they could tie and steal my soul. They approached like a sheep, but they were a wolf. The Bible warns us of wolves in sheep clothing.

Matthew 7:15 *Beware of false prophets, which come to you in sheep's clothing, but inwardly they are ravening wolves.*

Deuteronomy 18:15-22 *The LORD thy God will raise up unto thee a Prophet from the midst of thee, of thy brethren, like unto me; unto him ye shall hearken; According to all that thou desiredst of the LORD thy God in Horeb in the day of the assembly, saying, Let me not hear again the voice of the LORD my God, neither let me see this great fire any more, that I die not. And the LORD said unto me, They have well spoken that which they have spoken. I will raise them up a Prophet from among their brethren, like unto thee, and will put my words in his mouth; and he shall speak unto them all that I shall command him. And it shall come to pass, that whosoever will not hearken unto my words which he shall speak in my name, I will require it of him. But the prophet, which shall presume to speak a word in my name, which I have not commanded him to speak, or that shall speak in the name of other gods, even that prophet shall die. And if thou say in thine heart, How shall we know the word which the LORD hath not spoken? When a prophet speaketh in the name of the LORD, if the thing follow not, nor come to pass, that is the thing which the LORD hath not spoken, but the prophet hath spoken it presumptuously: thou shalt not be afraid of him.*

That word *afraid* is *gur* in Hebrew and means, "*to turn aside from the road (for a lodging or any other purpose), to shrink, to run.*" This is not a ministry where you eat the meat and throw away the bones. It is a ministry you should be RUNNING from like I did in my dream. I did not hang around to see if God would show up or to see if the prophet would say something to put me back at ease again. I RAN to a higher place in God. Decreeing you rightfully discern in this hour and know when to separate yourself for God's glory.

Chapter 18

WITCHCRAFT VERSUS PROPHETIC ACTS

Some people try to justify engaging in witchcraft and curious arts by comparing them to some of the prophetic acts and symbolisms prophets performed in the Bible or some of the signs and wonders the apostles manifested in the New Testament. Please understand that prophetic acts and curious arts are two vastly different things. Prophetic acts are/were led by divine direction from God and had specific symbolism and purpose. The signs and wonders of the apostles were made possible through the leading and miracle working power of the Holy Spirit that was in them. This was not the prophets or the apostles seeking signs for self-glory, personal gain, to assert control over situations or over the lives of others, heal or cure themselves or others, do harm to others. It was God leading them to be a sign and a wonder to draw people back into or into covenant with him.

Isaiah 8:18 *Behold, I and the children whom the LORD hath given me are for signs and for wonders in Israel from the LORD of hosts, which dwelleth in mount Zion.*

Acts 1:8 *But ye shall receive power, after that the Holy Ghost is come upon you: and ye shall be witnesses unto me both in Jerusalem, and in all Judaea, and in Samaria, and unto the uttermost part of the earth.*

Also, when God performs prophetic acts, miracles, signs, and wonders, the operations and results are not witchcraft. Even if a person is brought into strong delusion, under a curse, experience affliction or calamity, etc., this is due to the judgment of not adhering to the warnings that was made known through the prophetic acts - not the working of witchcraft itself. The negative or judgmental impact of the prophet acts are due to the consequences of sin and not yielding to the will and purpose of God - not the working of witchcraft itself. These judgments legalities are found in his word to which God does not steer from. He has established standards and principles that express his character, nature, will, and purpose. These standards and principles do not change even though God himself is an evolving God.

Psalms 55:19 *God will hear and answer them— Even the one who sits enthroned from of old— Selah. With whom there is no change, And who do not fear God.*

Psalm 102:27 *But You are the same, And Your years will not come to an end.*

Malachi 3:6 *For I, the Lord, do not change; therefore you, O sons of Jacob, are not consumed.*

Hebrews 13:8 *Jesus Christ is the same yesterday and today and forever.*

James 1:17 *Every good thing given and every perfect gift is from above, coming down from the Father of lights, with whom there is no variation or shifting shadow.*

Daniel 7:14 *And to Him was given dominion, Glory and a kingdom, That all the peoples, nations and men of every language might serve Him. His dominion is an everlasting dominion which will not pass away; And His kingdom is one which will not be destroyed.*

It is important to further note that God does not have ill will or a motive of harm when he is warning people through prophetic acts. His hope is that people will turn from their wicked ways so that the judgment of the word will not come upon them. We keep saying God does not do things contrary to his word and blaming it on his sovereignty, but this is error and a misunderstanding of God and his scriptures. God would never operate in witchcraft. Let us take a moment to explore strong delusion to clarify this truth.

2Thessalonians 2:8-12 *And then shall that Wicked be revealed, whom the Lord shall consume with the spirit of his mouth, and shall destroy with the brightness of his coming: Even him, whose coming is after the working of Satan with all power and signs and lying wonders, And with all deceivableness of unrighteousness in them that perish; because they received not the love of the truth, that they might be saved. And for this cause God shall send them strong delusion, that they should believe a lie: That they all might be damned who believed not the truth, but had pleasure in unrighteousness.*

<u>Delusion</u> is *plane* in Greek and means:
1. objectively, fraudulence; subjectively, a straying from orthodoxy or piety,
2. deceit, to deceive, delusion, error,
3. a wandering, a straying about,
   a) one led astray from the right way, roams hither and thither,
   b) metaph. mental straying,
      1. error, wrong opinion relative to morals or religion,
   c) error which shows itself in action, a wrong mode of acting,
   d) error, that which leads into error, deceit, or fraud.

God was not operating or sending witchcraft; strong delusion was sent as judgment for not coming out of sin.

Due to the heightened level of witchcraft that has been released in the earth, and people being driven by intellect, self-thought, and self-teaching, opinions that strengthen their ideologies, the fascination with gimmicks and signs, and the charismatic witchcraft that needs to be purified from the church, I would suggest avoiding seeking to win a witch, warlock, or anyone or to Christ through the idea or premise that they can still engage in supernatural powers once saved. A person first must want to put God first as Lord and savior and want to be drawn to him, not what they can receive from him. There are many scriptures that warn of being fascinated with signs and wonders, only wanting to see signs and wonders, how we can be fooled and misled by signs and wonders, and how signs and wonders being exalted above God is a sin.

Simon, the sorcerer, was rebuked by Apostle Peter for wanting to purchase the Holy Spirit because of his fascination with the signs being performed. It was revealed that he got saved because of the sign and not because of a heart for God.

Acts 18:12 *But when they believed Philip preaching the things concerning the kingdom of God, and the name of Jesus Christ, they were baptized, both men and women. Then Simon himself* *believed also: and when he was baptized, he continued with Philip, and wondered, beholding the miracles and signs which were done. Now when the apostles which were at Jerusalem heard that Samaria had received the word of God, they sent unto them Peter and John: Who, when they were come down, prayed for them, that they might receive the Holy Ghost:*

(For as yet he was fallen upon none of them: only they were baptized in the name of the Lord Jesus.) Then laid they their hands on them, and they received the Holy Ghost. And when Simon saw that through laying on of the apostles' hands the Holy Ghost was given, he offered them money, Saying, Give me also this power, that on whomsoever I lay hands, he may receive the Holy Ghost. But Peter said unto him, Thy money perish with thee, because thou hast thought that the gift of God may be purchased with money. Thou hast neither part nor lot in this matter: for thy heart is not right in the sight of God. Repent therefore of this thy wickedness, and pray God, if perhaps the thought of thine heart thou art in the gall of bitterness, and in the bond of iniquity. Then answered Simon, and said, Pray ye to the Lord for me, that none of these things which ye have spoken come upon me.

Apostle Peter told Simon to repent of his wickedness.

<u>Wickedness</u> is *kaki* in Greek and means:
1. badness, i.e. (subjectively) depravity, or (actively) malignity, or (passively) trouble,
2. evil, naughtiness, wickedness, malice, maliciousness, ill-will,
3. desire to injure, depravity, wickedness that is not ashamed to break laws.

Witchcraft operates through ill will, ill intent, and regardless of the appearance of good, its very nature is to injure its prey and deprive them of true righteousness and salvation.

The Old Testament believers were fascinated with signs and always seeking them. Even in God's efforts to answer their prayers without signs, they still wanted signs. And when God did not answer them as fast as they felt, they yielded to witchcraft in effort to make their own god, answer their prayers, manifest their own results. This is the reason Jesus said in **John 4:48**, *"Then said Jesus unto him, Except ye see signs and wonders, ye will not believe."* He was trying to point the people to the savior, but they were so conditioned by signs and wonders that they could not see the savior was right in their midst. Nothing wrong with wanting the greater works of God, but when they cloud our ability to discern God, we will not believe unless they are in operation, we want them more than we want God, and become our god, we have yielded to witchcraft and idolatry.

I will admit that I continuously seek God to perform miracles consistently. But my relationship with him is not dependent on manifestation. Did you catch that? My relationship is not dependent on manifestation. My relationship is solid whether he performs a sign or a wonder or not. I believe the reason we do not see more miracles, signs, and wonders, are because there is too much mixture in the body of Christ, and because people are more drawn to signs than to God himself. One fact about the prophets of old is that the signs they performed were not always flamboyant. They endured hardship, affliction, and even persecution as they demonstrated the prophetic acts of God. They were also sold out in covenant with God. So not matter what the results or outcome of the sign or wonder was, they remained rooted and grounded in covenant with him. We do not have that currently. Many do not stand in faith and covenant with God. If God does not respond, then many prophets turn to the world, to people, to alternative acts that are or border on witchcraft to produce results. We are so in a time of needing to return to our first love - returning to God, returning to loving him, and allowing the signs of our love to flow from our covenant with him.

Revelations 2:1-7 *"To the angel of the church of Ephesus write, 'These things says He who holds the seven stars in His right hand, who walks in the midst of the seven golden lampstands: "I know your works, your labor, your patience, and that you cannot [c]bear those who are evil. And you have tested those who say they are apostles and are not, and have found them liars; and you have persevered and have patience, and have labored for My name's sake and have not become weary. Nevertheless I have this against you, that you have left your first love. Remember therefore from where you have fallen; repent and do the first works, or else I will come to you quickly and remove your lampstand from its place—unless you repent. But this you have, that you hate the deeds of the Nicolaitans, which I also hate.*

The greatest sign and wonder someone can perform is the ability to believe and faithfully live through the truth that Jesus Christ died for their sins, rose again, and sits on the right hand of the Father with all power in his hand. When you live this, it produces God and his kingdom, and draws souls into salvation with him. Seek to get people to live this truth so that they can live and demonstrate the greatest sign ever performed.

Peter's shadow healing and Paul's handkerchief's healing is not witchcraft, but God was choosing to use these apostles to do extraordinary miracles.

Acts 5:15 *The Amplified Bible So that they [even] kept carrying out the sick into the streets and placing them on couches and sleeping pads, [in the hope] that as Peter passed by, at least his shadow might fall on some of them.*

Acts 19:11-12 The Amplified Bible *And God did unusual and extraordinary miracles by the hands of Paul, So that handkerchiefs or towels or aprons which had touched his skin were carried away and put upon the sick, and their diseases left them and the evil spirits came out of them.*

Paul going to heaven was not him engaging in astral projection. Astral projection is an intentional out of body experience of using an exaltation of one's consciousness to translate their soul into the spirit realm. Through this curious art, a person's soul can travel upon the spiritual planes and ley lines in the spirit to engage in witchcraft activity. Paul clearly was not seeking to translate. The Holy Spirit was leading him. It was also for the purposes of God revealing revelation to him. It was not him illegally entering the spirit realms to seek some higher level of consciousness or engaging in curious acts independent of God's leading and participation.

2Corinthians 12:1-4 *It is not expedient for me doubtless to glory. I will come to visions and revelations of the Lord. I knew a man in Christ above fourteen years ago, (whether in the body, I cannot tell; or whether out of the body, I cannot tell: God knoweth;) such an one* *caught up to the third heaven. And I knew such a man, (whether in the body, or out of the body, I cannot tell: God knoweth;) How that he was caught up into paradise, and heard unspeakable words, which it is not lawful for a man to utter.*

How we present the gospel is vital to the motives to which people enter salvation. Their heart must be for God and for entering covenant relationship with him. Preaching Jesus Christ as the only way to salvation and only using signs and wonders as God leads is the safest and purest way to draw souls to the truth of God and the purpose of living for him. Any other motive is witchcraft and is also erred doctrine that does not guide them to God but to the kingdom of darkness that they already serve.

1Corinthians 2:2-5 The Amplified Bible *For I determined not to know any thing among you, save Jesus Christ, and him crucified. And I was with you in weakness, and in fear, and in much trembling And my speech and my preaching was not with enticing words of man's wisdom, but in demonstration of the Spirit and of power: That your faith should not stand in the wisdom of men, but in the power of God.*

Chapter 19

POLITICAL DEMON DEALING

My spiritual overseer, Apostle Jackie Green has adamantly stated that God has called her to the United States. No matter who is president and what political party is dominant in the White House, she has consistently prayed, sent letters, released prophecy, trained, and raised up prayer warriors, to intercede for the United States for over 25 years. Never have I experienced someone who has a pure heart, humble compassion, and godly agenda, for their nation and the assignment God has granted to their hands. I have attended events where she has wept for America and over presidents, have rebuked us for prayerlessness, a lack of compassion and focus on properly governing the nation God has allowed us to live in, for not having God's heart and an agape love for our nation and whatever president that was in office at that time. Her posture is always about being a gate keeper to the nation God has birthed her in and called her to. There is no other agenda to her disposition.

John 4:34 *Jesus saith unto them, My meat is to do the will of him that sent me, and to finish his work.*

With such a determined faithful stance, at no time has Apostle Green, ever told those she is training and overseeing who to vote for, demanded that we vote for a particular president or political party, chastise us for note voting if that is our choice, or release judgment upon us for not voting for her candidate or political party. As an apostle, she will train and educate us on the political parties and the operation of laws and judicial system and teach us how to hear God for ourselves concerning who to vote for. Her declaration has always been "vote your conscience and what God is saying to you, but fervently pray for whoever is in office and for your nation." Apostle Green understands that God is in control and can use whoever takes the seat in the White House. She also understands that we live in this world, but we govern from a greater authority and sphere. Even with the recent national upheavals of 2020, with President Donald Trump being in office, her mandate has been "Prayer for the USA and those called to govern it."

Proverbs 21:1 *The king's heart is a stream of water in the hand of the LORD; he turns it wherever he will.*

Job 12:23-25 *He makes nations great, and destroys them; he enlarges nations, and disperses them.*

2Chronicles 7:14 *If my people, who are called by my name, will humble themselves and pray and seek my face and turn from their wicked ways, then I will hear from heaven, and I will forgive their sin and will heal their land.*

1Timothy 2:1-2 *I urge, then, first of all, that petitions, prayers, intercession, and thanksgiving be made for all people— for kings and all those in authority, that we may live peaceful and quiet lives in all godliness and holiness.*

Romans 13:1 *Let everyone be subject to the governing authorities, for there is no authority except that which God has established. The authorities that exist have been established by God.*

I love that Apostle Green says, "vote your conscience and what God is saying to you." Both factors are key to hearing God clearly and not succumbing to demon dealing. Our conscience is part of our soul which house what we believe is morally right or wrong. Our conscience can become polluted by the world, media, people, experiences, relationships, interactions, personal ideologies, desires, and motives. Seeking God for his will and purpose guides us to a place of truth about what is in our conscience, what is not of him, what needs to be cleansed, so we can operate through the conviction of the Holy Spirit, while maintaining a balance perspective regarding our conscience.

1Timothy 4:1-2 *Now the Spirit speaketh expressly, that in the latter times some shall depart from the faith, giving heed to seducing spirits, and doctrines of devils; Speaking lies in hypocrisy; having their conscience seared with a hot iron.*

I do believe God can give prophecy, dreams, revelation, and insight regarding politics and how he plans to work in a nation through political leaders and political parties. I also believe that their needs to be godly candidates raised up, trained, and equipped to enter these arenas to impact laws and policies and be a voice for God in the lives of people, regions, and spheres. However, people who are only driven by their conscience become seared to the truth and conviction of the Holy Spirit. They become driven by their emotions and what they believe is morally correct in their own eyes. They deal their conscience as the word of God, thus seducing people with hypocritical dogmas that are full of lies, condemnation, deceit, and damnation. These doctrines appear to have good intent, godly rhetoric, divine foretelling, but are full of mixture, compromise, and dissimulation. There is no doubt that certain polices and laws grieve God and can result in judgment upon the nation. However, the manner to which these doctrines are released, create chaos, confusion, division, and discrediting within the body of Christ and nation. They operate through tactics of bullying, control, manipulation, exacerbated fear, and end time terror, while demanding political alliance. Many to witchcraft tactics where they are releasing curses and spells to those who do not believe or regard their prophecies or actions. No matter how much the political leaders, parties, and doctrines prove integral, deceitful, erred, lack the character, nature, and fruit of God, these hypocritical believers engage in conspiracy theories, claim demonic interference, contend they and their followers are experiencing spiritual warfare, and unleash raging condemnation and judgement on anyone who attempts to hold them accountable.

Jeremiah 14:14 *Then the LORD said unto me, The prophets prophesy lies in my name: I sent them not, neither have I commanded them, neither spake unto them: they prophesy unto you a false vision and divination, and a thing of nought, and the deceit of their heart.*

Jeremiah 23:16 *Thus saith the LORD of hosts, Hearken not unto the words of the prophets that prophesy unto you: they make you vain: they speak a vision of their own heart, and not out of the mouth of the LORD.*

Jeremiah 29:8 *For thus saith the LORD of hosts, the God of Israel; Let not your prophets and your diviners, that be in the midst of you, deceive you, neither hearken to your dreams which ye cause to be dreamed.*

1John 4:1-5 *Beloved, believe not every spirit, but try the spirits whether they are of God: because many false prophets are gone out into the world. Hereby know ye the Spirit of God: Every spirit that confesseth that Jesus Christ is come in the flesh is of God: And every spirit that confesseth not that Jesus Christ is come in the flesh is not of God: and this is that spirit of antichrist, whereof ye have heard that it should come; and even now already is it in the world. Ye are of God, little children, and have overcome them: because greater is he that is in you, than he that is in the world. They are of the world: therefore speak they of the world, and the world heareth them.*

I believe the posture of my overseer, Apostle Green is what God would require of us as saints when praying for the president, political leaders, the White House, and our nation. Though God is all for nations, he is not part of this world. He is Kingdom. HIS government is HIS kingdom. In the Bible days, nations ruled by godly men, use to strive to align their laws and standards to what God desired. This has changed as man has sought to rule nations by what they desire and think best, and only want to seek God when they or the nation is in turmoil.

Politics is a world system. Even with United States of America has been one of the most affluent, successful, and advanced, nations in the earth, it is no different in how it deals God. Because it sprinkles God here and there, we contend that it is a God-fearing nation. Though, it strives to have some decency and human fiber, the system is not godly and is not rooted in biblical principles. The US Constitution is a secular document that does not contain any mention of Jesus Christ or Christianity. The main law that mentions religion is the First Amendment which protects our right to choose and establish our religious exercise. This law also protects free speech, not just for Christians but for ALL people, the press, assembly, and right to petition the government for a redress of grievances which means people can serve any god their choosing. Many of the Founding Fathers of the United States considered themselves religious, drew from their religious convictions to answer many political questions, the laws and policies of the United States are created based on what benefits the nation and All mankind. They are not created to benefit Christians, sustain a biblical standard, nor to draw souls to Jesus Christ. This is the reason it is difficult for believers to fully support the Republican and Democratic parties with a biblical stance. There will always be laws and policies that are formed due to what it best for world's system as it relates to the nation and ALL mankind, or even the elite which are the rich and those who dominate these systems. As it relates to the rich and the elite, the laws and principles are also designed for the rich and elite to get richer at the expense of anyone or anything that can advance its agenda. The United States was built upon using the poor and enslaved to grow the country for the rich and the elite. This goes for both the Republican and Democratic party. It has always been this way. The only difference now in 2020, is that many are just now realizing the severity of the impact of the system. There has also been an impact on some of the privileged realizing that if they are not the rich and elite, they too have been sacrificed and oppressed by the way these systems have been designed to operate.

These world's system will never fully come under the subjection of God. Though God has commanded us to go into the world, meaning earth, to preach the gospel and save souls, he is not requiring us to change the world's system into a godly system. Aside for people, there is nothing about the world's systems that God wants to save and keep for himself.

NOT ONE THING! ONLY SOULS!

John 3:16 For God so loved the world, that he gave his only begotten Son, that whosoever believeth in him should not perish, but have everlasting life. For God sent not his Son into the world to condemn the world; but that the world through him might be saved.

Jesus came to save souls in the earth, not to save the world's system.

Mark 16:15-18 And he said unto them, Go ye into all the world, and preach the gospel to every creature. He that believeth and is baptized shall be saved; but he that believeth not shall be damned. And these signs shall follow them that believe; In my name shall they cast out devils; they shall speak with new tongues; They shall take up serpents; and if they drink any deadly thing, it shall not hurt them; they shall lay hands on the sick, and they shall recover.

Jesus sent the disciples into the world to save souls not the world's system.

Matthew 28:20 Go ye therefore, and teach all nations, baptizing them in the name of the Father, and of the Son, and of the Holy Ghost: Teaching them to observe all things whatsoever I have commanded you: and, lo, I am with you alway, even unto the end of the world. Amen.

Jesus told the disciples to go teach, which means to disciple, instruct, make a pupil out of those within nations. Once they are learned regarding him, baptize them so that they could be saved and live for him. Jesus understood that the world was impacted by saving souls. He was draining the world's system by drawing people into him government, not trying to keep people tied to the world and its' system.

Acts 1:8 But you will receive power when the Holy Spirit comes upon you, and you will be My witnesses in Jerusalem, and in all Judea and Samaria, and to the ends of the earth."

This word *witness* means *martyr* in the Greek. Our lives have died for the sake of the gospel. People should witness someone that is dead to the world and full of God's powerful Holy Spirit.

Mark 13:9-10 But take heed to yourselves: for they shall deliver you up to councils; and in the synagogues ye shall be beaten: and ye shall be brought before rulers and kings for my sake, for a testimony against them. And the gospel must first be published among all nations.

The world's government will seek to persecute us for the gospel's sake. They will not be trying to give us a position or opportunity to overtake them. This is the reason we must remain focus on preaching the gospel and using our gifts and callings to establish God's government in the earth by creating our own systems, not overtaking their system. Our focus is not to be part of their system. Our focus is to preach God's word so we can save souls. Whether we impact laws or not, the world's system will always seek to silence the gospel from being fully proclaimed. We will always have to publish the gospel whether the world receives us or not. We are not dependent or living on world systems and laws, but on God.

2Corinthians 6:14-18 *Be ye not unequally yoked together with unbelievers: for what fellowship hath righteousness with unrighteousness? and what communion hath light with darkness? And what concord hath Christ with Belial? or what part hath he that believeth with an infidel? And what agreement hath the temple of God with idols? for ye are the temple of the living God; as God hath said, I will dwell in them, and walk in them; and I will be their God, and they shall be my people. Wherefore come out from among them, and be ye separate, saith the Lord, and touch not the unclean thing; and I will receive you, And will be a Father unto you, and ye shall be my sons and daughters, saith the Lord Almighty.*

That word *separate* means to *sever and to have a clear boundary*. Though there are things in the world that mimic God and his government or appear good, we are to be separate from the world and the world's system. We are not to commune and participate in anything that has form or a little bit of God but is rooted in the world. It should be clear that God is in us, we belong to him, and our dealings are to glorify him.

Come out means to *cast out or to depart*. When we try to make the world's system be a godly system we have not come out from among a thing. We want what the world has, and we are striving to make it our own. We become soul tied and covenant to it, while trying to put a God twist on it. Saying God created everything, and the devil is just a counterfeit will not make it be godly. This mindset only deceives us and those who yield to this falsehood. Resulting in defiling us and them because it is tied and rooted to the world. Only a severing separates us from the world.

Mathew 10:14:15 *And whosoever shall not receive you, nor hear your words, when ye depart out of that house or city, shake off the dust of your feet. Verily I say unto you, It shall be more tolerable for the land of Sodom and Gomorrah in the day of judgment, than for that city.*

When we are shaking the dust off our feet, we are expressing extreme contempt and refusing to have any further dealings with whatever or whoever it is that rejected us and the gospel of Jesus Christ within us. We are not to be challenged because they did not receive us; for they are not the ultimate government. Though they may think they are judging and ostracizing us, we are judging them. We were never trying to be received but were saving them from being destroyed for being apart.

John 17:13-21 *And now come I to thee; and these things I speak in the world, that they might have my joy fulfilled in themselves. I have given them thy word; and the world hath hated them, because they are not of the world, even as I am not of the world. I pray not that thou shouldest take them out of the world, but that thou shouldest keep them from the evil. They are not of the world, even as I am not of the world. Sanctify them through thy truth: thy word is truth. As thou hast sent me into the world, even so have I also sent them into the world. And for their sakes I sanctify myself, that they also might be sanctified through the truth. Neither pray I for these* *alone, but for them also which shall believe on me through their word; That they all may be one; as thou, Father, art in me, and I in thee, that they also may be one in us: that the world may believe that thou hast sent me.*

Jesus said we are to be sanctified in truth so that we can be protected by the evil on and can be identified as those who are not of this world. So that it will be clear that we belong to his kingdom.

Matthew 5:13-15 *Ye are the salt of the earth: but if the salt have lost his savor, wherewith shall it be salted? it is thenceforth good for nothing, but to be cast out, and to be trodden under foot of men. Ye are the light of the world. A city that is set on an hill cannot be hid. Neither do men light a candle, and put it under a bushel, but on a candlestick; and it giveth light unto all that are in the house. Let your light so shine before men, that they may see your good works, and glorify your Father which is in heaven.*

Revelations 11:15 *Then the seventh angel sounded: And there were loud voices in heaven, saying, "The kingdoms of this world have become the kingdoms of our Lord and of His Christ, and He shall reign forever and ever!"*

Our stance as kingdom citizens is for the coming season when Jesus will return and use our workings of preaching the gospel and saving souls, and what we have established through creating reform through our gifts and callings, to totally overthrow the world's systems such that God's kingdom is the only one that remains. God's intent is not to keep the world's systems and make them his. But to destroy them so that only his kingdom remains.

Hebrews 12:25-27 *See that ye refuse not him that speaketh. For if they escaped not who refused him that spake on earth, much more shall not we escape, if we turn away from him that speaketh from heaven: Whose voice then shook the earth: but now he hath promised, saying, Yet once more I shake not the earth only, but also heaven. And this word, Yet once more, signifieth the removing of those things that are shaken, as of things that are made, that those things which cannot be shaken may remain.*

Chapter 20

THE POWER OF ALGORITHMS
Written By: Prophet Reenita Keys, Marketing Specialist

We live in a world that is constantly changing. The innovation of technology is moving so fast, the human brain may not have the capacity to outperform the artificial intelligence being released into the earth. If you are technologically savvy, advanced, or merely a novice, we cannot deny that technology does not wait on society to approve its global SHIFTS.

The world we once knew a decade ago has changed whether we like it or not. Many individuals do not realize that various forms of technology have been engineered in such a way it infiltrates our personal data to make us a product. Have you logged onto Pinterest, Facebook, or Tik Tok, and realized you have been interacting with the application for over an hour because of posts, videos, pictures that seem to know what your current interest are? Have you ever visited a website to consider purchasing a product and the same item you were thinking about buying follows you to Facebook or other online sites? More than likely, the answer to either one of these questions is "yes." Social media platforms have been engineered with various algorithms. Algorithms are a series of codes or operations that help identify user behaviors, what is relevant and important to the user, and what the user is likely to engage in, invest in, or purchase. Algorithms help drive the success of a social media platform. Each day, when you are using social media it is strategically guessing what you would be interested in. One of the main goals of the algorithm is to keep you on the platform as long as it can and so you can invest financially in that product.

Algorithms change over time to mirror new trends and interests. The way we interacted on Facebook a decade ago is not the same way we interact with the platform today. There are various stages and goals an algorithm will focus on. When a platform is created, the algorithm's purpose is to build loyal users and to promote influencers. The algorithm knows that if it can build influencers within a platform, the greater the user base. If one consistently shares content, there is a chance the platform will deem you an influencer. When this happens, algorithms share videos organically to their user base. This is why we tend to see someone's content at the top of our timelines when we open our social media apps. It is a crafty way to get you hooked on that app as it is feeding you content that is important to you! You will then become a loyal user, while not even realizing that an algorithm has drawn you in.

While hooking the user, an algorithm in its infancy stage is working to build a big user base. Timing and money are crucial and needful for social media. The focus eventually SHIFTS from building a user database to generating revenue. Have you noticed each time you are using Facebook you at least see one ad? Platforms will start bombarding users with ads because they are hooked to the content. Or they have tracked the user online and now know what ailments, issues, challenges, interests, they need solutions for. Ads for those products are released on that users feed to spark an interest in possibly purchasing that product. This causes users to utilize social media and the internet more because they have now been programmed to know that the internet has answers for them. Such unconscious programming can cause addictions to social media sites and internet usage where users are drawn to constantly check their apps, stroll media timelines, and search online for topics and products. Individuals may not realize they have become addicted because of the psychological techniques that are involved. The longer the system can keep you on a platform, the greater the number of ads you are consuming, which increases the drive to use apps and the internet. It is important to know that if you are not paying for a product, you are more than likely the product. Social media platforms generate leads for various businesses and corporations with the intent to make money. At the end of the day, it is a business although it is a powerful tool that connects people around the world. It is a weapon that has the capacity to SHIFT average joes into millionaires and users are the products that make average joes rich and famous.

Algorithms change as the user changes. It also changes to accommodate trends. We are being watched around the clock by algorithms. Our behaviors are being modified based on what we are being fed. Algorithms support the users, but its end goal is to support the platform itself. We have been manipulated unknowingly because media sites claim it is our page, our space, and about us, but really it is about them - the power and financial wealth of their platform. Every so often, it is good to take a break from social media to purge and reset from all the various forms of subtle manipulation we have come into agreement with unbeknownst to ourselves. Taking time away from social platforms is not only best for your own good but society. I suggest this because there is no way around the truth that the way algorithms operate cause a bewitching that impacts our beliefs, desires, will, and habits. Habitually, algorithms are manipulating us by sending slight changes to our media feed to see how we will react and to cause us to react, to prick our perspective and to SHIFT our perspective. Have you ever received an advertisement or post that made you question how it landed on your timeline? Or made you question what you believe about God, life, your health, family, etc.? I have personally encountered these changes where I blatantly noticed the difference and had to reorder my truths versus what was being proposed to me. Such propositions can cause us to doubt God, sway from truth, engage in new age activities, yield to addictions, and sins. Algorithms are looking for quick responses and it does not care if the content is positive or negative. Algorithms naturally take the negativity and amplify it. Negative responses tend to rise faster than positive responses. This is how social media can introduce negative people to each other. Have you ever had negative feedback in the comment section of your post? Random people you have never interacted with come out of nowhere wanting to intrude their opinions onto you. These people are nowhere to be found when you are talking about other subjects they may not disagree with. Algorithms may see negative media getting more responses than positive news and categorize people's pages to connect and combat with one another. With so many opinions swirling around, you can easily take on someone else's views and belief systems without searching things out for yourself. Or become offended and angry about a matter that causes you trauma, frustration, mind racing, and soul wounds, where ordinarily in real life, you would not be challenged by such matters. Taking time away from social media can unclog these webbings and keep you in a balanced and healthy place with God, rooted in his principles and truths.

Some social media platforms have confessed that they have utilized addictive schemes in their platform. This level of manipulation can cause thousands of people to show addictive behaviors without realizing it. Various brands conduct manipulative schemes with some of their paid ads. The more you see their product the more you are prone to think about it and eventually make the purchase. Things can become strange and wicked when it comes to these sorts of mind and eye deceptions, seductions, and manipulations. The universal business model is designed to addict you and to sell you to third-party channels without you realizing it.

I am not saying that everything about algorithms is wicked and demonic. I want you to give you key foundational information so you can discern when boundaries are being crossed, so you can be more aware of your interactions on the internet, and how the internet is engaging and targeting you.

Today, individuals do not take the time to fact check some of the news they are being fed. With this type of behavior, it is easy to digest fake news and function under a confirmation bias. Years ago, citizens around the world were dependent upon news channels, newspapers, and magazines for their daily dose of media. The audience knew the various biases these outlets had, and it allowed us to take the meat and leave the bones. Unfortunately, when it comes to algorithms, we do not know what the algorithm is choosing not to show us. Algorithms take a handful of decisions we make and extract data from our social media behavior and data to generalize truths about what we are potentially important to us.

Now that you understand algorithms, I want to move on to discuss cookies. When you visit a webpage for the first time, you are asked if it is okay to save cookies on your browser. Usually, when this notification pops up, we casually click "Okay" without realizing what we agreed to. You are probably asking yourself, "what is a cookie?" A cookie is a string of letters and numbers formed together to create a unique ID. This special ID helps the site remember you to create a better experience. On the other hand, cookies make it possible for products to follow you around the internet. The engineering behind cookies, allow companies to band together to track and remember everything we do online. They become the center of our warfare when it comes to the protection of our personal data and privacy. If websites did not use cookies, we would not have the ability to save login information nor experience many other benefits we may not think about. Did you know that cookies can track your location, time spent on a website, items you placed in your cart, and any details you deliberately give to that website? Cookies can track the number of times you visit a website. When you visit websites multiple times, cookies collect your data and tell the website you are the same visitor. First-party cookies are solely used on the site you are interacting with directly. They are used for renting, shopping, banking, and so much more. They have played a key role in the advancement of the digital world we live in today. Banner ads were created because of the invention of cookies. When we look at society today, our online experience runs on ads. Brands work with various social media platforms to strategically deliver their ads to their ideal customers. Brands and social media platforms are seeking to know as much as they can about your online behavior to make money from you.

First-party cookies were created to be placed and retrieved only by the direct site you were interacting with. Brands and social media platforms began collaborating behind-the-scenes to increase sales and conversion rates. As a result, third-party cookies were created. Have you visited a website and a notification instantly popped up giving you a spill about third-party cookies? We have become desensitized and familiar with the first-party cookies notification that we most likely clicked "okay" and ignored what we agreed to. We just clicked the necessary buttons to get back to our online experience that may or may not result in a purchase.

Usually, third-party cookie notifications give you two options.

Option 1: The user can customize the type of cookies they allow to track their online experience with a website or decline.

Option 2: The user pushes "I agree" or "okay" accepting the use of third-party cookies.

Third-party cookies give brands the ability to tell social media platforms to show their ads to people who visited their website in the last week, month, or whatever frequency they want to use. This is how products, goods, and services can show up on your timeline multiple times and follow you on other websites. When cookies were created, the engineers did not anticipate for websites to abuse the use of cookies hosted by third parties. Over a decade ago, no one knew third-party elements would have the ability to save their own cookies to your browser to ultimately spy on you. Third-party elements can save cookies onto your browser each time you access their domain. They can access the data from the site you are on and every site that uses that same third-party element. This is called tracking! For example, you access multiple sites through Facebook clicking on different products. Facebook stores that information into their database and sells it to companies inquiring about you. Things SHIFTED from multiple sites knowing your online behavior to just a few sites knowing it all! The main purpose of this SHIFT was to deliver manipulated personalized ads to each user.

Over the years, various browsers have made changes to protect its users against third-party Cookies by blocking them by default. This makes it more difficult for the middleman to know that the person who was shopping for a new house on one site, bought new clothes on another site, and looked for a new physician on different site are all the same person. Companies will always attempt to find a loophole to weasel their way in to obtain this type of data. They can find loopholes that usurp your privacy settings because they have billions of dollars budgeted for ad spend. Some social media companies can give corporations codes that mimic the identity of a first-party cookie. Corporations know you cannot block the use of first-party cookies because the website would not work without them. Companies are creating additional tools that work behind the scenes to make sure third-party cookies are not turned off. You are merely just a product to them! There are billions of dollars at stake.

Chapter 21

MEDIA DEMON DEALING

Media is one of the biggest soul stealing demon dealers of this day. We can expect in the coming days for free speech to be amended with great stipulations and grave consequences. With the rise of social media, truth has been replaced with a lot of ideologies that are causing upheavals, historical smearing and confusion, and misrepresentation of what is morally and ethically appropriate. Public opinion has become the judge, jury, law, and executioner, while the justice system and the law are striving to appease to gain some since of trust and control over society. The media has become so full of gossip, drama, confusion, slander, betrayal, accusations, manipulation, lawlessness, and heartlessness. They fuel societal and social media ideologies with fake news, half-truths, blatant lies, or biased truths. They hide behind the First Amendment so there are no consequences for their actions.

CANCEL CULTURE
Cancel culture (or call-out culture) is a modern form of boycotting, refusal to support/promote the work of, silencing, shaming, punishing, and ostracizing, in which someone is thrust out of social, professional, religious, and personal circles - whether online, on social media, in the real world, or both. Those who are subject to this ostracism are said to be "canceled." A person, business, organization, ministry, etc., can be canceled for whatever reason the culture decides is warranted. There is no regard to the impact canceling someone has on their mental and physical wellbeing, their family and loved ones, their professional careers, any good they have done in the earth, or the fact that most cancel culture acts stem from offenses, personal opinions, and differences. There are also no consequences to the person or entity being physically stalked and their lives being violently threatened and attacked due to being canceled.

Cancel culture has lacks the fruit of restoration or reconciliation, so in this fashion, canceling someone can be an eternal exile that a person may never come back from. When someone is being canceled, people jump on the bandwagon with little to no information and aide in bullying, condemning, destroying, and ostracizing a person. Even if others come to the defense of the canceled person or entity, the damage tends to override any rectifying that is done. The words, abuse, and damage are done. The person or entity is forced to endure the experience and work on rebuilding what was lost or starting over in a new genre. This makes cancel culture extremely dangerous, especially because people and entities are judged in the eyes of the public and even with repentance, receiving prosecution, they are never fully able to recover from the stigma of being canceled. This experience becomes what defines them regardless of the changes they make to their lives and entities. For even if the cancel culture acknowledged their good, they do it, while referring to the reason they were canceled in the first place.

CYBER BULLYING ATTACKS
Cyber bullying aborts the opportunity for true justice. Cyber bullying is the use of electronic communication to bully, intimidate, negatively expose a person, or bring and release contempt,

typically by sending messages, posting messages, or releasing video and audio regarding the person.

Despite there being a law of free speech, cyber and media bullying is used to strip the person of their right to speak their opinion, belief, and to be different. Once the person is the current trending topic, then the cyber and media bullies come to help destroy that person's life. These pathways are used to put the person in an unfavorable light where those who once supported them and even those who are just now learning who the person is, will give divided opinion, shun, slander, betray, vilify, and ostracize, that person; thus, causing a catastrophe and reproach to the person's name, character, career, opportunities, life, and ultimately their destiny. Cyber and media bullying is a controlling spirit seeking to kill the person's purpose and calling.

***Psalm** 75:7 But God is the judge: he putteth down one, and setteth up another.*

Anyone, including believers, can be subject to cyber bullying at any time. And with the modernization of cancel culture, cyber bullying can ruin a person by disparaging their name. Cyber bullying appears justified and lawful, but in most cases, it is emotional petty outrage and lawlessness. It is so easy to succumb to cyber bullying by jumping on the bandwagon and killing someone's reputation, career, and life with no real legality. It is also quite easy to be swayed to engage in cyber bullying without knowing all the facts, not being discerning, and receiving the opinions of the cyber bullies as truth and law.

The following spirits operate through cyber bullies and the cancel culture:

- **Spirit of the World** - Using worldly ways and anti-Christ tactics to resolve issues.
- **Celebrity Spirit** – Excessive and unhealthy drive to be famous, renown, widely honored and validated, publicly known, be the center of attention and to receive a lot of public attention, whether positive or negative.
- **Fame Spirit** - Selling and sacrificing one's soul and the soul of others for popularity, fame, and fortune.
- **Lying Spirit** - Telling false truths, half-truths, biased truths; deceiving and tricking others with false information.
- **Spirits of Offense** - Being annoyed, irritated, angered, wounded, and resentful to a point of wanting to defend, punish, avenge, and engage in revenge.
- **Spirit of the Villain & Revenge** - Operating in cruelty, maliciousness, wickedness, to vilify a person, place, or thing.
- **Gossiping Spirits** - Engage in idle talk, familiar talk, rumors, share secrets or information, about the personal or private affairs of others; there is no concern for whether the info is true or how it impact the person, loved ones, or parties involved.
- **Blog Gossipers & Cyber Reporters** - People who claim they are called to exposed, gossip, slander, destroy the lives of people they deem to be entertainment worthy, cancel worthy, or caught in wrongdoing; they will claim this is their life's purpose or God called them to this self-imposed career. They may claim to be believers and put a God twist or use scriptures wrongly to justify their actions.

- **Spirit of Slander & Backbiting** - Maliciously and falsely defaming, belittling, damaging, and destroying the identity, success, reputation, wellbeing, of a person or entity.
- **Spirits of Strife** - Creating or engaging in vigorous or bitter conflict, discord, quarreling, competition, rivalry, or antagonism.
- **Spirits of Betrayal** - Exposing or delivering someone to an enemy through treachery or disloyalty, revealing information or violating the confidence of a person or entity, hurtfully wounding a person or entity in a way that is contrary to one's normal character or behavior.
- **Gang Spirits** - Groups of people conspiring, gossiping, bullying another person or entity; having your associates join posts, videos, etc., for the purposes of strengthening one's point of view or vilifying a person or entity. Different groups of people conflicting with one another when they disagree, to a point of operating towards one another like literal opposing gangs. These groups may go back and forth conflicting with one another, cyber bullying one another, threatening one another, slandering one another, gossiping about one another, and canceling one another.
- **Accuser of the Brethren** - Impute a charge of wrongdoing or offense; impose guilt or blame; often without just cause or facts, or regard of the ramifications of public exposure.
- **Spirits of Rejection** - Refusal to recognize, the differences, opinions, or rights of others; seek to cast off or castrate because of rebuffing of a person or entity.
- **Spirits of Rebellion** - Open, organized, or reckless, armed resistance and defiance to authority, rules, regulations, or the rights of others.
- **Spirits of Lawlessness** - Engaging in reckless, unrestrained, and illegal behavior with no regard to the law or consequences.
- **Respect of Persons** - deciding who should be honored and who should be cancels; esteeming others because of personal approval while destroying others due to disapproval.
- **Ease Dropping & Tracking Spirits** - Following posts, blogs, website activity, reviewing videos, tracking friends and whereabouts on social media sites and online; using this information to cyber bully or cancel the person.
- **Stalking Spirits** - Tracking, watching, gaining entail, and harassing a person or entity in an aggressive, threatening, intimidating, or illegal manner.
- **Confederate & Siege Spirits** - Spirits from that different spheres and regions collaborating to surround, barricade, isolate, a person or entity while releasing an attack from every side; this attack fortifies or overthrows a person's ability to fight back, get back on their feet and gain momentum, or recover from what is being unleashed against them.
- **Blocking Spirits** - Hinders, stifles, deters, delays, blocks the process, progress, potential, and opportunities of a person.
- **Spirits of Murder & Suicide** - Attacking a person to the degree that they are killed physically, emotionally, and spiritually, or to a point where they want to kill or do kill themselves; Attacking a person where people literally stalk, threaten, attack, and kill these people in real life.
- **Destiny Killing Spirits** - Spirits that steal, kill, and destroy the plan and purpose of God for someone's life; destroys a person's success and advancement in life.

It is no doubt that social media and the internet in general expose the character, nature, and heart of a person. This is because we are operating in spiritual realms where our spirits, minds, and souls, are engaging one to another in the fullness of its existence. We are operating through spiritual realms and through the essence of our spirit to which we exist. Many in the body of Christ have resorted to engaging in cancel culture, cyber bullying, gang banging and using the media stories to as a spiritual gage to speak what they deem to be divine prophecies, apostolic revelations, and end time insights. When the media is exposed for releasing false information, these believers do not repent for their actions. Despite *Ephesians 5:21* saying we are to submit to one another in the fear of the Lord, they lack accountability and reject accountability. Instead, they yield to conspiracy theories, increasing in falsehoods, or demon dealing the next big story as God. When being held accountable by anyone who questions their false information and ungodly activities, they become offended, vengeful, cyber bullies and cancel culture dealers. They and their followers rally to bully and cower the person into retracting from exposing them, while continuing to lobby a false ungodly agenda. Often, these soul stealers increase with fostering their falsehoods to draw more likeminded followers so they can hide amid them to avoid accountability and responsibility for their actions. The followers serve as their cushion, support pillars, and erred proof, that what they are doing is of God even though God has nothing to do with it. These types of actions have a lot to do with the connections, opportunities, success, and financial gain, these soul stealers have achieved because of these agendas, and not wanting to lose or give back what they have attained. Such behavior has become all too common and is its own cancel culture because it is canceling out God's true agenda and lobbying demonic anti-Christ agendas. Cancel culture as well, rejects restoration, reconciliation, and redemption, freewill, and the right to have difference of opinions. This is umbilical. God is not about gossip, slander, false rhetoric, or hindering freewill. He is not about destroying and banishing. He is not about controlling a person's freewill or dispelling the opportunity for reproof and atonement. God is also about us resolving conflicts in a healthy manner. Believers need to learn biblical and applicable conflict resolution and communication skills so they can resolve challenges in person and on social media in a godly manner.

Colossians 2:8 *Beware lest any man spoil you through philosophy and vain deceit, after the tradition of men, after the rudiments of the world, and not after Christ.*

Romans 12.2 *And be not conformed to this world: but be ye transformed by the renewing of your mind, that ye may prove what is that good, and acceptable, and perfect, will of God.*
Ephesians 4:14-15 *That we henceforth be no more children, tossed to and fro, and carried about with every wind of doctrine, by the sleight of men, and cunning craftiness, whereby they lie in wait to deceive; But speaking the truth in love, may grow up into him in all things, which is the head, even Christ:*

2Timothy 4:3-4 *Preach the word; be instant in season, out of season; reprove, rebuke, exhort with all longsuffering and doctrine. For the time will come when they will not endure sound doctrine; but after their own lusts shall they heap to themselves teachers, having itching ears; And they shall turn away their ears from the truth, and shall be turned unto fables.*

Galatians 6:1 The Amplified Bible *Brothers, if anyone is caught in any sin, you who are spiritual [that is, you who are responsive to the guidance of the Spirit] are to restore such a person in a spirit of gentleness [not with a sense of superiority or self-righteousness], keeping a watchful eye on yourself, so that you are not tempted as well.*

Matthew 12:35-36 *But I say unto you, That every idle word that men shall speak, they shall give account thereof in the day of judgment. For by thy words thou shalt be justified, and by thy words thou shalt be condemned.*

Ephesians 4:29 *Let no corrupting talk come out of your mouths, but only such as is good for building up, as fits the occasion, that it may give grace to those who hear.*

Philippians 2:3 *Let nothing be done through strife or vainglory; but in lowliness of mind let each esteem other better than themselves.*

James 1:26 *If anyone thinks he is religious and does not bridle his tongue but deceives his heart, this person's religion is worthless.*

Titus 3:2 *To speak evil of no one, to avoid quarreling, to be gentle, and to show perfect courtesy toward all people.*

Colossians 2:13 *Bear with each other and forgive one another if any of you has a grievance against someone. Forgive as the Lord forgave you.*

Luke 17:3 *So watch yourselves. "If your brother or sister sins against you, rebuke them; and if they repent, forgive them.*

2Corinthians 5:18-21 *this is from God, who reconciled us to himself through Christ and gave us the ministry of reconciliation: that God was reconciling the world to himself in Christ, not counting people's sins against them. And he has committed to us the message of reconciliation. We are therefore Christ's ambassadors, as though God were making his appeal through us. We implore you on Christ's behalf: Be reconciled to God. God made him who had no sin to be sin for us, so that in him we might become the righteousness of God.*

Matthew 18:15-17 *Moreover if thy brother shall trespass against thee, go and tell him his fault between thee and him alone: if he shall hear thee, thou hast gained thy brother. But if he will not hear thee, then take with thee one or two more, that in the mouth of two or three witnesses every word may be established. And if he shall neglect to hear them, tell it unto the church: but if he neglect to hear the church, let him be unto thee as a heathen man and a publican.*

From 2015 to 2020, society has become more media driven. With the reset of 2020, due to Covid-19, many ministries were forced to use media as a form ministry since churches were closed or restricted due to the pandemic. But even before the pandemic, God was urging the church to build not just in their communities but via media – to use social media and online services to spread the gospel, train, equip, and disciple souls. Before 2020, there was a resistance to this SHIFT. Now this SHIFT is needed like never before. Many ministries and believers have embraced the change and are building huge media platforms, while others are using media because they have too, and hoping to return to the old church traditional in-service paradigm. God is igniting revival reform and media is part of his mission and movement. God is striving to do is to build his own media system that draws people out of mainstream media idolatry, to his true government. With this SHIFT comes great responsibility, a pursuit for holiness, righteousness, the character, nature, and fear of the Lord like never before. It will be essential for believers to govern their platforms in a godly manner and really be mindful, and strategic about what they post, respond to, how they respond, release via video, blogs, and streaming. Believers must resist engaging in cyber bullying, cancel culture and media assassination, while releasing and being examples of God's word. Our focus must be to draw souls to God's kingdom by delivering, healing, saving, restoring, and setting people free. Though in this world, we are not of it - and are not to behave like it or build it.

BUILD GOD'S MEDIA MOUNTAIN!

Chapter 22

ENTERTAINMENT DEMON DEALING

Aligning with The Apostolic Volume 5 contends that:

Hollywood is not just a geographic place anymore, but a huge entertainment industry that reaches the world, for good or ill. Aided increasingly by foreign investments, it is the United States of America's voice to people everywhere, especially the youth.

Hollywood is the epic center for entertainment, glitz, and glamour for America and the world at large. It is defined as the place for making a person's dreams come true, and is society's exemplar for appearance, fashion, fame, fortune, success, what is morally and ethically right and appropriate. Hollywood is its own sphere within the entertainment system and its own region inside of California. I also believe that its webbing has entangled the world at large so it is a massive principality that while we are ignorantly thinking we are just being entertained, it is subtly seeking to rule us and the world. Hollywood, the internet, and social media is changing the morals, values, laws and standards of society and the world at large, and we are the puppets it seeks to manipulate for rulership and gain.

Though there are some believers in Hollywood and some biblically based artistries are manufactured there, Hollywood is a secular industry that has no interest in sacrificing its fame and glam for God. This is where many believers who enter Hollywood error. They think they can infiltrate and change the system. They soon realize that Hollywood is not a little demon imp, but a major principality that will contend for its rulership. Believers also realize that they must sacrifice themselves to sustain in the system of Hollywood. Their gift makes room for them, but Hollywood is its own god and master. And we know from the Bible that it is impossible to serve two masters. The righteous believer either will bow to Hollywood or maintain their godly standards and accept whatever doors can be open to them. Most times, these doors are not as wide and prosperous as doors that have no godly or moral boundaries.

Moments of encouragement and salvation are two entirely different realms.

Due to having to sell out and feed the idolatrous well of Hollywood, a believer has trouble with fully serving God without compromise, and with walking in their true purpose and calling. Hollywood can handle and wants the fruit of the person's gift, but not their purpose and calling as a believer or carrier of the gospel of Jesus Christ. This is because Hollywood is not about saving souls but sacrificing them for its own glory. Our calling is not the gift, but what the gift does to save, deliver, and heal souls. The gift often becomes an offering to the idol god of Hollywood so that a person can be used on that platform. And since there is no separating the gift from the person, the person is sacrificed right along with their gift. A believer may think they are saving souls by being able to encourage someone every now and again. But encouragement and salvation are two vastly different things. So is thinking you are ministering salvation when your soul is also in jeopardy because it is tied to an idolatrous system.

1Kings 18:21 *And Elijah came to all the people, and said, "How long will you falter between two opinions? If the LORD is God, follow Him; but if Baal, follow him." But the people answered him not a word.*

Matthew 6:24 *"No one can serve two masters; for either he will hate the one and love the other, or else he will be loyal to the one and despise the other. You cannot serve God and mammon.*

Mammon is an inordinate spirit that is rooted in an insatiable greed for riches, wealth, and gain. This spirit is opposed to God because it becomes god in a person's life. It has people relying on them and thinking that if God does not come through in their lives, this spirit will provide what they need. Our society is driven by the spirit for mammon through the need for material goods, wealth, success, and power. The inability to be processed with God where he is guiding their destiny and success causes people to yield to the spirit of mammon. They succumb the plan B's of life, while sacrificing their true destiny, integrity, and soul, for wealth and gain. The spirit of mammon operates as a gluttonous spirit. It, therefore, cannot be satisfied. This causes people to have to keep pursuing fame and riches to keep what they have gained and to maintain the lifestyle they have SHIFTED into. There soul is also tied to mammon so no matter how much success, material goods, and money they obtain, there is a drive to always be the best, and to obtain more and more goods and wealth for pleasure, and power. Mammon steals the person's satisfaction for life and self-value. There is no satisfaction unless they are fulfilling some goal that is driven to feed their mammon identity.

James 4:4 *You adulteresses! Do you not know that friendship with the world is hostility toward God? Therefore, whoever chooses to be a friend of the world renders himself an enemy of God.*

Revelation 3:15-18 The Amplified Bible *I know your [record of] works and what you are doing; you are neither cold nor hot. Would that you were cold or hot! So, because you are lukewarm and neither cold nor hot, I will spew you out of My mouth! For you say, I am rich; I have prospered and grown wealthy, and I am in need of nothing; and you do not realize and understand that you are wretched, pitiable, poor, blind, and naked. Therefore I counsel you to purchase from Me gold refined and tested by fire, that you may be [truly] wealthy, and white clothes to clothe you and to keep the shame of your nudity from being seen, and salve to put on your eyes, that you may see.*

The system of Hollywood is not designed to promote destiny. It is designed to sacrifice a person's gift and forfeit destiny. A person either conform, tolerate its licentiousness, yield to mixture or blatant sin, get out, or be put out of Hollywood. Often believers are forced to justify some of the acts, behaviors, and job tasks as just work which is difficult when it requires blaspheming God and/or displaying oneself in an immoral light for roles, fame, and platform. There gift gets them their as they become entrapped in the world's ways of trying to be the best on Hollywood's platform, that they never SHIFT to true purpose. Hollywood reinvents their purpose. Because their gift flourishes, the person and all of us onlookers contend this is destiny, yet the person has sold their soul or soul tied their soul to the devil. How is that true destiny?

Godly entertainers have complained of not being paid comparable wages to their peers and if they are minority this confounds matters. Some believers who are producers manage to get a movie cast into mainstream media, but often it cannot compete with the godless movies that are released. Many saints do not support these movies; some even contend they are bland, boring, poorly acted, and unentertaining. This is because Hollywood has become our standard for entertainment, rather than us becoming the standard for holiness. This results in many godly producers conforming to Hollywood standards to make movies. Though they aim to keep an uplifting message or godly theme, they lose the godly standard of holiness and righteous. They make money but not at the expense of looking like and demon dealing the character and nature of the world.

Hollywood cannot handle a true vessel of God walking in purpose as to do so the person would have to preach about the very things that they are a part of. Hollywood will not have a person vilifying their brand of sin and idolatry.

2Corinthians 6:14-18 Do not be unequally yoked with unbelievers [do not make mismated alliances with them or come under a different yoke with them, inconsistent with your faith]. For what partnership have right living and right standing with God with iniquity and lawlessness? Or how can light have fellowship with darkness? What harmony can there be between Christ and Belial [the devil]? Or what has a believer in common with an unbeliever? What agreement [can there be between] a temple of God and idols? For we are the temple of the living God; even as God said, I will dwell in and with and among them and will walk in and with and among them, and I will be their God, and they shall be My people. So, come out from among [unbelievers], and separate (sever) yourselves from them, says the Lord, and touch not [any] unclean thing; then I will receive you kindly and treat you with favor, And will be a Father unto you, and ye shall be my sons and daughters, saith the Lord Almighty.

Belial is a name for Satan and represents anything that is worthless, wicked, or connected to Satan and his demonic systems. Hollywood is a system of Belial. This is the reason most believers do not expose the truth about their experiences in Hollywood. Many of them are shamed and embarrassed regarding how they had to sell out for fame. About how others wanted what they have but have no clue of the demonic sacrifice. About how people try to use them for their fame and fortune with no clue to what they are exposing themselves to. Many entertainers do not speak out until they have made their fame and fortune, and are exiting their career, or they have become fed up and can no longer live by the idolatrous restraints Hollywood has placed on their soul and destiny. In these instances, they are seen as traitors, are often threatened, and ostracized for exposing the truth about the inner workings of the entertainment system. Because of this, many people in Hollywood are so broken and oppressed in their soul despite having fame, fortune, and success. It comes with a price. One that steals, kills, and destroy the soul, rather than build, heal, and empowers it.

Hollywood is too perverse to be infiltrated and taken over for God. Believers need to build their own Hollywood rather than trying to be part of a sphere that is rooted in idolatry, perversion, sin, and mocks and scoffs at godly beliefs and principles. The more liberal the world becomes; the more liberal Hollywood gets with revealing the true roots of its origin and the character and nature of the people who produce its filth. Biblically, there were some regions God said to destroy or to have nothing to do with. Even Jesus told the disciples to shake the dust off their shoe when they go in places where they were not welcomed. Why do believers today think they can just infiltrate systems and take a mountain that God never owned or want?

Isaiah 47:1-4 New Century Version (NCV)
God Will Destroy Babylon
The Lord says, "City of Babylon, go down and sit in the dirt. People of Babylon sit on the ground. You are no longer the ruler. You will no longer be called tender or beautiful. You must use large stones to grind grain into flour. Remove your veil and your nice skirts. Uncover your legs and cross the rivers. People will see your nakedness; they will see your shame. I will punish you; I will punish every one of you." Our Savior is named the Lord All-Powerful; he is the Holy One of Israel.

Jeremiah 51:6 *Flee from Babylon! Run for your lives! Do not be destroyed because of her sins. It is time for the LORD's vengeance; he will repay her what she deserves.*

God does not want Hollywood; he wants to demolish it. Many believers do not want to demolish Hollywood because they want fame and fortune and secretly live through many of the Hollywood entertainers, even the secular ones. They do not want to admit this truth, but it is the reality of their heart. So instead of seeking to destroy it they submit to just trying to have influence. But God is not trying to just have influence in the world, he is striving to save souls and to establish his kingdom. He is not trying to share space with the devil. And until we grasp this mindset, we will keep trying to infiltrate through the world's systems rather than using our gifts, callings, visions, and platform to usurp and destroy demonic kingdoms (e.g., pull down strongholds scripture), while building through God's kingdom. When we are lights, we are not yoked to idolatry but to God and his platform. So, though we are infiltrating the enemy's camp, they cannot control or dictate our gift, legislate what we say and stand for, and cannot demolish our calling and destiny. We are not on their plain. We do not work for them. We work for God. We are not to share space but to be light that annihilated darkness.

The book "*Aligning with The Apostolic Volume V*" contends, that Hollywood can be redeemed. Much of this premise if based on statistics, ministry, and information from 1999 and before. They seemed to have been able to infiltrate Hollywood and have an impact on movies by displaying respectable morals and standards that align with Christian views. But here we are some 21 years later and cartoons, movies, TV shows, music, from Hollywood are being inundated with sadistic perversion, sex trafficking, child trafficking, pornography, senseless murder and suicide, homosexuality, transgender narratives, identity theft, witchcraft, idolatry, new age beliefs and practices. Hollywood is producing some of the most perverse and violent movies of all time. Musical artists are producing some of the most idolatrous, witchcraft, demonically infested music of all time. People are desensitized to these movies and musical lyrics and are beginning to the view them as normal entertainment and even appropriate behavior. The lines are so blurred that the boundary between right and wrong is thin; most straddle the line for thrills and to feed their drive for happiness, lust, and entertainment.

- Christian reality TV shows attempting to be more relevant and socially acceptable than godly. Focused more on entertaining rather than wining souls. Presenting more worldly and sinful issues and lifestyles than godly restraint and holiness.
- Secular entertainers singing Christian music at their concerts, media platforms, etc., while dressed provocatively and/or half naked. They contend to be displaying their Christian roots or their personal love for God, as believers contend their worship is God inspired.
- Secular entertainers thanking God for their fame and success, while living and working a life of perversion, idolatry, witchcraft, and sin.
- Believers idolize, worship, and lust after secular entertainers. They deem them as role models, defend their sins and idols tries, use them and their work in sermon illustration, pattern their lives and brands after them, and allow their children to be entertained and by their music, movies, and lifestyles.
- When you ask Christian youth who their role model is, they are naming Hollywood entertainers who live and build a fortune through perversion, sin, idolatry, with graft; these entertainers are clearly against God and his word but have God's people and generations soul tied to them.
- It is not uncommon to view social media and have believers posting and commenting as these entertainers receive their rewards, perform their music, movie, and tv roles, while living vicariously through the sinful lives that they demon deal to the world.
- Many ministry leaders invite these entertainers to their ministries to give motivational speeches to their members, entertain them with comedy, acting, secular music, and will even have these entertainers leading them in worship to Christian music, knowing that they live wretched lives in everyday life. They will have these entertainers teaching them tips and strategies regarding how to become rich and famous, knowing that what they do in their careers does not edify God or his kingdom.
- Entertainers are performing with idolatrous and witchcraft symbols and symbolisms in their movies, music, and videos. They have clearly soul their soul to the devil for fame and fortune while contending they are followers of the one true and living God. Believers defend these idolatrous and witchcraft work by contending sits their job and not their life. There is no regard to the truth that the entire entertainment system is rooted in idolatry and is a mountain of the devil.

2Kings 17:41 *So these nations worshiped the LORD but also served their idols, and to this day their children and grandchildren continue to do as their fathers did.*

Let us talk a moment about allowing secular entertainers into our pulpits and ministry events to empower, teach, sing, play instruments, and/or lead our congregants into worship. Social media and culture trends have made it easy for gifts to flourish. People equate large crowds, popularity and fame, fortune of materialistic things and worldly wealth, to God approving and even being the visionary of particular movements. To justify allowing entertainers in our pulpits, we use rhetoric like:

- We are all human.
- God is still working in them.
- We cannot judge someone's walk.

Gifts will operate regardless of the person's lifestyle or relationship with the Lord. However, gifts do not save people. It is the anointing that breaks the yoke.

Isaiah 10:27 *And it shall come to pass in that day, that his burden shall be taken away from off thy shoulder, and his yoke from off thy neck, and the yoke shall be destroyed because of the anointing.*

David was chosen to play the Harp for Saul when he was oppressed with an evil spirit. David not only had the gift but the anointing to break the yoke of mental illness off Saul.

1Samuel 16:15-18 *And Saul's servants said unto him, Behold now, an evil spirit from God troubleth thee. Let our lord now command thy servants, which are before thee, to seek out a man, who is a cunning player on an harp: and it shall come to pass, when the evil spirit from God is upon thee, that he shall play with his hand, and thou shalt be well. And Saul said unto his servants, Provide me now a man that can play well, and bring him to me. Then answered one of the servants, and said, Behold, I have seen a son of Jesse the Bethlehemite, that is cunning in playing, and a mighty valiant man, and a man of war, and prudent in matters, and a comely person, and the LORD is with him.*

- **Cunning** (yada) - Skilled, learned, sharp.
- **Valiant Man** (gibbôr - haiyl) - Strong, mighty, brave, chief, champion in one's own right, able to excel, virtuous, wealthy, rich in character and identity, a force, an army, efficient, worthy.
- **Man of War** (milḥâmâ) - Warrior, fighter, engaged of battle and war.
- **Prudent** (byin) - Teacher, eloquent, informed, diligent, discerning, knowledgeable, and honoring regarding the things of God, purposed, power.
- **Comely** (toar) - Beautiful, favored, goodly.
- **The Lord Was with Him** (yhwh) - the self-Existent or Eternal, the Lord, Jehovah, the existing One.

Saul's servant did not get him any harp player; he knew just the type of harp playing - a cunning, prudent, comely, God covenant minstrel - to break Saul through. For even as David would appear charismatic, he had on great benefit and that was, "THE LORD WAS WITH HIM!"

These characteristics let us know that David was skilled but also possessed the Spirit, heart, favor, essence, and relationship of God. His lifestyle, character, and nature demonstrated that he was not only talented, but God was evident in his life. This enabled David to not just be a cunning harp player, but one who manifested deliverance and healing. He was able to eat against the evil spirit that oppressed Saul and break him through to wellness.

Secular entertainers have the gift and talent. They are cunning at what they do. And we are even moved with emotions by their gifts and talents. But only the anointing breaks the yoke. Only God being with a person - not just during a concert - but journeying with them in a daily evident lifestyle, endows the gifted with an anointing to war for someone's soul and manifests deliverance and healing. Many secular arts have roots in gospel music and love to sing gospel music and talk about God, but this does not equate to a discipled lifestyle of journeying in covenant with God. God does not want us to start out with him then leave him and go work for the devil, then return to him every now and again when we need a spiritual pick me up or when we are feeling convicted about leaving our roots and lifestyles. There is such a desensitization of this that many secular artists will begin to sing godly music at their concerts. The event is secular, they are half naked, gyrating and performing all kinds of sexual acts and perverse dance movements, then they will throw in a couple of Christian songs and contend they was worshipping God and leading people to Christ. People in the audience are crying, and claiming they are giving their lives back to God. Some secular entertainers will even contend that God told them this was their way of ministering for him and drawing souls to his kingdom. When these videos go viral, believers will defend this type of behavior and contend God is working on the secular entertainer and that they are being used of God. This type of confusion causes people to become lukewarm and think it is okay to live in sin and claim a discipled lifestyle in God. However, a discipled lifestyle is one that lives fully for God. Even a person who claims to be a minister of the gospel where they are leading people to Christ is not just making people feel good with an emotional word or song. They understand that they are making people disciples of God.

Matthew 28:16-20 *Then the eleven disciples went away into Galilee, into a mountain where Jesus had appointed them. And when they saw him, they worshipped him: but some doubted. And Jesus came and spake unto them, saying, All power is given unto me in heaven and in earth Go ye therefore, and teach all nations, baptizing them in the name of the Father, and of the Son, and of the Holy Ghost: Teaching them to observe all things whatsoever I have commanded you: and, lo, I am with you alway, even unto the end of the world. Amen.*

<u>Teach is *mathēteuō* in the Greek and means:</u>
1. to become a pupil; transitively, to disciple, i.e., enroll as scholar,
2. be disciple, instruct, teach, to make disciples,
3. to be a disciple of one, to follow his precepts and instructions.

<u>Observe is *tēreō* in the Greek and means:</u>
1. a watch, to guard (from loss or injury, properly, by keeping the eye upon; hold fast, keep(-er), (pre-, re-)serve, watch, reserve, preserve,
2. to attend to carefully, take care of, to guard,
3. metaph. to keep, one in the state in which he is to observe, to reserve: to undergo something.

In this passage of scripture, we have Jesus manifesting himself after the resurrection to the disciples who had set under is training and teaching for the three years that he did ministry. When they saw him, they worshipped him, yet still some doubted it was him. People can worship, and still doubt who God is and whether they want to embrace him. Jesus let the disciples know that all power in heaven and earth had been given to them and that they were to go into all the nations, baptizing, teaching, and SHIFTING people into observing - living - he life of one who new truth.

People can be given encouraging, empowering insights and truths about life and about God, but only one who is truly discipled can impart discipleship into others, and even then, people must observe by being representatives of the teachings they have received to be considered God's true disciples. A feel-good song or word does not do this. Only a lifestyle surrendered to God SHIFTS this into existence.

Even as we have discussed secular entertainment, we must also explore gospel entertainers. Gospel music can be traced back to the 17th century and consisted of hymns and sacred songs, often performed in cappella. After World War II, gospel music became mainstream. Concerts became more common and elaborate, SHIFTING from church settings and small events to major auditoriums.

__Jude 1:3-4__ Beloved, when I gave all diligence to write unto you of the common salvation, it was needful for me to write unto you, and exhort you that ye should earnestly contend for the faith which was once delivered unto the saints. For there are certain men crept in unawares, who were before of old ordained to this condemnation, ungodly men, turning the grace of our God into lasciviousness, and denying the only Lord God, and our Lord Jesus Christ.

__John 3:19__ And this is the condemnation, that light is come into the world, and men loved darkness rather than light, because their deeds were evil.

Chapter 23

INTERFAITH PERSECTIVE
By: Dr. Kathy Williams

I am a retired prison chaplain. The legalities of my role in the correctional system included providing time and space for those religious practices that have been identified by the State. The scope of religious services is to provide religious, spiritual, and moral support to individuals who are incarcerated. My life has been forever enriched by the opportunity to have dialogue and interaction in an interfaith setting. Periodically, I have had individuals approach me with an accusatory statement of, "How can you say you are a Christian and interact with all those other religions?" The answer is simple and can be summarized with ***2Corinthians 5:20***, "Now then we are ambassadors for Christ . . .." An ambassador is one who goes to other nations and has familiarized themselves with the culture, including food, dress, customs, language, and so on; HOWEVER, the ambassador never loses sight of their own citizenship.

My reputation was always that I was going to go above and beyond in making sure each religious group had the essentials needed so that they could fully practice their faith. I sat in during their services in a supervisory role but often took part in the discussions. That includes Wicca, Asatru (a white supremacist-based religion), Islam, Judaism, Buddhism, Native American, Hebrew Israelite, and much more. The only group that was not permitted to gather as a group were Satanists. We had a third-generation Satanist who had been baptized in the blood and urine of a prostitute when he was a child. I treated everyone with respect and had an open door for counseling and conversations. I met with the inmate leaders of the groups as well as the participants and listened respectfully as they shared how their religion was meaningful to them. There were many times that we could include in the discussion our similarities, such as praying to the four directions or use of anointing oil. It left the door open for dialogue.

One thing life has taught me well is simply that where a person is does not compare to where they will always be. If we cannot walk with a person where they are, then we have no right to be part of the rest of their journey. Accepting a person does not equate to agreeing with their choices. Choices may change, but the reality is that people in our society are searching everywhere for acceptance. One of the most powerful moments as a chaplain came when a young man who wanted to change from Christianity to Wicca explained his choice to me like this, "Chaplain Williams, I would rather serve a god who can't answer my prayers as to serve the God who won't answer my prayers." As we talked. he shared that he had recently been turned down for early release. He felt like he had done everything right, and there was no reward in it. Any mature Christian would surely have to admit that they have felt that same discouragement at some point in their walk with the Lord. Amen, somebody?

It has also been my experience that many individuals who practice faiths other than Christianity were raised in Christianity and experienced condemnation and church hurt to the extent that discouragement drove them out. Those who practice Wicca often include Christ as one of their deities. Is that an oxymoron? To say the least! Gerald Gardner, the founder of Wicca, would not support mixing Christ and Wiccan practices. I use this group as an example of people who have experienced rejection to the extent that their response is to create an aura that often invites rejection. It is as if the capacity to control the rejection becomes an identity which then translates to spiritual alliances. There is much more that I could share concerning specific faith groups, but for now it suffices to say that people have not changed from the beginning of time. Human beings have an innate need to be included. That is the root of how Satan deceived Eve as he suggested to her that God was leaving her out by not allowing Eve and Adam to eat of the forbidden tree.

The contents of this book remind me of the prophet Jeremiah's assignment. The spectrum of his calling included instructions to tear down and pluck up followed by the task of building up and planting. The author has carefully presented chapters that disassemble and dissect various spiritual practices so that those who are sincerely committed to practicing Christianity in its clearest form will not purposefully or inadvertently incorporate ideologies that will eventually taint their spiritual identity. My prayer is that the readers will not just read but study the contents and challenge themselves to greater depths of serving the kingdom of God as one of its ambassadors.

Dr. Kathy E. Williams

Chapter 24

SHIFTING TO FREEDOM

As you are spending time studying and meditating on the biblical truths and scriptures, take time to journal what God is revealing to you.

Spend time with God identifying, repenting, and renouncing, sin issues, witchcraft, idolatry, occultism, and paganism.

Break all soul ties, curses, dedications, covenants, hexes, and vexes, with these acts and practices.

Bind and cast out all personal and generational spirits God reveals as it relates to these practices.

Through renunciation, nullify and break all cycles, patterns, and strongholds, personally and generationally that Holy Spirit reveals to you.

Spend consistent time soaking and washing yourself in the blood of Jesus to purify yourself from the workings of these practices.

Spend consistent time asking and allowing the Holy Spirit to come fill you with his fruit, character, nature, deliverance fire, and healing power.

REJECT BEING LIKE THE WORLD

We must resist the devil, the world, and lusting for that which draws us from God. We cannot just abstain from the world but fall out of agreement with worldly and demonic ways and have a drive to be restored in the innocence and newness of God. That means not holding on to worldly things and worldly ways, while striving to find some way to fit them in our lives or save them for a time where we think they would be lawful; such as putting a God twist on them to try to make them appropriate or holy, holding on to desires until marriage when we think it's undefiled or approved by God, or when we are mature enough to not totally yield to them, but still yielding subtly to the sin propensity of them. Abstaining using willpower is not deliverance. Only seeking sanctification, consecration, and a total divorcing from sin by literally putting to death its workings, is proof of true restoration of innocence unto salvation. When we justify sin and ungodly practices, we have not fully died with Jesus Christ where we resurrect into our new man. Dying to the flesh and sun issues is vital to SHIFTING out of witchcraft, occult, paganism, and idolatry.

Ezekiel 36:26 *I will give you a new heart and put a new spirit within you; I will remove your heart of stone and give you a heart of flesh.*

Matthew 6:24 *No one can serve two masters, for either he will hate the one and love the other, or he will be devoted to the one and despise the other. You cannot serve God and money.*

John 3:3 *Jesus replied, "Truly, truly, I tell you, no one can see the kingdom of God unless he is born again."*

John 15:18-21 *If the world hates you, know that it has hated me before it hated you. If you were of the world, the world would love you as its own; but because you are not of the world, but I chose you out of the world, therefore the world hates you. Remember the word that I said to you: 'A servant is not greater than his master.' If they persecuted me, they will also persecute you. If they kept my word, they will also keep yours. But all these things they will do to you on account of my name, because they do not know him who sent me.*

John 12:26 *I have come into the world as light, so that whoever believes in me may not remain in darkness.*

Acts 3:19 *Repent, then, and turn to God, so that your sins may be wiped out, that times of refreshing may come from the Lord.*

Acts 15:20 *Instead we should write to them, telling them to abstain from food polluted by idols, from sexual immorality, from the meat of strangled animals and from blood.*

Romans 6:4 *Therefore we are buried with him by baptism into death: that like as Christ was raised up from the dead by the glory of the Father, even so we also should walk in newness of life.*

Romans 6:6 *Knowing this, that our old self was crucified with Him, in order that our body of sin might be done away with, so that we would no longer be slaves to sin.*

Romans 8:36 *As it is written, For thy sake we are killed all the day long; we are accounted as sheep for the slaughter.*

Romans 12:2 *Do not conform to the pattern of this world, but be transformed by the renewing of your mind. Then you will be able to test and approve what God's will is—his good, pleasing and perfect will.*

1Corinthians 6:12 The New Living Bible *You say, "I am allowed to do anything"—but not everything is good for you. And even though "I am allowed to do anything," I must not become a slave to anything.*

1Corinthians 6:18 *Flee fornication. Every sin that a man doeth is without the body; but he that committeth fornication sinneth against his own body.*

1Corinthians 10:23 *All things are lawful for me, but all things are not expedient: all things are lawful for me, but all things edify not.*

2Corinthians 2:4-11 *For we who live are constantly being delivered over to death for Jesus' sake, so that the life of Jesus also may be manifested in our mortal flesh.*

2Corinthians 5:17 *Therefore if any man be in Christ, he is a new creature: old things are passed away; behold, all things are become new.*

James 4:4 *You adulterous people! Do you not know that friendship with the world is enmity with God? Therefore whoever wishes to be a friend of the world makes himself an enemy of God.*

James 4:7 *Submit yourselves therefore to God. Resist the devil, and he will flee from you.*

1John 15-17 *Do not love the world or the things in the world. If anyone loves the world, the love of the Father is not in him. For all that is in the world—the desires of the flesh and the desires of the eyes and pride in possessions—is not from the Father but is from the world. And the world is passing away along with its desires, but whoever does the will of God abides forever.*

Colossians 2:8 *See to it that no one takes you captive by philosophy and empty deceit, according to human tradition, according to the elemental spirits of the world, and not according to Christ.*

Colossians 3:5-10 The Amplified Bible *So kill (deaden, deprive of power) the evil desire lurking in your members [those animal impulses and all that is earthly in you that is employed in sin]: sexual vice, impurity, sensual appetites, unholy desires, and all greed and covetousness, for that is idolatry (the deifying of self and other created things instead of God). It is on account of these [very sins] that the [holy] anger of God is ever coming upon the sons of disobedience (those who are obstinately opposed to the divine will),*
Among whom you also once walked, when you were living in and addicted to [such practices].

But now put away and rid yourselves [completely] of all these things: anger, rage, bad feeling toward others, curses and slander, and foulmouthed abuse and shameful utterances from your lips! Do not lie to one another, for you have stripped off the old (unregenerate) self with its evil practices, And have clothed yourselves with the new [spiritual self], which is [ever in the process of being] renewed and remolded into [fuller and more perfect knowledge upon] knowledge after the image (the likeness) of Him Who created it.

Galatians 2:20 *I have been crucified with Christ; and it is no longer I who live, but Christ lives in me; and the life which I now live in the flesh I live by faith in the Son of God, who loved me and gave Himself up for me.*

Galatians 5:19-21 New Living Bible *When you follow the desires of your sinful nature, the results are very clear: sexual immorality, impurity, lustful pleasures, idolatry, sorcery, hostility, quarreling, jealousy, outbursts of anger, selfish ambition, dissension, division, envy, drunkenness, wild parties, and other sins like these. Let me tell you again, as I have before, that anyone living that sort of life will not inherit the Kingdom of God.*

1Peter 2:11-12 The Amplified Bible *Beloved, I implore you as aliens and strangers and exiles [in this world] to abstain from the sensual urges (the evil desires, the passions of the flesh,* *your lower nature) that wage war against the soul. Conduct yourselves properly (honorably, righteously) among the Gentiles, so that, although they may slander you as evildoers, [yet] they may by witnessing your good deeds [come to] glorify God in the day of inspection [when God shall look upon you wanderers as a pastor or shepherd looks over his flock].*

2Timothy 2:11 *It is a trustworthy statement: For if we died with Him, we will also live with Him.*

Philippians 1:21 *For to me, to live is Christ and to die is gain.*

LIVE A LIFE OF DAILY REPENTANCE & CONVICTION

We must understand that even our righteousness is filthy and live a life of daily repentance and wanting to be convicted of everything that does not please God. Repentance is not stating sorrow for your transgression. Repentance entails an actual turning and living a lifestyle conducive to God's will and purposes. A genuine desire to be in the will of God and practicing it as a lifestyle is a demonstration of the true fruit of repentance.

Proverbs 28:13 *He that covereth his sins shall not prosper: but whoso confesseth and forsaketh them shall have mercy.*

Isaiah 64:6 *But we are all as an unclean thing, and all our righteousnesses are as filthy rags; and we all do fade as a leaf; and our iniquities, like the wind, have taken us away.*

2Chronicles 7:14 *If my people, which are called by my name, shall humble themselves, and pray, and seek my face, and turn from their wicked ways; then will I hear from heaven, and will forgive their sin, and will heal their land.*

Joel 2:13 *And rend your heart, and not your garments, and turn unto the Lord your God: for he is gracious and merciful, slow to anger, and of great kindness, and repenteth him of the evil.*

Matthew 3:8 *Bring forth therefore fruits meet for repentance.*

Matthew 4:17 *From that time Jesus began to preach, and to say, Repent: for the kingdom of heaven is at hand.*

Luke 13:3 *I tell you, Nay: but, except ye repent, ye shall all likewise perish.*

1John 1:9 *If we confess our sins, he is faithful and just to forgive us our sins, and to cleanse us from all unrighteousness.*

Acts 3:19 *Repent ye therefore, and be converted, that your sins may be blotted out, when the times of refreshing shall come from the presence of the Lord.*

James 7:8 *Draw nigh to God, and he will draw nigh to you. Cleanse your hands, ye sinners; and purify your hearts, ye double minded.*

Revelations 3:19 As many as I love, I rebuke and chasten: be zealous therefore, and repent.

DESIRE TO PLEASE GOD
SHIFT where you desire to please God, to be obedient to his scriptures, will, and purpose, and wanting to be and have what he has ordained for your life.

Psalm 40:8 I delight to do thy will, O my God: yea, thy law is within my heart.

Psalm 73:25-28 The Amplified Bible Whom have I in heaven but You? And I have no delight or desire on earth besides You. My flesh and my heart may fail, but God is the Rock and firm Strength of my heart and my Portion forever. For behold, those who are far from You shall perish; You will destroy all who are false to You and like [spiritual] harlots depart from You. But it is good for me to draw near to God; I have put my trust in the Lord God and made Him my refuge, that I may tell of all Your works.

Isaiah 26:9 At night my soul longs for You, Indeed, my spirit within me seeks You diligently; For when the earth experiences Your judgments the inhabitants of the world learn righteousness.

John 4:34 Jesus saith unto them, My meat is to do the will of him that sent me, and to finish his work.

John 5:30 I can do nothing by Myself; I judge only as I hear. And My judgment is just, because I do not seek My own will, but the will of Him who sent Me.

HATE WHAT GOD HATES
Sometimes we may have to pray to love the things God loves and to hate the things God hates and to practice living what pleases God in order SHIFT out of these workings.

Leviticus 20:22-26 The Amplified Bible You shall therefore keep all My statutes and all My ordinances and do them, that the land where I am bringing you to dwell may not vomit you out [as it did those before you]. You shall not walk in the customs of the nation which I am casting out before you; for they did all these things, and therefore I was wearied and grieved by them. But I have said to you, You shall inherit their land, and I will give it to you to possess, a land flowing with milk and honey. I am the Lord your God, Who has separated you from the peoples.

You shall therefore make a distinction between the clean beast and the unclean, and between the unclean fowl and the clean; and you shall not make yourselves detestable with beast or with bird or with anything with which the ground teems or that creeps, which I have set apart from you as unclean. And you shall be holy to Me; for I the Lord am holy, and have separated you from the peoples, that you should be Mine.

Leviticus 26:30 *I then will destroy your high places, and cut down your incense altars, and heap your remains on the remains of your idols, for My soul shall abhor you.*

Proverbs 6:16-19 *These six things doth the Lord hate: yea, seven are an abomination unto him: A proud look, a lying tongue, and hands that shed innocent blood, an heart that deviseth wicked imaginations, feet that be swift in running to mischief, a false witness that speaketh lies, and he that soweth discord among brethren.*

Proverbs 8:18 *The fear of the LORD is to hate evil: pride, and arrogancy, and the evil way, and the froward mouth, do I hate."*

Revelations 21:8 The Amplified Bible *But as for the cowards and the ignoble and the contemptible and the cravenly lacking in courage and the cowardly submissive, and as for the unbelieving and faithless, and as for the depraved and defiled with abominations, and as for murderers and the lewd and adulterous and the practicers of magic arts and the idolaters (those who give supreme devotion to anyone or anything other than God) and all liars (those who knowingly convey untruth by word or deed)—[all of these shall have] their part in the lake that blazes with fire and brimstone. This is the second death.*

We also must trust what God's word says and cast down our desires, will, and tendencies to do things our way.

Ezekiel 18:24 The Amplified Bible *But if the righteous man turns away from his righteousness and commits iniquity and does according to all the abominations that the wicked man does, shall he live? None of his righteous deeds which he has done shall be remembered. In his trespass that he has trespassed and in his sin that he has sinned, in them shall he die.*

DESIRE HOLINESS, PURITY & FEAR OF GOD
We must want, love, and honor holiness and purity, and have a fear and reverence for the Lord and the things of the Lord.

Leviticus 20:7 *You shall consecrate yourselves therefore and be holy, for I am the Lord your God.*

Psalm 19:9 *The fear of the LORD is pure, enduring forever. The decrees of the LORD are firm, and all of them are righteous.*

Psalm 25:3-4 *Who may ascend the mountain of the LORD? Who may stand in his holy place? The one who has clean hands and a pure heart, who does not trust in an idol or swear by a false god.*

Psalm 34:9 *O fear the Lord, you His saints; For to those who fear Him there is no want.*

Psalm 51:10-12 Create in me a pure heart, O God, and renew a steadfast spirit within me. Do not cast me from your presence or take your Holy Spirit from me. Restore to me the joy of your salvation and grant me a willing spirit, to sustain me.

Psalm 111:10 *The fear of the LORD is the beginning of wisdom: a good understanding have all they that do his commandments: his praise endureth for ever.*

Psalm 119:9 *How can a young person stay on the path of purity? By living according to your word.*

Proverbs 1:7 *The fear of the LORD is the beginning of knowledge: but fools despise wisdom and instruction.*

Proverbs 9:10 *The fear of the LORD is the beginning of wisdom: and the knowledge of the holy is understanding.*

Proverbs 14:27 *The fear of the LORD is a fountain of life, to depart from the snares of death.*

Proverbs 16:6 *By mercy and truth iniquity is purged: and by the fear of the LORD men depart from evil.*

Proverbs 19:23 *The fear of the LORD tendeth to life: and he that hath it shall abide satisfied; he shall not be visited with evil.*

Proverbs 22:4 *By humility and the fear of the LORD are riches, and honour, and life.*

Mathew 5:8 *Blessed are the pure in heart, for they will see God.*

Romans 13:14 *Rather, clothe yourselves with the Lord Jesus Christ, and do not think about how to gratify the desires of the flesh.*

1Timothy 4:12 *Don't let anyone look down on you because you are young, but set an example for the believers in speech, in conduct, in love, in faith and in purity.*

Philippians 4:8 *Finally, brothers and sisters, whatever is true, whatever is noble, whatever is right, whatever is pure, whatever is lovely, whatever is admirable—if anything is excellent or praiseworthy—think about such things.*

1Peter 15:16 *But as he which hath called you is holy, so be ye holy in all manner of conversation; Because it is written, Be ye holy; for I am holy.*

DESIRE TRUTH
You must desire truth and not reject it when it is presented to you.

Psalm 26 *VINDICATE ME, O Lord, for I have walked in my integrity; I have [expectantly] trusted in, leaned on, and relied on the Lord without wavering and I shall not slide. Examine me, O Lord, and prove me; test my heart and my mind. For Your loving-kindness is before my eyes, and I have walked in Your truth [faithfully]. I do not sit with false persons, nor fellowship with pretenders; I hate the company of evildoers and will not sit with the wicked. I will wash my hands in innocence, and go about Your altar, O Lord, That I may make the voice of thanksgiving heard and may tell of all Your wondrous works. Lord, I love the habitation of Your house, and the place where Your glory dwells. Gather me not with sinners and sweep me not away [with them], nor my life with bloodthirsty men, In whose hands is wickedness, and their right hands are full of bribes. But as for me, I will walk in my integrity redeem me and be merciful and gracious to me. My foot stands on an even place; in the congregations will I bless the Lord.*

Psalm 51:6 *Behold, thou desirest truth in the inward parts: and in the hidden part thou shalt make me to know wisdom.*

John 4:24 *God is a Spirit: and they that worship him must worship him in spirit and in truth.*

John 16:13 *Howbeit when he, the Spirit of truth, is come, he will guide you into all truth: for he shall not speak of himself; but whatsoever he shall hear, that shall he speak: and he will shew you things to come.*

John 17:17 *Sanctify them through thy truth: thy word is truth.*

James 1:5 *If any of you lack wisdom, let him ask of God, that giveth to all men liberally, and upbraideth not; and it shall be given him.*

2Timothy 2:15-19 The Amplified Bible *Study and be eager and do your utmost to present yourself to God approved (tested by trial), a workman who has no cause to be ashamed, correctly analyzing and accurately dividing [rightly handling and skillfully teaching] the Word of Truth. But avoid all empty (vain, useless, idle) talk, for it will lead people into more and more ungodliness. And their teaching [will devour; it] will eat its way like cancer or spread like gangrene. So it is with Hymenaeus and Philetus,*

Who have missed the mark and swerved from the truth by arguing that the resurrection has already taken place. They are undermining the faith of some. But the firm foundation of (laid by) God stands, sure and unshaken, bearing this seal (inscription): The Lord knows those who are His, and, Let everyone who names [himself by] the name of the Lord give up all iniquity and stand aloof from it.

2Timothy 3:16-17 The Amplified Bible *Every Scripture is God-breathed (given by His inspiration) and profitable for instruction, for reproof and conviction of sin, for correction of error and discipline in obedience, [and] for training in righteousness (in holy living, in conformity to God's will in thought, purpose, and action), So that the man of God may be complete and proficient, well fitted and thoroughly equipped for every good work.*

SHIFTING INTO GENERATIONAL HERITAGE
We want to SHIFT out of generational bondages and false and erred family customs and traditions. These obligations block to true blessings and inheritance of God from coming upon you and your family line. This may require defying family monarchs and revealing or SHIFTING from other secret family sins and covenants, rejecting family traditions, beliefs, and behaviors that are rooted in mixture, disobedience to God, idolatry, witchcraft, paganism, and the occult. Jesus Christ came to set us free from all sin and curses and to divide family's so that we would be against what is not of him, such that his blessings can be restored upon our lives and lineages.

Genesis 17.7: And I will establish My covenant between Me and you and your descendants after you in their generations, for an everlasting covenant, to be God to you and your descendants after you.

Exodus 20:5 You shall not bow down to them or serve them, for I the Lord your God am a jealous God, visiting the iniquity of the fathers on the children to the third and the fourth generation of those who hate me.

Exodus 34:7 Keeping steadfast love for thousands, forgiving iniquity and transgression and sin, but who will by no means clear the guilty, visiting the iniquity of the fathers on the children and the children's children, to the third and the fourth generation.

Numbers 14:18 The Lord is slow to anger and abounding in steadfast love, forgiving iniquity and transgression, but he will by no means clear the guilty, visiting the iniquity of the fathers on the children, to the third and the fourth generation.

Deuteronomy 5:9 You shall not bow down to them or serve them; for I the Lord your God am a jealous God, visiting the iniquity of the fathers on the children to the third and fourth generation of those who hate me.

2Kings 10.30 And the Lord said to Jehu, "Because you have done well in doing what is right in My sight, and have done to the house of Ahab all that was in My heart, your sons shall sit on the throne of Israel to the fourth generation.

Psalm 22:30 Posterity shall serve Him; they shall tell of the Lord to the next generation.

Psalm 78.4 We will not hide them from their children, telling to the generation to come the praises of the Lord, And His strength and His wonderful works that He has done.

Psalm 145:4 One generation shall praise thy works to another, and shall declare thy mighty acts.

Joel 1.3 Tell your children about it, and let your children tell their children, and their children the next generation.

Proverbs 13:2-22 *Evil pursueth sinners: but to the righteous good shall be repayed. A good man leaveth an inheritance to his children's children: and the wealth of the sinner is laid up for the just.*

Jeremiah 32:18 *You show steadfast love to thousands, but you repay the guilt of fathers to their children after them, O great and mighty God, whose name is the Lord of hosts.*

Matthew 16:24-25 *Then Jesus told his disciples, "If anyone would come after me, let him deny himself and take up his cross and follow me. 25 For whoever would save his life will lose it, but whoever loses his life for my sake will find it.*

John 1:9 *If we confess our sins, he is faithful and just to forgive us our sins and to cleanse us from all unrighteousness.*

Luke 1:16-17 *And many of the children of Israel shall he turn to the Lord their God. And he shall go before him in the spirit and power of Elias, to turn the hearts of the fathers to the children, and the disobedient to the wisdom of the just; to make ready a people prepared for the Lord.*

Luke 12:51-53 *Do you suppose that I have come to give peace upon earth? No, I say to you, but rather division; For from now on in one house there will be five divided [among themselves], three against two and two against three. They will be divided, father against son and son against father, mother against daughter and daughter against mother, mother-in-law against her daughter-in-law and daughter-in-law against her mother-in-law.*

HAVE TRUE ACCOUNTABILITY
Accountability allows others to speak truth to us while also helping us to govern and cover our souls. True accountability is not someone who will speak what we want to hear or justify our sins for fear of hurting our feelings or having us disconnect from them. True accountability is someone who will speak truth because they are more concerned about us not going to hell than pleasing our flesh, desires, or remaining in good graces with us. This person is also striving to live a life pleasing to God and is seeking not to compromise his will and word while dying to their own self-gratification. Seek to have such a person in your life that can journey with you in truth. Seek to honor them in a way where you can accept rebuke, chastisement, and instruction for correcting anything that is ungodly in your life.

Proverbs 27:17 *Iron sharpeneth iron; so a man sharpeneth the countenance of his friend.*

Ecclesiastes 4:9-12 *Two are better than one; because they have a good reward for their labour. For if they fall, the one will lift up his fellow: but woe to him that is alone when he falleth; for he hath not another to help him up. Again, if two lie together, then they have heat: but how can one be warm alone? And if one prevail against him, two shall withstand him; and a threefold cord is not quickly broken.*

James 5:16 *Confess your faults one to another, and pray one for another, that ye may be healed. The effectual fervent prayer of a righteous man availeth much.*

Hebrews 3:17 *Have confidence in your leaders and submit to their authority, because they keep watch over you as those who must give an account. Do this so that their work will be a joy, not a burden, for that would be of no benefit to you.*

LIVE A LIFE OF HUMILITY
Humility enables you to live under the grace, dignity, honor, and reverence's fear of the Lord. Honor postures you to want to hear God's instruction and to please him with your life choices.

Proverbs 15:3 *Wisdom's instruction is to fear the LORD, and humility comes before honor.*

Proverbs 22:4 *Humility is the fear of the LORD; its wages are riches and honor and life.*

Proverbs 29:23 *A man's pride will bring him low, but a humble spirit will obtain honor.*

Psalm 24:9 *He guides the humble in what is right and teaches them his way.*

Psalm 149:4 *For the LORD takes delight in his people; he crowns the humble with victory.*

James 4:10 *Humble yourselves in the presence of the Lord, and He will exalt you.*

1Peter 5:6 *Humble yourselves, therefore, under God's mighty hand, so that in due time He may exalt you.*

Colossians 3:12 *Therefore, as God's chosen people, holy and dearly loved, clothe yourselves with compassion, kindness, humility, gentleness and patience.*

Chapter 24

SOUL STEALER DELIVERANCE PRAYER

Even though you will use the scriptures above to pray detailed prayers with God, pray this prayer aloud as a sealant to what God is in your life and generations. Anytime during this prayer where you can be specific regarding practices you knowingly engaged in, please do so.

Lord, thank you for the revelation in this book and the deliverance that has taken place in my life, sphere of influence, and generational line. Thank you that when you set me free, I am free indeed and that through your freedom no foe can overturn. Thank you, Lord Jesus, that deliverance is the children's bread. I partake and feast off your deliverance bread even now with tangible miracles, signs, and wonders following me.

In your matchless name Jesus, I repent for all forms of personal and generational witchcraft, occultism, idolatry, and paganism. I lose your blood into me and my generational line. I wash and soak in the redemptive power of your blood and your works on the cross. I repent for the sins of my ancestors on my mother side and father side a hundred generations back. I repent for every dedication, covenant, and oath, made to demons, sacrifices made on witchcraft altars, and any sacrifices and alignments made to the demonic kingdom concerning our lives, mantles, callings, and destinies. I repent for any harm released to others on these altars. I break these dedications, covenants, and oaths in the name of Jesus and decree that me and my family line are SHIFTING eternally out of agreement with them and their workings in our bloodline by the atonement of your cross and your resurrection power.

I repent for every form of witchcraft, ancestral worship, hero worship, conjuring and communing with the dead, traditional, and cultural practice I and my family line have engaged in that does not align with you and your word. I lose your blood to cleanse and set us free and decree an annulment of these practices, their loyalties, false obligation, systematic family hierarchy, monarchy, all forms of control, manipulation, lies, myths, errors in the name of Jesus. I rise as a bloodline breaker and kingdom heir against everything in me and my family line that does not represent you. I decree I died with Jesus Christ and rose in resurrection power in sonship with you Jesus. Jesus Christ is my Lord and savior and is the ultimate authority to which I am loyal to and who governs my life. I declare enmity against every witchcraft power, idol, and familiar spirit, poltergeists, that seeks to control me and my family line and say NO MORE in Jesus name. You are renounced and cast out in Jesus name. Your assignment and legal right are broken through his working in me and for me in Jesus name.

I renounce all religious doctrines rooted in gimmicks, charismatic witchcraft, error, misinterpretation and misrepresentation of the scripture, manmade justifications and systems, ungodly dogmas in the name of Jesus. I come out of agreement with every way man and the devil use your kingdom, your word, and your name to pimp, prostitute, monetize, discredit, cast suspicion on you Jesus Christ, your word, and your kingdom. I repent for all twisted and religious perversions, erred thinking, political religious demonization, church witchcraft, being a church witch or warlock, rebellion, rejection, Jezebel, Athaliah, and Saul tendencies and proclivities, and every way it was imparted into me and taught to me in the name of Jesus. I forgive those who operated in this manner towards me and repent for every way I operated in this manner towards you and others. I reject these idolatrous ways, cast them down, and lift you up Jesus Christ as Lord and Savior of my life, the only Lord and Savior in heaven in earth, and the only way to eternal life with you.

I repent for all acts centered around seeking different ways to eternal life, communing with demons, the universe, the stars, the moon, the sun, the elements of the earth, in effort to ascend into a higher consciousness. I recognize that this is not of you, and I fall out of agreement with it. I admit that it is an idolatrous practice, and I eradicate it from my life and lineage. I repent for every way I have opened a third eye in my life and for every demonic portal that is opened within my consciousness and around my sphere. In Jesus Christ matchless name, I close all these portals and command them to be eternally shut closed by the authority of Jesus Christ. I break covenant and soul ties with all idols and demons attached to these portals and renounce them as spirit guides and gods of my life. I decree they fall like Dagon today as I lift you, Jesus Christ, as Lord and banner over my life, sphere, and generational line. I repent for all astral projection activities, acts of engaging in soul soaring, riding the witch's broom, sunbathing, astrology, numerology, horoscope practices, psychic powers, magister, candle magic, black magic, spell casting, voodoo, hoodoo, root working, yoga, all forms of mystical meditation, pharmakeia, and any other acts that are connected to ascending into higher forms of consciousness (name them).

I renounce all idolatrous and cult organizations and false religions (name them and renounce them). I renounce every covenant, oath, and dedication I made to be in the organization, with members and demonic forces attached to the organization. I SHIFT my allegiance to Jesus Christ only and his kingdom. Jesus Christ cleanse my mind, body, and soul - make me whole. Jesus Christ, renew in me a clean heart and a right spirit while giving me your mind and thoughts. Jesus Christ put your Holy Spirit, your character, your nature, your renewed identity in me, and restore me in the fullness of salvation. I rededicate my life to you and commit to only wanting you Jesus Christ. I accept you as my personal savior and give my life to you. I decree I only want to love the things you love, hate the things you hate, live a life feasting on pleasing you, and SHIFT into loving, honoring, and obeying you.

I humble myself to you Jesus and SHIFT to seek you daily to learn you and your ways and understand my destiny and calling in you. It is only in you that I move, breathe, and have my very own being. I SHIFT to humbling myself under your mighty hand and allow you to guide me into all truth, living through truth, and being enlightened, equipped, empowered, and directed by the dreams and visions of your truth. Thank you for your deliverance and healing power and for making me brand new in you. Thank you for making me a new creature and for my kingdom life of journeying in covenant as a lifestyle with you. In Jesus name I decree it is so. Amen! SHIFT!

SOUL STEALER TEST

Unmasking the Power of the Scouts Volume II

Multiple Choice
1. How do demon dealers transform themselves into apostles of Christ?
    a. They take an oath and dedicate their lives to Christ.
    b. They transform themselves in appearance, figure, and operation, even though their motive is deceitful and ungodly.
    c. They take on an office of high ranking in the spirit realm and deem it their duty to operate like God's sent one even though the devil sent them.
    d. Both B and C
2. In the Old Testament, scouting was used as a ____ tactic against the enemy. In the New Testament, scouting was used as a tactic to _____ Jesus Christ for the purposes of crucifying him and to spy on the disciples.
    a. Defensive; protect
    b. Hostile; overthrow
    c. Warfare; seize
    d. None of the above
3. Which of the following describes the characteristics of a scout:
    a. Scouts encourage others to see God's hand in a situation or to see a situation like God sees it.
    b. Scouts are self-sacrificing to the cause, good of the vision, and the people.
    c. Scouts are fearless and can detect the salvation of the Lord in a situation.
    d. All of the above
4. _____ level warfare involves casting demons out of individuals, places, and things.
    a. Occult
    b. Ground
    c. Strategic
    d. Tactical
5. _____ level warfare involves witchcraft, idolatry, or strategic organizations that are really powers of darkness, or spiritual wickedness in high places within a community or region. Examples, Freemasonry, Sororities, Fraternities, New Age Practices, Buddhism, Tibetan, Yoga, etc.
    a. Ground
    b. Strategic
    c. Tactical
    d. Occult

6. Strategic Level Warfare is where principalities and territorial spirits are assigned by Satan to:
    a. directly bind, influence, and govern the activities of communities, regions, states, and nations.
    b. Overtake the rulers of the world and their governance.
    c. coordinate demonic activities in political, governmental, economic, financial, educational, business, and entertainment arenas.
    d. Both A and C

Match the Following to the Appropriate Definition:
7. _____ are demonic forces, evil spirits or devils that possess, depress, oppress, torment, influence, or stronghold a person, place, or thing.
8. _____ are demonically possessed, demonically depressed, demonically gripping clutches, barriers, fortresses, walls, or entanglements that harass, influence, hinder and/or prevent a person from being free to walk in the full salvation of the Lord.
9. _____ are satanic princes and territorial spirits ruling over a nation, city, region, and community for the purposes of establishing Satan's demonic plan in people's lives and spheres.
10. _____ are high ranking supernatural demons or demonic influences that cause evil and sin in the world.
11. _____ are demonic forces that govern deception and manipulative hardships and catastrophes that are generally produced by witchcraft, manipulation of the weather and worldly systems; they operate in cultures and countries such that idolatry and sin reign in the earth.
12. _____ are evil plots and deceptions, and demonic attacks directed in and against the church and God's people for the purposes of hindering, contaminating and demolishing God's will in the earth.
    a. **Spiritual wickedness in high places**
    b. **Powers**
    c. **Strongholds**
    d. **Demons**
    e. **Principalities**
    f. **Rulers of Darkness**
13. David said it is good when God does not have to impute one to iniquity and that we are blessed when we confess our sins. Impute means:
    a. God is allowing us to get away with our sins
    b. God wants us to embrace our sins
    c. God called us out on our sin
    d. God wants us to soak in our wrongdoings

14. _____ and _____ has enabled them to be more efficient with unifying and asserting their right to free speech and openly practicing their beliefs, while contesting and even demanding imprisonment of those who believe contrary to them.
    a. Radio and social media
    b. Internet and Social Media
    c. Newspaper and Internet
    d. Newspaper and Magazines

15. New Age participants usually are:
    a. very intellectual, explorers, informational pursuers, spiritual, yet lack submission to authority.
    b. high strung renegades who have a divine calling, but have been drawn away from God's original plan and intent of leadership for their lives
    c. deem themselves Christians who desire to hold on to their cultural or ethic roots and customs, or whose pursuit of greater knowledge, healing, and power, has caused them to believe and delve into in different paths to eternal life.
    d. All of the above.

16. After reading the scripture below, what does the scripture tell us about the importance of our obedience.
    1 Chronicles 22:7-10 *And David said to Solomon, My son, as for me, it was in my mind to build an house unto the name of the LORD my God: But the word of the LORD came to me, saying, Thou hast shed blood abundantly, and hast made great wars: thou shalt not build an house unto my name, because thou hast shed much blood upon the earth in my sight. Behold, a son shall be born to thee, who shall be a man of rest; and I will give him rest from all his enemies round about: for his name shall be Solomon, and I will give peace and quietness unto Israel in his days. He shall build a house for my name; and he shall be my son, and I will be his father; and I will establish the throne of his kingdom over Israel for ever.*
    a. that our obedience is more important than our thoughts, desires, and intent of our hearts.
    b. That our obedience release warfare.
    c. That our obedience allows us to navigate through life clearly.
    d. That our obedience reveals God's heart to us.

17. Which of the following can Christians NOT do regarding the use of incense, perfume, and herbs and spices:
    a. incense and candles to set the ambiance within an environment and for prayer
    b. can wear perfume as a fragrance and grooming
    c. used in witchcraft ceremonies, rituals, spells, incantations, sacrifices, to ward off evil and demonic forces, God deems that strange fire.
    d. can groom and cook food with our spices and herbs; use them as a healing aide

18. Which definition(s) best describes an occult
    a. The dark practices they are drawn too and difficulty fitting into popular culture tends to be the reason they experience gloominess, depression, sadness, and loneliness.
    b. practices include the ability to manipulate natural laws with the intent to navigate life experiences, produce luck, favor, fame, fortune, impact someone else's life, engage in wicked or evil practices.
    c. practices are designed to worship, serve, live, and build the kingdom of Satan.
    d. Both B and C
19. What is the difference between Goths and Emos.
    a. Goth culture draw ideologies and dark concepts from B movies, Gothic literature, horror films, vampire cults and traditional mythology; the emo culture include despair, depression, heart break, sensitivity and easily triggered, introversion, and self-loathing.
    b. Goth culture derives from Africa and draw ideologies from mummification practices; Emo culture derives from Mayan tribal practices.
    c. Goth culture uses different ideologies and practices surrounding beliefs, knowledge, and use of supernatural forces or beings, magic, divination, witchcraft, and alchemy; Emo culture practitioners have a strong dislike, hatred, and distrust for humankind; are angry at society, at someone, or about life issues; are rebelling against laws, rules, and regulations that they believe violate how they feel, think, or believe
    d. None of the above
20. The Yoruba religion believes in _____, which is reincarnation within the family. Many believe when a baby is born and resembles a dead relative, he or she is the reincarnation of that person.
    a. Oshun
    b. Atunwa
    c. Ajogun
    d. Ashe
21. Becoming a Freemason requires achieving three ceremonial stages called degrees, which have their roots in medieval craftsmanship of apprentice, fellow craft, and master Mason. What are the three ceremonial stages, or degrees called?
    a. youth, manhood, and age
    b. courage, manhood, and age
    c. sacrifice, overachieving and age
    d. none of the above
22. What two organizations are sororities and fraternities founded from?
    a. Occultism and Satanism
    b. RASTAFARIANISM and Yoruba
    c. Free Masonry and Easter Star
    d. None of the above

23. Rebellious believers are:
   a. Hear the word, but implement it how they see fit, according to their own desires, what benefits them and those they are aiming to please.
   b. Tend to act first, then repent, pray, and seek to hear God after they realized they have disobeyed him, and is risking the repercussions of their actions.
   c. Will continue in their position unrepentant to save face with the people yet knowing God has rejected them.
   d. All of the Above

24. God's glory is:
   a. substance that has the character, nature, identity, weight, and authority of God.
   b. ascribing glory we are literally giving people God
   c. Both A and B
   d. None of the Above

25. In regard to the political system, the reason we must remain focused on preaching the gospel and using our gifts and callings to
   a. establish God's government in the earth by creating our own systems, not overtaking their system.
   b. Overtake their system and take the system by force.
   c. Infiltrate their system by going undercover and declaring the word of the Lord
   d. None of the above

True or False Questions

26. One of the mandates as a scout is to deal with spiritual wickedness in high places and to pull down high places.
   a. True
   b. False

27. Demonic spirits can attack in the following ways: Oppress, Suppress, Negatively influence, and Possess.
   a. True
   b. False

28. As scouts, one must study witchcraft. Know your authority and gain intel on how witchcraft operates so you can quickly discern and dispel its workings.
   a. True
   b. False

29. Conviction can be described as a feeling or emotion, guilt, shame or condemnation, a quickening because it is flesh that may or may be responding to our spirit.
   a. True
   b. False

30. To have a clean heart created within you, you have to first acknowledge that your heart needs to be clean and then ask God to do the work. You must seek deliverance and healing even when you have not committed blatant or conscious sin or think you are pure before God.
    a. True
    b. False
31. In Proverbs 4:23, in the King James Bible says Keep thy heart with all diligence; for out of it are the issues of life. Issues entail whatever challenges, questions, concerns, perceptions, proceedings, wounds, pains, circumstances, experiences we have in occurring in our lives.
    a. True
    b. False
32. A boundary is a line that gives us unlimited and unbounding access in an area of distinction.
    a. True
    b. False
33. The first demon dealer was the devil.
    a. True
    b. False
34. Inordinacy can lead to obsessive and compulsive thoughts and behaviors that can make us appear or act double-minded or mentally unstable and can lead to idolatry as now we are striving to be our own god by striving to fulfill our desires at the expense of God's will and plan for our lives.
    a. True
    b. False
35. we do have authority in the spirit realm to not tolerate witches and witchcraft, and to release God's judgment on those who engage in witchcraft or operate as witches.
    a. True
    b. False
36. In Genesis 11:4, Nimrod and his kingdom striving to build a city and a tower to reach heaven. God had to advance their language and scattered them abroad upon the earth, so they would understand one another, and would be able to complete this task.
    a. True
    b. False
37. The New Age Movement encompasses new modern practices, witchcraft practices, occult practices in a modern context. These practices include sorcery, pursue astrology for divine guidance, magic, witchcraft, communication with the dead, worship of Satan, sacrifices to idols and demons and much more.
    a. True
    b. False

38. New Age participants us the following scriptures to justify their belief that all humans are gods: Psalm 82:6 I have said, Ye are gods; and all of you are children of the most High and John 10:34 Jesus answered them, Is it not written in your law, I said, Ye are gods?
    a. True
    b. False

39. There is a difference between astral projection and guided translation of the Holy Spirit.
    a. True
    b. False

40. A vision board is a great way to become successful by visualizing what the person wants in their life and how they plan on accomplishing it.
    a. True
    b. False

41. Our inability to train and even govern these people, their gifts, and heavenly realms, confound matters for the body of Christ and expose us to being infiltrated by witches and warlocks who the devil send to steal, kill, and destroy people and ministries.
    a. True
    b. False

42. When rebellion operates in members and ministries, it closes the door to witchcraft.
    a. True
    b. False

43. Algorithms are a series of codes or operations that help identify user behaviors, what is relevant and important to the user, and what the user is likely to engage in, invest in, or purchase.
    a. True
    b. False

44. First-party elements have the ability to save cookies onto your browser each time you access their domain. They can access the data from the site you are on and every site that uses that same third-party element. This is called tracking!
    a. True
    b. False

45. . Cyber bullying is the use of electronic communication to bully, intimidate, negatively expose a person, or bring and release contempt, typically by sending messages, posting messages, or releasing video and audio regarding the person.
    a. True
    b. False

46. Cyber and media bullying is a controlling spirit seeking to kill the person's purpose and calling.
    a. True
    b. False

47. The Celebrity Spirit is Selling and sacrificing one's soul and the soul of others for popularity, fame, and fortune.
    a. True
    b. False
48. It is doubt that social media and the internet in general expose the character, nature, and heart of a person. This is because we are operating in spiritual realms where our spirits, minds, and souls, are engaging one to another in the fullness of its existence.
    a. True
    b. False
49. God is striving to do is to build his own media system that draws people out of mainstream media idolatry, to his true government.
    a. True
    b. False
50. Our calling is not the gift, but what the gift does to save, deliver, and heal souls. The gift often times becomes an offering to the idol god of Hollywood so that a person can be used on that platform.
    a. True
    b. False
51. New Age practitioners claim they have healing and protection powers, although there is no scientific evidence to support this theory. The claim is that they have unique mystical healing powers that cure ailments protect against illness, disease, and injury, provide mental and emotional wellness, balance, and stability, promotes creativity, and awakens spiritual consciousness.
    a. True
    b. False
52. The following scripture is a symbolizing of remembrance but is not a literal act of drinking blood or eating body parts, whether Jesus or otherwise. Mark 14:22-25 *And as they were eating, he took bread, and after blessing it broke it and gave it to them, and said, "Take; this is my body." And he took a cup, and when he had given thanks he gave it to them, and they all drank of it. And he said to them, "This is my blood of the covenant, which is poured out for many. Truly, I say to you, I will not drink again of the fruit of the vine until that day when I drink it new in the kingdom of God."*
    a. True
    b. False
53. Some idolatrous religions believe incenses and candles provides a light for their god to engage them, raise vibration levels, draw energy from the sun, draw spirit guides and certain spirits into the atmosphere, dispels evil and demons, brings protection, purifying the person and the atmosphere, stimulate the sexual drive, enhance memory, can be lit as a sacrifice to gods for certain purposes (e.g., for luck, prosperity, love, friendship, wellness).
    a. True
    b. False

54. Herbalism is one of the most ancient medical systems in the earth and can be correlated with the history of medicine. Also known as phytotherapy or botanical medicine, herbalism entails the practice of making or prescribing plant based herbal remedies for medical conditions.
    a. True
    b. False
55. Is the following statement true or false regarding the Black Hebrew Israelites: They equate their uprising to reclaiming the people of the lost tribe of Israel and taking their rightful place in the earth so they can reign when God returns to restore their rulership.
    a. True
    b. False
56. Black Hebrew Israelites accept the images of a white Jesus and believe these images were created to steal their ordained identity. They believe Jesus is a black man according to Revelation 1:15. Black Hebrew Israelites accept Christian and pagan holidays regard them as idolatrous and demonic. They celebrate the Passover but have adopted their own ideologies regarding many biblical symbols, feasts, and celebrations.
    a. True
    b. False
57. Orishas are human beings that already existed in the spirit world at creation, who become incarnated beings that live on earth.
    a. True
    b. False
58. The artist Rihanna invoked the goddess Orshun in several of her musical and movie projects. She also compares herself to Oshun throughout the movie "Black Is King" and in her visual imagery album entitled "Lemonade."
    a. True
    b. False
59. As Christ followers, anything that is not aligning with God and his word is error or false.
    a. True
    b. False
60. The charismatic person's words, charisma, and the manner to which they utilize the scriptures and principles of God, operate like witchcraft spells to woo, and subdue people under their powers, while building their personal kingdoms.
    a. True
    b. False
61. Babylonians are worldly, manmade, and demonic systems with self-focused and idolatrous agendas. They present a true sense of godliness, liberty, and freedom, but truthfully Babylon is idolatrous, oppressive, and evil. The focus is fame, fortune, pleasure, and success.
    a. True
    b. False

62. The following is a Characteristic of a Church Warlock: Strives to get close to leaders so they can acquire inside information, become a leader themselves, be in position to control others, and usurp authority to fulfill their purpose.
    a. True
    b. False
63. The following is a Characteristic of a Church Witch: Is not interested in unity, fellowship, togetherness, but utilize these methods to gain the favor of people, to infiltrate groups and become a lead voice over people.
    a. True
    b. False
64. The purpose of a Watchmen is to be stationed at specific places within the room before service, during high levels of deliverance, healing, and worship within the service, and at altar calls. Their goal is not to personally pray for people, but to pray for the atmosphere to be pliable for deliverance healing, to pray protection prayers as the ministry was going forth, pray and encourage those God revealed to come to the altar for salvation, baptism, and prayer, and to watch, pray, and intervene regarding suspicious activity within the pews and at the altar.
    a. True
    b. False
65. Some saints are now rogue witches and warlocks because they were taught how to steward their gifts and powers of the prophetic, seed, etc. in the church or in life.
    a. True
    b. False
66. Lack of teaching and training of translating and traveling in spiritual realms for ministry and warfare purposes, and prophetic and supernatural dreams and encounters, cause people to find their own interpretation and education in these areas. Done void of Holy Ghost direction, they open their lives to spirit guides and demon activity that turn them in Christian witches and warlocks.
    a. True
    b. False
67. Failure to really bring physical and emotional wellness, deal with life issues, admit and heal church issues, has caused a disbelief and mistrust in God and the church.
    a. True
    b. False
68. Yoga meditation is a type of meditation that is designed to heighten and enhance a person's awareness of their connection to the universe. The premise is that cosmic meditation causes heighten spiritual awareness, divine consciousness, and awakening by receiving energy, enlightenment, and spiritual and natural power from different regions, spheres, and properties (e.g., sun, moon, stars, galaxies), in the universe.
    a. True
    b. False

69. Reiki practitioners use their hands to massage the body and operate through specific verbal mantras and blessings they speak out loud to clear negative energy from the body for the perceived purposes of raising a person's vibration, bringing harmony and balance to one's mind, open and balance energy Kundalini chakras, bringing mental, emotional, and spiritual healing and balance.
    a. True
    b. False
70. Anything that overtakes our identity, becomes excessive, or something we feel we cannot live without, should be a caution to really go before God and see if deliverance and healing is needed.
    a. True
    b. False
71. An incantation is a strong wish, desire, motive, intent, or compilation of words rooted in magical powers that can be worked by simply pointing a finger, meditating, and willing a situation to occur, performing a ritual using various tools, herbs, and crystals, or drawing from energies, vibrations, and demonic powers to complete its workings.
    a. True
    b. False
72. A charm is a ritual utterance or potion used for the purposes of attracting, magnetizing, or connecting, to a desired person, object, or experience.
    a. True
    b. False
73. Regarding the practice of smudging, a person is actually invoking demons and calling more demons into their life, rather than casting them out.
    a. True
    b. False
74. The All Lives Matters movement, is essential to racial reform and enlightening the public on racial injustices. The movement is not designed to exclude other races, but to emphasize the lack of necessary action and attention brought to the systematic racism and violence Black people are enduring.
    a. True
    b. False
75. Regarding algorithms, Individuals may not realize they have become addicted because of the psychological techniques that are involved. The longer the system can keep you on a platform, the greater the number of ads you are consuming, which increases the drive to use apps and the internet.
    a. True
    b. False

SOUL STEALER ANSWER KEY

Unmasking the Power of the Scouts Volume II

Multiple Choice
1. How do demon dealers transform themselves into apostles of Christ?
    a. They take an oath and dedicate their lives to Christ.
    b. They transform themselves in appearance, figure, and operation, even though their motive is deceitful and ungodly.
    c. They take on an office of high ranking in the spirit realm and deem it their duty to operate like God's sent one even though the devil sent them.
    d. Both B and C
2. In the Old Testament, scouting was used as a ____ tactic against the enemy. In the New Testament, scouting was used as a tactic to _____ Jesus Christ for the purposes of crucifying him and to spy on the disciples.
    a. Defensive; protect
    b. Hostile; overthrow
    c. Warfare; seize
    d. None of the above
3. Which of the following describes the characteristics of a scout:
    a. Scouts encourage others to see God's hand in a situation or to see a situation like God sees it.
    b. Scouts are self-sacrificing to the cause, good of the vision, and the people.
    c. Scouts are fearless and can detect the salvation of the Lord in a situation.
    d. All of the above
4. _____ level warfare involves casting demons out of individuals, places, and things.
    a. Occult
    b. Ground
    c. Strategic
    d. Tactical
5. _____ level warfare involves witchcraft, idolatry, or strategic organizations that are really powers of darkness, or spiritual wickedness in high places within a community or region. Examples, Freemasonry, Sororities, Fraternities, New Age Practices, Buddhism, Tibetan, Yoga, etc.
    a. Ground
    b. Strategic
    c. Tactical
    d. Occult

6. Strategic Level Warfare is where principalities and territorial spirits are assigned by Satan to:
   a. directly bind, influence, and govern the activities of communities, regions, states, and nations.
   b. Overtake the rulers of the world and their governance.
   c. coordinate demonic activities in political, governmental, economic, financial, educational, business, and entertainment arenas.
   d. Both A and C

Match the Following to the appropriate Definition:
7. __D__ are demonic forces, evil spirits or devils that possess, depress, oppress, torment, influence, or stronghold a person, place, or thing.
8. __C__ are demonically possessed, demonically depressed, demonically gripping clutches, barriers, fortresses, walls, or entanglements that harass, influence, hinder and/or prevent a person from being free to walk in the full salvation of the Lord
9. __E__ are satanic princes and territorial spirits ruling over a nation, city, region, and community for the purposes of establishing Satan's demonic plan in people's lives and spheres.
10. __B__ are high ranking supernatural demons or demonic influences that cause evil and sin in the world.
11. __F__ are demonic forces that govern deception and manipulative hardships and catastrophes that are generally produced by witchcraft, manipulation of the weather and worldly systems; they operate in cultures and countries such that idolatry and sin reign in the earth.
12. __A__ are evil plots and deceptions, and demonic attacks directed in and against the church and God's people for the purposes of hindering, contaminating and demolishing God's will in the earth.
    a. **Spiritual wickedness in high places**
    b. **Powers**
    c. **Strongholds**
    d. **Demons**
    e. **Principalities**
    f. **Rulers of Darkness**
13. David said it is good when God does not have to impute one to iniquity and that we are blessed when we confess our sins. Impute means:
    a. God is allowing us to get away with our sins
    b. God wants us to embrace our sins
    c. God called us out on our sin
    d. God wants us to soak in our wrongdoings

14. _____ and _____ has enabled them to be more efficient with unifying and asserting their right to free speech and openly practicing their beliefs, while contesting and even demanding imprisonment of those who believe contrary to them.
    a. Radio and social media
    b. Internet and Social Media
    c. Newspaper and Internet
    d. Newspaper and Magazines
15. New Age participants usually are:
    a. very intellectual, explorers, informational pursuers, spiritual, yet lack submission to authority.
    b. high strung renegades who have a divine calling, but have been drawn away from God's original plan and intent of leadership for their lives
    c. deem themselves Christians who desire to hold on to their cultural or ethic roots and customs, or whose pursuit of greater knowledge, healing, and power, has caused them to believe and delve into in different paths to eternal life.
    d. All of the above.
16. After reading the scripture below, what does the scripture tell us about the importance of our obedience.

    1 Chronicles 22:7-10 *And David said to Solomon, My son, as for me, it was in my mind to build an house unto the name of the LORD my God: But the word of the LORD came to me, saying, Thou hast shed blood abundantly, and hast made great wars: thou shalt not build an house unto my name, because thou hast shed much blood upon the earth in my sight. Behold, a son shall be born to thee, who shall be a man of rest; and I will give him rest from all his enemies round about: for his name shall be Solomon, and I will give peace and quietness unto Israel in his days. He shall build a house for my name; and he shall be my son, and I will be his father; and I will establish the throne of his kingdom over Israel for ever.*
    a. that our obedience is more important than our thoughts, desires, and intent of our hearts.
    b. That our obedience release warfare.
    c. That our obedience allows us to navigate through life clearly.
    d. That our obedience reveals God's heart to us.
17. Which of the following can Christians NOT do regarding the use of incense, perfume, and herbs and spices:
    a. incense and candles to set the ambiance within an environment and for prayer
    b. can wear perfume as a fragrance and grooming
    c. used in witchcraft ceremonies, rituals, spells, incantations, sacrifices, to ward off evil and demonic forces, God deems that strange fire.
    d. can groom and cook food with our spices and herbs; use them as a healing aide

18. Which definition(s) best describes an occult
    a. The dark practices they are drawn too and difficulty fitting into popular culture tends to be the reason they experience gloominess, depression, sadness, and loneliness.
    b. practices include the ability to manipulate natural laws with the intent to navigate life experiences, produce luck, favor, fame, fortune, impact someone else's life, engage in wicked or evil practices.
    c. practices are designed to worship, serve, live, and build the kingdom of Satan.
    d. Both B and C
19. What is the difference between Goths and Emos.
    a. Goth culture draw ideologies and dark concepts from B movies, Gothic literature, horror films, vampire cults and traditional mythology; the emo culture include despair, depression, heart break, sensitivity and easily triggered, introversion, and self-loathing.
    b. Goth culture derives from Africa and draw ideologies from mummification practices; Emo culture derives from Mayan tribal practices.
    c. Goth culture uses different ideologies and practices surrounding beliefs, knowledge, and use of supernatural forces or beings, magic, divination, witchcraft, and alchemy; Emo culture practitioners have a strong dislike, hatred, and distrust for humankind; are angry at society, at someone, or about life issues; are rebelling against laws, rules, and regulations that they believe violate how they feel, think, or believe
    d. None of the above
20. The Yoruba religion believes in _____, which is reincarnation within the family. Many believe when a baby is born and resembles a dead relative, he or she is the reincarnation of that person.
    a. Oshun
    b. Atunwa
    c. Ajogun
    d. Ashe
21. Becoming a Freemason requires achieving three ceremonial stages called degrees, which have their roots in medieval craftsmanship of apprentice, fellow craft, and master Mason. What are the three ceremonial stages, or degrees called?
    a. youth, manhood, and age
    b. courage, manhood, and age
    c. sacrifice, overachieving and age
    d. none of the above
22. What two organizations are sororities and fraternities founded from?
    a. Occultism and Satanism
    b. RASTAFARIANISM and Yoruba
    c. Free Masonry and Easter Star
    d. None of the above

23. Rebellious believers are:
    a. Hear the word, but implement it how they see fit, according to their own desires, what benefits them and those they are aiming to please.
    b. Tend to act first, then repent, pray, and seek to hear God after they realized they have disobeyed him, and is risking the repercussions of their actions.
    c. Will continue in their position unrepentant to save face with the people, yet knowing God has rejected them.
    d. All of the Above
24. God's glory is:
    a. substance that has the character, nature, identity, weight, and authority of God.
    b. ascribing glory we are literally giving people God
    c. Both A and B
    d. None of the Above
25. In regard to the political system, the reason we must remain focused on preaching the gospel and using our gifts and callings to
    a. establish God's government in the earth by creating our own systems, not overtaking their system.
    b. Overtake their system and take the system by force.
    c. Infiltrate their system by going undercover and declaring the word of the Lord
    d. None of the above

True or False Questions

26. One of the mandates as a scout is to deal with spiritual wickedness in high places and to pull down high places.
    a. True
    b. False
27. demonic spirits can attack in the following ways: Oppress, Suppress, Negatively influence, and Possess.
    a. True
    b. False
28. As scouts, one must study witchcraft, know your authority, and gain intel on how witchcraft operates so you can quickly discern and dispel its workings.
    a. True
    b. False
29. Conviction can be described as a feeling or emotion, guilt, shame or condemnation, a quickening because it is flesh that may or may be responding to our spirit.
    a. True
    b. False

30. To have a clean heart created within you, you have to first acknowledge that your heart needs to be clean and then ask God to do the work. You must seek deliverance and healing even when you have not committed blatant or conscious sin or think you are pure before God.
    a. **True**
    b. False
31. In Proverbs 4:23, in the King James Bible says Keep thy heart with all diligence; for out of it are the issues of life. Issues entail whatever challenges, questions, concerns, perceptions, proceedings, wounds, pains, circumstances, experiences we have in occurring in our lives.
    a. **True**
    b. False
32. A boundary is a line that gives us unlimited and unbounding access in an area of distinction.
    a. True
    b. **False**
33. The first demon dealer was the devil.
    a. **True**
    b. False
34. Inordinacy can lead to obsessive and compulsive thoughts and behaviors that can make us appear or act double-minded or mentally unstable and can lead to idolatry as now we are striving to be our own god by striving to fulfill our desires at the expense of God's will and plan for our lives.
    a. **True**
    b. False
35. we do have authority in the spirit realm to not tolerate witches and witchcraft, and to release God's judgment on those who engage in witchcraft or operate as witches.
    a. **True**
    b. False
36. In Genesis 11:4, Nimrod and his kingdom striving to build a city and a tower to reach heaven. God had to advance their language and scattered them abroad upon the earth, so they would understand one another, and would be able to complete this task.
    a. True
    b. **False**
37. The New Age Movement encompasses new modern practices, witchcraft practices, occult practices in a modern context. These practices include sorcery, pursue astrology for divine guidance, magic, witchcraft, communication with the dead, worship of Satan, sacrifices to idols and demons and much more.
    a. True
    b. **False**

38. New Age participants us the following scriptures to justify their belief that all humans are gods: Psalm 82:6 I have said, Ye are gods; and all of you are children of the most High and John 10:34 Jesus answered them, Is it not written in your law, I said, Ye are gods?
    a. True
    b. False
39. There is a difference between astral projection and guided translation of the Holy Spirit.
    a. True
    b. False
40. A vision board is a great way to become successful by visualizing what the person wants in their life and how they plan on accomplishing it.
    a. True
    b. False
41. Our inability to train and even govern these people, their gifts, and heavenly realms, confound matters for the body of Christ and expose us to being infiltrated by witches and warlocks who the devil send to steal, kill, and destroy people and ministries.
    a. True
    b. False
42. When rebellion operates in members and ministries, it closes the door to witchcraft.
    a. True
    b. False
43. Algorithms are a series of codes or operations that help identify user behaviors, what is relevant and important to the user, and what the user is likely to engage in, invest in, or purchase.
    a. True
    b. False
44. First-party elements have the ability to save cookies onto your browser each time you access their domain. They can access the data from the site you are on and every site that uses that same third-party element. This is called tracking!
    a. True
    b. False
45. . Cyber bullying is the use of electronic communication to bully, intimidate, negatively expose a person, or bring and release contempt, typically by sending messages, posting messages, or releasing video and audio regarding the person.
    a. True
    b. False
46. Cyber and media bullying is a controlling spirit seeking to kill the person's purpose and calling.
    a. True
    b. False
47. The Celebrity Spirit is Selling and sacrificing one's soul and the soul of others for popularity, fame, and fortune.
    a. True
    b. False

48. It is doubt that social media and the internet in general expose the character, nature, and heart of a person. This is because we are operating in spiritual realms where our spirits, minds, and souls, are engaging one to another in the fullness of its existence.
    a. True
    b. False
49. God is striving to do is to build his own media system that draws people out of mainstream media idolatry, to his true government.
    a. True
    b. False
50. Our calling is not the gift, but what the gift does to save, deliver, and heal souls. The gift oftentimes becomes an offering to the idol god of Hollywood so that a person can be used on that platform.
    a. True
    b. False
51. New Age practitioners claim they have healing and protection powers, although there is no scientific evidence to support this theory. The claim is that they have unique mystical healing powers that cure ailments protect against illness, disease, and injury, provide mental and emotional wellness, balance, and stability, promotes creativity, and awakens spiritual consciousness.
    a. True
    b. False
52. The following scripture is a symbolizing of remembrance but is not a literal act of drinking blood or eating body parts, whether Jesus or otherwise. Mark 14:22-25 *And as they were eating, he took bread, and after blessing it broke it and gave it to them, and said, "Take; this is my body." And he took a cup, and when he had given thanks he gave it to them, and they all drank of it. And he said to them, "This is my blood of the covenant, which is poured out for many. Truly, I say to you, I will not drink again of the fruit of the vine until that day when I drink it new in the kingdom of God."*
    a. True
    b. False
53. Some idolatrous religions believe incenses and candles provides a light for their god to engage them, raise vibration levels, draw energy from the sun, draw spirit guides and certain spirits into the atmosphere, dispels evil and demons, brings protection, purifying the person and the atmosphere, stimulate the sexual drive, enhance memory, can be lit as a sacrifice to gods for certain purposes (e.g., for luck, prosperity, love, friendship, wellness).
    a. True
    b. False
54. Herbalism is one of the most ancient medical systems in the earth and can be correlated with the history of medicine. Also known as phytotherapy or botanical medicine, herbalism entails the practice of making or prescribing plant based herbal remedies for medical conditions.
    a. True

b. False
55. Is the following statement true or false regarding the Black Hebrew Israelites: They equate their uprising to reclaiming the people of the lost tribe of Israel and taking their rightful place in the earth so they can reign when God returns to restore their rulership.
　　a. True
　　b. False
56. Black Hebrew Israelites accept the images of a white Jesus and believe these images were created to steal their ordained identity. They believe Jesus is a black man according to Revelation 1:15. Black Hebrew Israelites accept Christian and pagan holidays regard them as idolatrous and demonic. They celebrate the Passover but have adopted their own ideologies regarding many biblical symbols, feasts, and celebrations.
　　a. True
　　b. False
57. Orishas are human beings that already existed in the spirit world at creation, who become incarnated beings that live on earth.
　　a. True
　　b. False
58. The artist Rihanna invoked the goddess Orshun in several of her musical and movie projects. She also compares herself to Oshun throughout the movie "Black Is King" and in her visual imagery album entitled "Lemonade."
　　a. True
　　b. False
59. . As Christ followers, anything that is not aligning with God and his word is error or false.
　　a. True
　　b. False
60. The charismatic person's words, charisma, and the manner to which they utilize the scriptures and principles of God, operate like witchcraft spells to woo, and subdue people under their powers, while building their personal kingdoms.
　　a. True
　　b. False
61. Babylonians are worldly, manmade, and demonic systems with self-focused and idolatrous agendas. They present a true sense of godliness, liberty, and freedom, but truthfully Babylon is idolatrous, oppressive, and evil. The focus is fame, fortune, pleasure, and success.
　　a. True
　　b. False
62. The following is a Characteristic of a Church Warlock: Strives to get close to leaders so they can acquire inside information, become a leader themselves, be in position to control others, and usurp authority to fulfill their purpose.
　　a. True
　　b. False

63. The following is a Characteristic of a Church Witch: Is not interested in unity, fellowship, togetherness, but utilize these methods to gain the favor of people, to infiltrate groups and become a lead voice over people.
    a. True
    b. False
64. The purpose of a Watchmen is to Every service be stationed at specific places within the room before service, during high levels of deliverance, healing, and worship within the service, and at altar calls. Their goal was not to personally pray for people, but to pray for the atmosphere to be pliable for deliverance healing, to pray protection prayers as the ministry was going forth, pray and encourage those God revealed to come to the altar for salvation, baptism, and prayer, and to watch, pray, and intervene regarding suspicious activity within the pews and at the altar.
    a. True
    b. False
65. Some saints are now rogue witches and warlocks because they were taught how to steward their gifts and powers of the prophetic, seed, etc. in the church or in life.
    a. True
    b. False
66. Lack of teaching and training of translating and traveling in spiritual realms for ministry and warfare purposes, and prophetic and supernatural dreams and encounters, cause people to find their own interpretation and education in these areas. Done void of Holy Ghost direction, they open their lives to spirit guides and demon activity that turn them in Christian witches and warlocks.
    a. True
    b. False
67. Failure to really bring physical and emotional wellness, deal with life issues, admit and heal church issues, has caused a disbelief and mistrust in God and the church.
    a. True
    b. False
68. Yoga meditation is a type of meditation that is designed to heighten and enhance a person's awareness of their connection to the universe. The premise is that cosmic meditation causes heighten spiritual awareness, divine consciousness, and awakening by receiving energy, enlightenment, and spiritual and natural power from different regions, spheres, and properties (e.g., sun, moon, stars, galaxies), in the universe.
    a. True
    b. False
69. Reiki practitioners use their hands to massage the body and operate through specific verbal mantras and blessings they speak out loud to clear negative energy from the body for the perceived purposes of raising a person's vibration, bringing harmony and balance to one's mind, open and balance energy Kundalini chakras, bringing mental, emotional, and spiritual healing and balance.
    a. True
    b. False

70. Anything that overtakes our identity, becomes excessive, or something we feel we cannot live without, should be a caution to really go before God and see if deliverance and healing is needed.
    a. **True**
    b. False
71. An incantation is a strong wish, desire, motive, intent, or compilation of words rooted in magical powers that can be worked by simply pointing a finger, meditating, and willing a situation to occur, performing a ritual using various tools, herbs, and crystals, or drawing from energies, vibrations, and demonic powers to complete its workings.
    a. True
    b. **False**
72. A charm is a ritual utterance or potion used for the purposes of attracting, magnetizing, or connecting, to a desired person, object, or experience.
    a. **True**
    b. False
73. In regard to the practice of smudging, a person is actually invoking demons and calling more demons into their life, rather than casting them out.
    a. **True**
    b. False
74. The All Lives Matters movement, is essential to racial reform and enlightening the public on racial injustices. The movement is not designed to exclude other races, but to emphasize the lack of necessary action and attention brought to the systematic racism and violence Black people are enduring.
    a. True
    b. **False**
75. Regarding algorithms, Individuals may not realize they have become addicted because of the psychological techniques that are involved. The longer the system can keep you on a platform, the greater the number of ads you are consuming, which increases the drive to use apps and the internet.
    a. **True**
    b. False

SOUL STEALER DEFINITION INDEX

Demon Dealing - on page 1	Leviathan - on page 102
Scouting Demonic Operations - on page 4	Incantations, Charms - on page 103
Demon Rankings - on page 7	Spell Casting, Emoji Casting - on page 103
Truth About Convictions - on page 9	Hashtag Spell Casting - on page 104
Honoring The Boundaries of God - on page 13	Days Of The Week Witchcraft - on page 105
New Age Movement - on page 27	Chakras & Yoga - on page 106
Mysticism - on page 35	Sound Bowls - on page 110
Consciousness - on page 36	Manifestation & Mood Rings - on page 110
Disposition - on page 36	Reiki - on page 110
Waves - on page 37	Acupuncture - on page 111
Vibes Or Vibrations - on page 37	Henna Tattoos - on page 112
Energies - on page 38	Bleaching - on page 113
Stay Woke - on page 40	Adornment - on page 114
Privilege & Entitlement - on page 41	Yoruba Waist Beads - on page 115
Witchcraft Definition & Tables - on page 42	Hypnotism, Mesmerism - on page 116
Altars - on page 45	Tarot Cards - on page 116
Third Eye - on page 46	Clairvoyance - on page 118
Extraordinary Six Sense - on page 49	Chain Letters - on page 118
Astral Projection - on page 49	Palm Reading - on page 119
Shapeshifting & Alter Egos - on page 50	Dolls - on page 119
New Age or Intrinsic Meditation - on page 51	Numerology - on page 119
Vision Dream Boards - on page 52	Angel Numbers - on page 121
Mastering Manifestation - on page 55	Sun & Moon (Sunbathing) - on page 122
Divination - on page 59	Transcendental Meditation - on page 123
Telepathy - on page 59	Alchemy - on page 123
Astrology Worship & Horoscopes - on page 61	Potion & Salves - on page 124
Spirit Guides - on page 61	Root Workers & Doctors - on page 125
Hero Or Cult Worship - on page 62	Poltergeist - on page 126:
Ancestral Worship - on page 64	Idolatrous Rationale - on page 127
Reincarnation - on page 69	The Ethnicity of Jesus - on page 129
Curious Arts - on page 70	Demon Dealing Organizations - on page 133
Incense & Candles - on page 76	Occultism - on page 133
Perfumes & Anointing Oils - on page 76	Satanism, Idolatry, & Atheism - on page 133
Spices & Herbs - on page 84	Goth & Emo Movement - on page 135
Sage Workings - on page 85	Rastafarianism - on page 137
Warding - on page 87	Black Hebrew Israelites - on page 137
Casting Out Devils & Godly Protection - on page 80	Yoruba Religion - on page 140
Blood Rituals & The Blook of Jesus - on page 88	Sangomas - on page 142
Crystals & Stones - on page 92	Free Masonry - on page 142
Pharmakeia - on page 93	Eastern Stars - on page 144
List of Pharmakeia Drugs —on page 94	Greek Organizations - on page 144
Marijuana - on page 98	Feminist Movement - on page 146
All Forms Of Magic - on page 101	Goddess Movement & Worship - on page 149

SOUL STEALER DEFINITION INDEX CONT.

All Forms Of White Supremacy - on page 150
Black Supremacy - on page 153
Black Lives Matter - on page 154
NAACP - on page 159
Scientology - on page 160
Types Of Witches - on page 161
Types Of Warlocks - on page 163
Cosmic Meditation & Celestial Activity - on page 164
How Churches Create Witches - on page 168
Witches Infiltrating The Church - on page 170
Characteristics Of A Church Witch - on page 173
Warlocks Infiltrating The Church - on page 175
Characteristics Of A Church Warlock - on page 175
Babylon Christianity - on page 177
Communing With Deceased Relatives & Familiar Spirits - on page 182
Charismatic Witchcraft - on page 195
Christian Gimmicks - on page 199
Witchcraft Versus Prophetic Gifts - on page 204
Political Demon Dealing - on page 209
The Power Of Algorithms - on page 215
Media Demon Dealing - on page 219
Cancel Culture - on page 219
Cyber Bullying Attacks - on page 219
Entertainment Demon Dealing - on page 225
Interfaith Perspective - on page 233
Shifting To Freedom - on page 235
Soul Stealer Deliverance Prayer - on page 246
Soul Stealer Test - on page 248
Soul Stealer Answer Key - on page 259

REFERENCES

Website Resources

    Allaboutspirituality.org
    Blueletterbible.com
    Biblestudytools.com
    Dictionary.com
    Olivetree.com
    Strong's Exhaustive Bible Concordance Online Bible Study Tools

Book Resources

Apostolic Mantle by Taquetta Baker
The Great Awakening! Igniting Regional Revival by Taquetta Baker
Unmasking the Power of The Scouts Volume I by Taquetta Baker
Eradicating The Powers Of Racism by Taquetta Baker
Aligning with The Apostolic Volume V by Dr. Bruce Cook
Church Planters Spiritual Warfare Manual by Apostle Jackie Green

Consultant Resources

Front Cover Photo by Reenita Breeona Keys.
Reenitakeys@gmail.com
Connect With her on Facebook.

Back Cover Photo By Deborah Settles.
Debsettles@gmail.com
Connect With her on Facebook.

Editing by Dr. Kathy Williams.
Lkone49kw@yahoo.com
dr24k_williams TikTok

Kingdom Shifters Product Line

Products available at kingdomshiftingbooks.com and amazon.com	
Books (Paperback, Kindle, and e-books available)	
Healing the Wounded Leader	There is an App for That
Apostolic Governing	Dance from Heaven to Earth
Apostolic Mantle	Annihilating Church Hurt
Release the Vision	Discerning the Voice of God
Sustaining The Vision	Feasting in His Presence
Birthing Books That Shift Generations	Prayers that Shift Atmospheres
Atmosphere Changes (Weaponry)	Dismantling Homosexuality
Strategies for Eradicating Racism	Let There Be Sight
Kingdom Shifters Decree That Thang	Kingdom Watchman Builder on the Wall
Kingdom Heirs Decree That Thang	Kingdom Keys to Governing Relationships
Fivefold Operations – Manuals I, II, and III	Unmasking the Power of the Scouts – Volumes I and II
Deliverance from the Suicide	Kingdom Wellness Counseling & Mentoring Mantle
Books for Liturgical / Interpretive Dance Ministries	
Dance & Fivefold Ministry	Dance from Heaven to Earth
Spirits that Attack Dance Ministers	Dancers! Dancers! Dancers! Decree That Thang
CD's	
Decree That Thang	Kingdom Heirs Decree That Thang
Teaching and Worship	

www.ingramcontent.com/pod-product-compliance
Lightning Source LLC
Chambersburg PA
CBHW080727230426
43665CB00020B/2645